MW01620900

Demetrio Paparoni

ERETICA

The Transcendent and the Profane in Contemporary Art

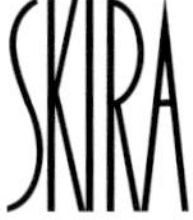

Cover
Marc Quinn, *Angel*, 2006

Design
Mauro Luccarini

Editing
Emanuela Di Lallo

Layout
Paola Pellegatta

Translations
Christopher "Shanti" Evans and Jeffrey Jennings, Language Consulting Congressi, Milan

First published in Italy in 2007
by Skira Editore S.p.A.
Palazzo Casati Stampa
via Torino 61
20123 Milano
Italy
www.skira.net

© 2007 Arthur C. Danto
for his text
© 2007 Vito Mancuso
for his text
© 2007 Gianni Mercurio
for his text
© 2007 Demetrio Paparoni
for his text
© 2007 Pierre Riches
for his text
© 2007 Arturo Schwarz
for his text
© 2007 Gore Vidal for his text
Georges Bataille, *L'histoire de l'érotisme*, © Editions Gallimard
Georges Bataille, *L'Erotisme*, © 1957 Editions de Minuit
Jean Baudrillard et François L'Yvonnet, *D'un fragment l'autre*, © Albin Michel 2001
Roger Caillois, *L'homme et le sacré*, © Editions Gallimard
George Hersey, *The Evolution of allure*, © 1996 MIT Press
David Morgan, *Visual Piety*, © 1997 University of California Press
© 2007 Skira editore, Milan
© Marina Abramović, Monica Bonvicini, Gérard Garouste, Andreas Gursky, Thomas Ruff, David Salle, Doug Starn by SIAE 2007
© Andy Warhol Foundation for the Visual Arts by SIAE 2007

The publisher is at the disposal of the entitled parties as regards all unidentified iconographic and literary sources.

All rights reserved under international copyright conventions. No part of this book may be reproduced or utilized in any form or by any means, electronic or mechanical, including photocopying, recording, or any information storage and retrieval system, without permission in writing from the publisher.

Printed and bound in Italy.
First edition

ISBN 978-88-6130-069-9

Distributed in North America by Rizzoli International Publications, Inc., 300 Park Avenue South, New York, NY 10010, USA.
Distributed elsewhere in the world by Thames and Hudson Ltd., 181A High Holborn, London WC1V 7QX, United Kingdom.

Contents

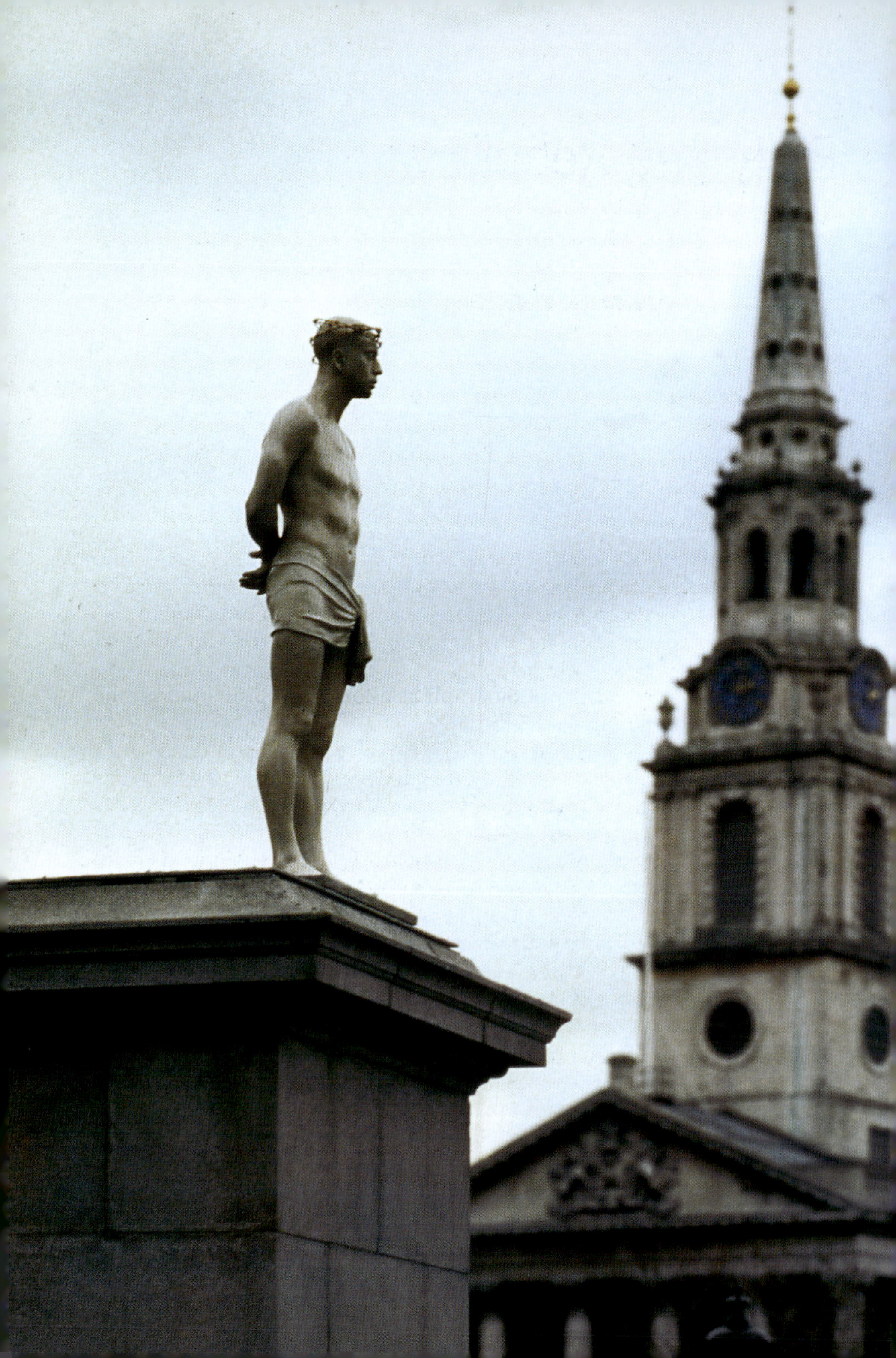

Piety and Rebellion

Demetrio Paparoni

Only recently has the course of the evolution of the post-modern in art become clear. Like modernism, the art of the period from the 1980s to our own day has been characterized by a succession of contrasting movements and tendencies, heading in unexpected directions. Today we have reached the third generation of the post-modern. Placing the accent on the painted picture and the photograph as a form of representation, the first of these generations revisited the themes of the sacred and of history, often in an ironic key, but rejected the concept of narration, seen as old hat. In fact modernism wanted to set art free from the classical properties of representation, such as perspective, foreshortening, chiaroscuro and physiognomy, all elements that contribute to defining a narrative. In short, art was expected to express its own truth, independently of social factors. In the 1980s these elements were rejected on the strength of a belated avant-gardist attitude. Yet it was in the 1980s that the preconditions were created for a free art, liberated from schemes dictated by the historical avant-gardes: it was from that moment on that, in parallel to the spread of the internet and satellite TV, art tended to coincide and overlap with external reality.

Narration burst back onto the scene in an unprecedented fashion in the art of the 1990s. The seal was set on this shift principally by Matthew Barney's *Cremaster* cycle and Damien Hirst's dissected animals immersed in formaldehyde; but there were also the crude realism of Andres Serrano, who photographed corpses in mortuaries, the psycho-

Mark Wallinger *Ecce Homo*, 1999. Marbleised resin, barbed wire and gold leaf, life size. Installation in Trafalgar Square, London

logical portraits painted by John Currin and the dramatically realistic ones of Jenny Saville.

Cremaster is a complex cycle of films, photos, sculptures and drawings that, while cut loose from the constraints of the logical and temporal narrative structure, superimposed sacred, anthropological, historical, social, political and journalistic elements in a fantastic way. Above all *Cremaster* reclaimed the symbology of the religious works of the past. The cadavers of real animals exhibited by Hirst, on the other hand, are the crudest, most realistic and truthful vision of the death that has ever been presented. We are accustomed to seeing carcasses of animals at the butcher's and are not scandalized by the existence of slaughterhouses, and yet display of the dead body in an art gallery gives it a different symbolic value. The animal carcasses of Rembrandt, Velázquez, Soutine, Serrano or Saville, like the bowels painted by Bacon (who claimed to have reached a turning-point in his art when he saw the entrails of an animal run over by a car), still belong to the realm of representation, but not those of Hirst, which fall within the sphere of presentation. While not a painter, Hirst is the direct heir of Bacon, taking from him the idea that killing an animal in an abattoir is the closest thing you can get to a crucifixion. His rotting head of a cow, covered with flies, embodies the torments and existential dramas of the contemporary human being with the same tension as can be found in Bacon's paintings.

By exhibiting cabinets or cupboards filled with medicines, Hirst draws attention to people's unconditional faith in medical science: 'Basically, you can tell what kind of a doctor they are by the way they organize their drugs', says Hirst, '… so I quite liked the idea that to a hell of a lot of people [my medicine cabinets] looked so confident, but then to somebody who knows what's going on, you know, it's a mess. […] In the medicine cabinets the bottles are packaged like formal sculptures, perfectly organized. […] I've always liked the idea that art could cure people. I'm obsessed by the body, I like the fact that there are all these things connected with the organism inside a medicine cabinet…'[1]

Very different is the illness depicted in the paintings of Currin and Saville — schizophrenia and mental disorders in the people portrayed by the former, existential torment in the ones portrayed by the latter. Creating a sense of unease in the observer, their pictures show that it is precisely through a powerful narrative and psychological structure that today's painting expresses the spirit of the time. Their relationship with

Mark Wallinger *Ecce Homo* (detail), 1999. Marbleised resin, barbed wire and gold leaf, life size

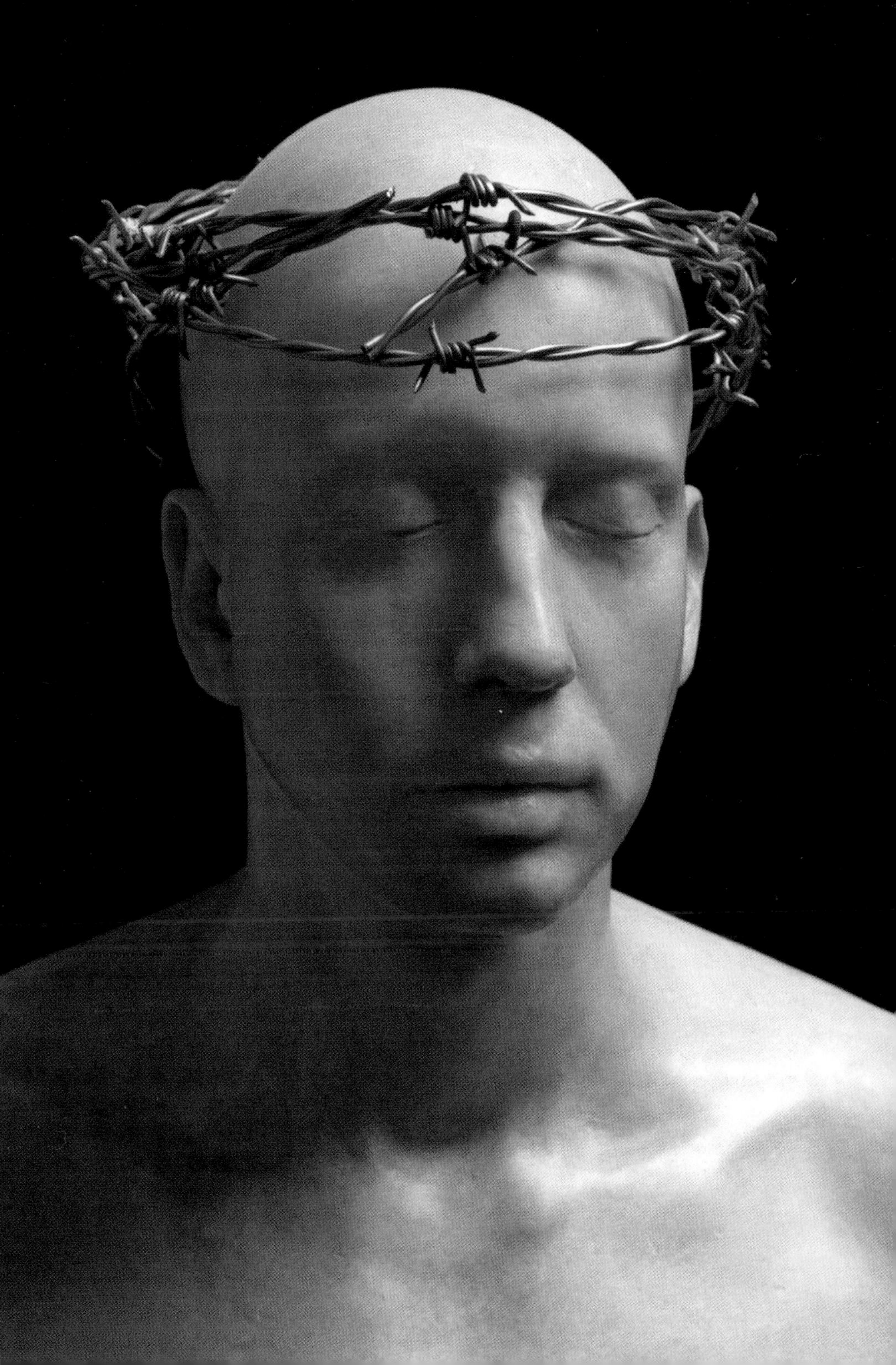

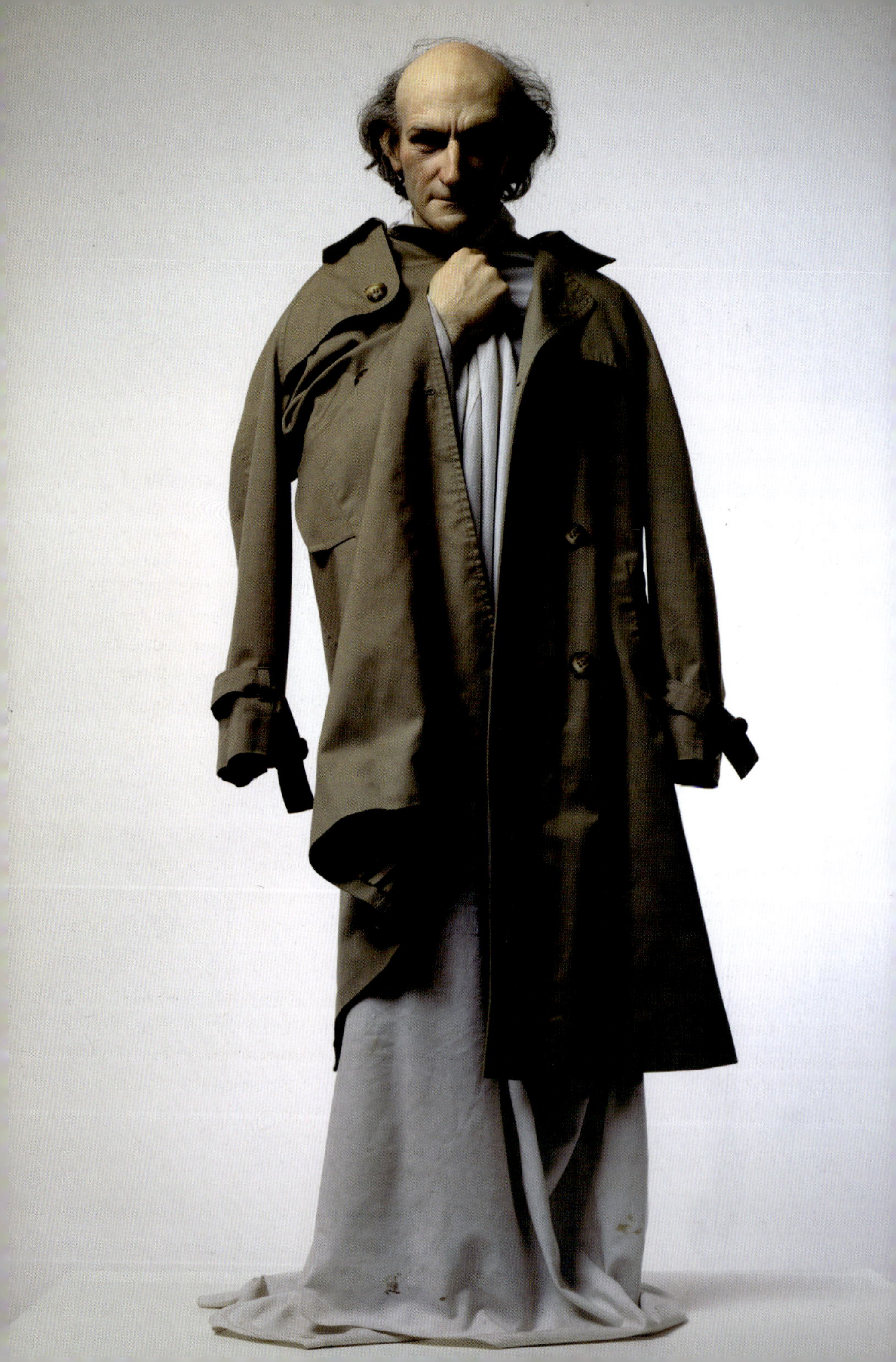

tradition, that of the pre-modern era as well as that of the twentieth century, remains strong: in Currin we find echoes of the style of Lucas Cranach in an unprecedented combination with stylistic features of the figures painted by illustrator Norman Rockwell; in Saville the tension of Bacon finds expression through the rapid brushwork of de Kooning.

With Barney's *Cremaster*, Hirst's series of dead animals and medicine cabinets and the narrative paintings of Currin and Saville, we have reached the second generation of the post-modern. With his or her load of stories to tell, the human being has once again become the subject of the work, confronting the transcendent. Unlike in the past, however, the theme of death is filtered through the illusion of immortality created by new technologies.

In the 1990s the planet-wide spread of the internet and satellite TV strengthened the conviction that technology can do anything, even give us immortality. Art turned its attention to the bionic body, to the phenomenon that Jeffrey Deitch has so aptly called 'post-human'. The third generation of post-modern artists (obviously we are not talking in terms of age here) was born with the end of the 'post-human'. It stemmed from the realization that the body is anything but a machine whose parts can be replaced, from the realization that the youth offered by surgery is a pathetic illusion. Above all, there was an understanding that the aspiration to a perfect or in some way manipulated body concealed the perilous idea of the superman.

As Jeffrey Deitch puts it: 'The matter-of-fact acceptance of one's "natural" look and one's "natural" personality is being replaced by a growing sense that it is normal to reinvent oneself. […] There is a new sense that one can simply construct the new self that one wants, freed from the constraints of one's past and one's inherited genetic code.'[2] In support of this thesis four authoritative museum directors went on to say: 'The advances in biogenetics and informatics and the consequent metamorphoses in patterns of social behaviour are shifting the boundaries in relation to which the end of the human is celebrated and the post-human begins. The emerging world in which plastic surgery, genetic reconstruction and the grafting of electronic components onto the brain will become common practice may very soon be seen as a further stage in the Darwinian evolution of the human being. Technological innovations like these will also begin to radically alter the structure of social interactions'.[3] It is undeniable that science has achieved extraordinary results through the development of advanced

Ron Mueck *Untitled* (*Standing Man*). Silicone, acrylic, polyurethane, foam rubber and fabric, 116 x 50.8 x 38.1 cm

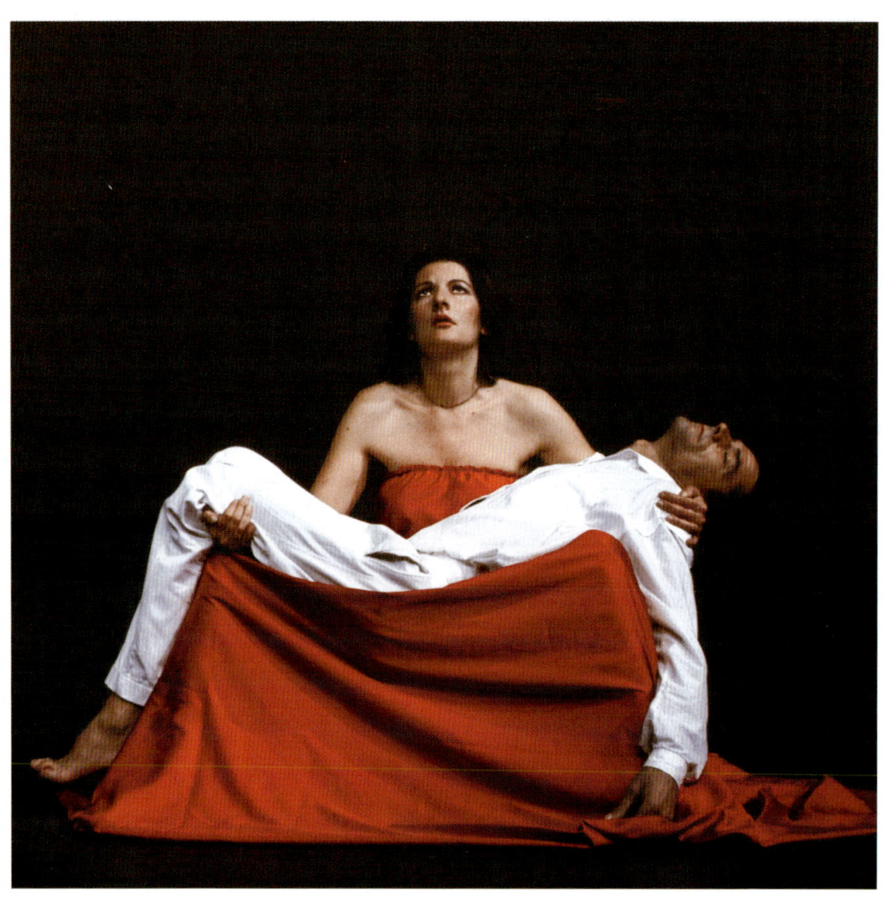

Marina Abramović *Pietà*, 2002 (taken from the performance *Anima Mundi*, 1983). Photographic print, 180 x 180 cm

micro-technologies. Yet to make the claim that these results could modify social relationships was more than rash, as the art of the third post-modern generation has demonstrated by tackling themes like that of the *Pietà* or reconstructing ancient rites of propitiation: the more science pushes us forwards, the more art forges links with tradition. What has changed, if anything, is the relationship of individuals with themselves, but this is only true for those who decide to appear different from what they really are. The world is for the most part indifferent towards those who alter their own bodies, whether out of pure hedonism or necessity.

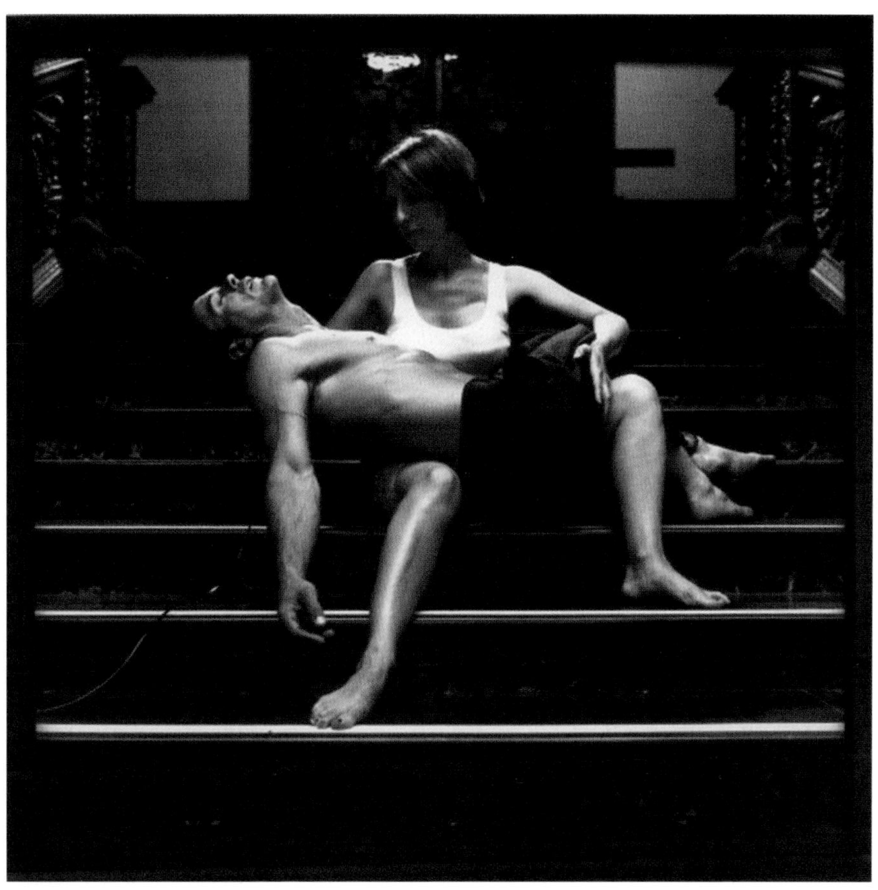

Sam Taylor-Wood *Pietà*, 2001. Photographic print, 128 x 128 cm

As is well-known, after the fall of the Berlin Wall and the end of the struggle between Soviet communism and Western capitalism, the concept of history has been reincarnated in the conflicts opened by ethical questions connected with biogenetics. It was these new conflicts related to the moral sphere that gave rise in the 1990s to works like those of Cindy Sherman or Jake and Dinos Chapman, who even took on, obviously each in his or her own way, the theme of civil war, and thus of violence between fellow human beings. In a series of photographic works produced at the beginning of the 1990s, Cindy Sherman looked at the relationship of indi-

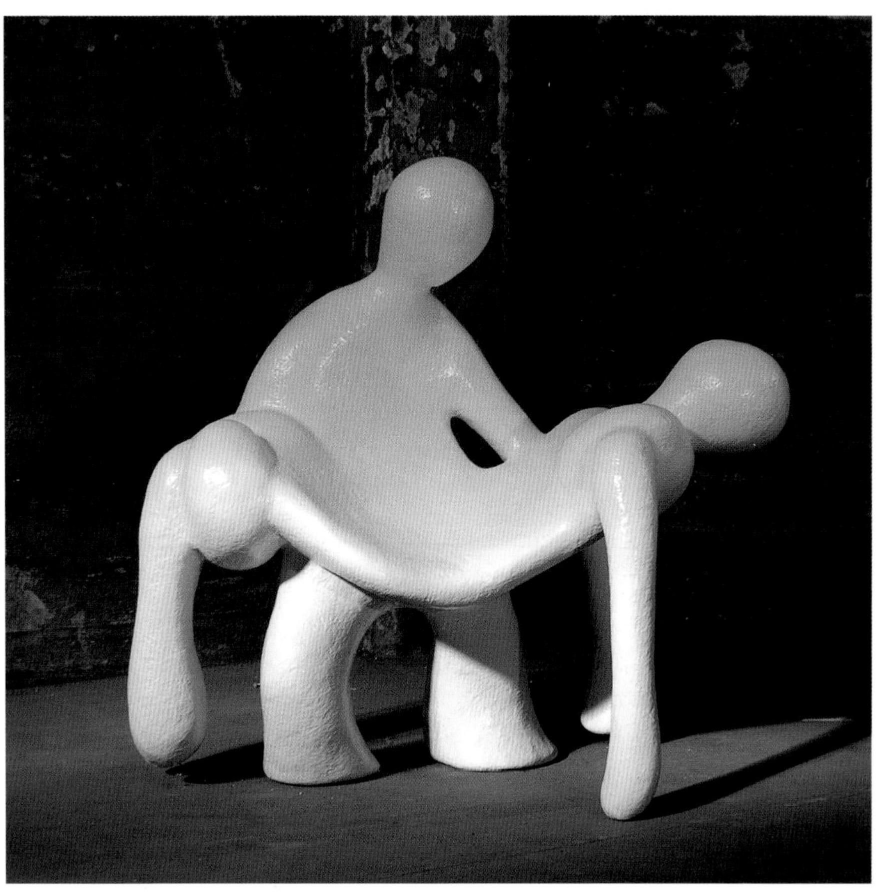

Atelier Van Lieshout *Caretaker*, 2005. Fibreglass, 80 x 90 x 60 cm

viduals with society and with themselves. She took pictures of herself in the guise of characters from famous films or historical figures taken from paintings of the past, constructed scenes with medical dummies and photographed parts of the human anatomy stained with blood and dirt. Not unlike Francis Bacon, who has had a strong influence on much recent art, she stresses that the world around the individual can have the characteristics of hell. In her work the disassembled bodies of dummies waiting to be put back together again express anything but trust in biogenetics or plastic surgery, rejecting the argument that it is completely painless for human beings to reinvent themselves. This is in clear contradiction with the theses of those who have linked her work to the theories of the post-human.

If at the outset Sherman frequently photographed herself dressed up as historical figures, her recent self-portraits show her in the guise of the clown. The clown is a figure characterized by its non-sense, it is an allegory of the worthlessness of being. Gratuitousness, non-sense or lack of meaning are the elements of a theatrical figure that does not coincide with the existential reality of whoever wears its costume. Justifying his professional identity by making fun of himself, the clown is an anti-person, an allegorical overthrowing of the self. He is a contradictory figure because, in destroying any hope of a consistent and harmonious world, he reveals the absurdity of existence. Yet his laughter, or the laughter he provokes, points us towards a shred of truth, of which the mask is the visible secret behind which absence is concealed. So the clown's mask is the skull, which serves as an emblem of the representation of the human being in some of Sherman's other works: a human being that also appears in the guise of a mutant who undergoes, against his will, a terrible genetic transformation.

Damien Hirst, Dinos and Jake Chapman, Marc Quinn and Bernardi Roig are obsessed with death and immortality. For the Spanish sculptor Roig human beings are always alone, wrestling with their own fears and their own disputed identity. The flames that spring from the eyes of his figures, blackening their faces with smoke, is a pregnant metaphor (the narrative) of a fire that burns the soul and the mind.

Roig regards eroticism as a perpetual challenge to death. As with Currin and Saville, there is nothing celestial about the nude in his work. It is never sensual, but concerns the emotional sphere and excludes lust.

Marc Quinn has created a sculpture of his own head out of frozen blood. And has moulded the head of his son out of his placenta and umbilical cord. In this way he stresses the transitoriness of existence: unlike sculptures in marble or paintings in oil, where the representation contains no genetic memory, his work includes the DNA of its subject, incorporating the whole of its being. It is the same desire to bring a living element into the work that prompts Roig to have real flames coming out of the eyes of his sculptures.

Skulls and skeletal figures appear in the work of many contemporary artists, performing the function of a symbol of human transience. Skulls and skeletons have always been a mirror in which what we will become is reflected. Linked to Christianity, this representation of death found its highest expression at a time scarred by the terrible plague of the fourteenth century, and it retains its power today.

In early modernism the skull can be found in the art of Vincent van Gogh, James Ensor and Paul Cézanne, among others, and appears again in the twentieth century, especially in the work of Egon Schiele, Edvard Munch, Pablo Picasso, Otto Dix, Salvador Dalí and a few others. Although its form recurs in the paintings and sculptures of Western art — from the *danses macabres* and *ars moriendi* of the Middle Ages to Baroque iconography — what prevails in art is life and its positive values. Death is not the main subject of art: it is overshadowed by life.

Between the second half of the 1970s and the first half of the 1980s the figure of the skull was explored many times. One of the first artists to emphasize this subject was Andy Warhol who, by presenting it as if it were an X-ray, underlined its power as a mass image, not dissimilar in form to a commercial logo or an advertising poster. The idea was taken up, at the beginning of the 1980s, by the then young Italian painters Enzo Cucchi, Francesco Clemente and Mimmo Paladino: the first two evoked the *memento mori* of Catholic origin, seeing skulls as the ground on which we walk, while the other turned the skull into a tribal mask. Gerhard Richter also produced a series of pictures of skulls, in this case ambiguously occupying a space somewhere between the painting of Johannes Vermeer or Georges de La Tour and modern, mechanical photography.

Warhol's first *Skulls* date from 1976, those of Clemente, Cucchi and Paladino from 1979, those of Richter from 1983. That same year Robert Mapplethorpe photographed the sculpture of a skull, going on to portray a real one in 1988.

The 1980s saw the outbreak of the plague of AIDS, officially identified in the United States in 1982 and causing many deaths in the world of art as well. Ten years later, in 1992, Cindy Sherman took a picture of a skull decked out with flowers and jewellery as if in a genuine, but falsely alluring Baroque theatre of death. This work of Sherman's is the emblem of a decade scarred by a disease that, contracted for the most part through the injection of drugs with infected syringes or unprotected sexual relations, gave a whole new meaning to death. It should not be forgotten that in those years there were people who saw AIDS as an expression of God's wrath. Many reacted to these attitudes by denouncing the exploitation of the new plague to impose religious concepts and precepts that tended towards sexual and social discrimination. For Mapplethorpe, infected with AIDS, the skull, which he photographed on several occasions, was the antechamber of a terrible nightmare: he died in 1989, at the age of forty-three.

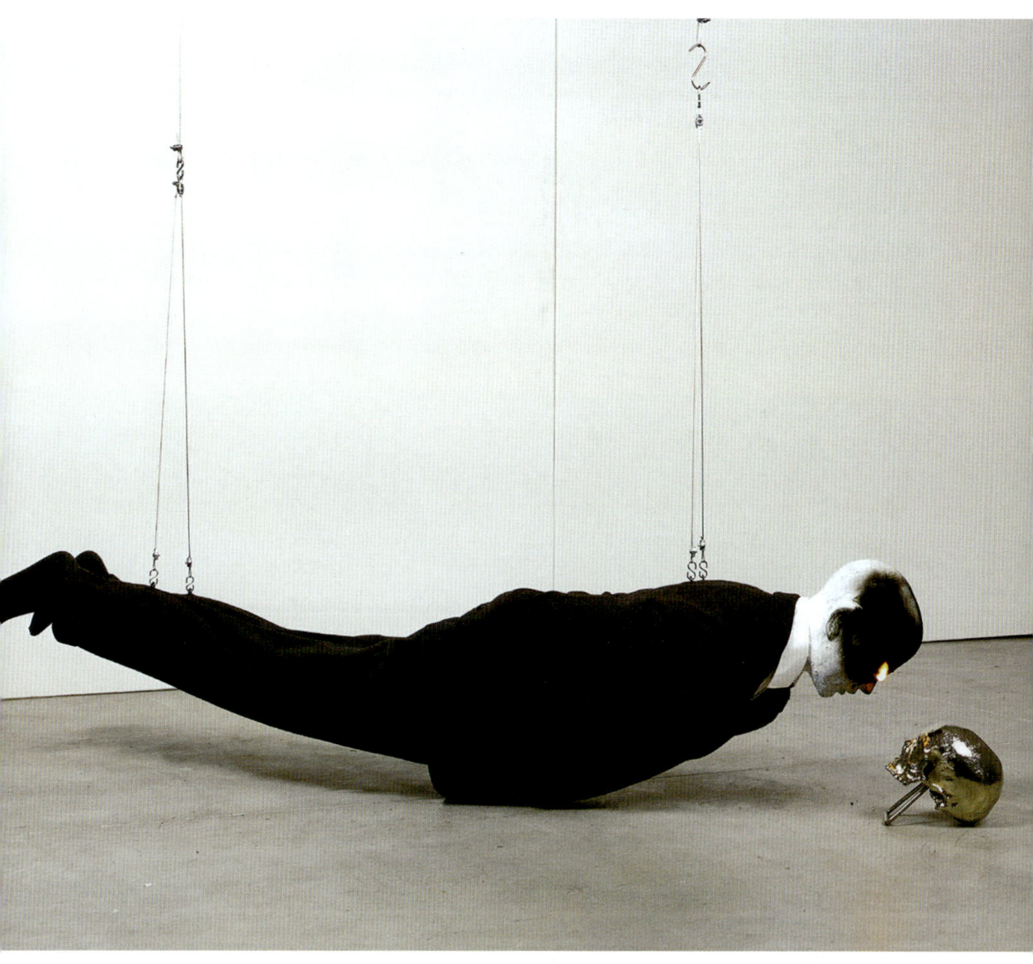

Bernardi Roig *Exercises in Levitation.* Bronze, fire, fabric, propane gas, silver leaf and cable, life size

One of Mapplethorpe's last self-portraits shows him with his face hollowed out by illness and holding a cane with a small skull at its end. Yet in Mapplethorpe's photographs there is no taste for the macabre, something which is present instead in the work of the Chapmans, who convey the cruelty of man to man in an explicit and gory way. Their work is reminiscent of scenes of trench warfare and some of Goya's pictures (for example *Cronus Devouring One of His Children*), rather than the crucifixion, the *Ecce Homo* and representations of hell. The Chapmans remind us that

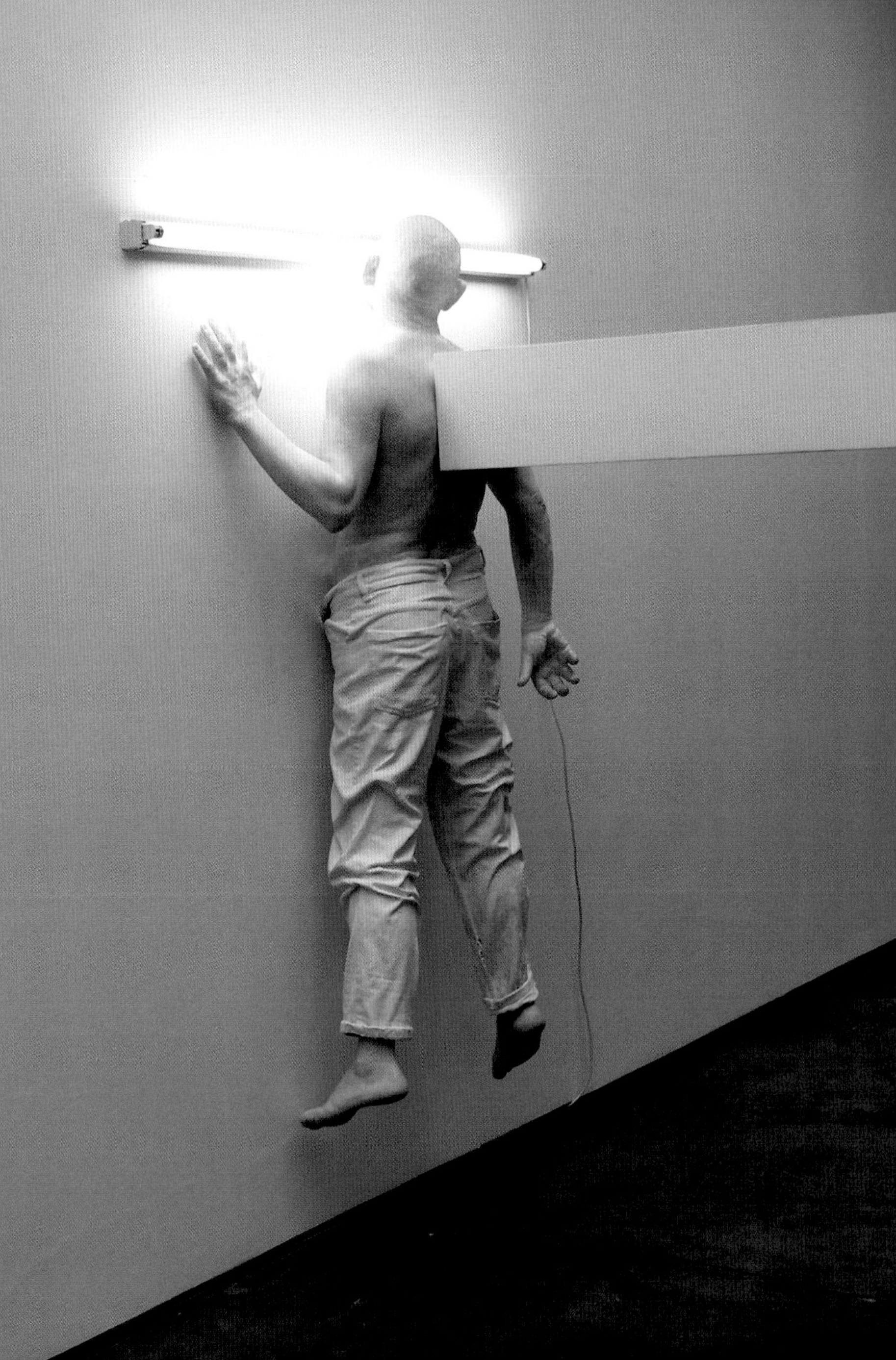

Bernardi Roig *Acteon*, 2004. Polyester resin, fluorescent light anc wall, variable dimensions

terrible wars have been waged in the name of the sacred. It suffices to think of the St Bartholomew's Day massacre of Protestants in France, or the genocide of peoples that missionaries wanted to convert to their religion at any cost.[4]

The different attitude towards scientific research into biogenetics has opened up new spaces of spirituality, expanding on the desire for transcendence that had already put in a timid appearance in the art of the 1980s and 1990s, although almost always in an ironic or political key. The situation today is very different, with an ever-growing tendency to tackle themes and subjects linked to religious iconography. Artists now resort in a no longer marginal way to images of Christ, biblical scenes, devils and angels, severed heads of St John, St Sebastian transfixed by arrows, the Pietà, the flood, mystical ecstasy, images of Buddha and portraits of religious authorities of our own day... Not that the art of the previous decades was wholly disinterested in these subjects, but this explicit demand for transcendence is now making itself felt with inescapable force.

But why was it that, from the end of the nineteenth century, i.e. the time of the second industrial revolution, up until the 1970s, with the exception of the exponents of Body Art and a few others, any reference to religious iconography, as well as to the blood and animal hidden in each of us, was banished from art? For it is with this that Western religious iconography is concerned, with human sacrifice and martyred bodies, with the suffering, transience and atonement with which the community identifies itself and which holds it together. How could it have happened that in the twentieth century artists were able to cut the umbilical cord that bound them to history, renouncing any investigation of religious feelings, and thus of a fundamental aspect of the human condition, in order to focus almost exclusively on the possibility of renewing the language? Did the art of much of the twentieth century really turn its back on any religious implications? It seems so.

In the first few decades of the last century, apart from a few, rare cases that stand out just because they are isolated (for example Max Beckman's extraordinary image of the deposition, *The Descent from the Cross* of 1917, or the *Crucifixions* of Marc Chagall, who saw the death of the Son of God on the cross as a personification of the persecuted Jew precisely because he was accused of having killed Christ himself), art concentrated almost solely on the development of new means of expression. A few decades earlier, towards the end of the nineteenth century, religious imagery had been used by Paul Gauguin (*The Yellow Christ* and *Calvary*, 1889), James Ensor (*Entry of Christ into Brussels*, 1888) and Edward

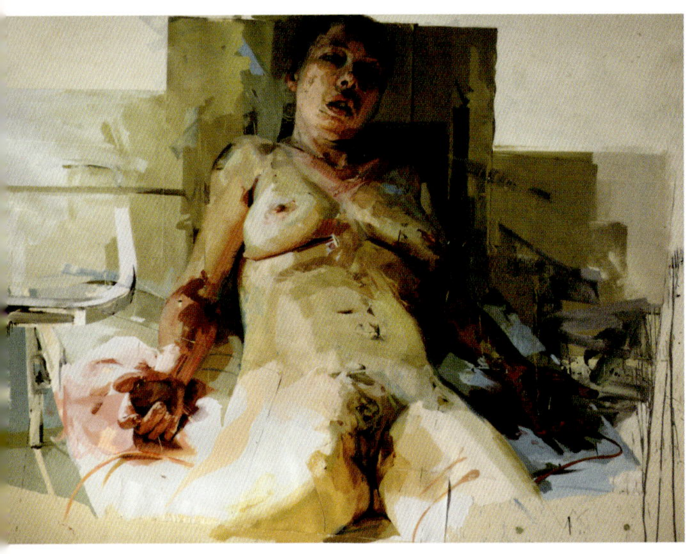

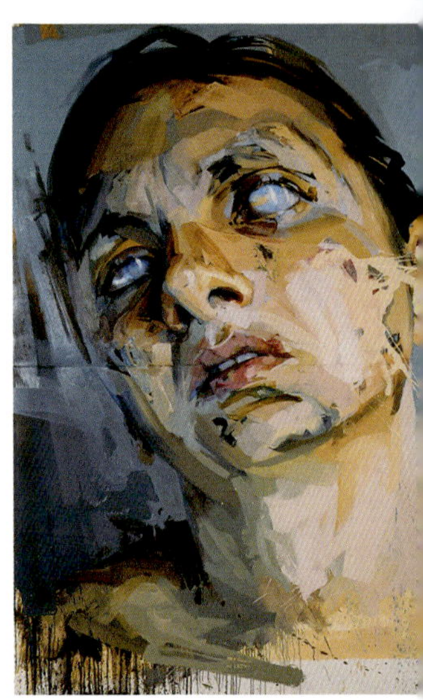

Munch (who painted the Madonna with bare breasts, 1894). But with the exception of Van Gogh — who was steeped in profound religious mysticism — the artists who ushered in modernism, like those who went on to define its parameters of style and content, did not draw on religious iconography in a manner faithful to the Holy Scriptures. They simply borrowed its universally recognized symbols to assert their own position as heretics on the religious as well as expressive plane: they contravened traditional religious dictates and disobeyed the rules of the languages utilized in the past to tackle those same themes. But they also transgressed with respect to their contemporaries, who tended to strip art of any reference to classical religious themes.

The exponents of the historic avant-garde movements rarely engaged with religious themes. Those who did, like Salvador Dalí, did so in the 1950s, at a time when the historic avant-garde had lost its subversive and renewing force. The chapel of the Rosary executed by Henri Matisse at Vence (1947–51) is also a late creation. Another heretical work which, by eliminating any representation of saints and martyrs and using forms and colours as a hymn to life itself, tended to remove any memory of the drama of the death of Christ on the cross from the place of worship.

The historic avant-garde movements had certainly not renounced the spiritual dimension, but this had been pushed into the background with respect to linguistic inventions and the processes of deconstruction of the

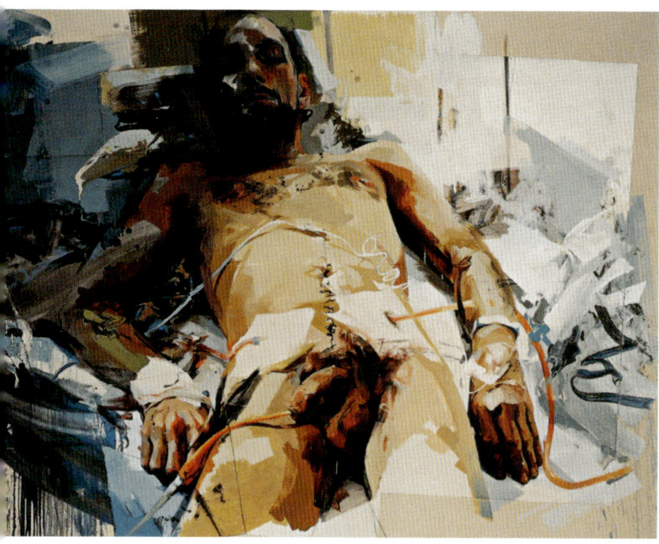

Jenny Saville

Atonement Studies
(panel 1), 2005–06
Oil on paper, 250 x 330 cm

Atonement Studies
(panel 2), 2005–06
Oil on paper, 251.5 x 185 cm

Atonement Studies
(panel 3), 2005–06
Oil on paper, 250 x 330 cm

image. Today, however, it is finding expression through the depiction of the human presence filtered by the medium of photography and an aesthetics influenced by modern techniques of computerized retouching.

In *The Dehumanization of Art* (1925), José Ortega y Gasset argued that modern art, embodying ideals contrasting with those of the masses, was by its very nature anti-popular. One of the reasons for this lack of popularity, explains Ortega, has been its dehumanization, the fact of its having been stripped of the human and animal figure. Wishing to see in the work nothing but the work, according to Ortega, modernity has treated art as a game, emphasizing its ironic dimension over the transcendental one. This argument did not find favour with the Surrealists and Expressionists, who in those same years, in opposition to the nihilism of the Dadaists, attempted to promote a sort of existential and social revolt by decoding the mechanisms of the unconscious in their work.

In order to place the accent on linguistic analysis, the historic avant-gardes had all too frequently renounced narration, and thus autobiographical content. So they ceased to speak of humanity, of the relationship with the body and with the transcendent, showing little interest in stirring the emotions of the public with the means used by the art of previous centuries. This is why Barney's *Cremaster* is the hinge between the twentieth and twenty-first centuries. The mass of visual information it presents us with harks back to the Baroque, but above all it is the clear-

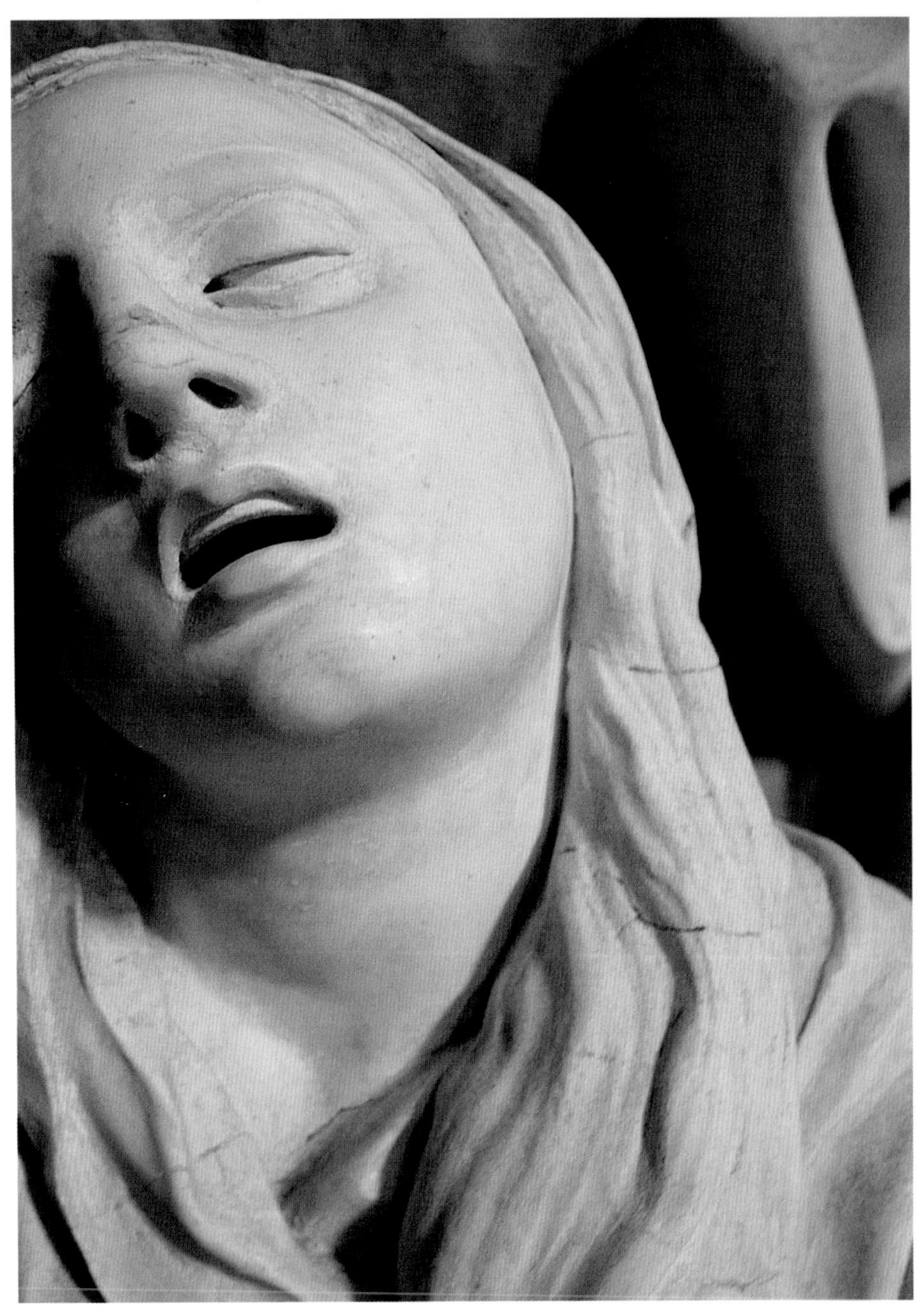

Giacomo Serpotta *Altar of the Holy Crucifix* (detail), 1720. Church of Santa Ninfa dei Crociferi, Palermo

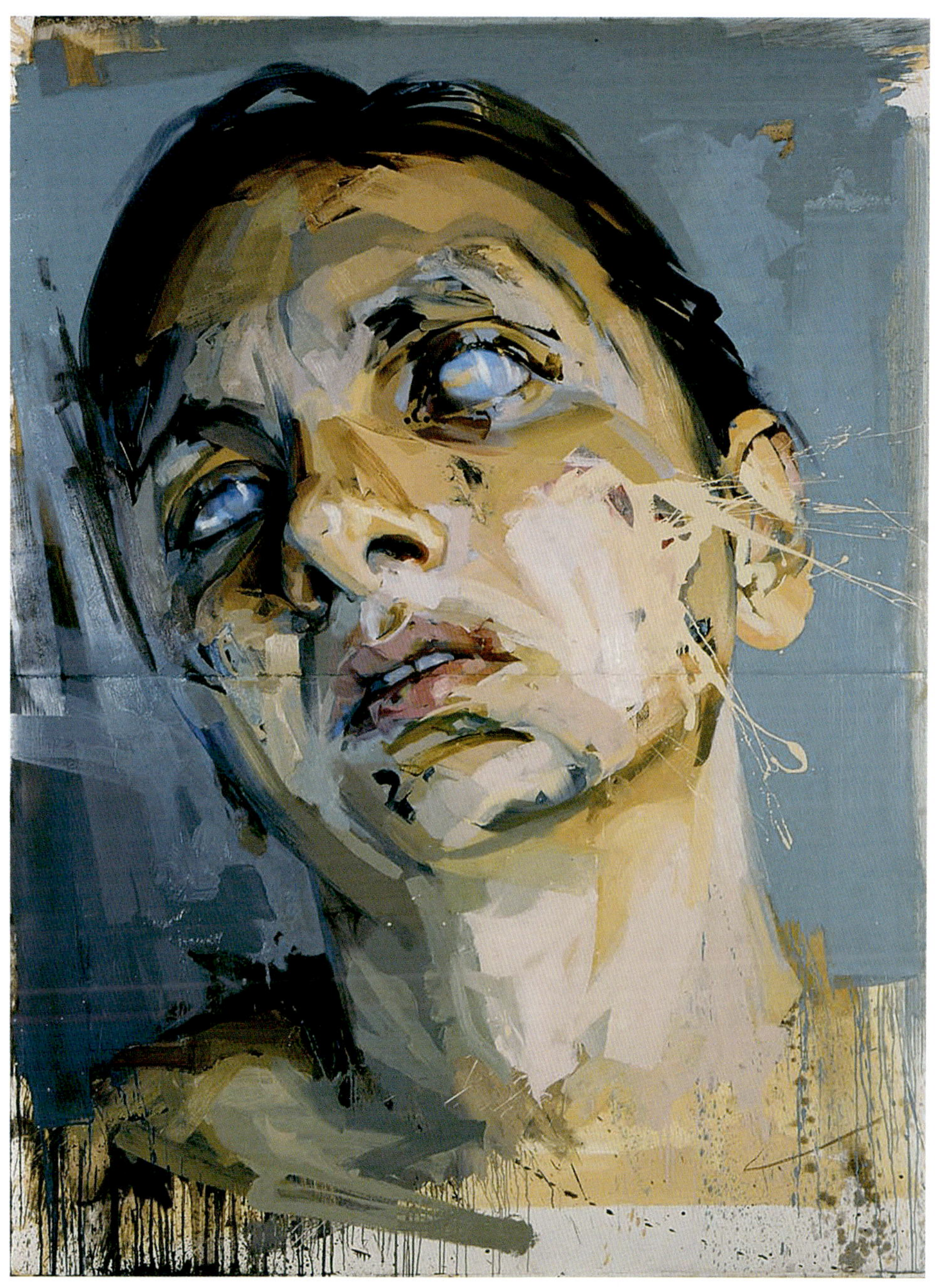

Jenny Saville *Atonement studies* (panel 2), 2005–06. Oil on paper, 251.5 x 185 cm

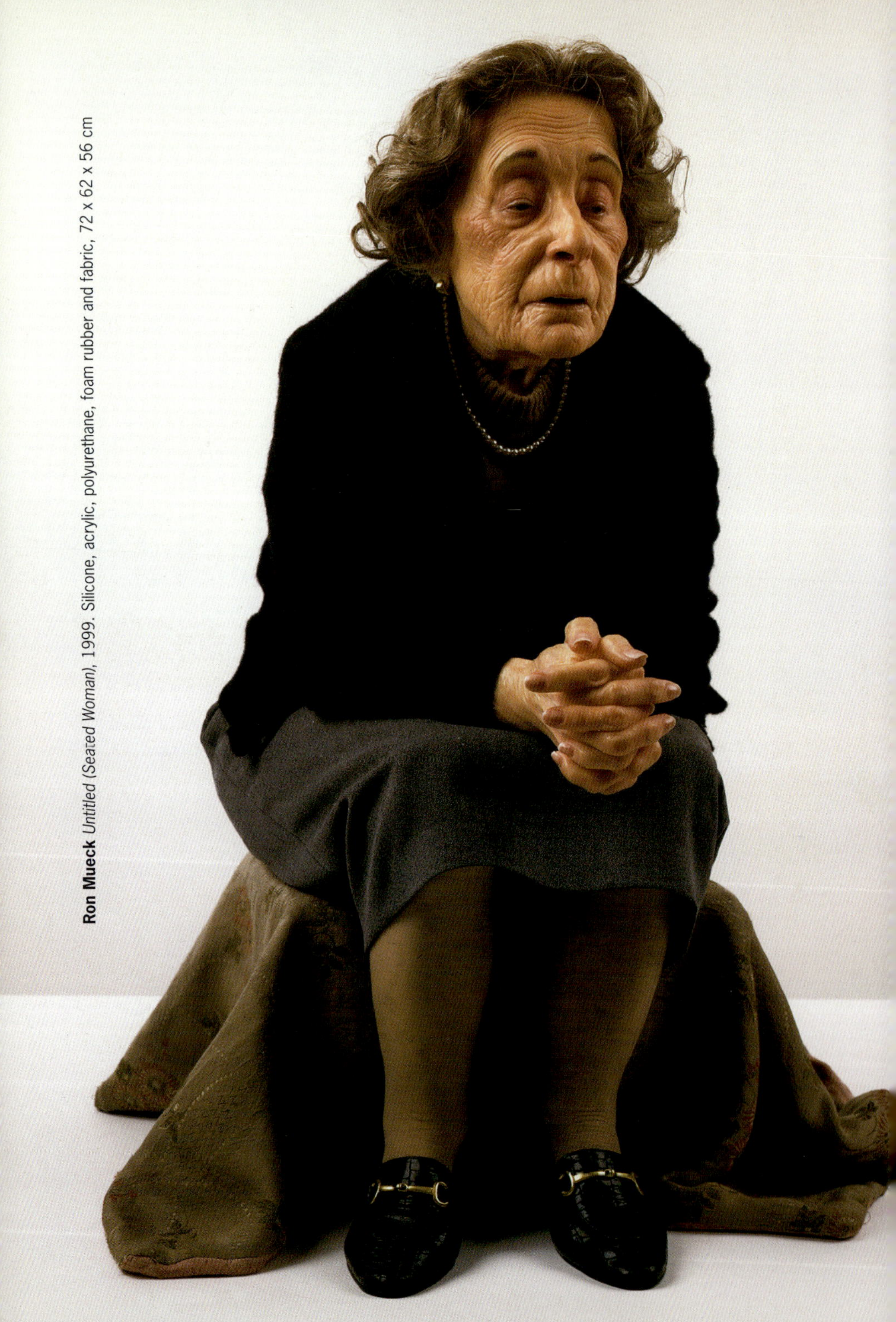

Ron Mueck *Untitled (Seated Woman)*, 1999. Silicone, acrylic, polyurethane, foam rubber and fabric, 72 x 62 x 56 cm

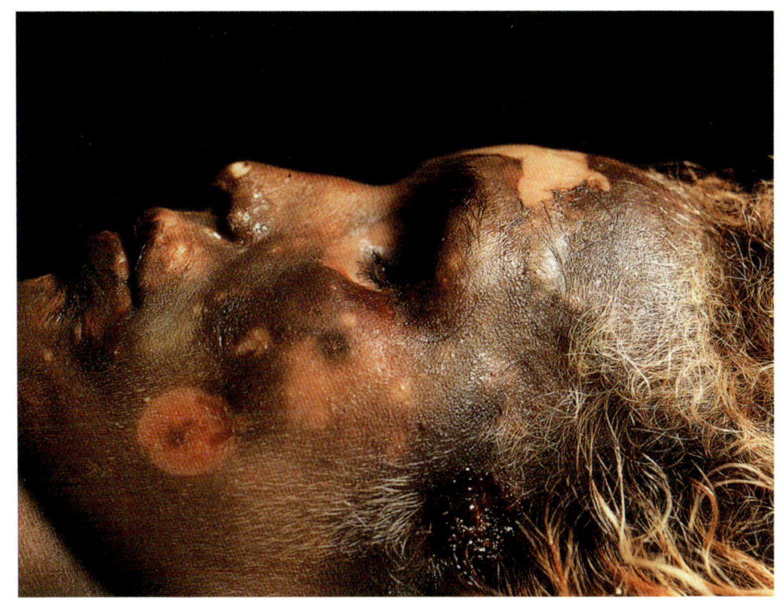

Andres Serrano *The Morgue (Jane Doe Killed by the Police)*, 1992. Cibachrome, 128 x 156 cm

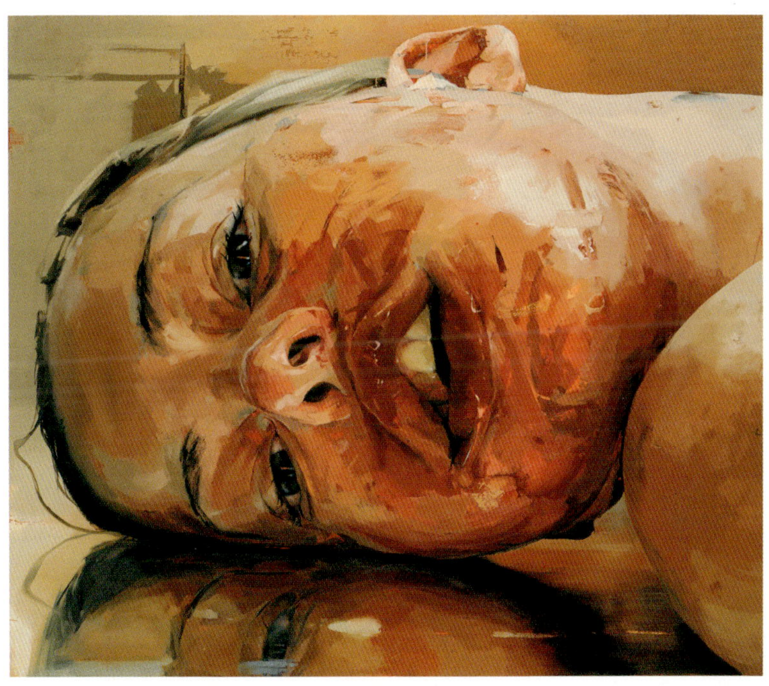

Jenny Saville *Reverse*, 2002–03. Oil on canvas, 213.4 x 243.8 cm

est manifestation of the revolution brought about by telecommunications in contemporary art. Barney displays a markedly religious attitude, even if it is cloaked in the profusion and overlap of the excessive amount of information provided. In art from the 1980s to the present we find explicit transpositions of the last supper (Vik Muniz, Hiroshi Sugimoto), the *Ecce Homo* (Mark Wallinger), the crucifixion (Andres Serrano, Damien Hirst, Robert Gober), Michelangelo's *Pietà* (Marina Abramović, Sam Taylor-Wood, Atelier Van Lieshout), St John Decollate and St Sebastian (Luigi Ontani, Cindy Sherman, Joel-Peter Witkin), the ecstasy of St Teresa (Jenny Saville) and Buddha (Michael Joo, Doug, Mike Starn, Sarah Charlesworth), as well as devils (Mike Kelley, John Bock) and angels (David Salle, Ron Mueck, Marc Quinn). However, any reference to the Holy Scriptures and religious iconography is a means to an end.

All religions raise questions that have no logical answers. The state of suspension generated by a culture that requires us to believe in intangible things opens a wound that a large section of humanity has tried (and is trying) to heal with faith. Looking at these works we realize that art is the salt that the artist rubs into the wound to make it stand out even more than it had in the past.

In demonstration of how works with religious subjects produced in the past are being treated today, in 2002 Marina Abramović created a photographic print of large dimensions out of a picture taken of a performance she gave in 1983 entitled *Anima Mundi*. Dressed in red, the artist holds in her arms her companion at the time, Ulay, dressed in white, both in Michelangelo's classic pose. Taking its cue from Chinese mythology, which holds that the universe was born from the fusion of a drop of woman's blood and a drop of sperm, this work draws on a series of performances based on the relationship between male (symbolized by white) and female (symbolized by red). It is significant to note that blood constitutes a reference to the menstrual cycle, and thus coincides with the period of infertility.

The theme of fertility returns in Abramović's video *Belgrade*, which is part of the cycle entitled *Balkan Erotic Epic*, where among other things we see a group of naked men copulating with the earth. In the same video, a group of women, young and old, perform a communal propitiatory rite in which they bare their vaginas and breasts to the rain. Writes Abramović: '*Balkan Erotic Epic* is based on my research into Balkan folk culture and its use of the erotic. It is through eroticism that the human tries to make himself equal with the gods. In folklore, the woman marrying the sun or the man marrying the moon is [an effort] to preserve the secret of the creative energy and to get in touch through eroticism with indestructible cosmic forces. People believed that in the erotic there was something superhuman that [didn't] come from [them] but from the gods. Obscene objects and male and female genitals [had] a very important function in the fertility and agricultural rites of Balkan peasants. They were used very explicitly for a variety of purposes. Women would show in the rituals openly their vaginas, bottoms, breasts and menstrual blood. Men would show openly in the rituals their bottoms and penises in acts of masturbation and ejaculation'.[5]

What meaning do rites of this kind have in our day? What induces an artist to conjure up outdated and anachronistic rituals? The archetypal motivations have not changed. They are, now as in the past, apotropaic rites. What has changed is the state of mind of the propitiator, who sets out to retrace the spiritual journey of her ancestors more to analyze the language they used than to get closer to the divine.

The theme of pity, as represented in particular by Michelangelo's sculpture of the *Pietà* in St Peter's, has recently been taken up by Sam Taylor-Wood and the Atelier Van Lieshout. The *Pietà*, a depiction of the Virgin Mary supporting the body of the dead Jesus, reflects an emotional tie, a fertile anxiety over the injustice inflicted on Christ. In the work of art the theme of the *Pietà* takes on the symbolic value of commutative justice acting on the despair and sorrow suffered by people. Unlike justice however, which is a value related to the whole community, pity is an individual sentiment that goes beyond social obligations.

The reference to justice is necessary in so far as justice is intended to make moral amends for suffering by conferring on innocence or guilt the status of a social truth. For Christianity justice is moral equity before God, indicating an ethical and loving attitude towards the other. This implies that out of benevolence or mercy a wrong may also be forgiven without getting anything in return. Consequently, rather than responding to the laws of a collective moral economy, the feeling of pity is only found at the individual level. By forgiving a person that someone else has judged guilty, the sense of compassion sanctions a loving opening towards the other, an initiation into grace.

The implications of this theme of religious origin lend themselves to interpretation in a political key, as happens in Sam Taylor-Wood's *Pietà* (2001), in which the artist holds the actor Robert Downey Jr. in her arms in the classic Michelangelesque pose. Draped across her lap, the actor conveys an impression of exhaustion due to physical pain. Rather than the drama of death by crucifixion, however, what we perceive here is a subtle

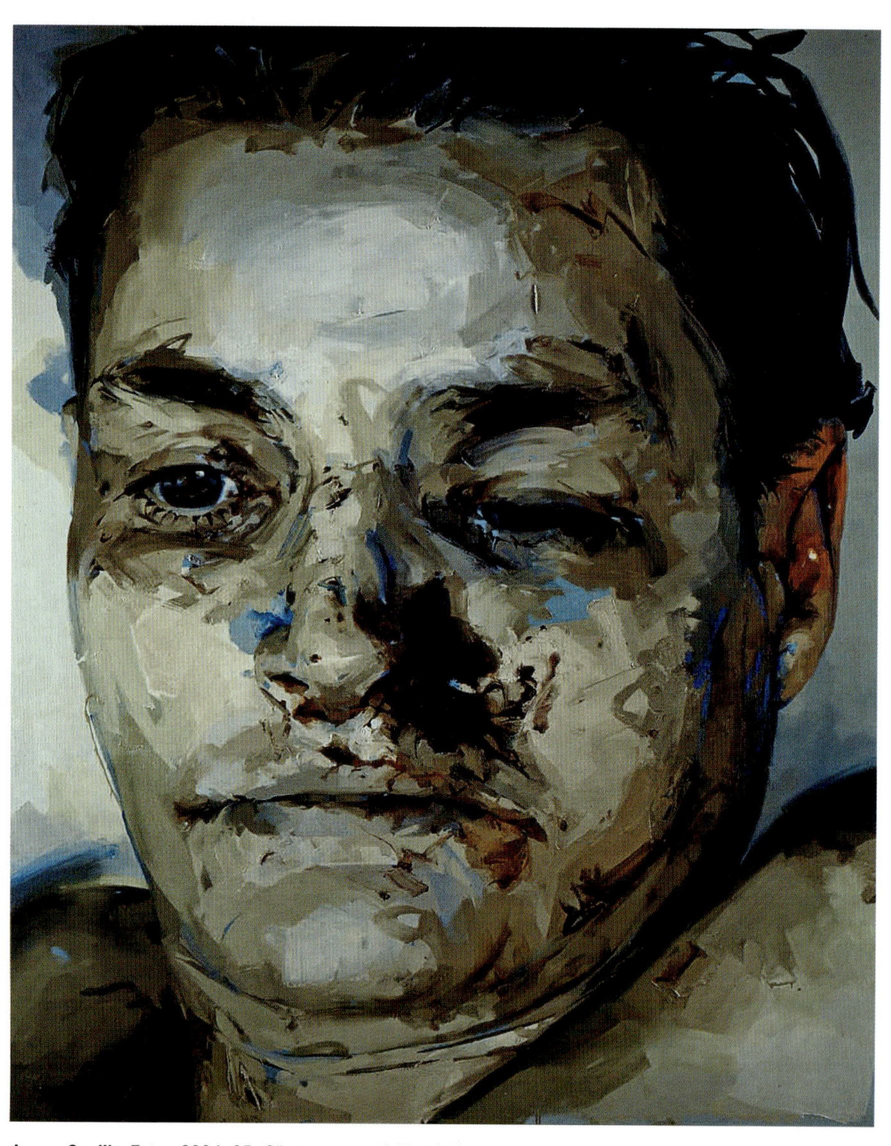

Jenny Saville *Entry*, 2004–05. Oil on canvas, 240 x 191 cm

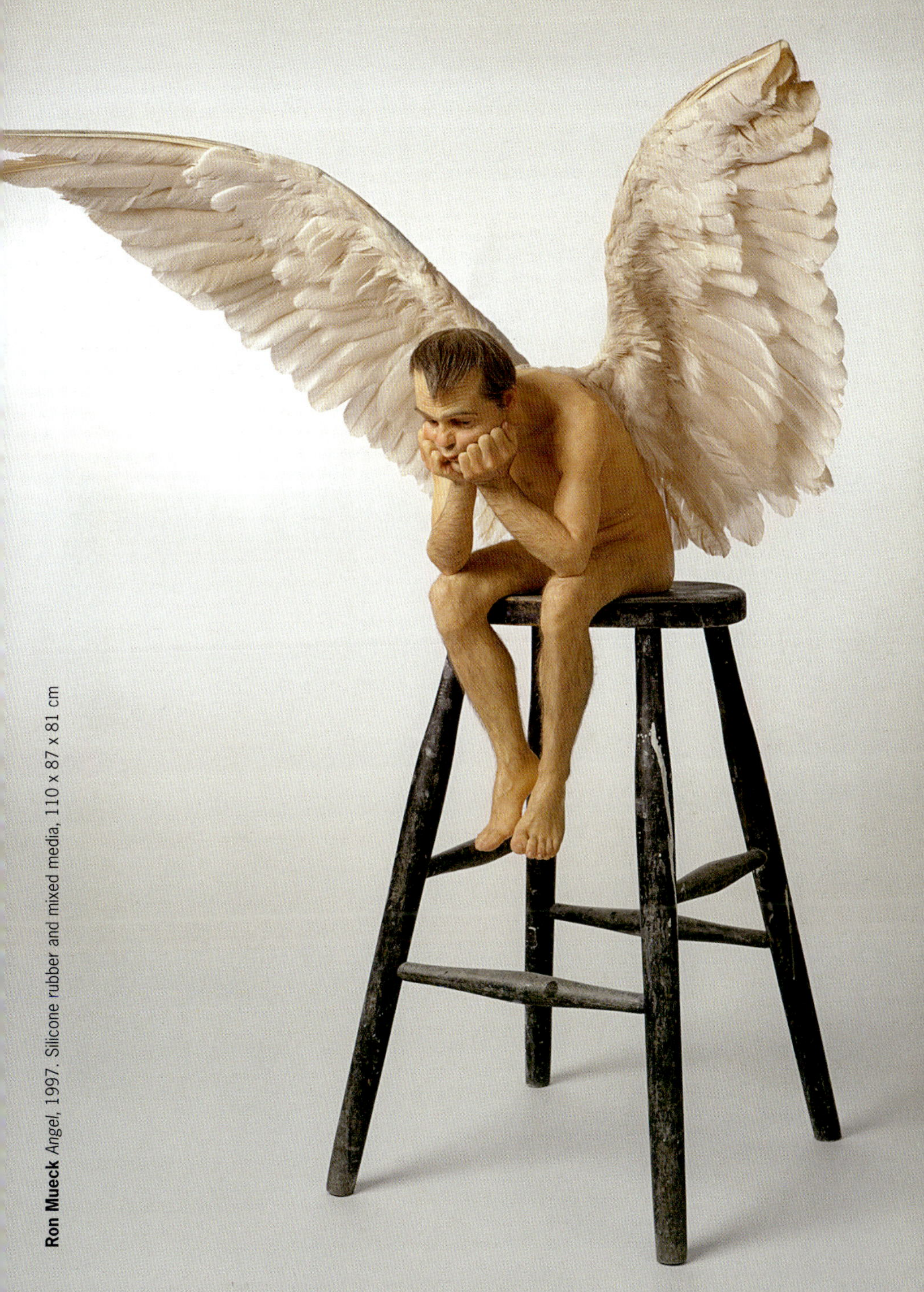

Ron Mueck *Angel*, 1997. Silicone rubber and mixed media, 110 x 87 x 81 cm

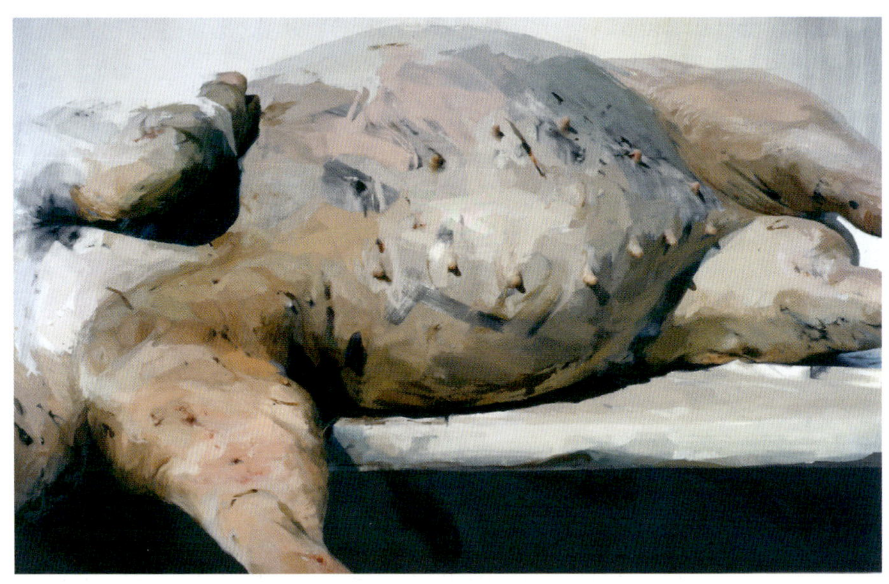

Jenny Saville *Host*, 2000. Oil on canvas, 304.8 x 457.2 cm

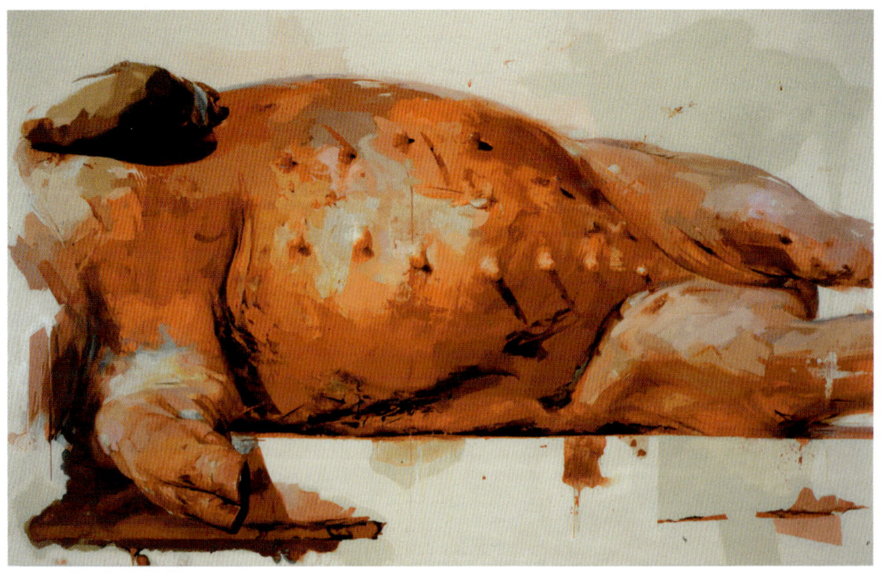

Jenny Saville *Suspension*, 2002–03. Oil on canvas, 292.2 x 453.1 cm

eroticism, accentuated by the uncovered parts of their bodies. The real subject of the work is the relationship between woman and man, a relationship characterized by eroticism, passion, sex and death.

The Atelier Van Lieshout's Michelangelesque *Pietà* stems from Joep van Lieshout's interest in the human body, considered both as architecture and as a complex organic unit, governed by biological changes capable of generating its mechanics. In the Atelier's sculptures and installations, on a large and small scale and always in a simple style, the human figure becomes a silhouette. As well as the body as a whole, Joep van Lieshout has reproduced its internal organs on a gigantic scale. The intention is to bring into the foreground the relationship between humanity and functionality that the body incarnates. What classical image expresses the idea of a humanity that believes it is possible to attain a better condition despite adversity better than Michelangelo's *Pietà*? Van Lieshout uses the *Pietà* as a symbol of collective religious feelings, a constructive sentiment that leads him to regard the life of a community organized on anarchic principles as a non-utopian possibility. This conviction has prompted Van Lieshout to found a micro-city, AVL-Ville, with a constitution that provides for the total freedom of the individual, made self-sufficient through the art of recycling.

The force with which subjects linked to religious iconography are re-emerging reflects an attention to themes common to all peoples and all cultures; but it is also a response to the post-modern artist's need to be popular. This does not mean that artists are adapting to the tastes of the public or refraining from presenting their own vision of the world: except for a few cases, their aim is not to shock but to affirm a new idea of beauty that affects not just the work but also the individual as such. This is the case with Marc Quinn, who at the end of the 1990s produced a series of sculptures in marble, as beautiful to look at as those of the Greek world we see in museums, often without arms or legs as a result of the damage they have suffered. Unlike ancient Greek and Roman sculptures, which express a desire for absolute perfection of the body, Marc Quinn's figures are born with missing parts as they are perfect replicas of gravely deformed people. In this way the artist is implicitly declaring that the conventional group mentality, which does not accept the representation of states outside the norm, asserts a conception of beauty that can turn into a cruel form of violence inflicted on people in these marginal situations.

In another series of sculptures, *Chemical Life Support* (2005), Quinn uses white polymer wax (which looks like the marble of classical sculptures in photographs, but is actually soft and produces a confusing visual

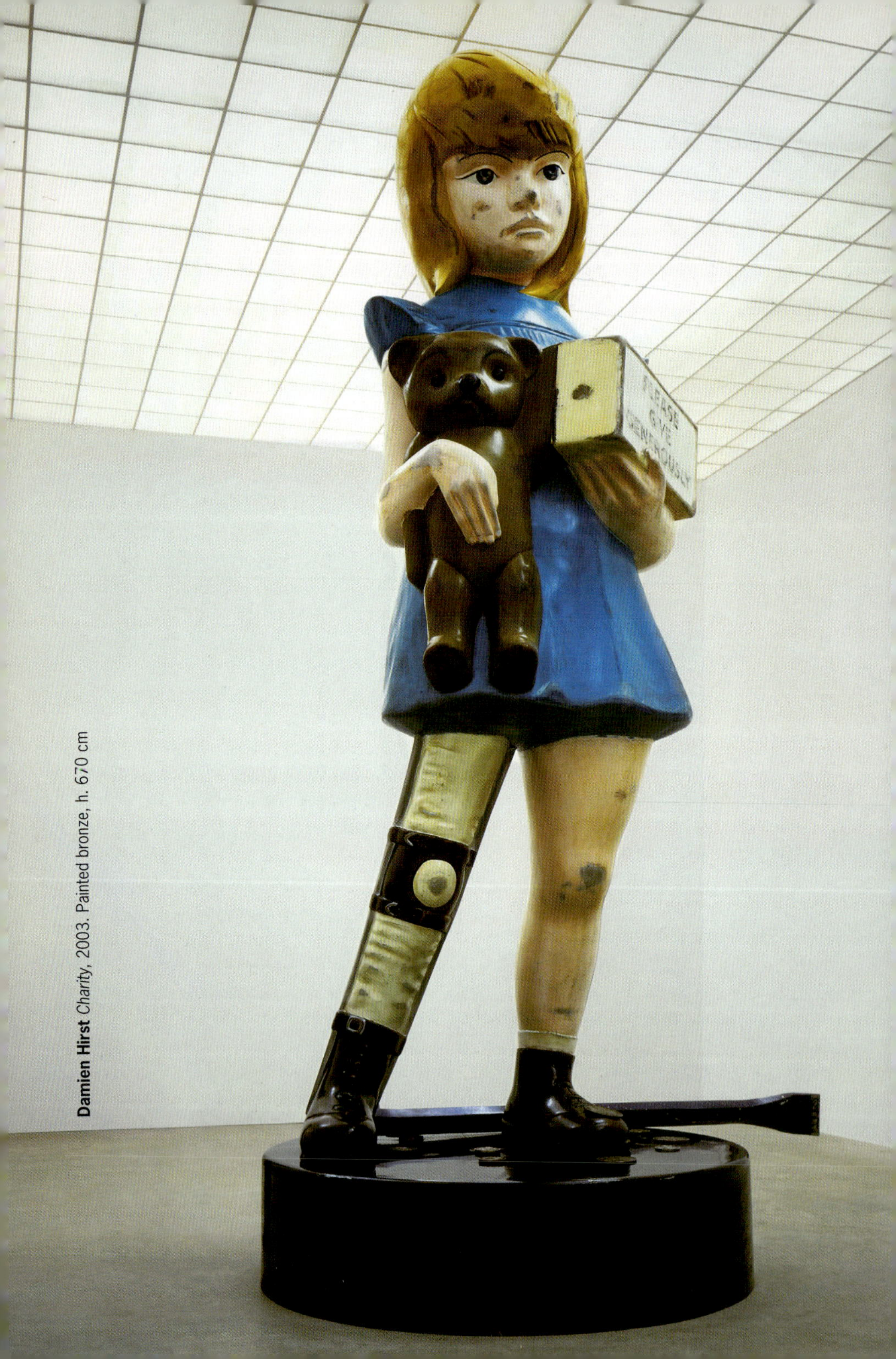

Damien Hirst *Charity*, 2003. Painted bronze, h. 670 cm

impression when seen from close-up), mixed with the drugs that each of his subjects has to take daily to stay alive. They are portrayed lying on the ground, in a sort of stupor, as if they were suspended between life and death (the models posed resting on a cushion, which was then eliminated in the sculpture). This further accentuates the sense of suspension in time and space. In other works Quinn uses high technology to immerse flowers and plants in silicone oil kept at a temperature of minus twenty degrees, thereby suspending them in a state between life and death: in reality the plants are already dead, even though they look perfectly healthy (silicone oil has the property of remaining fluid and transparent at that temperature). They decay the instant the current that powers the refrigerator is turned off. With these works Quinn is underlining our dependence on such artificial factors as electric power or medicine.

Thus humanity and nature are sacred figures in Marc Quinn's work, always in suspension between life and death, between health and sickness, between being themselves and being their own representation. Recently Quinn has been making sculptures of skeletons kneeling in prayer. One of these has its hands joined and is entitled *Waiting for God*, while the bone structure of the arms and legs of the other, *Waiting for Godot*, is deformed, so that it is unable to join its hands. In yet another version the praying skeleton is entitled *Angel*.

Waiting for Godot is the famous play by Samuel Beckett in which the two characters, Estragon and Vladimir, wait for someone who never comes. And the questions raised by the work of British artists like Marc Quinn, Damien Hirst, Jenny Saville, Mark Wallinger and Sam Taylor-Wood seem to be the same as Beckett's: What to do with life? How to get through it? In Beckett's work the existential disquiet is focused on the habits, the abysses of boredom and stupidity into which it casts us: suicide is presented as one of the easiest solutions. The ineluctability of fate resurfaces in the work of Marc Quinn, who by entitling one of his works *Waiting for Godot* speaks to us like Beckett of someone who, while awaited, is never going to turn up and whose name evokes that of God.

The same inevitability can be found in Mark Wallinger's *Angel*, a video showing the artist, wearing the dark glasses of a blind man, on an escalator that is taking him in the opposite direction to the one in which he wants to go. To his left and right, between people riding on other escalators, Wallinger has placed two rows of British flags in which the normal colours have been replaced by the orange and green of the Irish flag to underline the irreconcilability of nationalist Catholics and unionist Protestants. Wallinger's *Angel* is a work on destiny, faith and vision,

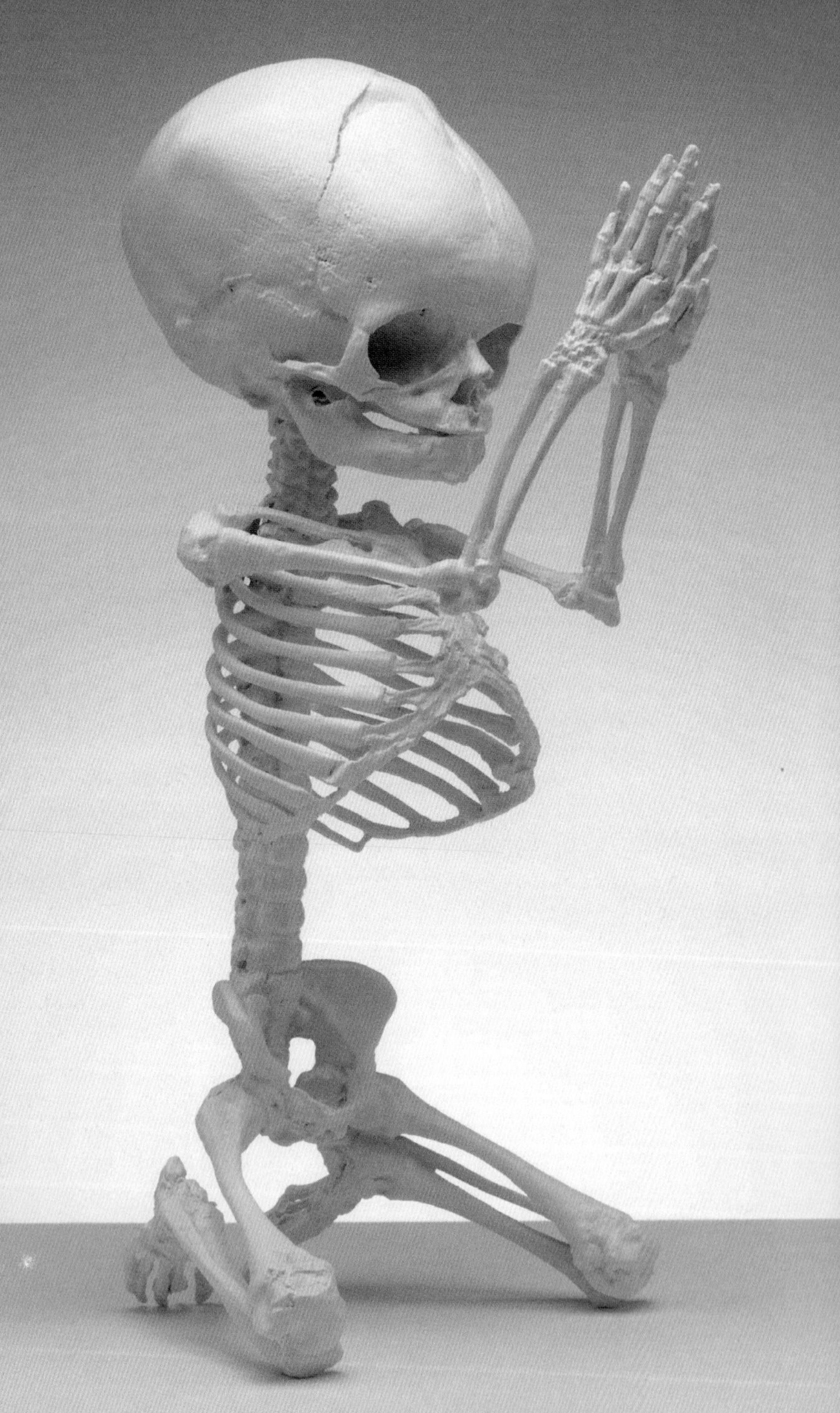

Marc Quinn *Angel*, 2006. Painted bronze, 30 x 14 x 16.5 cm

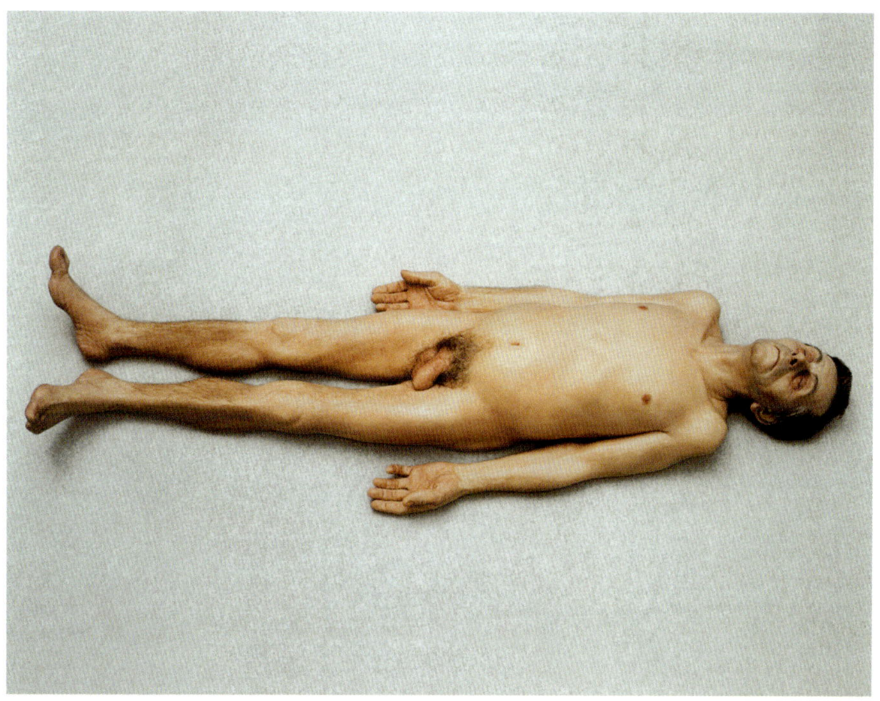

Ron Mueck *Dead Dad*, 1996–97. Silicone, acrylic, polyurethane and foam rubber, 20 x 102 x 38 cm

speaking to us of a blind man who, with no possibility of choice, is brought into a situation characterized by strong forms of incompatibility, as demonstrated by the improbable flags between which he passes.

And ineluctability is present in another *Angel* (1997), this time by Ron Mueck, a sculptor who accentuates the sense of the human solitude with an exaggerated realism. In Mueck the sentiment of pity is evident. His subjects have downcast eyes, as do those of the hyperrealistic sculptures of Duane Hanson (from the 1970s). The two artists bestow a sense of existential defeat on their subjects, but where Hanson makes the sculpture a perfect copy of the individual, which looks real, Mueck changes its scale. In this way he creates a sort of visual wrong-footing that brings the image back within the realm of representation. In this case the angel is a thin and disconsolate man, naked and seated on a giant stool with his legs dangling. The feathered wings on his shoulders, typical of the religious images of the past, are the only angelic feature. This sculpture, like others produced by the artist, conveys a sense of defeat in the face of death

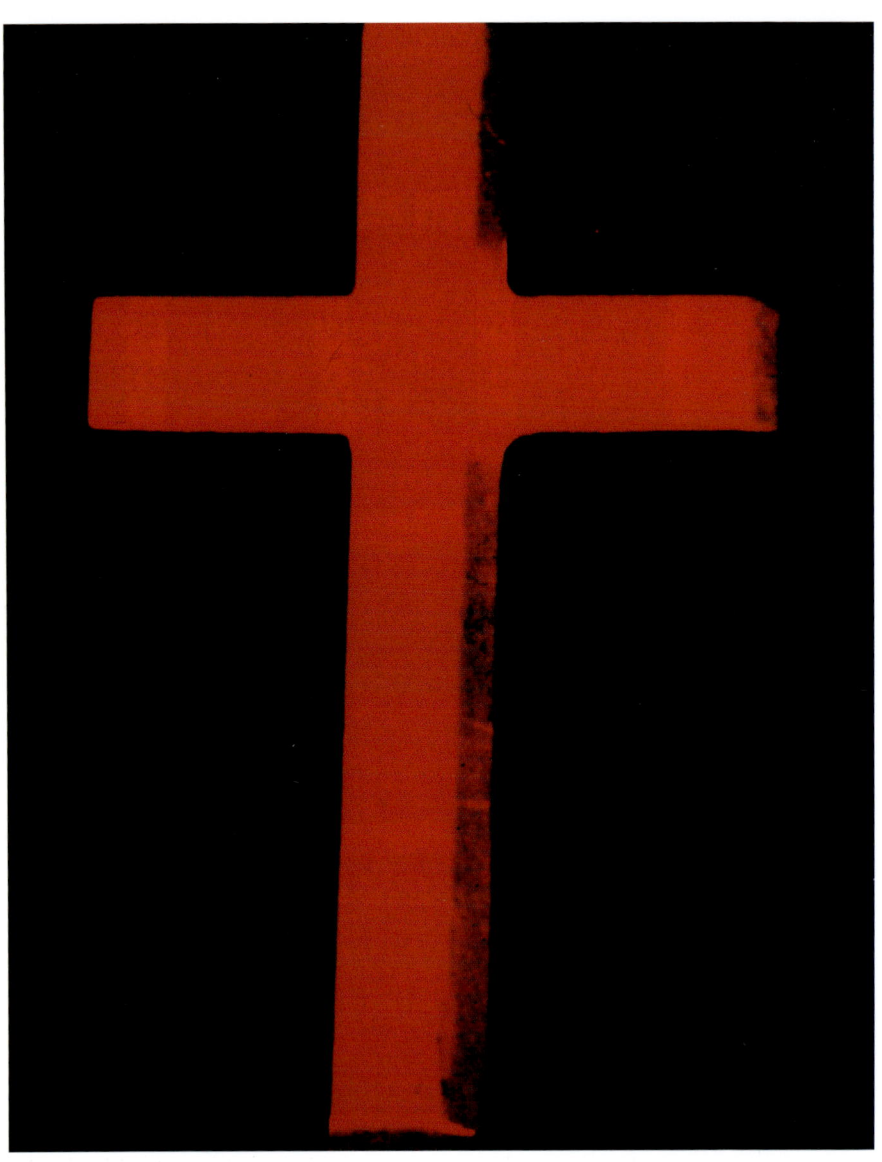

Andy Warhol *Cross*, 1982. Acrylic paints and silk-screen print on canvas, 228.6 x 177.8 cm

and of existence in general. Among the subjects of his sculptures are a very old woman sleeping with her mouth open, another seated in a position of prayer, a young woman about to give birth and one who has just given birth, still linked to her child by the umbilical cord. *Dead Dad* shows us a naked man, lying on his back. The realism of the subject makes this work a dramatic representation of death, while the small size of the figure accentuates the illusion of art. In this sense, Mueck and Hirst are profoundly different artists.

The human destiny of which Mueck, Hirst, Quinn, Wallinger and Saville speak is a sealed fate. Through their work they show that life is an appointment we cannot fail to keep, but also one whose phases we cannot determine. The final appointment is with death.

Rarely has death been represented in such an explicit manner as it was in the 1990s. Andres Serrano photographed corpses in mortuaries, Joel-Peter Witkin even brought cadavers into the studio. Both artists explained their choices as expressions of pity, but also as a way of showing the different forms through which evil manifests itself. Serrano and Witkin have also represented the figure of Christ. 'My first photographs', declares Witkin, 'were linked to contemporary images of Christ and of woman. Two basic poles. The reason I chose these images came from my personal need to see the "supernatural". The fact is I'm bound to life. The artists of the past painted according to a certain idea of holiness. As for me, a photographer of spiritual icons, I put the imagery of Christ back in its historical context. But at a certain point I expanded on things. I went further, in photography, taking "models", "people" who represent agony, joy, suffering, misery, even the desire to live'.[6]

The awareness of death is a constant in the work of Jenny Saville, who overlays the feeling of pity with that of rebellion. Her subjects are never dead, but they are often ill or seriously wounded individuals. There is a sort of resignation to suffering in them, but also a strong attachment to life. 'Death is the only real certainty of life and I want to look at life with eyes wide open',[7] says Saville, who in order to give greater realism to her paintings looks at medical publications in which disease is shown in an objective way, never interpreted emotionally. Her study of limbs mutilated by explosions, of war documents, is also associated with an interest in the manipulation of flesh by surgery. 'I use oil paint as a solid, tangible substance, that for me has in itself a reference to flesh', adds Saville, who right from the outset has drawn on the theories of Luce Irigaray.[8]

Saville substitutes the feeling of pity with a sense of justice. Her painting is political, in so far as she sees in the human being's condition of suf-

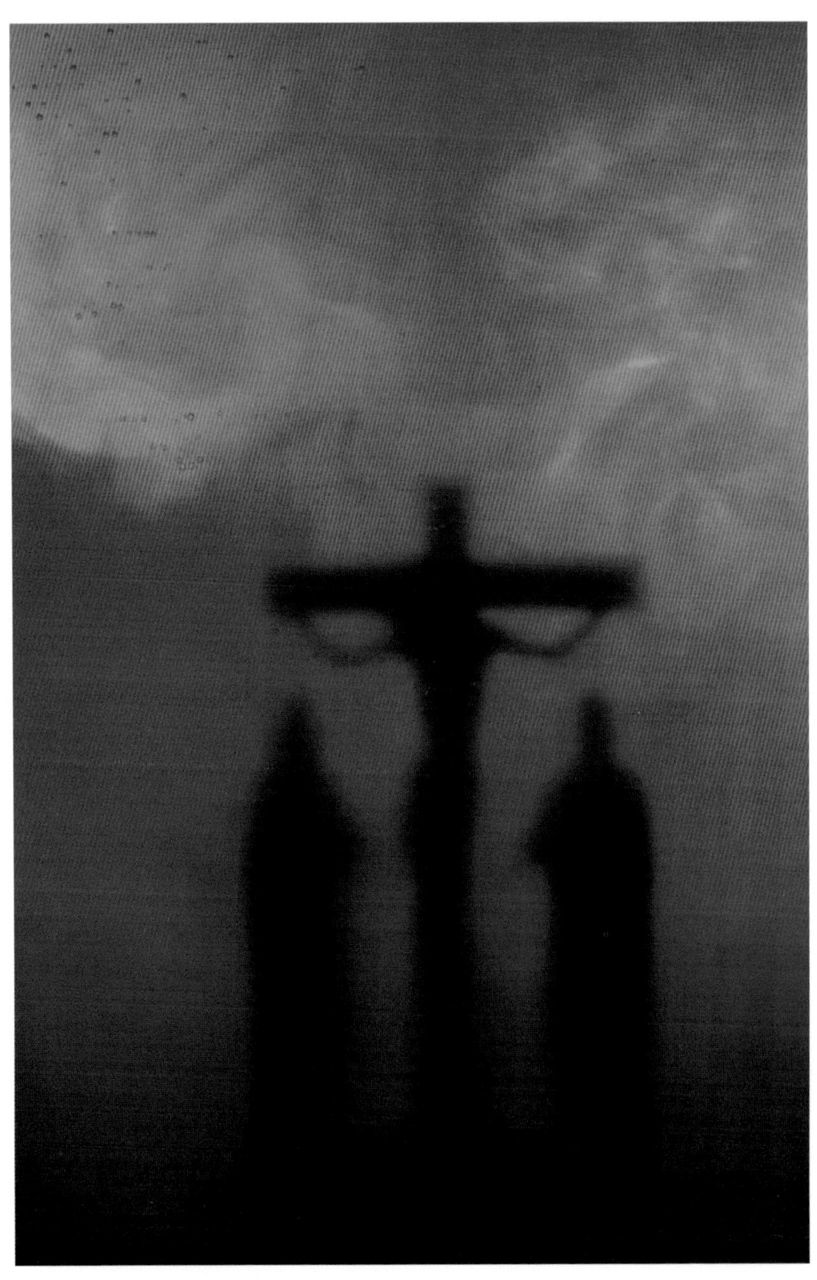

Andres Serrano *Crucifixion II*, 1987. Cibachrome, silicone and plexiglass, 101.6 x 69.9 cm

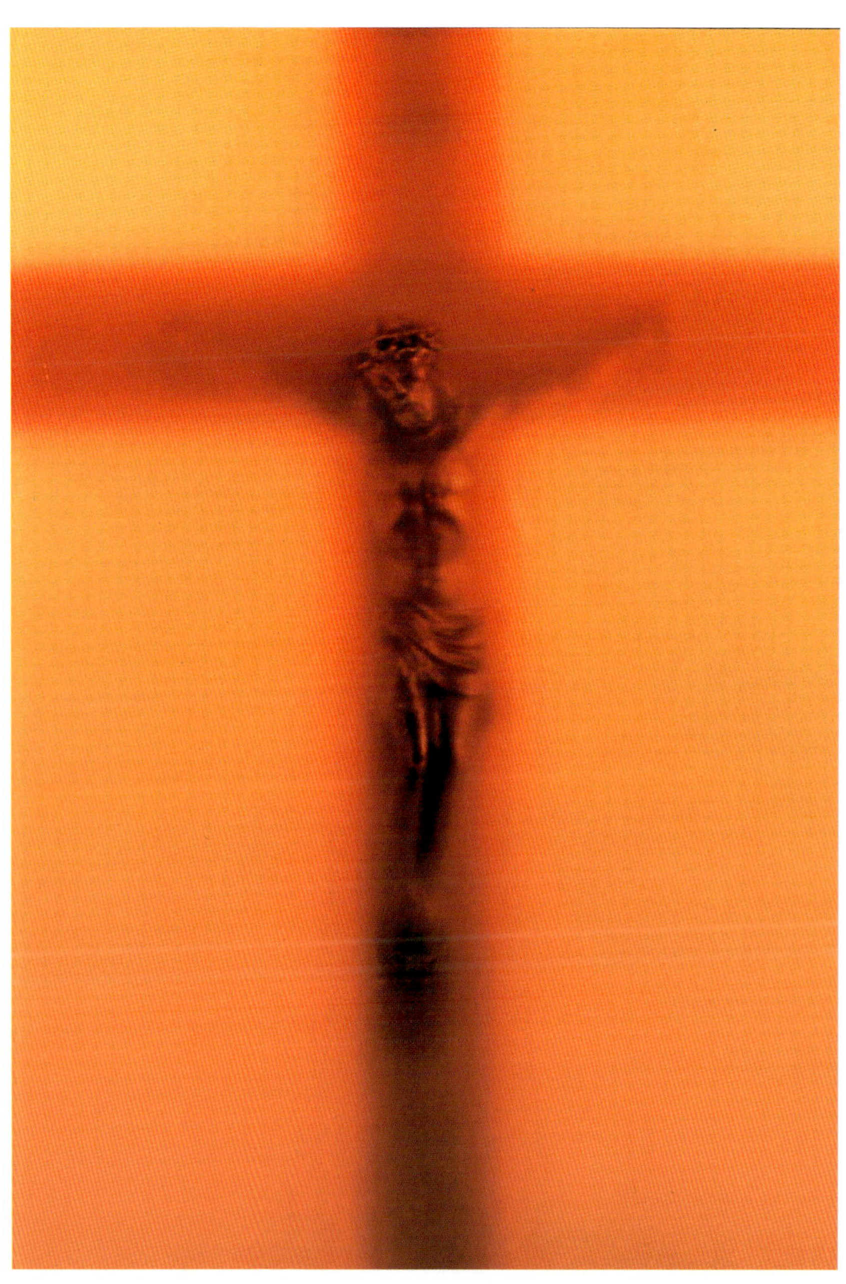

Andres Serrano *Piss Light*, 1987. Cibachrome, silicone and plexiglass, 101.6 x 69.9 cm

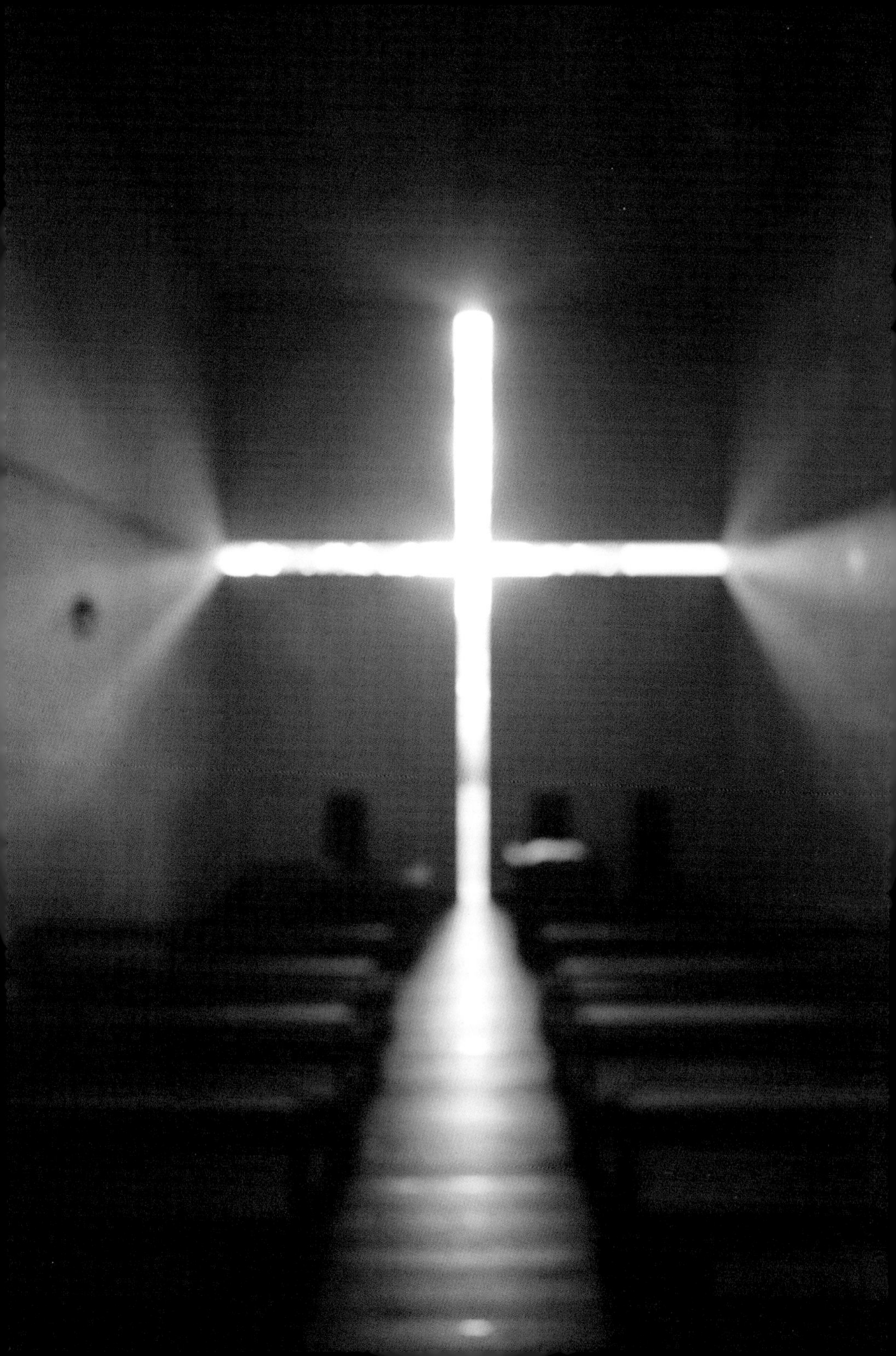

fering a lack of respect for diversity, an absence of fraternity, a failure of sympathy. Saville presents animals as human beings and human beings as animals. *Host*, for example, depicts the swollen belly of a mature sow, ready to give milk. The teats allude to the female body. The head is left out in order to create an ambiguity between the animal's body and that of a woman. The choice of a sow has other implications: in medieval images the pig is a symbol of lust, and it is regarded by both Muslims and Jews as an impure, dirty creature, a carrier of disease. Muslims even believe that if you come into contact with it just before you die the gates of heaven will be barred to you.

In the West the term 'pig' is one of the worst insults that can be addressed to a person. Despite this, modern science believes that it will be possible to transplant the organs of the pig into human beings. So the pig becomes a symbol of the sacrificial victim. It atones for sins that it has not committed, giving up part of itself to humans, who nevertheless treat it with repugnance.

Saville returned to the same subject two years later in a painting entitled *Suspension*, but this time the pig was covered with excoriations and dripping with blood. This second version of *Host* came as an emotional response to the attacks on the Twin Towers on 11 September 2001. The new title indicates that our life is at the mercy of events. Since that moment red has predominated in Saville's works, even when it is limited to a fleeting touch that does not fill the whole of the scene.[9]

Individuals become aware of death on the loss of a person they love, and yet Freud teaches us that even when faced with incontrovertible proof their unconscious goes on believing they will live forever. The child perceives an emotional loss in a different way from the adult. Both are deeply hurt, both tend to repress their suffering, but on the plane of the relationship with reality their defence mechanisms are profoundly different. Faced with death, adults tend not to lie to themselves, while children are able to deal with their grief through the stories told them by their parents, which help to console them even though they often do not correspond to the truth.

So we learn from the start that the fanciful story is a vital element, a driving force in our acquisition of myths, dreams, legends and the moral teachings implicit in them, passing through the trauma of death. Myths and legends are also elements common to all religions, however different their motivations.

Humanity has always utilized the mythical and religious story as a constructive and propulsive element for its existence, absorbing religion

Hiroshi Sugimoto *Church of the Light*, 1997 (arch. Tadao Ando). Silver gelatine print, 149.2 x 119.4 cm

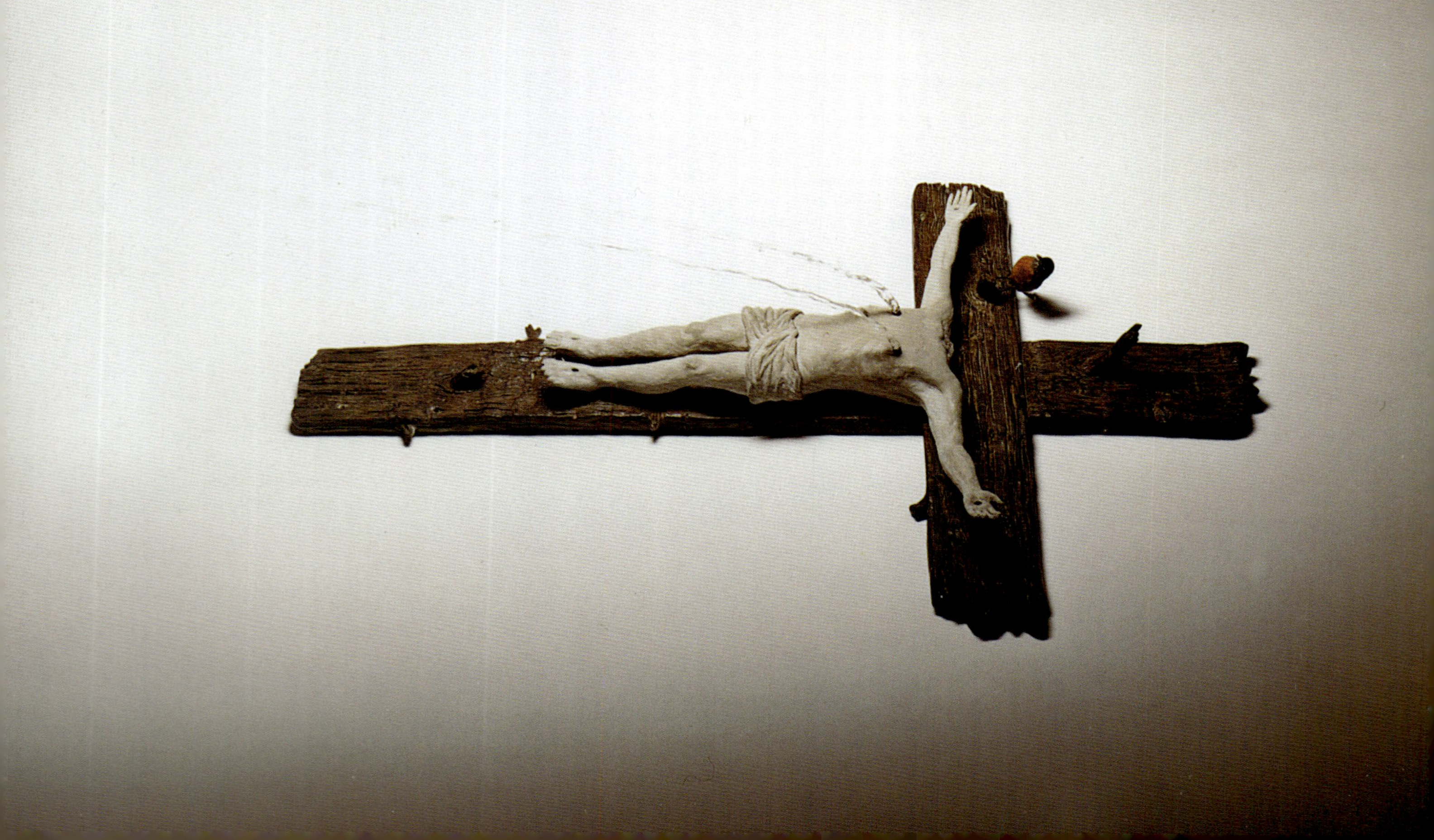

Robert Gober *Untitled* (detail), 2004–05. Bronze, artificial feathers, re-creation of American robin and water, 104 x 100 x 63 cm
Installation at the Matthew Marks Gallery, New York

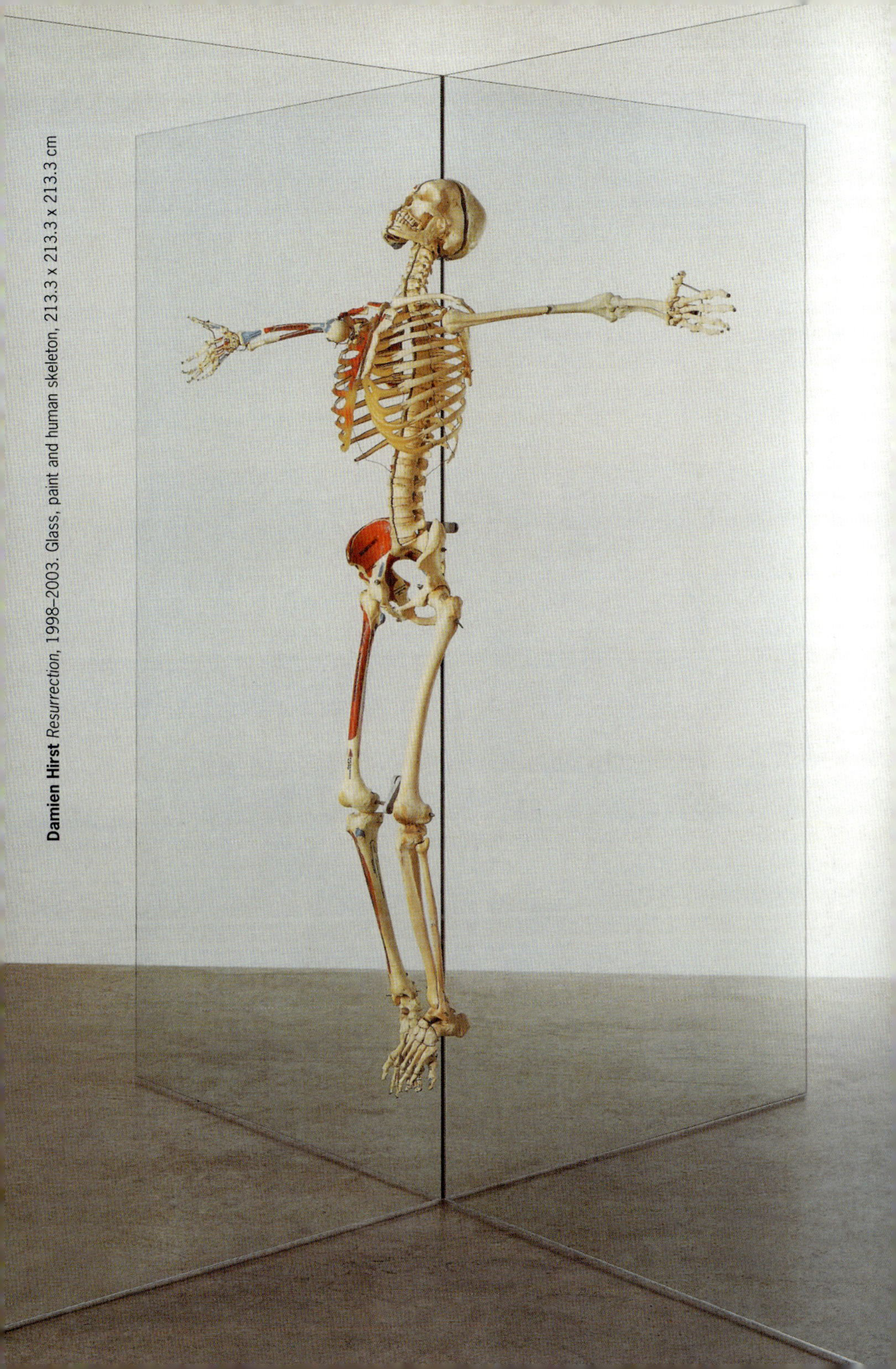

Damien Hirst *Resurrection*, 1998–2003. Glass, paint and human skeleton, 213.3 x 213.3 x 213.3 cm

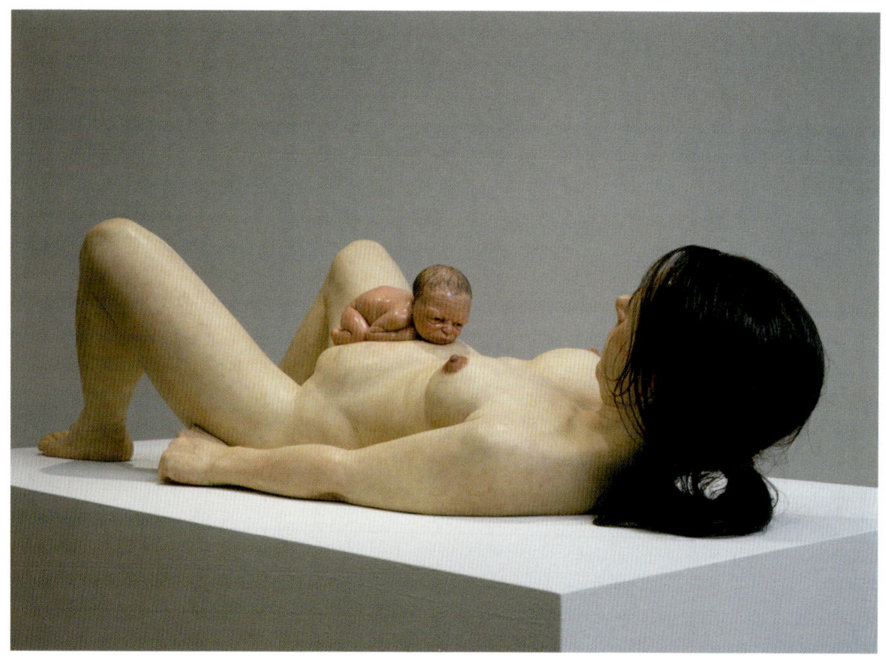

Ron Mueck *Mother and Child*, 2001–04. Silicone, acrylic, polyurethane and foam rubber, 24 x 89 x 38 cm

through art ever since the Palaeolithic and the time of the first paintings on the walls of the Lascaux grotto. This relationship is also stressed in the work of Hiroshi Sugimoto, who among other things has photographed a series of dioramas that show primitive man immersed in an archaic nature in which even the smallest occurrence can trigger fear and assume divine connotations. The relationship with death prevails, as is demonstrated by other works of his in which the camera, set up in a dark and empty cinema, shoots the entire length of a film, so that the flash of white light given off by the screen at the moment the film comes to an end will wipe out everything, leaving only the details of the hall visible. In this way the artist dwells on the end of every narration, showing that the end of a life does not mean the end of everything.

Another anthropological vision of the individual is offered by Tim Noble & Sue Webster, who based their cycle of realistic sculptures *The New Barbarians* on a museum-style reconstruction of one of the first species of hominids, the *Australopithecus afarensis*. Two naked, primitive figures, looking grotesque and defenceless, wander through a desolate land as if they were survivors of an apocalypse. Once again art confronts us with our

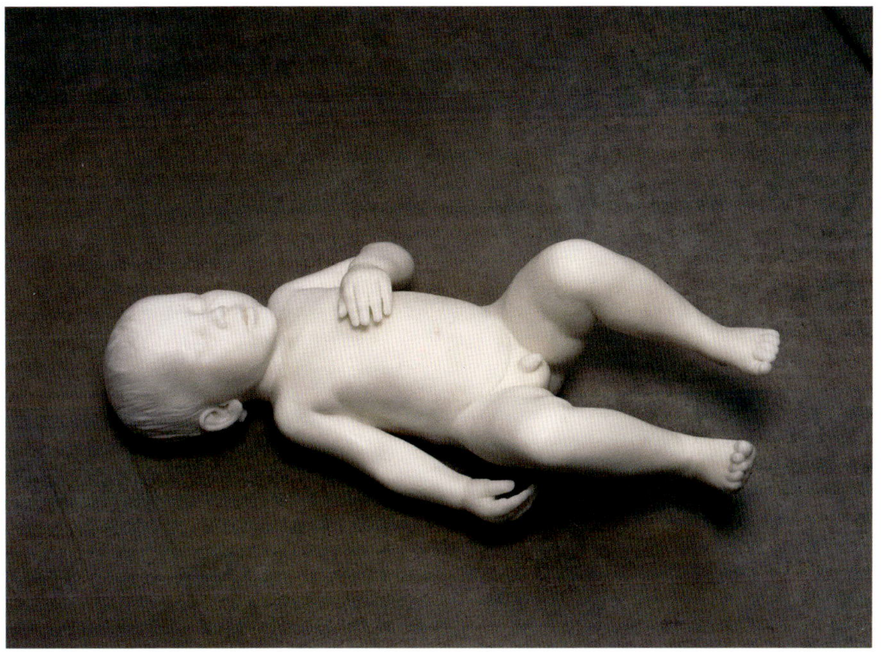

Marc Quinn *Innoscience*, 2004. Wax, synthetic polymer, dried glucose syrup, fractionated coconut oil, hybrid safflower oil and canola oil, mixed with assorted medicinal substances, 25 x 68 x 32.5 cm

nature, reminding us that our future might coincide with our origins. Anthropologists (from Lévi-Strauss to André Leroi-Gourhan) tell us that prehistoric human beings were not different from ourselves. They thought like us and also had a sense of the sacred, although their attitude towards it may have been more reverential and fearful. Above all they were afraid of natural events, in which they saw a mysterious and supernatural dimension. We are not astonished by an eclipse of the sun, a hurricane or a bolt of lightning setting fire to a tree or striking a person, nor do we associate this kind of event with the anger of the gods. But for early human beings the true source of religious feelings lay in the encounter with death, with the fear or attraction that it exercised, with its overcoming or its exaltation: the encounter with death is a formative experience, embracing a vast gamut of emotions capable of shaping not just the entire intellectual sphere of the individual, but also the spiritual and religious identity of a society.

In every culture it is the community that decides on the religious education to be imparted to the young. Every church and creed promulgates its own scriptures and requires faith. Questioning a sacred text has often been seen as an incitement to disorder. As can be seen from the Catholic church's

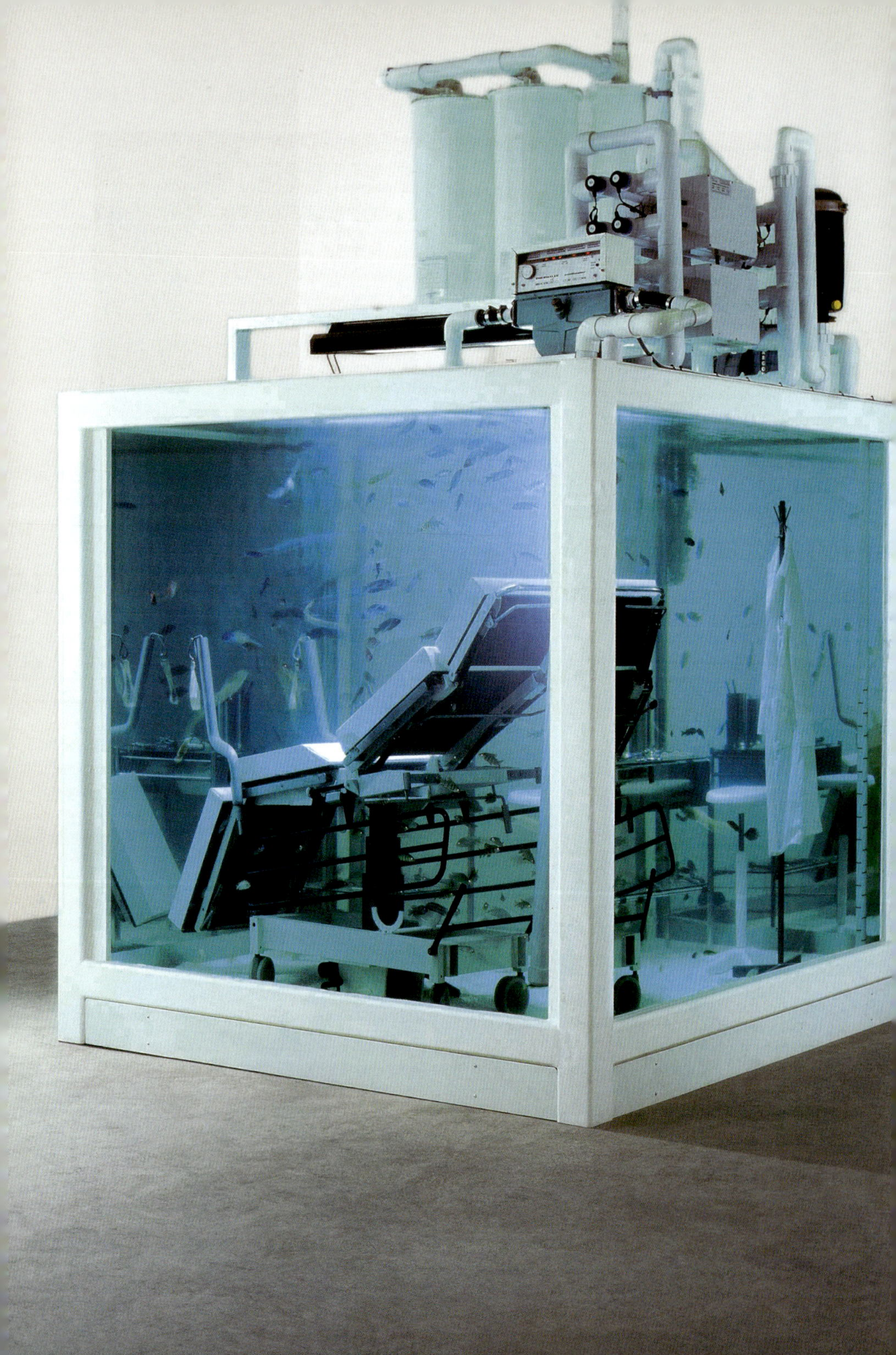

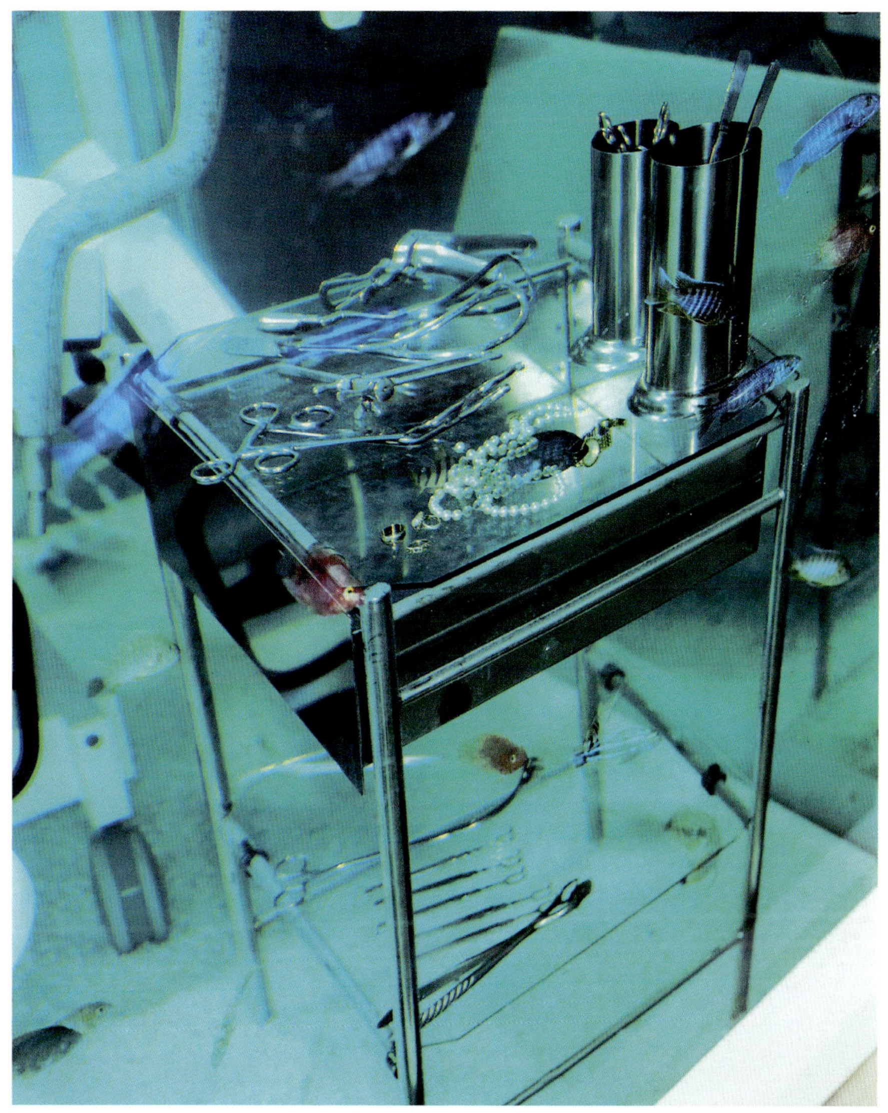

Damien Hirst *Lost Love*, 2000. Glass and steel fish tank, trolley, table, stool, surgical instruments, clothes hook with gown, jewellery and African river fish, 274 x 213 x 213 cm

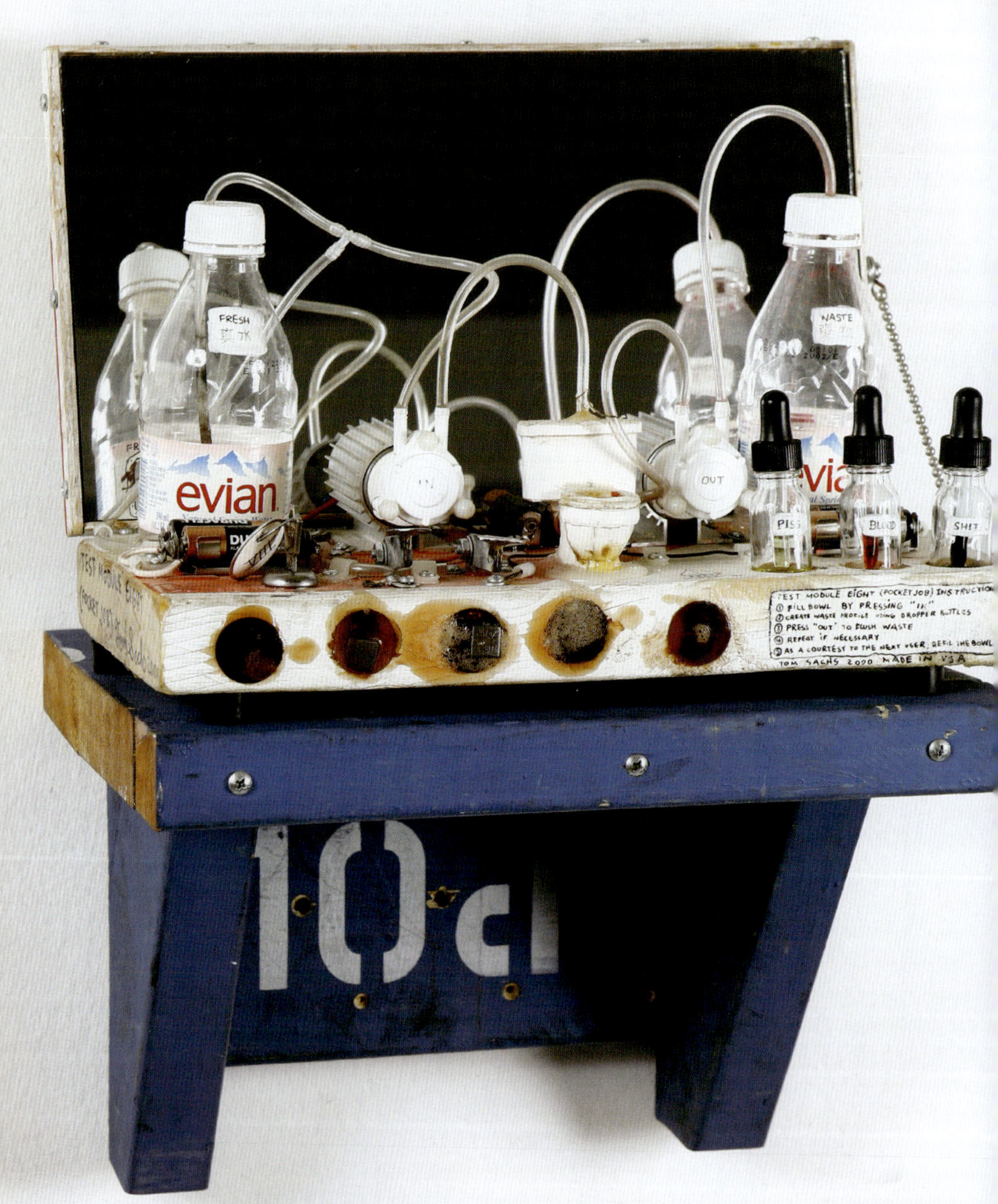

Tom Sachs *Test Module Eight*, 2000. Mixed media, 36 x 50 x 36 cm

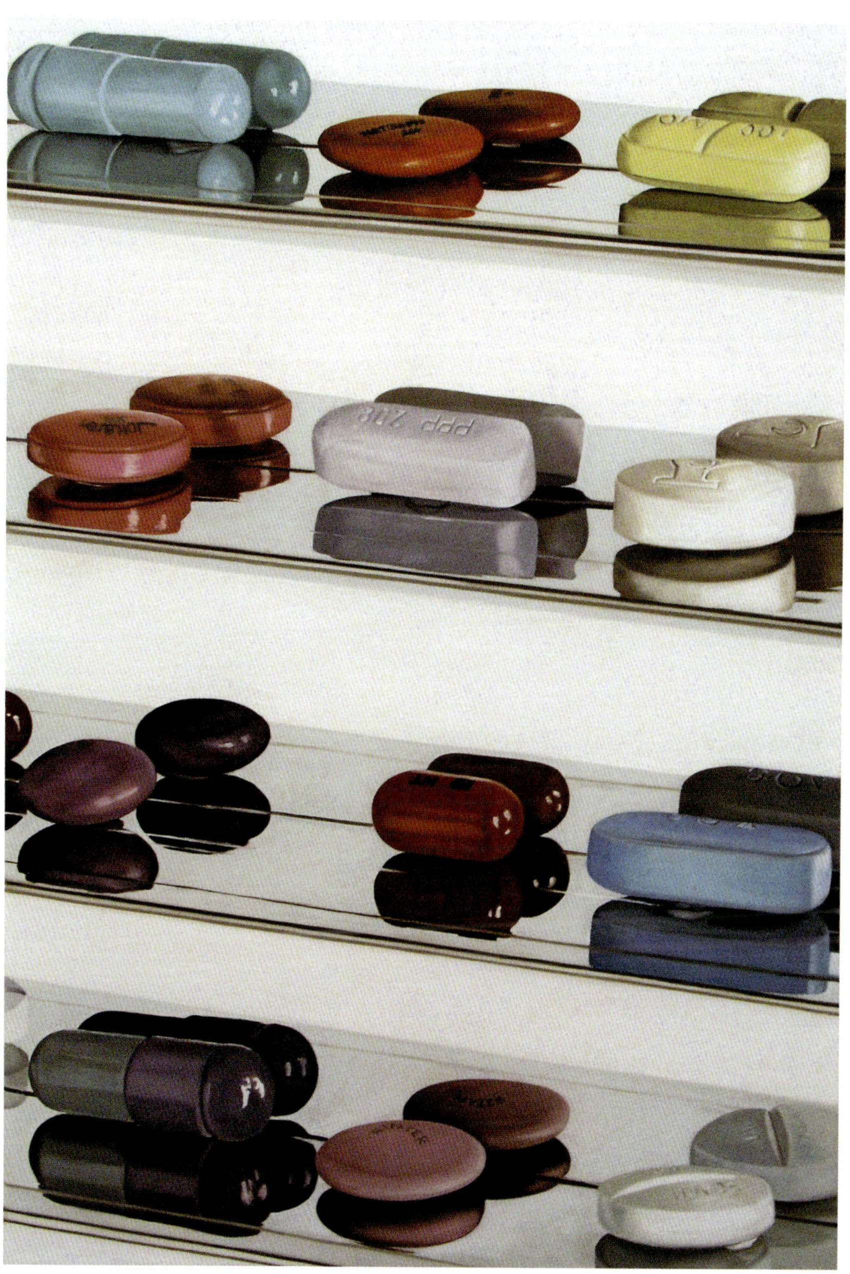

Damien Hirst *Twelve Pills*, 2004–05. Oil on canvas, 114.3 x 76.2 cm

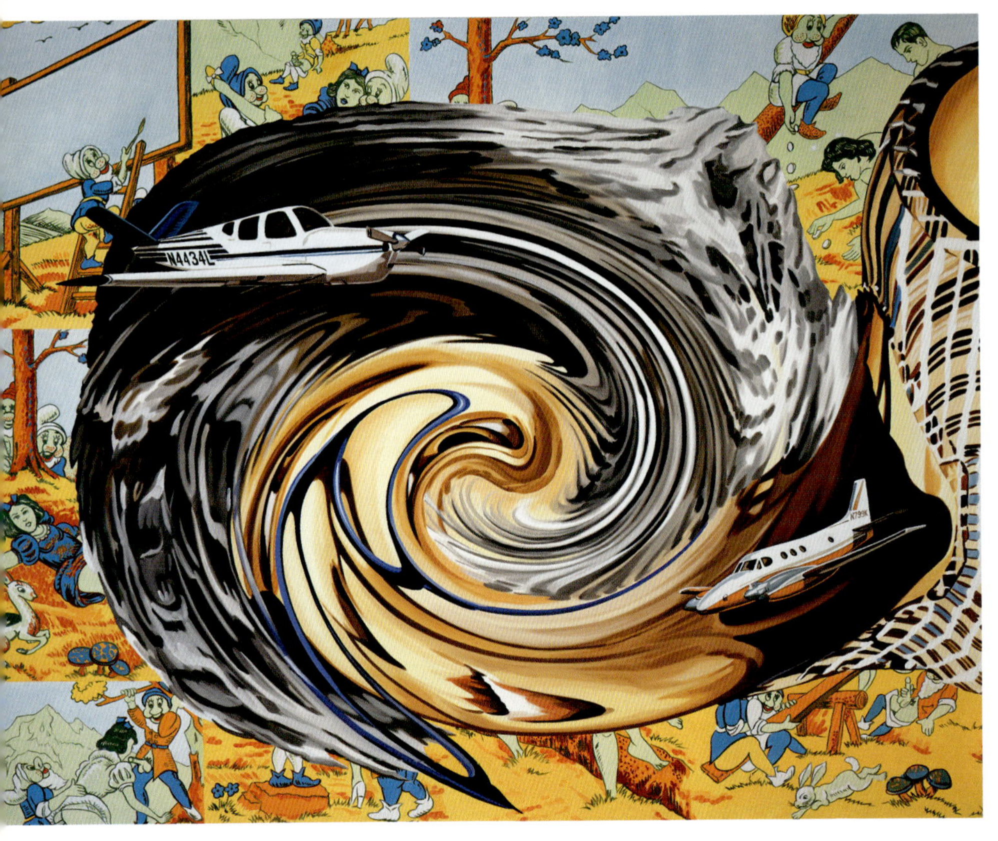

David Salle *Snow White*, 2004. Oil on linen, 96 x 120 cm

treatment of Giordano Bruno and Galileo Galilei and the expulsion of Spinoza by his Jewish community, this has social and political implications.

And yet the heretic does not necessarily deny the truth of the Holy Scriptures nor reject the interpretation and authority of the clergy. The crux of our relationship with divinity is the question of life before and after our death on earth: the vital impetus and not the fear of what awaits us after death is what has driven artists in the past to appropriate religious images above and beyond the requirements laid down by their clients. It is the same sense of emptiness that has prompted many artists in the last few decades to shift the centre of their interest to the more pregnant aspects of this world, transforming religious iconography into a sort of social and political history of humanity.

[1] D. Hirst and G. Burn, *On the Way to Work*, London, Faber and Faber: 2001. The latter part of the quotation has been translated from the Italian edition, *Manuale per giovani artisti*, Milan: Postmedia Books, 2004, pp. 22–23.
[2] J. Deitch, *Post Human*, exhibition catalogue (Castello di Rivoli), Turin, 1992, p. 146.
[3] A. B. Edelma, Z. Felix, I. Gianelli and D. Joannou, ibid., p. 145.
[4] There is a vast literature on this subject. As far as Latin America is concerned, the reader is referred to B. Díaz del Castillo, *The Conquest of New Spain* (1552), London: Penguin Books, 1963, and, for the inquisition, to B. Netanyahu, *The Origins of the Inquisition*, New York: Random House, 1995.
[5] M. Abramović, 'Balkan Erotic Epic', in *Balkan Epic*, exhibition catalogue (Hangar Bicocca, Milan), Milan: Skira, 2006, p. 64.
[6] J.-P. Witkin, *Flowers of Evil, Flowers of Morality*, conversation with P. Amine, exhibition catalogue (Infinito Ltd Gallery, Turin), Turin, 2002.
[7] Jenny Saville, conversation with the author, 2005.
[8] French philosopher and psychoanalyst close to the women's movement who was one of the first, in the 1960s, to challenge the ideas of Freud and Lacan. He held that it was through the figure of the father that a female or male child, entering into relationship with others by means of a web of social significances, became a true individual. The question directly concerns the way in which a woman perceives herself through her body and her speech, her projection of herself onto the other, her recognition and acceptance of herself within the parameters established by a culture created by male minds.
[9] The reference to *Host* and *Suspension* is taken from my earlier essay 'Jenny Saville and the Origin of the Wound', in *Damien Hirst, David Salle, Jenny Saville — The Bilotti Chapel*, exhibition catalogue (Museo Carlo Bilotti — Aranciera di Villa Borghese, Rome), Milan: Mondadori Electa, 2005.

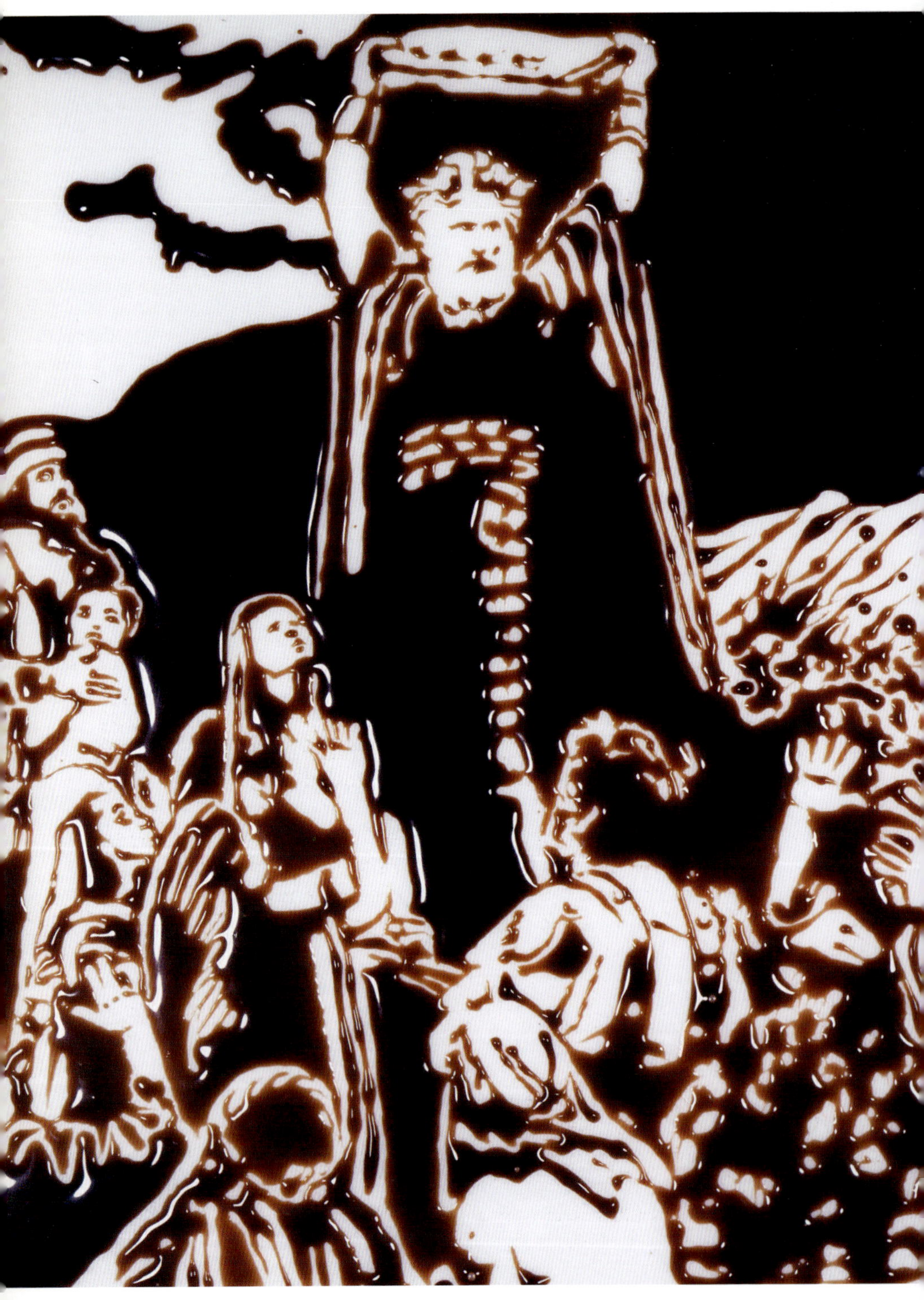

Perfection and Perdition

Gianni Mercurio

Perfection and perdition: it is out of these two concepts that the relationship between human beings and their God was born and has developed, to the point of turning into an intricate labyrinth. If on the one hand the idea of a benevolent and merciful God who sees and attends to everything and shows us the way is a comforting one, on the other rules, precepts and dogmas do not sit well with the intemperance of human nature. Defiance, the desire to choose different roads from the ones indicated to us, the need to venture beyond where it is permitted, in short, to disobey the Father, lead naturally to perdition, of which the Devil is the symbol *par excellence*. Satan the son turned out for his disobedience, not his betrayal; and still a son.

Devil and Demon are Greek words that were given a new meaning by Christianity, and following the transformation they have undergone over time gives us a clear idea of the evolution of the concept of evil. While the Devil is mentioned for the first time at the beginning of the Bible — the third chapter of Genesis tells the story of the temptation of Eve by the serpent — St Paul was the first to make clear the relationship between God, Satan and men: God wants to save his children, while the other strives to make men fall into perdition, during the time of their brief passage on the earth and forever in the next life. Lucifer, prince of those bodiless beings who, committing the sin of pride, left the house of the Father before the Father had created man, has a thousand faces. Each different. Each horrible. And those who claim to have actually seen him, like Luther, speak

Vik Muniz *Charlton Heston* (from the *Pictures of Chocolate* series), 1999. Cibachrome, 157 x 118 cm

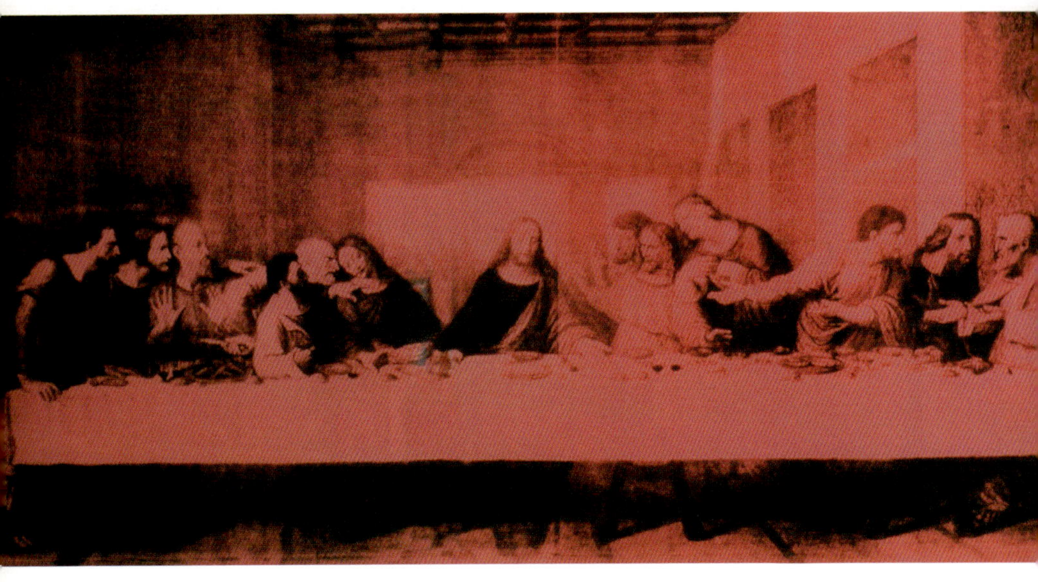

Andy Warhol *The Last Supper*, 1986. Acrylic paints and silk-screen print on canvas, 198.1 x 777.2 cm

of a foul being: the coarse face of evil. For Evil has a face and a body too. Crippled, lame, ugly. Obscene.

This is the morbid side. If beauty is attractive, the ugly, the depraved, is even more so.

With these premises, the myth of the Devil, of Evil, has become one of the most prominent subjects of sacred art. From Giotto at the Arena in Padua to Simone Martini and Orcagna in Florence's Santa Maria Novella, Luca Signorelli in the Cathedral of Orvieto and Michelangelo in the Sistine Chapel, artists have chosen to interpret the painful conflict of the eternal human struggle between Good and Evil. Between God and the Devil.

With the Renaissance came the great turning-point: Lucifer became a person. An individual. He was separated from the host of demons, of which he was still the leader, and his figure was slowly transformed. Now Lucifer was the one who had dared, the great rebel who had challenged the Father in an act of immense courage. While Tasso had written that in his eyes one read 'terror and death', Giambattista Marino spoke of mournful eyes in *La strage degli innocenti*. Satan looked mournful because his state of a fallen angel made him sad. Once very beautiful, his

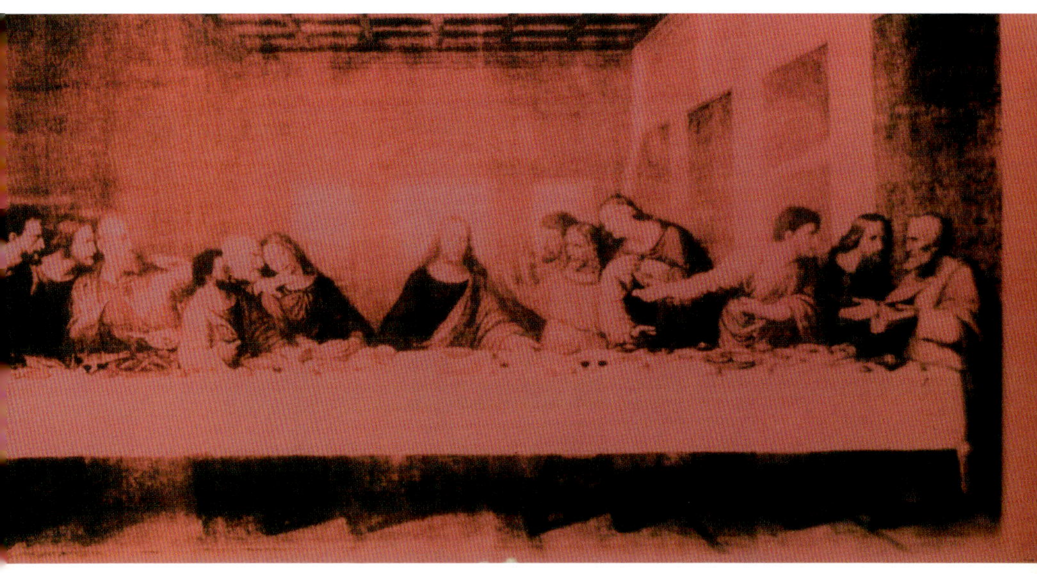

body now lived on earth, and his dealings with men, his absorption of the desires and sufferings of each of his victims, had changed him and made him monstrous. In *Paradise Lost*, Milton, who had read the *Strage degli innocenti* in Richard Crashaw's translation (*The Slaughter of the Innocents*), took the inspiration for his Satan 'majestic though in ruin' from Marino. Satan alone and abandoned. Satan beautiful and cursed. The Devil was beginning to exercise a certain appeal among writers and poets. In short, Lucifer went out and smartened himself up.

If Marlowe's Faust still carries with him the last traces of the mediaeval Christian tradition, with its vision of the great drama of the human being torn between Good and Evil, Goethe's Faust is free of any constraint. And above all it is he, Faust, who is the real protagonist. Along with the love that overcomes everything. Even Evil. Lucifer, or Mephistopheles as he appears in the legend of Faust, loses his strength, totters. His fiendishness is defeated by love. Lucifer is growing accustomed to men.

In the nineteenth century the Devil was dressed up again and became the companion of 'accursed' poets and writers, and of all those who saw

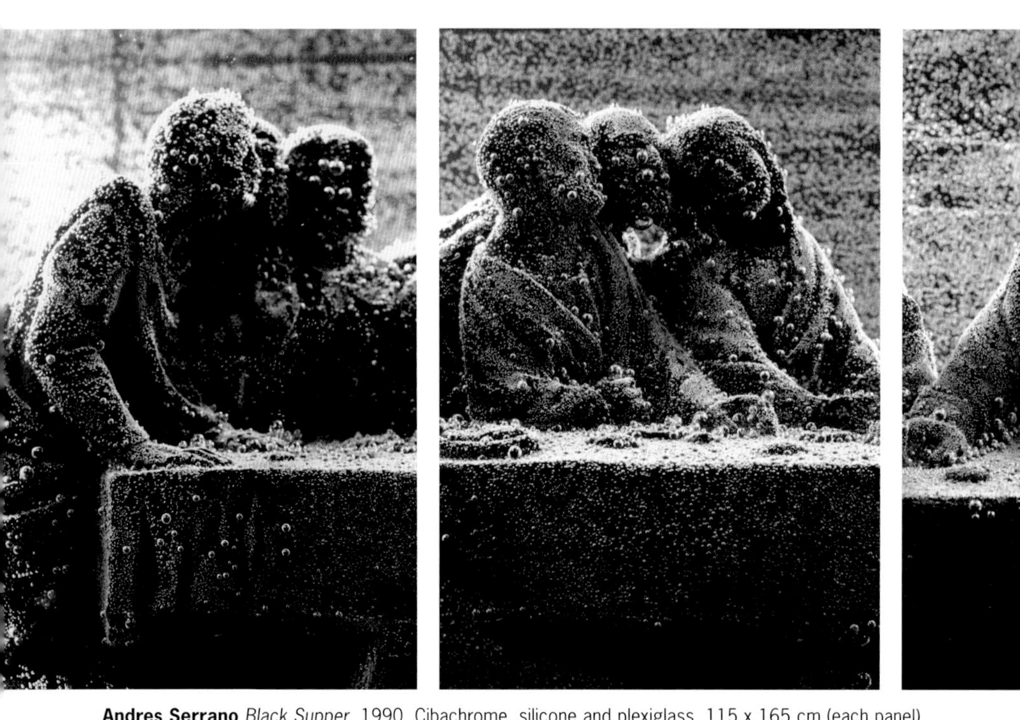

Andres Serrano *Black Supper*, 1990. Cibachrome, silicone and plexiglass, 115 x 165 cm (each panel)

him as a dark hero who no longer insinuated himself but fought his battle openly within a mediocre and stale society. It was here that the boundary between Good and Evil became unstable.

'O you, the most knowing, and loveliest of Angels', victim of God's jealousy, is how Baudelaire addressed Satan, appealing to him to 'take pity on my long misery'. For only he who has been vanquished feels compassion for the defeated.

His heart beats for human beings. God's heart, less so.

The fact was that, by living with them, Lucifer had learned to understand them. He knew everything about their nature, sensed their needs and desires. And being familiar with suffering on this earth, he sympathized with them.

Christ, on the other hand, had returned almost at once to his Heaven. He looked at human beings from on high, and had never really shared in their feelings.

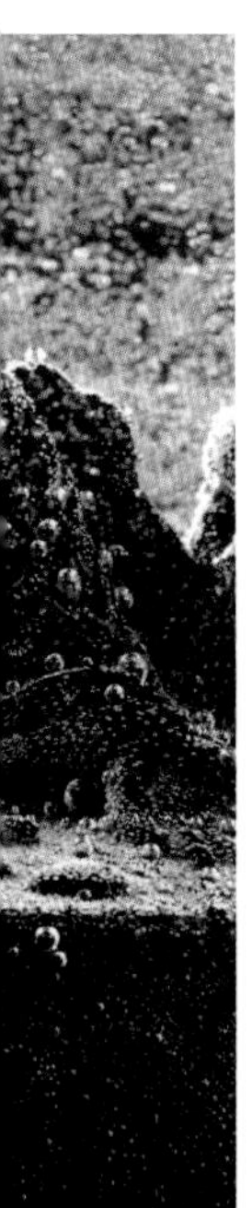
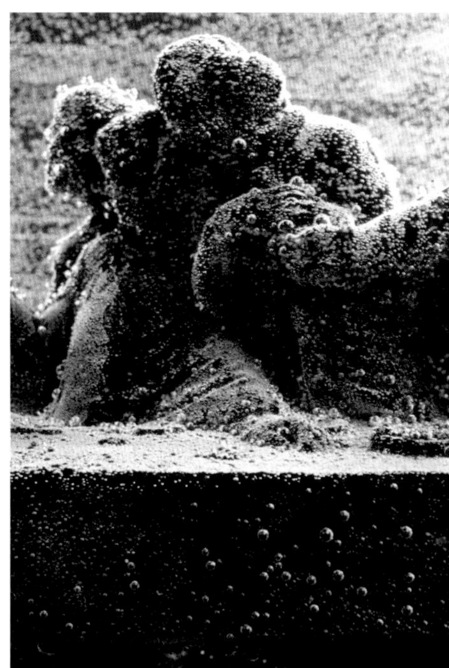
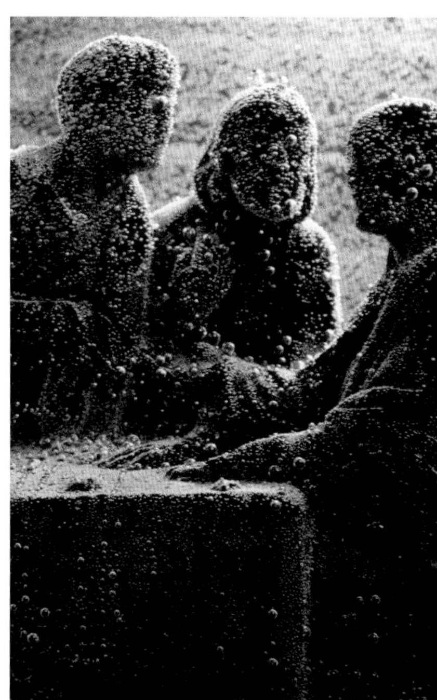

And yet, the two balanced one other. Thesis and antithesis. The existence of one sanctioned the existence of the other. Once again, Good necessary to Evil and vice versa. Both necessary to men.

Where is God today? And where is Satan? In this age of great killings, we no longer seek God in perfection but in the lacerated flesh and dull eyes of the dying.

Once more, perfection and perdition are two faces of the same coin: even artists are looking for them. Never has the world of art been in such turmoil. For if it is true that artists have the duty to reflect their time, to draw attention to the conflicts and the absurdities of life through their vision, and through the colours and forms that they choose, then never has there been as much work for them to do as there is now.

Angels and devils are figures that belong to the collective imagination. Filtered through the 'lowbrow culture' of the comic strip, as well as through images of them presented by certain old films in black and

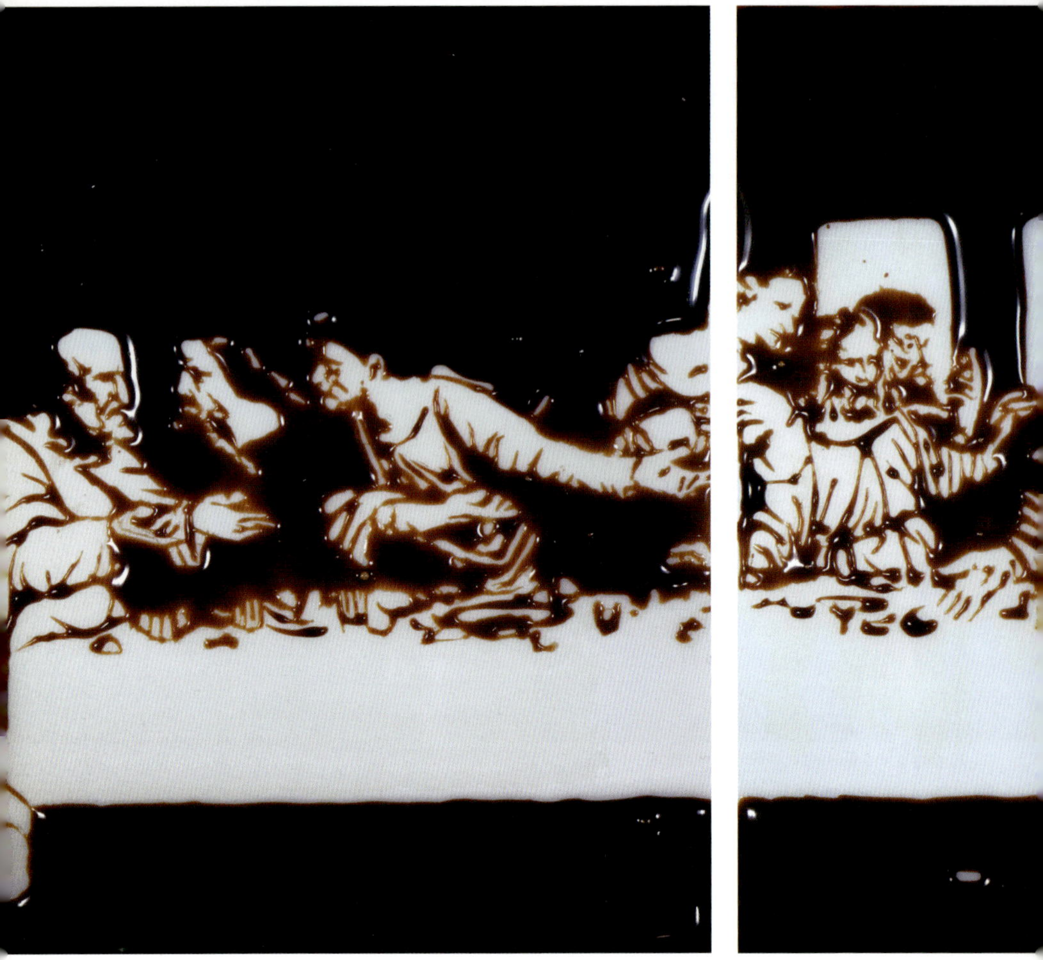

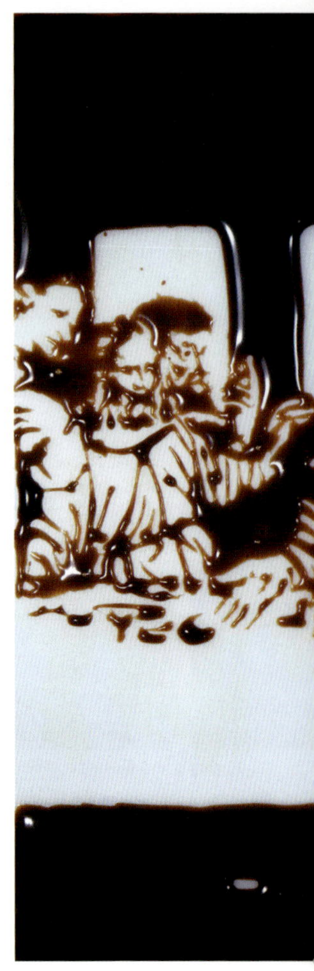

Vik Muniz *Milan (The Last Supper, after Andy Warhol)* (from the *Pictures of Chocolate* series), 1998.
3 cibachromes, 152.5 x 122 cm each

white, they have been transformed into pop icons in the work of contemporary artists.

Emblematic examples of this are provided by the performances and photos of Mike Kelley, and by David Salle's recent series of paintings devoted to the Sistine Chapel that include, among scenes drawn from the Holy Scriptures and the news, a devil in a straw hat and a polka-dot bowtie. His sardonic grin has ceased to terrify us, turning into a sort of logo of just one more product in the supermarket. More poetic, however,

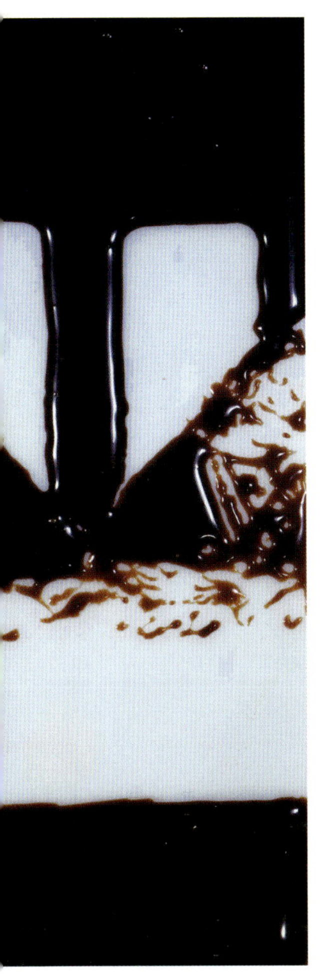

is the figure of the angel, never mocked, always poised between classical representation and innovation. It suffices to think of the angels of Ron Mueck and Marc Quinn, both looking dejected before scenes that are hidden from us but at which we can guess. And then we have the violence of the news reports, the reference to reality interacting with the fantastic dimension (Barney's *Cremaster*, Marc Quinn's sculptures of phocomelic people, the blind young woman portrayed by Jenny Saville who turns into a mystical figure), but also the sense of pity, and the sneer again, with

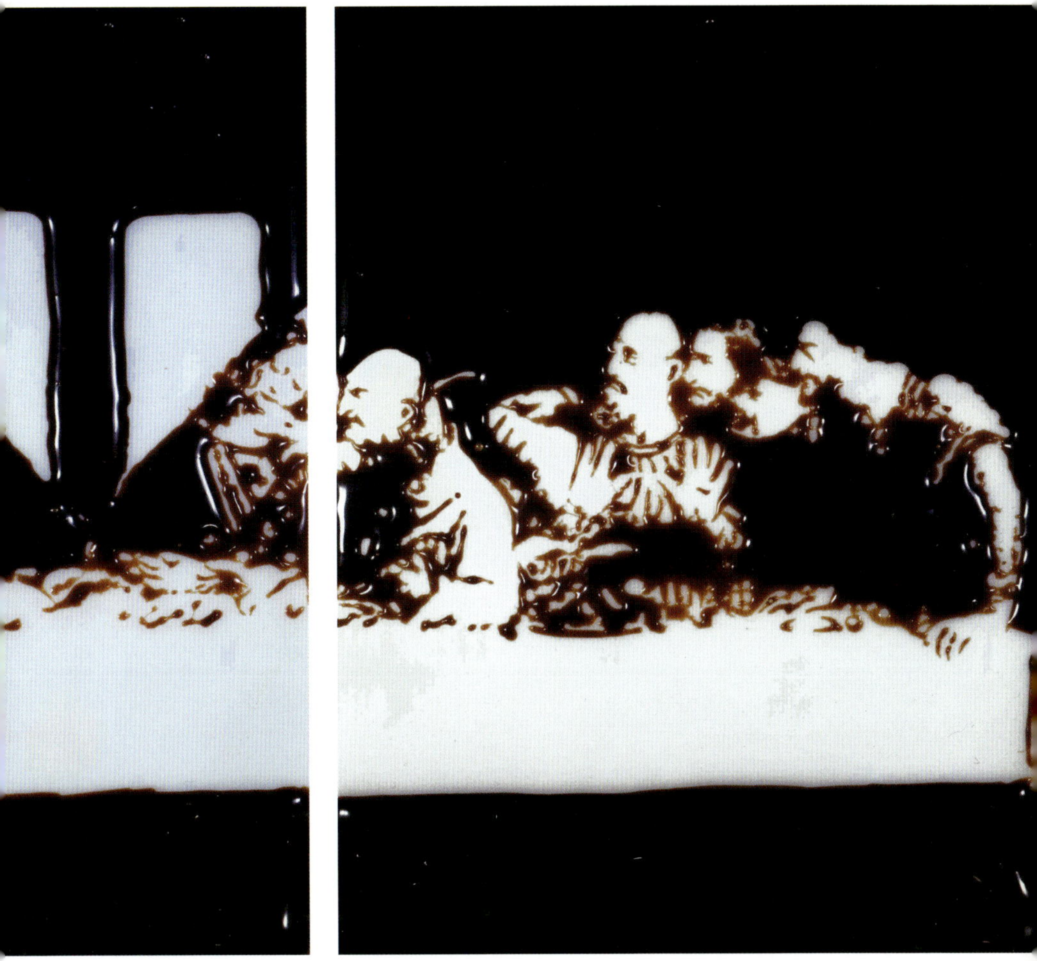

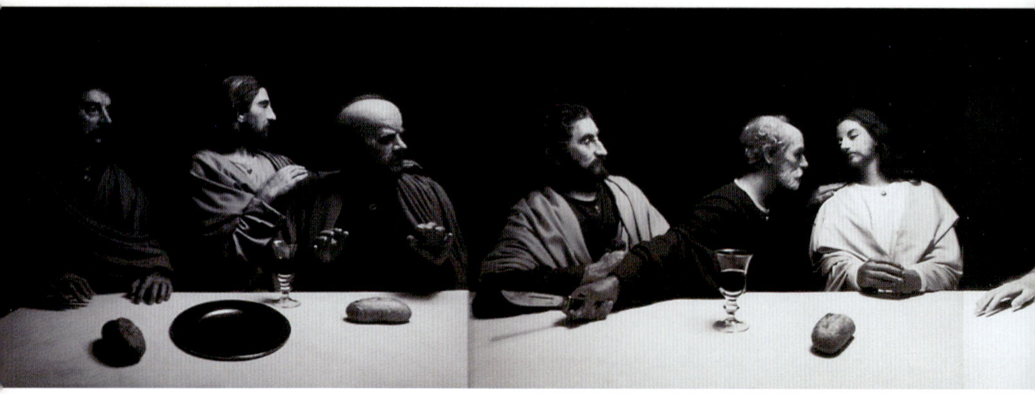

Hiroshi Sugimoto *The Last Supper*, 1999. Silver gelatine print, 118.1 x 706.1 cm (5 panels)

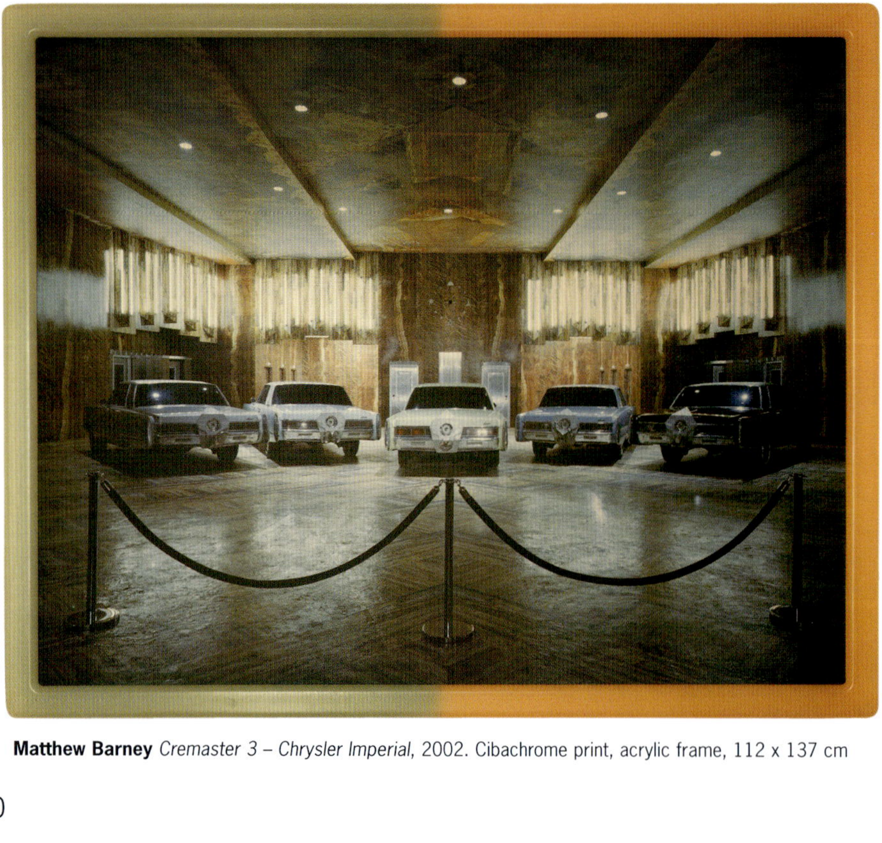

Matthew Barney *Cremaster 3 – Chrysler Imperial*, 2002. Cibachrome print, acrylic frame, 112 x 137 cm

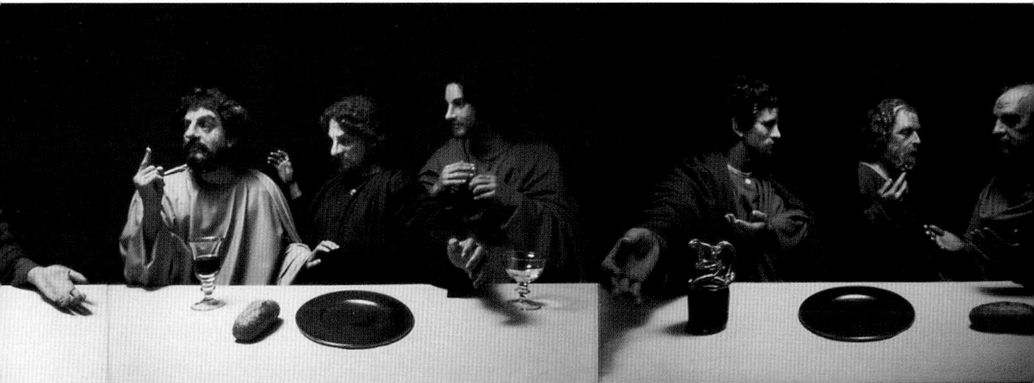

regard to the evil personified by Lucifer, who preserves his identity, even when he is reduced to a cartoon. There is a predominant pop background to today's culture, deriving from the relationship that images maintain with the media, which have modified their perception on the aesthetic plane as well as that of the content.

Recently Damien Hirst has produced four large pictures whose subjects are the four evangelists. He has taken a symbolistic intellectual approach to the theme: he makes explicit reference to the Holy Scriptures, but at the same time recalls the tension of Yves Klein. Vertical and monochrome, and painted with sand 'à la Tàpies', the works find their explanation in the details contained in the individual parts, like a secret waiting to be revealed. The butterflies pinned onto the canvas evoke death, and emblematically Hirst associates with them the first page of each of the Gospels, whose initial words he places on the vertical axes of the frames. And at the centre of each panel he has set a pen, indicating that there are still many sacred pages waiting to be written. So this is the possibility of reviving and rewriting the history of the sacred that, from Salle to Hirst, from Seville to Barney, from Kelley to Sugimoto (the list could be made much longer), and it constitutes one of the most significant new developments in contemporary art.

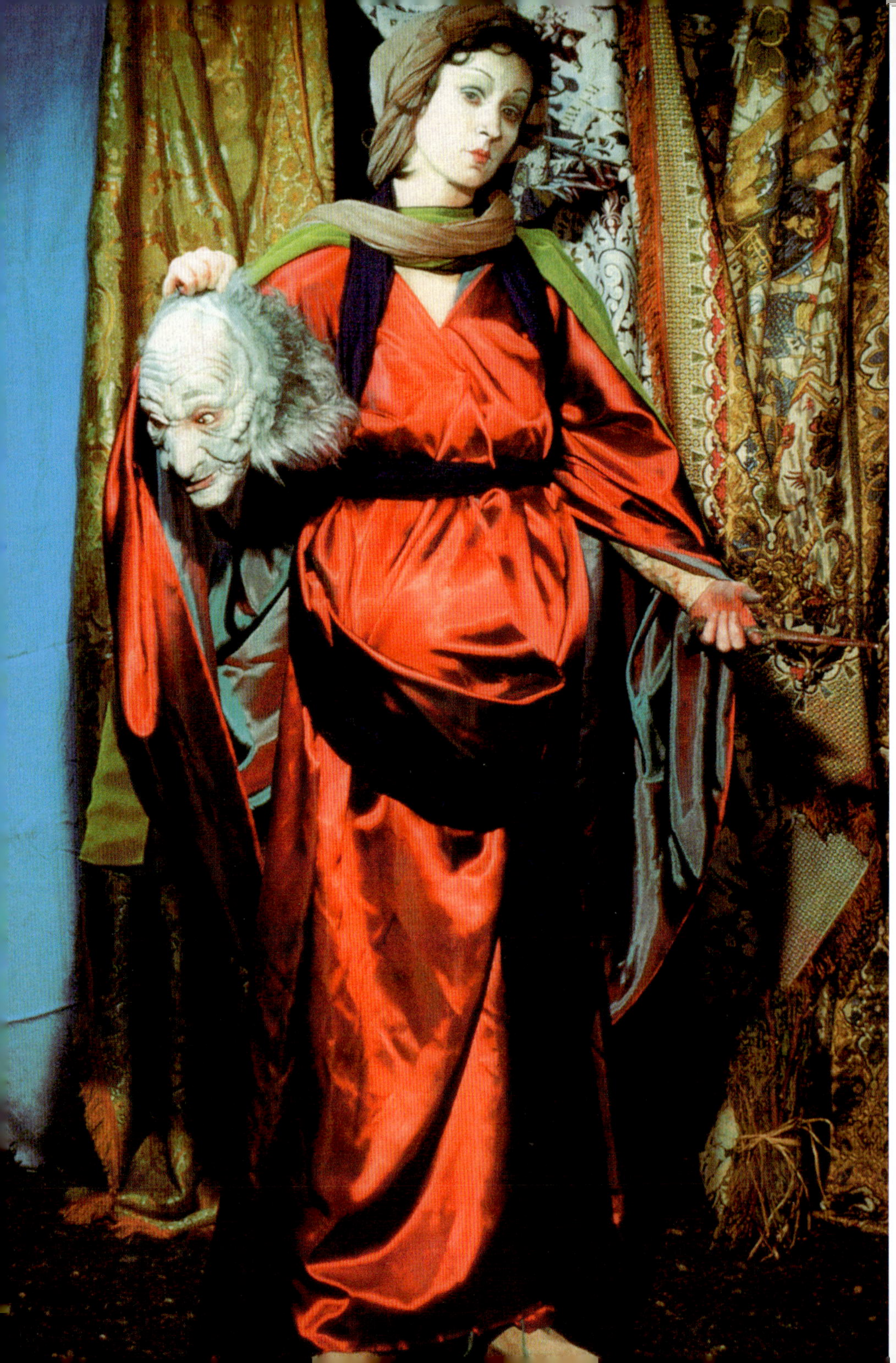

Sanctity and Depravity

Roger Caillois

... It turns out that depravity and sanctity, often rightly equated, both advise a certain prudence and represent the two poles of a frightening environment. It is for this reason that they are so often designated with just a single term even in the most advanced civilizations.The Greek word *hágos*, 'filth' or 'depravity', also means 'the sacrifice that cancels depravity'. The term *hágios*, or 'saint', also used to mean, the lexicographers tell us, 'depraved'. The distinction was effectuated later with the help of two symmetrical words, *hághes*, or 'pure', and *enaghés*, or 'cursed', the transparent composition of which denotes the ambiguity of the original word. The Greek *hosioún* and the Latin *espiare*, or 'expiate', are etymologically interpreted as 'causing to exit (from oneself) the sacred element (*hósios, pius*) that contracted depravity had introduced'. Expiation is the act that allows the criminal to resume his normal activity and his place in the profane community, shedding his sacred character, deconsecrating himself, as Maistre has observed.

It is all too well known that in Rome the word *sacer* designates, according to Ernout-Meillet's definition, 'the person or thing that cannot be touched without being soiled or soiling'. If someone is judged guilty of a crime against religion or the state, the assembly sends him out declaring him *sacer*. From that moment forward, while it is true that killing him entails a mystical risk (*nefas est*), the assassin is nonetheless innocent with respect to human law (*jus*) and is not condemned for homicide (*parricidii non damnatur*).

Cindy Sherman *Untitled #228*, 1990. Photographic print, 208.5 x 122 cm

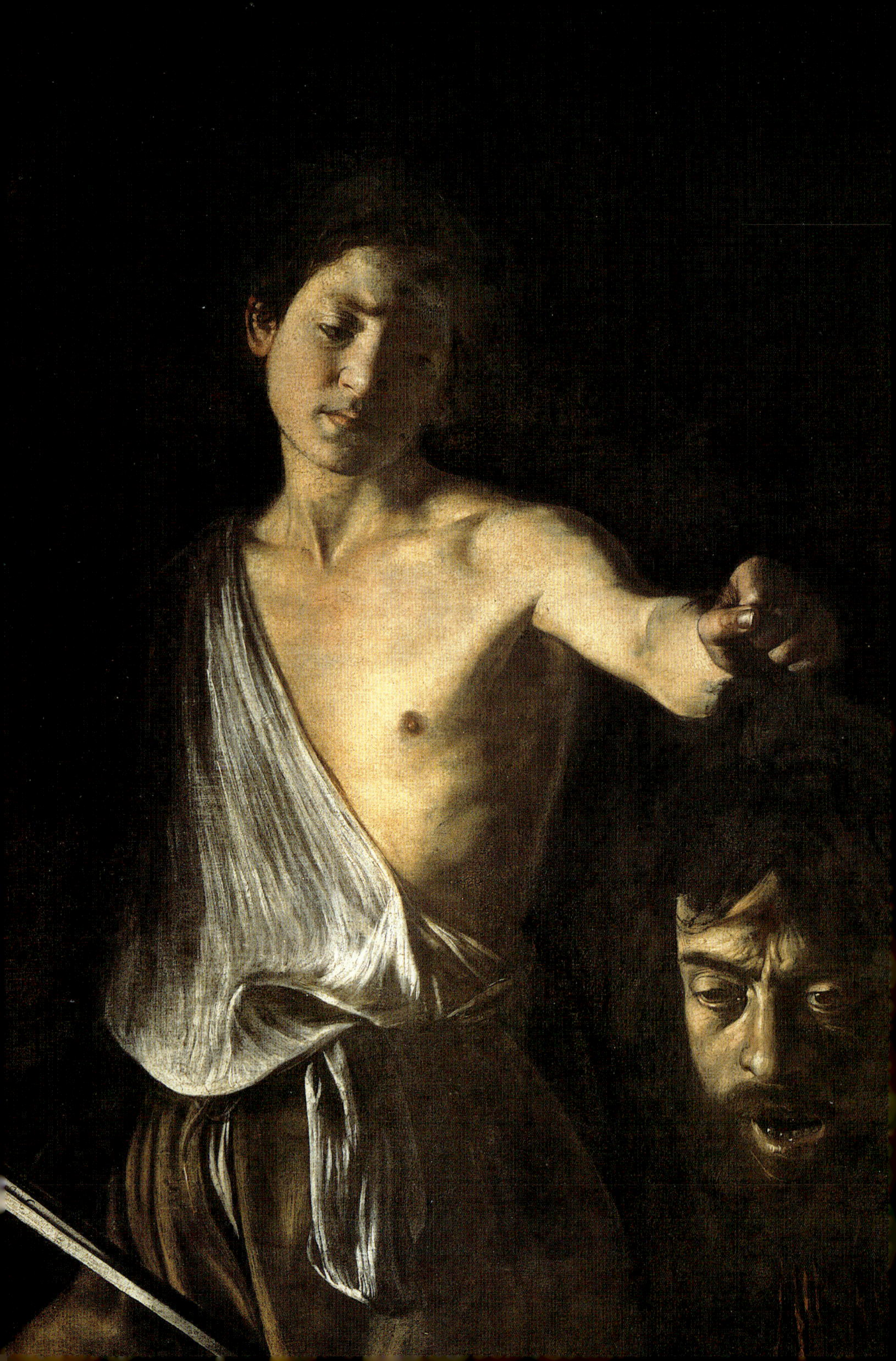

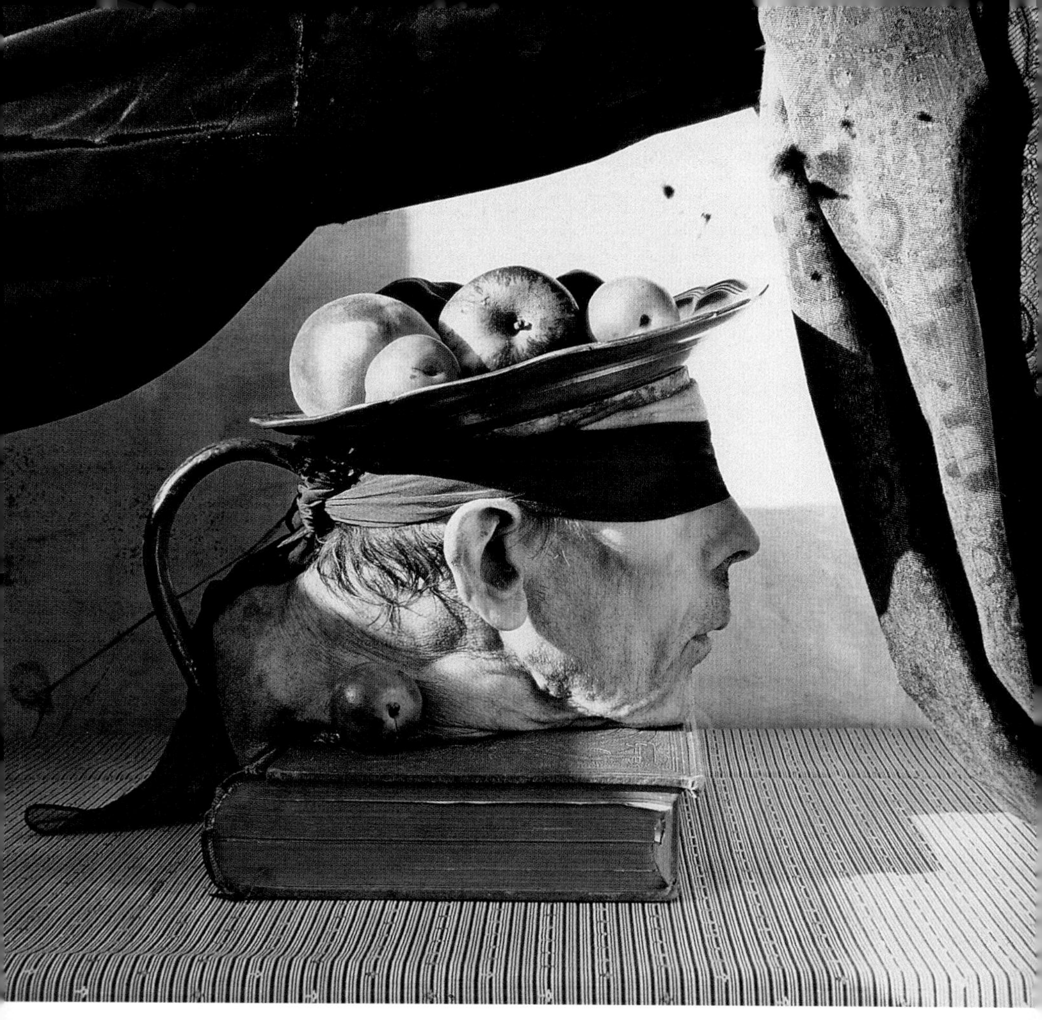

Joel-Peter Witkin *Story from a Book*, 1999. Silver salt print, 32 x 38.5 cm

Opposite
Caravaggio *David with the Head of Goliath*, 1605–06. Oil on canvas, 125 x 100 cm
Rome, Galleria Borghese

More primitive civilizations do not linguistically distinguish the prohibitions rooted in respect for sanctity from those inspired by fear of depravity. The same term evokes all the supernatural powers from which it is best, regardless of the reason, to keep a distance. The Polynesian word *tapu* and the Malaysian word *pamali* designate without distinction that which, blessed or cursed, is subtracted from shared use, or that which is not 'free'. Among native North Americans the word *dakota wakan* is used to refer indiscriminately to anything of any kind that is

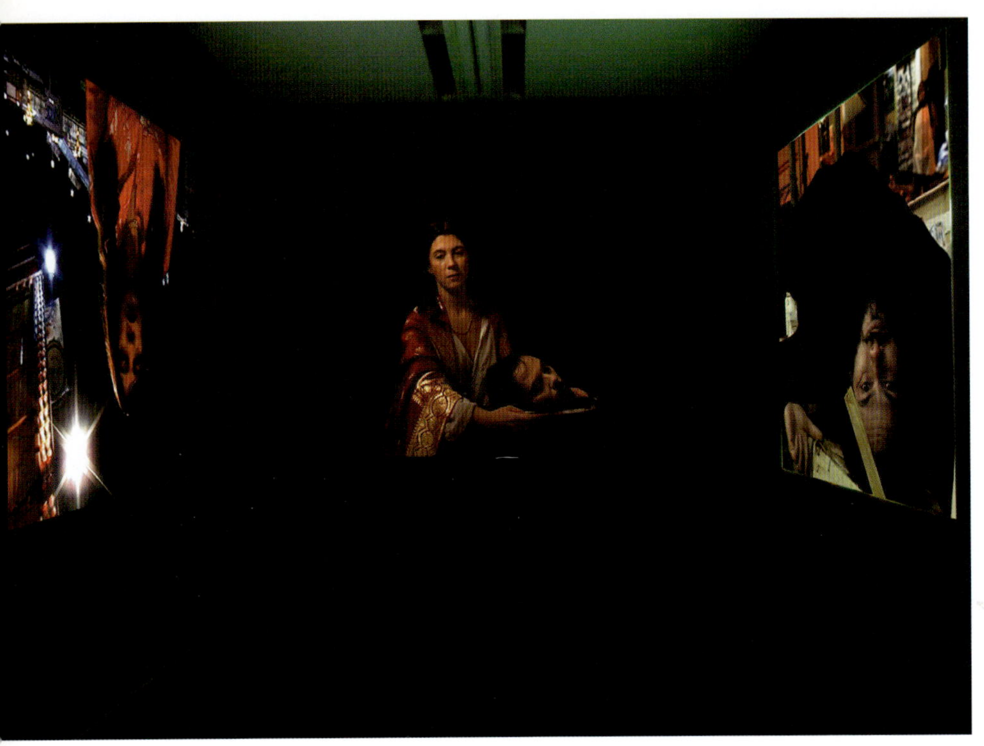

Ottonella Mocellin and Nicola Pellegrini *Togetherforever*, 2005. Video installation with three-channel sound, variable dimensions

awesome or incomprehensible. The natives use it to designate Christian missionaries and the Bible, but also for that paradigm of impurity represented by the woman during her menstrual cycle. The ancient Japanese used the word *kami* in a similar way for the divinities of Heaven and Earth, who are venerated for 'every evil and terrible being, so long as it is the object of general terror'. Yet *kami* is also all the qualities possessed by the virtue of effectiveness (*isao*).

The Dialectic of the Sacred

It is precisely this virtue (this *mana,* if one prefers the exotic term) that, in a state of quietude, elicits the ambivalent feelings we have just described. One is afraid of it and would like to utilize it. It repels and attracts at the same time. It is prohibited and dangerous: this is enough to make us wish to be near it and possess it, yet we simultaneously want to keep a respectful distance.

This is how, for example, the sacred character of a holy site (*hima*) is presented in the Semitic religions. It is prohibited to have sexual relations

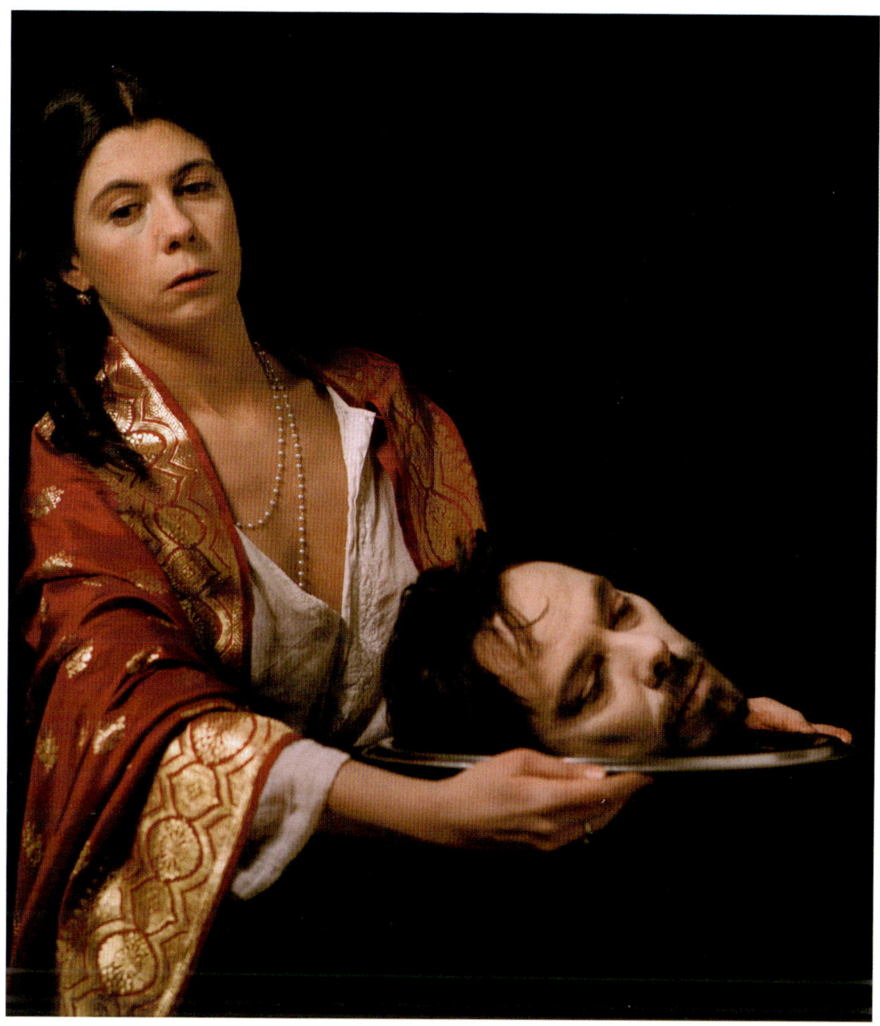

Ottonella Mocellin and Nicola Pellegrini *Una metafora in equilibrio sulla testa*, 2005.
Lambda print on aluminium, 125 x 162 cm

there, to hunt, to cut down trees or mow the grass. The action of justice ends at its boundaries: the criminal who takes refuge there is untouchable, consecrated by the holiness of the place; for the same reason, any domestic animal that wanders near it is lost to its owner. It is the quintessential place of danger, where no one ventures with impunity. However, its attractive aspect is powerfully evidenced in an Arab proverb: 'He who circles around the hima will end up falling in', which reminds us of the moth that

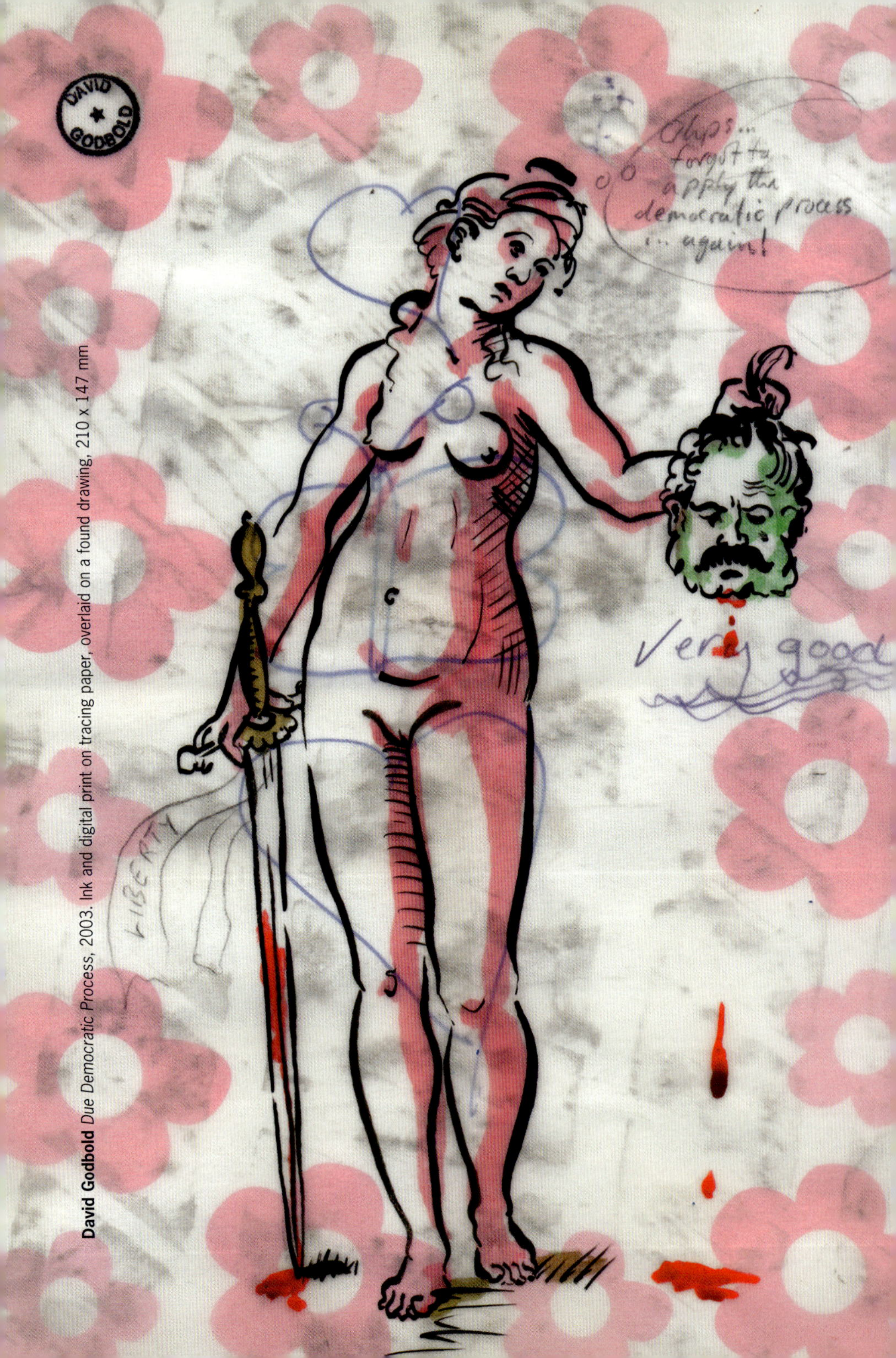

David Godbold *Due Democratic Process*, 2003. Ink and digital print on tracing paper, overlaid on a found drawing, 210 x 147 mm

cannot but burn itself in the flame. In the same way Martin Luther, speaking of the veneration of sacred places, states that it is mixed with fear. 'Yet', he adds, 'instead of fleeing, we move even closer.'

Fundamentally, the sacred inspires in the faithful the same sentiments that fire inspires in a child: the same fear of being burned, the same desire to light it. The same is true for emotion we feel before prohibited things, the belief that conquering them would bring us strength and prestige in the event of success, injury and death in the event of defeat. And just as fire produces good and evil at the same time, so does the sacred generate both propitious and nefarious actions, encompassing the opposite poles of pure and impure, sacred and sacrilegious, defining with their peculiar boundaries the very confines of the religious sphere.

Perhaps it is here that one can best grasp the essential movement of the dialectic of the sacred. Every force that incarnates it tends to be dissociated: its originary ambiguity is resolved in elements at once antagonistic and complementary, provoking the sentiments of respect and aversion, desire and fear, all inspired by its necessarily equivocal nature. But as soon as these polar extremes arise from the revelation of that nature, they provoke — each for its own part and to the extent that they possess the character of the sacred — the same ambivalent reactions that had separated them from one another. This rift of the sacred produces good and bad spirits, the priest and the warlock, Ormazd and Ahriman, God and the Devil, but the attitude of the faithful towards every one of these separations of the sacred reveals the same ambivalence as when they are confronted with its conjoined forms.

When St Augustine confronted the divine he was overcome by a shiver of horror along with a surge of love: '*Et inhorresco*', he writes, '*et inardesco*'. I shudder and I burn. He explains that his horror comes from recognizing the difference that separates his being from the sacred, while his ardour comes, on the other hand, from seeing their profound sameness. The theologian conserves this dual aspect of divinity, distinguishing in it two elements, one negative and one positive — the *tremendum* and the *fascinans*, to use R. Otto's terminology.

The *fascinans* corresponds to the seductive forms of the sacred, to Dionysian vertigo, ecstasy and transformative union. But it is also simply goodness, compassion and love for the divinity and his creatures, that which draws us irresistibly towards itself. The *tremendum*, conversely, represents the 'holy wrath', the inexorable justice of a 'jealous' God, before whom the humiliated sinner cowers, begging forgiveness. In the *Bhagavad Gita* it is Krishna who appears to the hero, Arjuna, terrified at

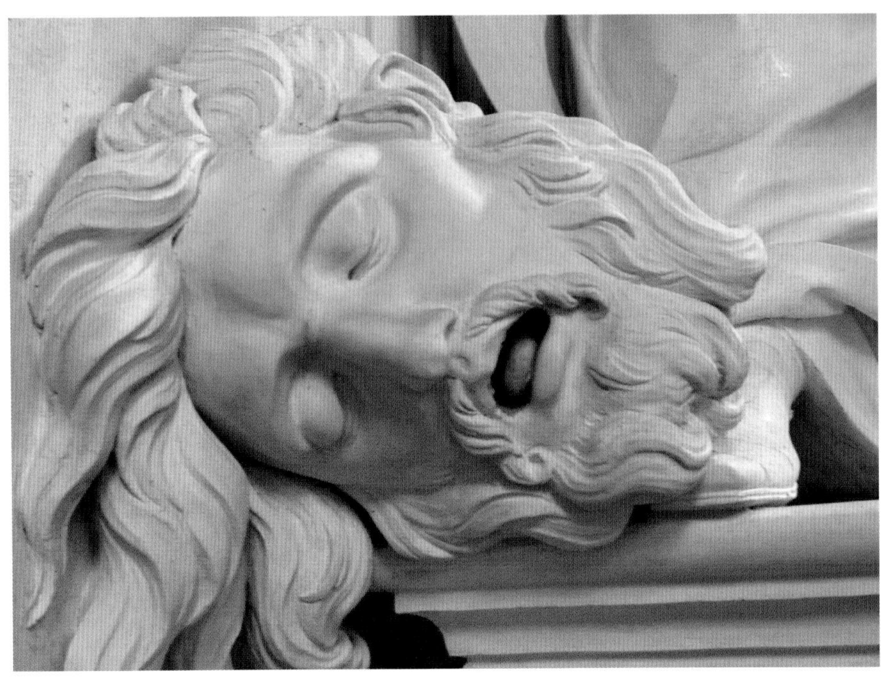

Giacomo Serpotta *Judith with the Head of Holofernes* (detail), 1717–18. Marble
Palermo, Oratorio del Santissimo Rosario in Santa Cita

the sight of humans falling in great numbers into the god's mouth, like a torrent rushing towards the ocean, 'like the insect that flies towards the mortal flame'. Some of them, their heads split open, remain stuck between his teeth, the god's tongue slurping up entire generations into his gullet. The other pole of the sacred — the demoniacal — which shares its terrible and dangerous aspects, suscitates in turn opposite feelings of repulsion and attraction, both of them equally irrational.

The Devil, for example, is not only he who cruelly punishes the damned in hell. He is also the one whose voice tempts the ascetic with earthly pleasures and delights, surely with the aim of making him transgress. And while any pact with the devil promises only transitory happiness, it is clear that it cannot be any other way. It is nonetheless noteworthy that the tormenter presents himself concurrently as seducer, and at times as consoler. Romanticism, which sought to celebrate Satan and Lucifer by attributing to them every seduction, was really only following the inherent logic of the sacred and the traits belonging to these figures. However, if the analysis of

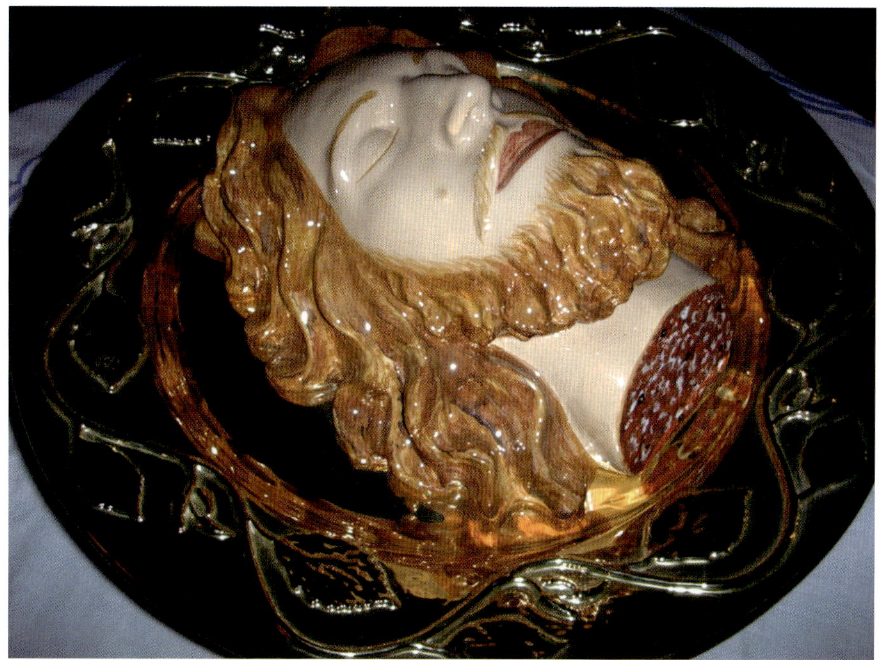

Luigi Ontani *Salamè*. Polychrome ceramic sculpture realized at the Bottega Gatti in Faenza, ø 50 x 34 cm

religion is organized in terms of the extreme and antagonistic limits represented in different forms by holiness and damnation, the essence of its function immediately appears to be determined by a double movement: the acquisition of purity and the elimination of depravity.

Acquisition and Abandonment of Purity

Purity is acquired by subjecting oneself to a set of ritual observances. First, as Durkheim clearly showed, is the progressive separation from the profane world in order to be able to enter the realm of the sacred without peril. One must abandon the human before accessing the divine. Consequently the cathartic rituals must be first and foremost practices of negation and abstention. These consist in the temporary renouncement of the various activities typical of the profane condition [...]: it is necessary to literally purify oneself in order to be worth of approaching the realm of the gods.

Roger Caillois, *L'homme et le sacré*, Éditions Gallimard, Paris 2006, pp. 45–50.

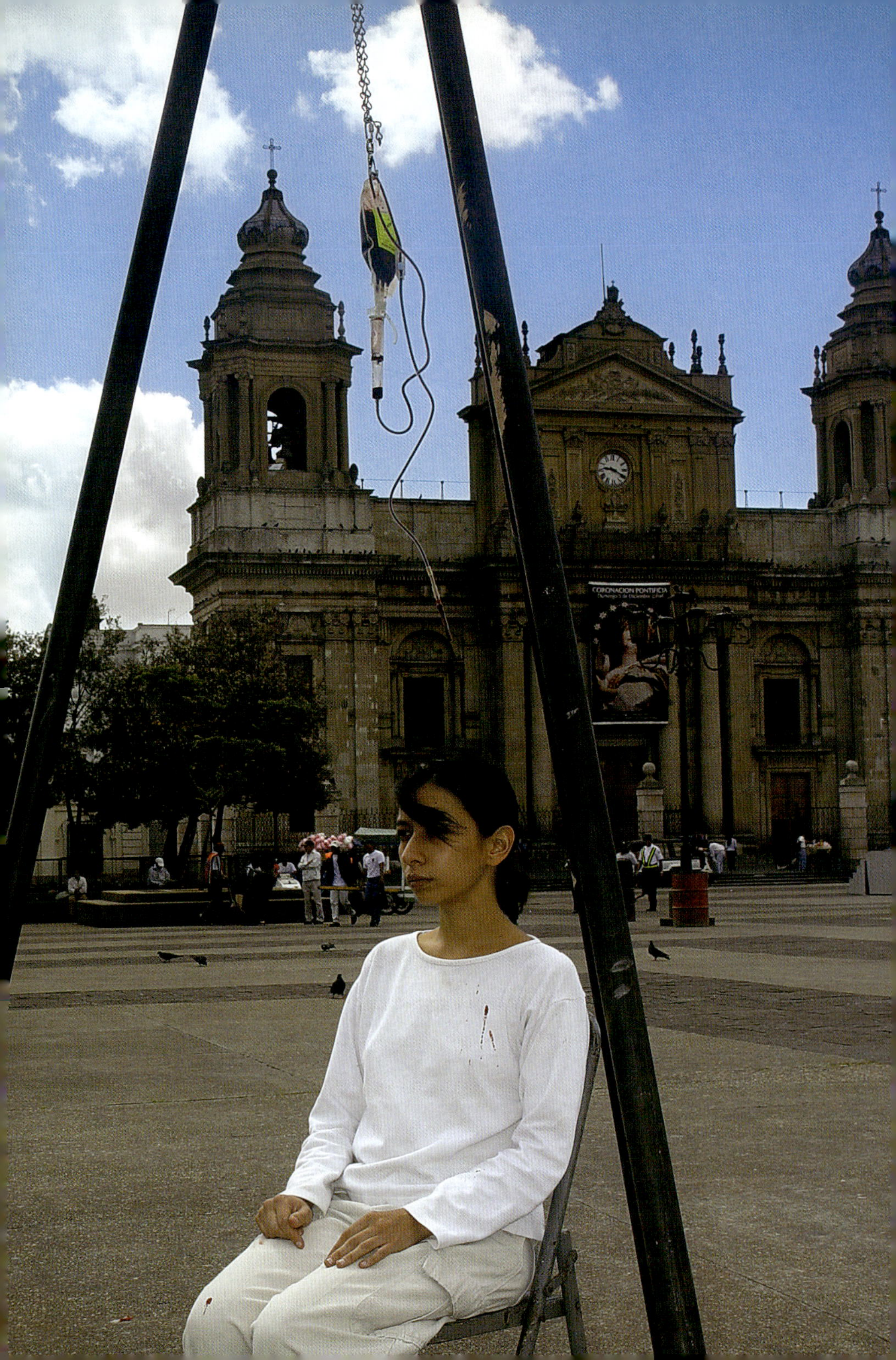
CORONACION PONTIFICIA

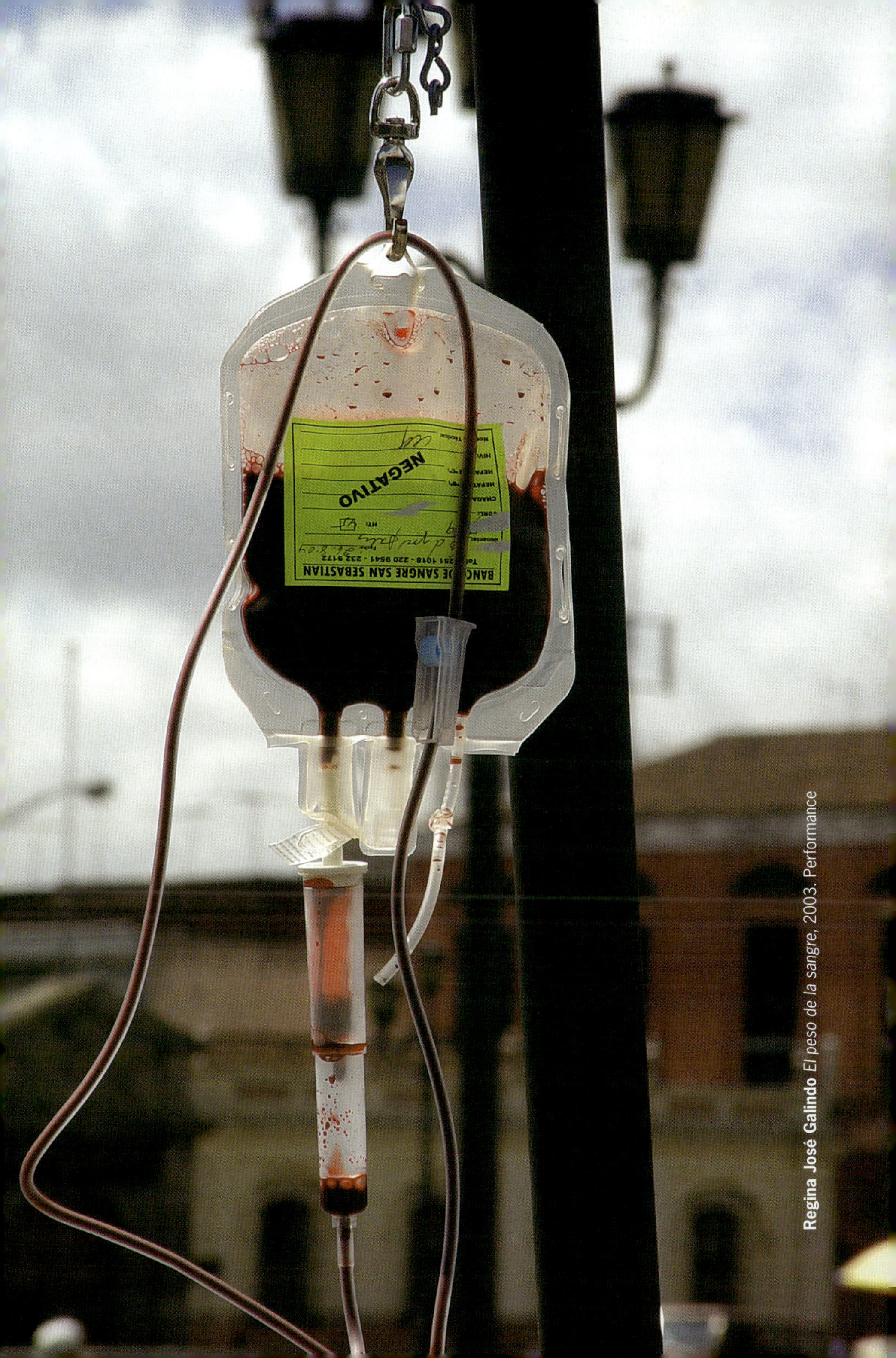

Regina José Galindo *El peso de la sangre*, 2003. Performance

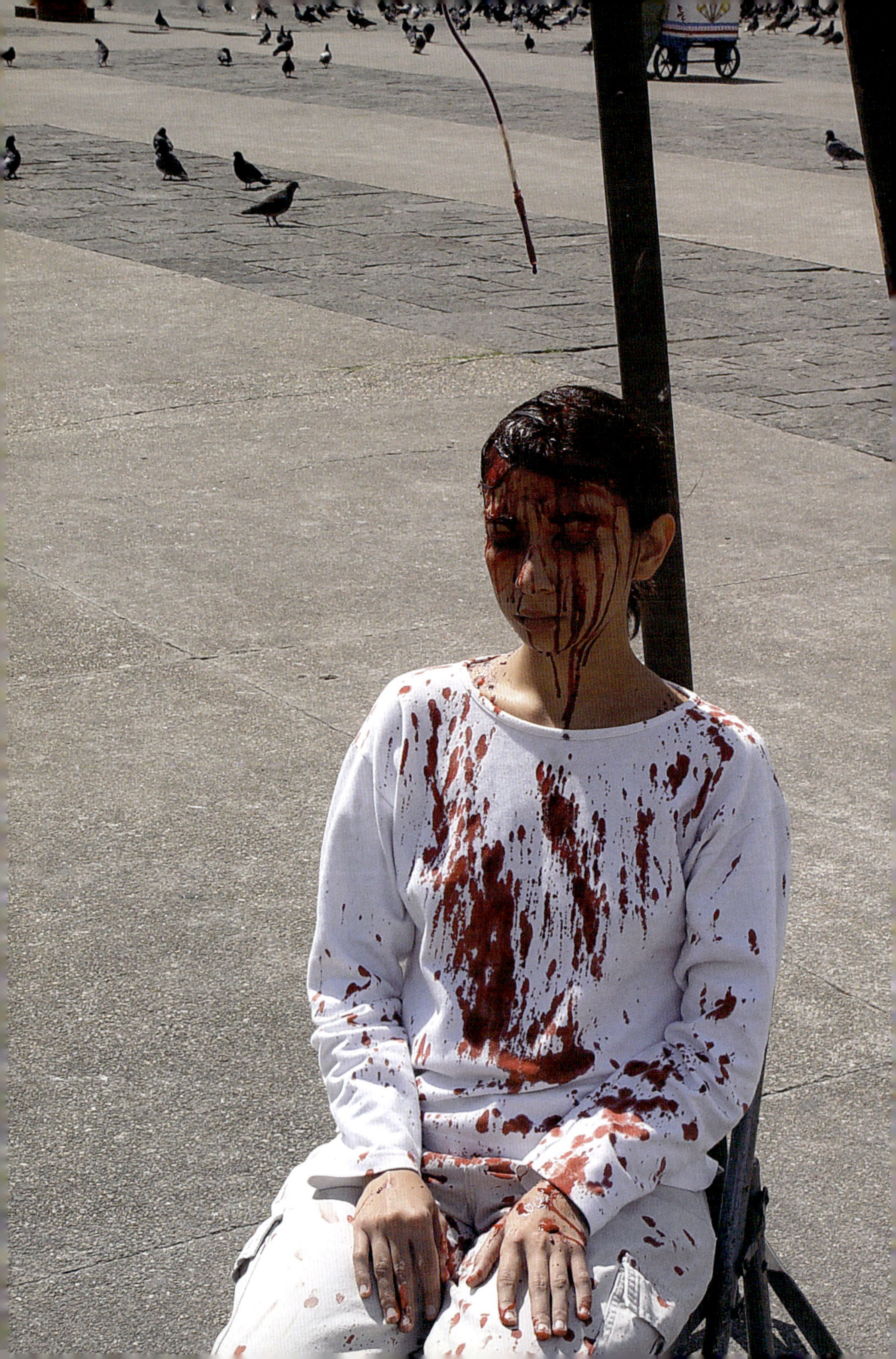

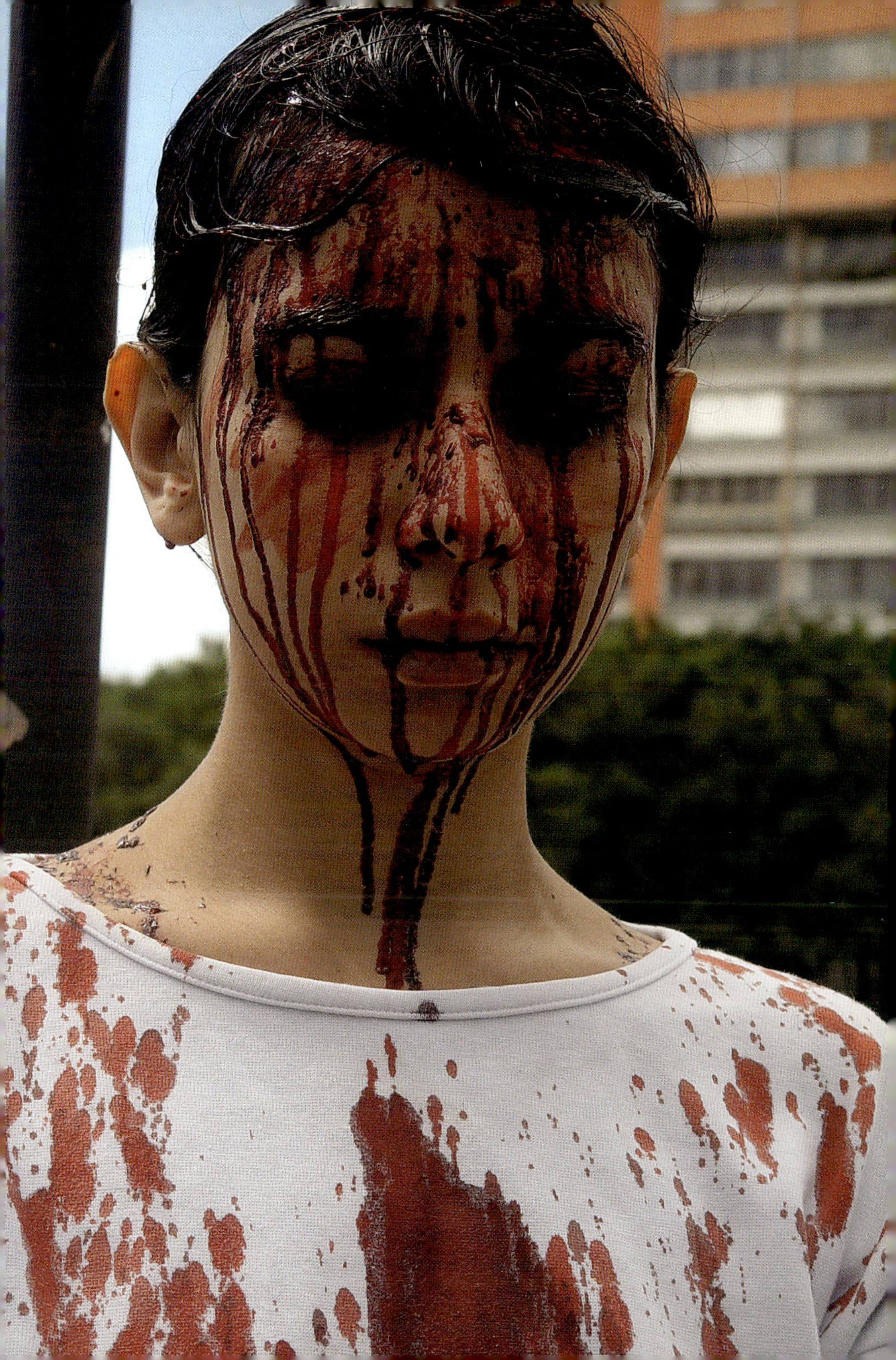

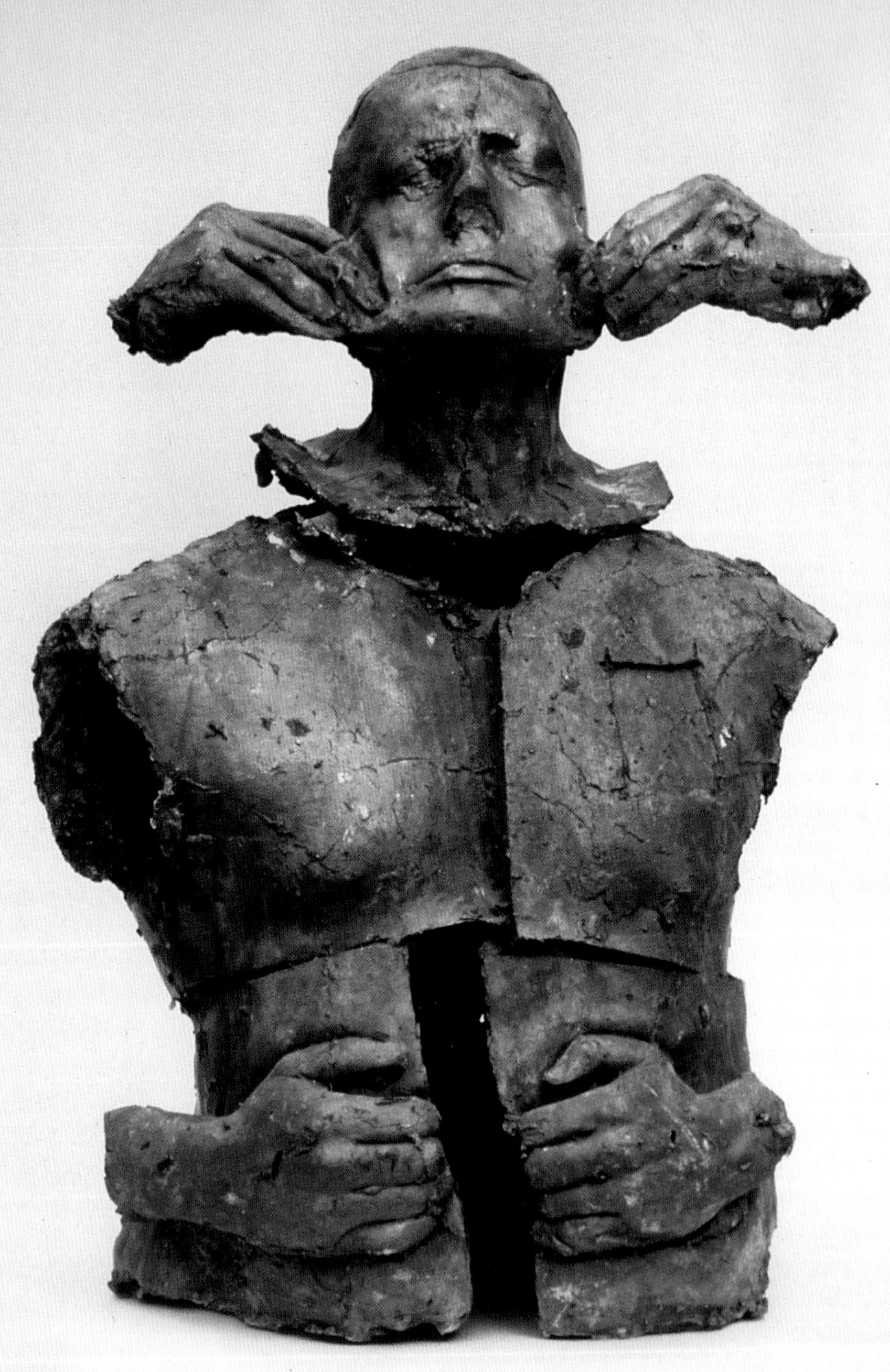

The Flesh in Sacrifice and in Love

Georges Bataille

… The reality of sacrifice generally consists in granting life and death, in bestowing on death the spark of the life, on life the heaviness, vertigo and opening of death. It is life mixed with death, but in it, at the same time, death is sign of life, opening onto the unlimited. Today, sacrifice lies outside the realm of our experiences: we have to substitute imagination for experience. But if sacrifice in itself and its religious significance elude us, we cannot ignore the reaction provoked by the spectacular elements that it offered: horror and disgust. We have to picture to ourselves an overcoming of disgust in sacrifice. But without sacred transfiguration, its aspects can in the end nauseate us when considered separately. Nowadays people are generally disgusted by the killing or butchering of animals: nothing that reminds them of it should appear in the dishes served at table. Thus it is possible to say that contemporary experience has inverted the rules of piety in sacrifice.

This inversion is significant if we bear in mind the similarity between the act of love and sacrifice. What the act of love and sacrifice reveal is flesh. Sacrifice substitutes the blind convulsion of the organs for the orderly life of the animal. The same thing happens with erotic convulsion: it liberates plethoric organs whose blind games continue beyond the reflective will of the lovers. The animal movements of the organs swollen with blood take the place of this reflective will. A violence that reason can no longer control drives these organs, it strains them to the point of spasm and suddenly the joy of hearts gives way to the overcoming of this storm. The

Marc Quinn *Emotional Detox (since V)*, 1994–95. Cast lead and wax, 86 x 52 x 36 cm

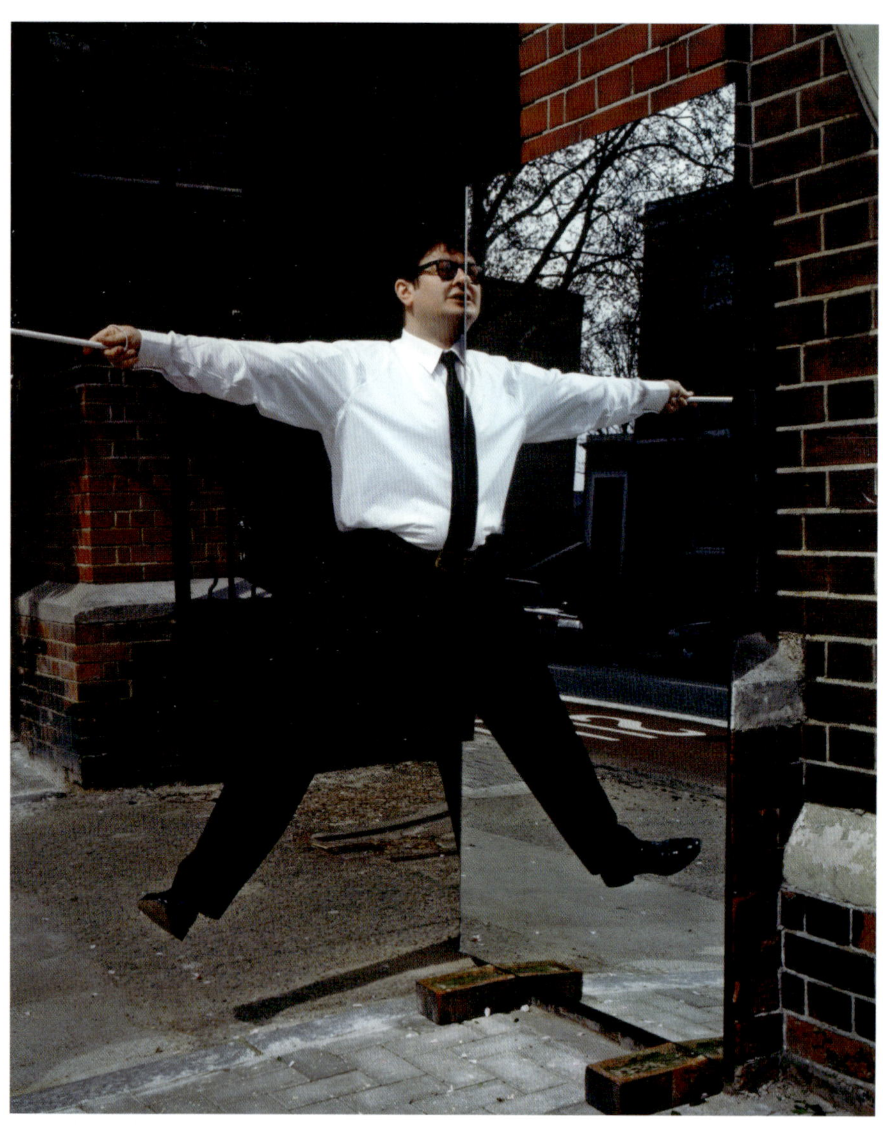

Mark Wallinger *The Word in the Desert*, 2000. Photographic print, 180 x 145 cm

movement of the flesh exceeds a limit owing to the absence of the will. The flesh is, in us, this excess that opposes the law of decency. The flesh is the enemy born from those who are obsessed by Christian prohibition, but if, as I believe, there is a vague and comprehensive prohibition that opposes sexual freedom in forms that vary with the time and the place, then the flesh is the expression of a return of this threatening freedom [...].

The Ultimate Meaning of Eroticism and Death

... If beauty, whose achievement spurns animality, is passionately desired, this happens because its possession introduces animal impurity into it. One desires it in order to be able to corrupt it. Not in and for itself, but for the joy experienced in the certainty of defiling it.

In the sacrifice, the victim was chosen in such a way that its perfection made the brutality of death perceptible. Human beauty, in the union of bodies, introduces the contrast between the purest humanity and the shameful animality of the organs. On the paradox of the filthy that is opposed to beauty in eroticism, Leonardo da Vinci's notebooks offer us this incisive comment: 'The act of copulation and the members of which it makes use are such filthiness that if it were not for the beauty of the faces, the ornaments of the participants and the unbridled impulse, nature would lose the human species'. Leonardo did not realize that the allurements of a beautiful face or fine clothing are effective to the extent to which this beautiful face heralds what the clothing conceals. What matters is to defile that face, its beauty. To defile it in the first place by laying bare the secret parts of a woman, and then by introducing the male organ into them. No one doubts the filthiness of the sexual act. Exactly like the death of sacrifice, the filthiness of copulation conveys a sense of anguish. But the greater the anguish — in relation to the force of the participants — the stronger is the awareness of going beyond the limits, which gives rise to a surge of joy. The fact that situations change according to tastes and habits cannot prevent the beauty (the humanity) of a woman generally helping to make perceptible — and disturbing — the animality of the sexual act. There is nothing more depressing, for a man, than the ugliness of a woman, against which the filthiness of the organs or the act does not stand out. Beauty has value chiefly because ugliness cannot be defiled, and the essence of eroticism lies in just this profanation. Humanity, expressive of prohibition, is transgressed in eroticism: it is transgressed, profaned, defiled. The greater the beauty, the deeper the profanation.

The possibilities appear so numerous, so elusive, that the picture of the various aspects is deceptive. Passing from one to the other, repetitions and

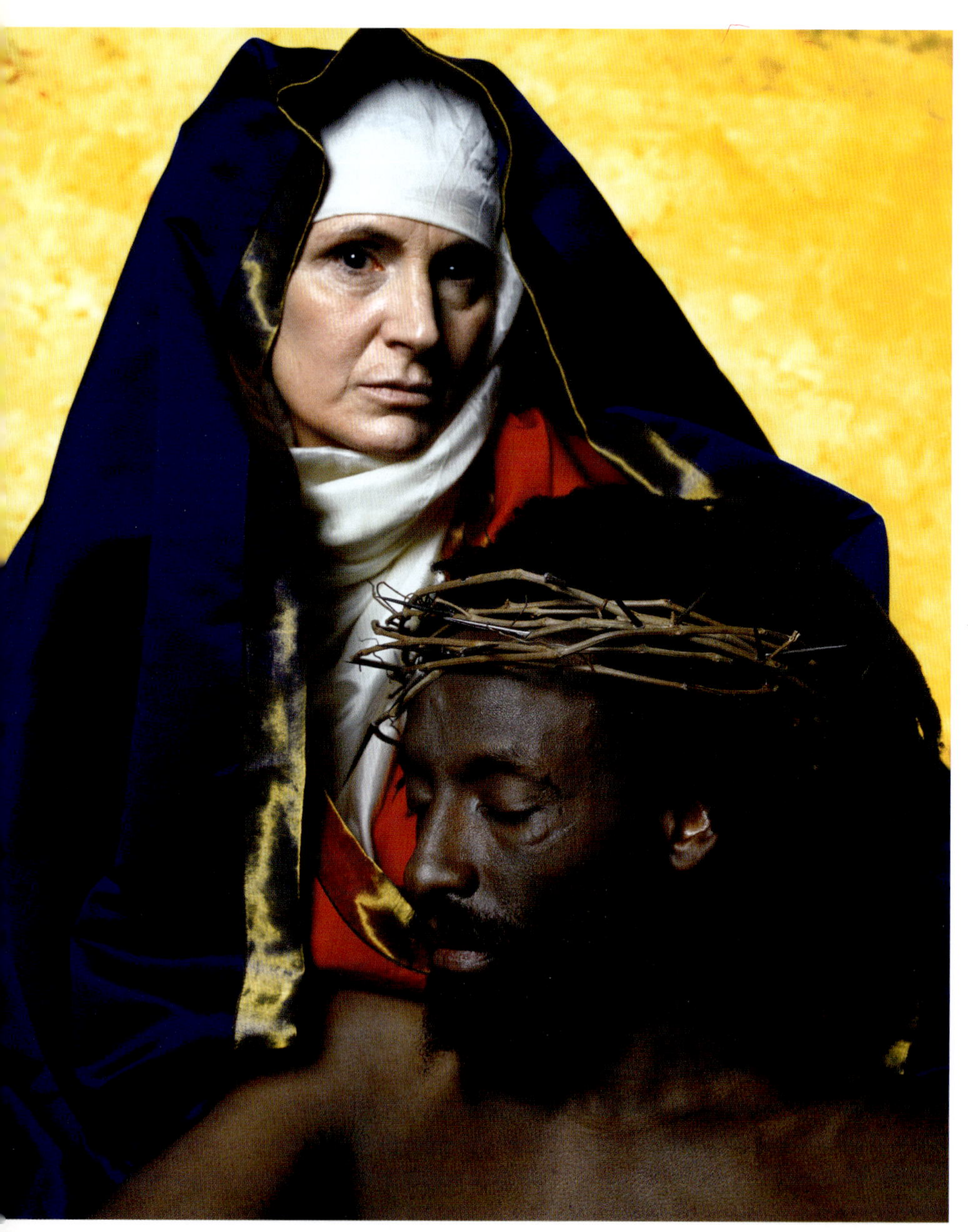

Andres Serrano *The Interpretation of Dreams (The Other Christ)*, 2001. Cibachrome, silicone, plexiglass

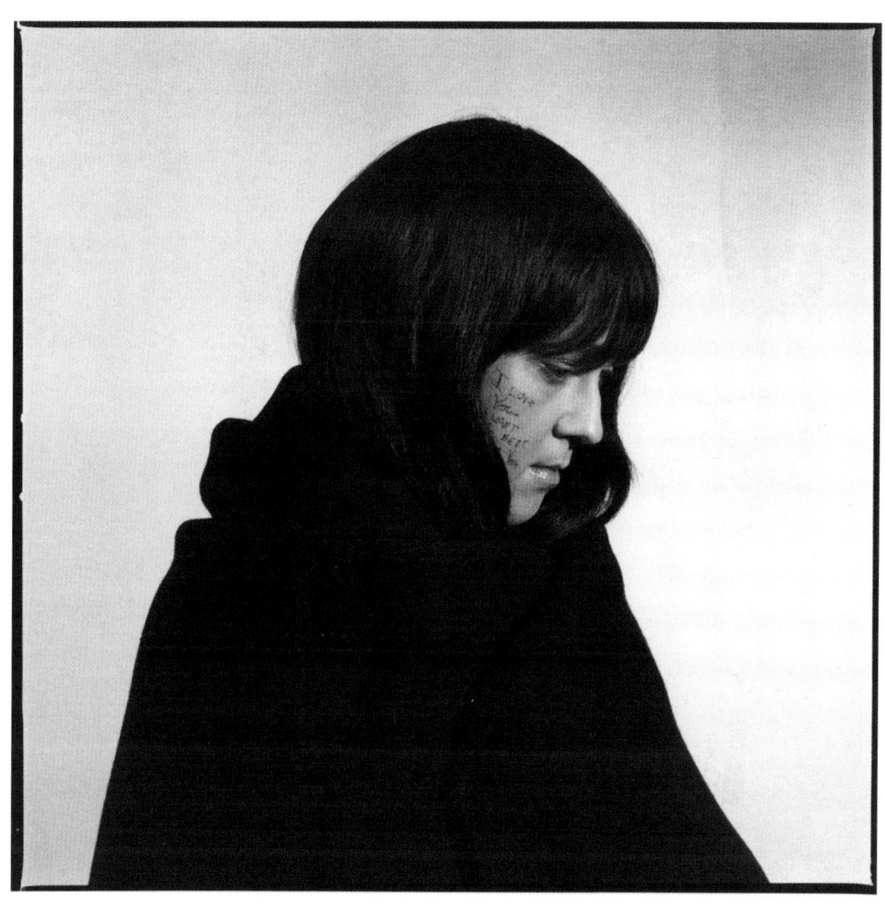

Antony Hegarty (with Don Felix Cervantes), *I Love You and I Want the Best For You*, 2005
Silver gelatine print, 91.5 x 91.5 cm

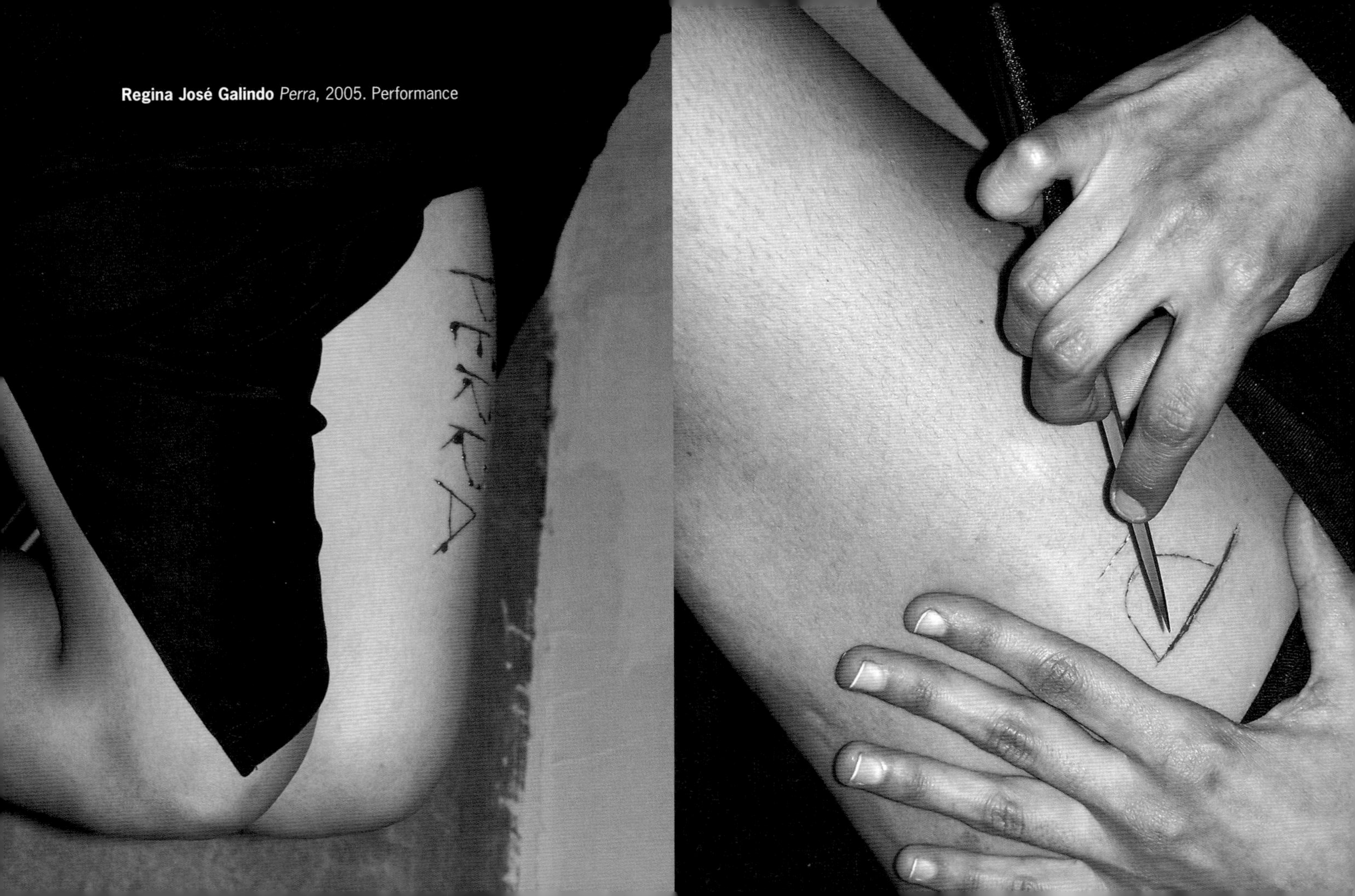

Regina José Galindo *Perra*, 2005. Performance

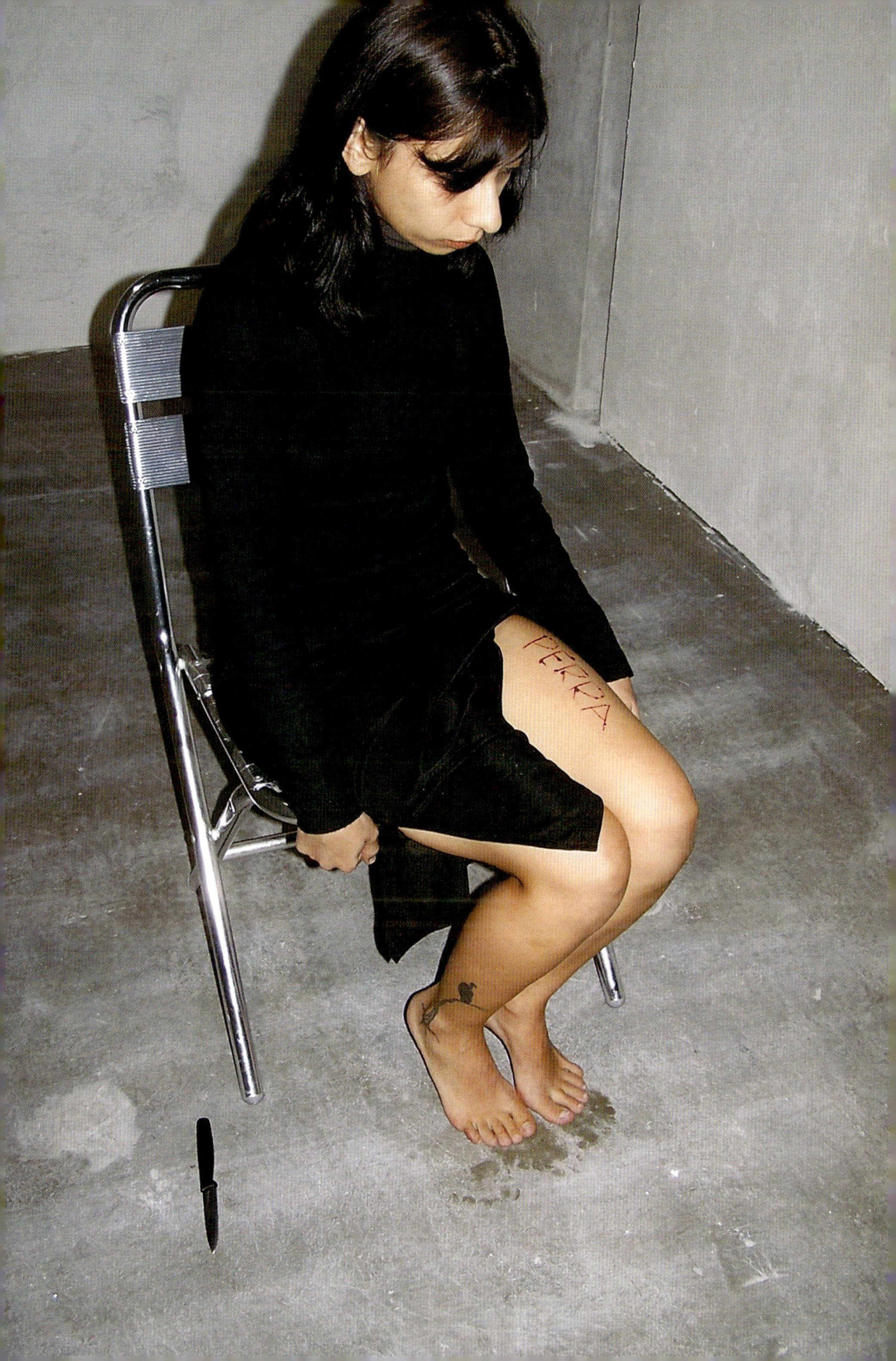
PERRA

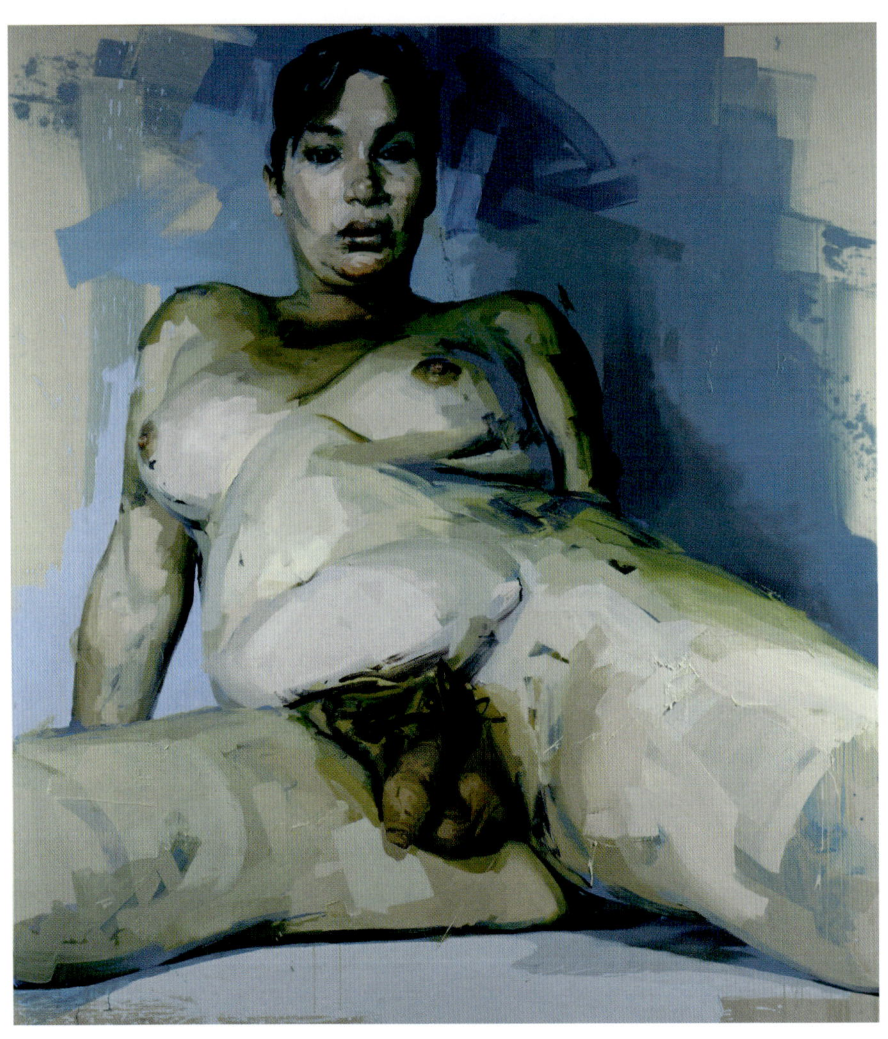

Jenny Saville *Passage*, 2004–05. Oil on canvas, 335.5 x 290.4 cm

contradictions are inevitable. But the movement, once understood, leaves nothing obscure. It is always an opposition in which we find the passage from compression to explosion. The means may change, but the violence remains the same, sometimes inspiring horror and sometimes attraction. Degraded humanity has the same significance as animality; profanation has the same significance as transgression.

In connection with beauty, I have spoken of profanation. I could also have spoken of transgression, since animality, as far as we are concerned, has the sense of transgression, for the animal ignores prohibition. But the feeling of profanation is more immediately comprehensible for us.

[...] Marriage is open to all forms of eroticism. Animality gets mixed up with decadence, and the object of desire can be distinguished, in the orgy, with a shocking precision.

Equally the need to make one fundamental truth perceptible cancels out another truth, that of reconciliation,[1] without which eroticism would not exist. I ought to have insisted on the turning imparted to the initial movement. In its vicissitudes, eroticism apparently detaches itself from its essence which binds it to the yearning for lost continuity. Human life cannot follow without shaking — without cheating — the movement that drags it towards death. I have represented it while it cheats — while it manoeuvres — along the streets of which I have spoken.

[1] Of desire and individual love, of the duration of life and the attraction of death, of sexual frenzy and concern for the children.

Georges Bataille, *L'erotisme*, Paris: Editions de Minuit, 1957. The above extracts have been translated from the Italian edition, *L'erotismo*, Milan: SE, 1986, pp. 89–90, 139–40.

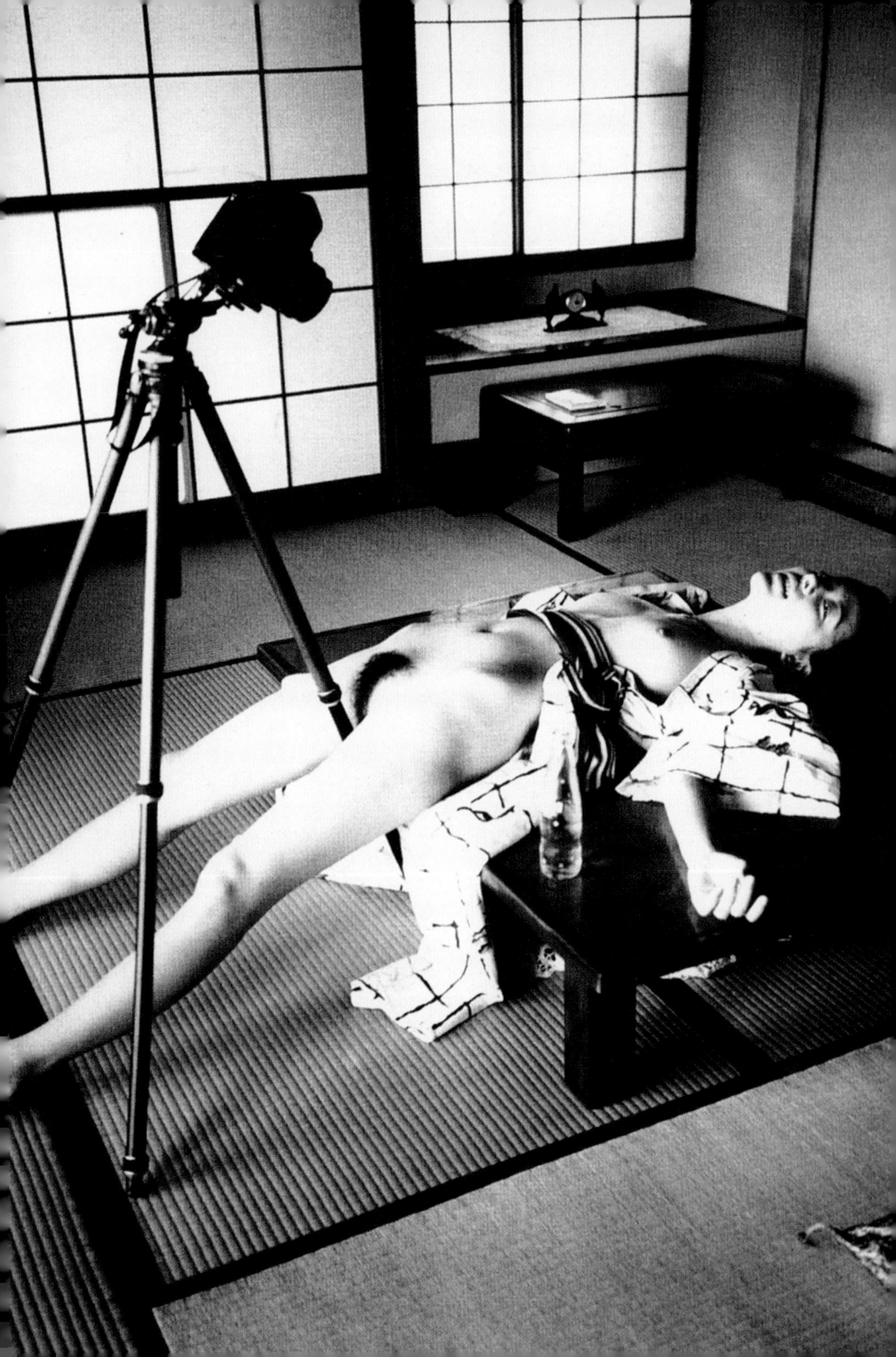

The Eroticism or Divinity of Evil versus the God of Good

Georges Bataille

The sovereignty of the devil presents two contrasting aspects. For believers it is a question of rivalry: the devil is jealous of God, and cannot admit his pre-eminence. But the *non serviam*, the refusal to have just a utilitarian value, to be an instrument in the world, does not always assume the vile significance referable to a confusion. The desire is to attain authenticity, the sovereignty without which an individual or an action have no value in themselves, but have a mere utility. The hammer is useful to someone driving a nail. And I can be useful even if I'm shining the shoes of passers-by, but between the shoeblack that I am and the passer-by are established, at least temporarily, the relations of the sovereign, or the master, with the servant. Let us suppose now that my subjection is not temporary and that the passer-by, whose shoes I am shining, will never return to me the service that I render him, by means of which, without doubt, I earn my living, but without ever being able to enjoy, in contrast to the passer-by, some superfluous shine. This shine has no utility, it has no meaning beyond itself, and yet it declares, along with my submission, the sovereignty of the passer-by. I am not saying that the only way to avoid being reduced to nothing more than my tin of polish and my brush is to refuse to carry out the services I render. And yet, if I accept without saying or thinking anything?… And above all: if the whole of humanity should observe that silence and that absence of thought?

To tell the truth, it is rare for the degradation of a human being to go so far: and yet it weighs on the whole of humanity. The gravest thing

Nobuyoshi Araki *Untitled* (from the *Fuyu-Koi: Love in Winter* series), 1997. Photographic print, 153 x 105 cm

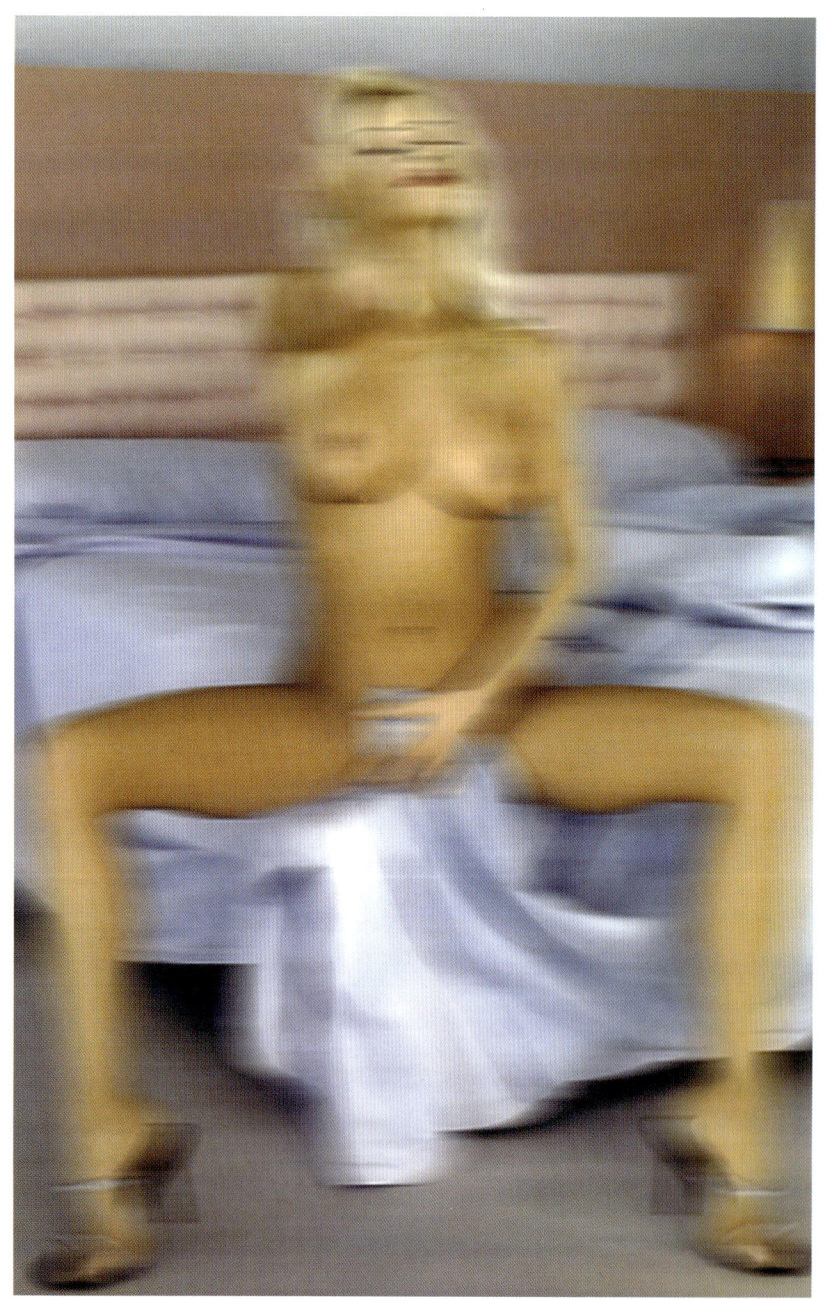

Thomas Ruff *Nudes TS 15*, 2003. Laserchrome mounted on frame, 161 x 110 cm

would be for the degradation to win out in the long run, reaching the point where it even affects the significance that humanity bestows on itself in general. Consequently what matters is not to lose sight of either the limits or the possibilities of the human being. No-one can contemplate the abolition of useful work, and yet man could not be reduced to it without suppressing himself.

Now, an ambiguity arises here, in connection with the God of good: he is the God of works, or the God of useful action. Within the Church itself, there has been an age-old struggle in support of the denial of the value of good works. Even for the Jansenist, however, the sovereignty of the faithful is indirect: he shares in that of God, even on condition of staying on his knees. I am not trying to say that submission, even to the God of works, excludes independence; but, to simplify, it is an independence of the other world: the sovereignty of which we are speaking is not given, it is only promised. In the process of its construction, Christianity has taken up, in a new form, the movement that opposed early men to nature. Christians spurned the pagan world, in which transgression balanced prohibition in order to form the whole. In this way, they experienced all over again that primary drama which was the passage from the animal to the human: they did this with an efficacy that was all the greater the more the ignominious death on the cross, before which they stood, maintained in them the moment of horror of transgression. Under such conditions, however, the whole only survived to the extent that Christianity did not succeed in destroying what it opposed: that pagan world which it regarded, not without some justification, with the horror that the early Christians had had of nature…

This provides an explanation of the wicked character that eroticism was to assume in Christian times. The witches' sabbath was the darkest form, in which games of nocturnal terror went hand in hand with licence. In which [there was] above all the wish for desire again and the awareness of doing evil.

The passage has been translated from the Italian edition of Georges Bataille, *Storia dell'erotismo. La parte maledetta II*, edited by F. Rella, Rome: Fazi Editore, 2006, pp. 108–09.

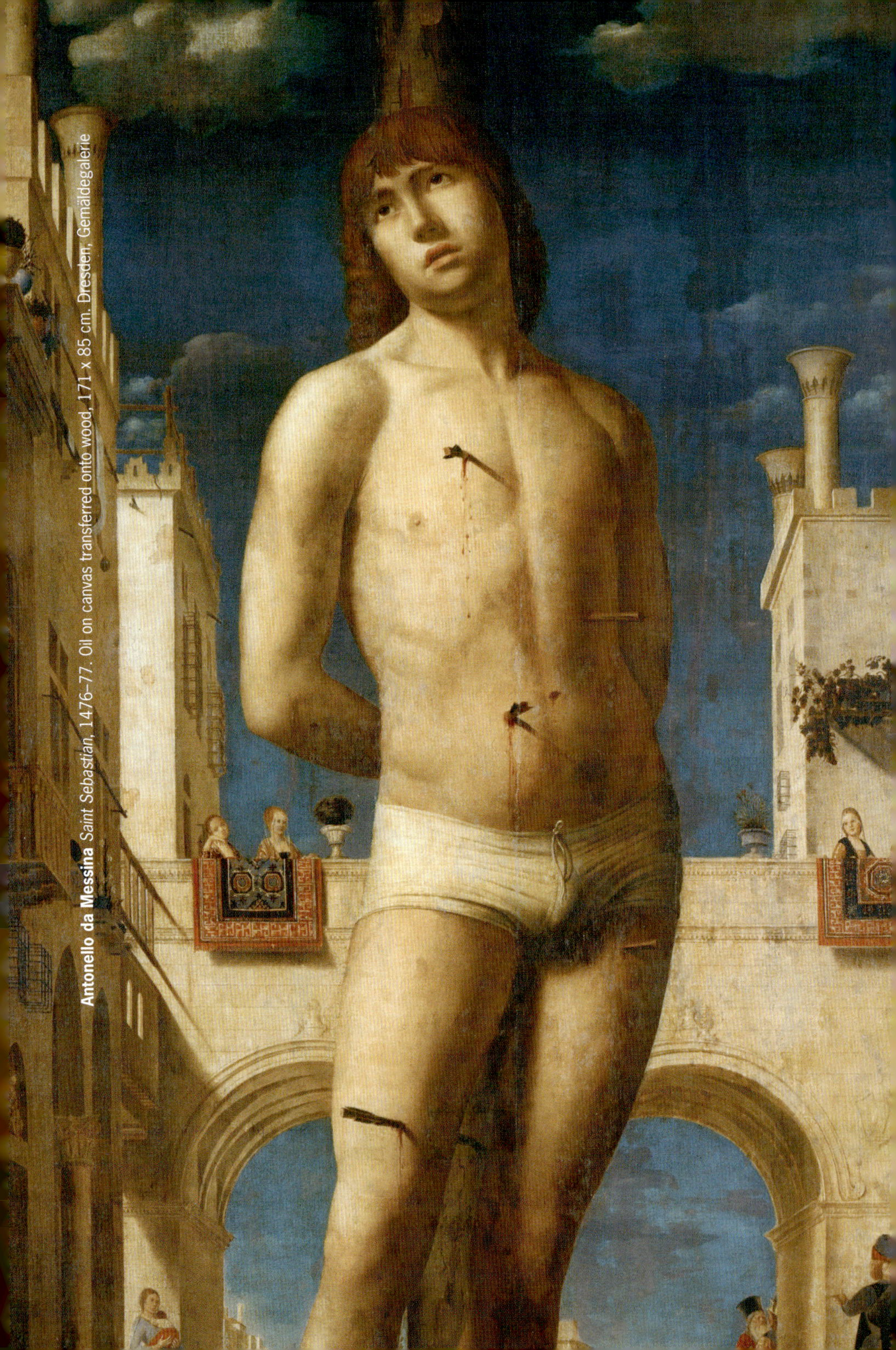

Antonello da Messina *Saint Sebastian*, 1476–77. Oil on canvas transferred onto wood, 171 x 85 cm. Dresden, Gemäldegalerie

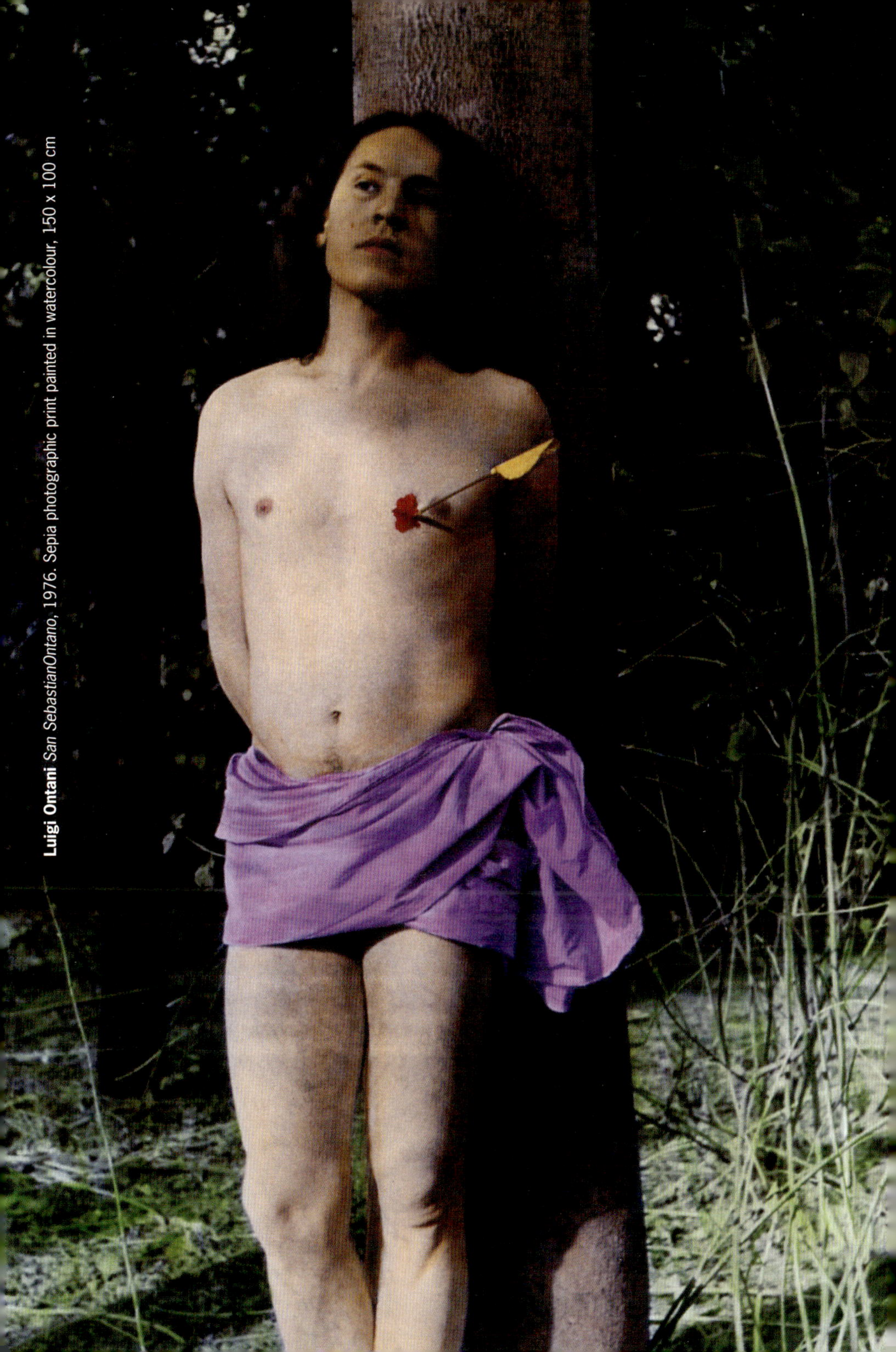

Luigi Ontani *San SebastianOntano*, 1976. Sepia photographic print painted in watercolour, 150 x 100 cm

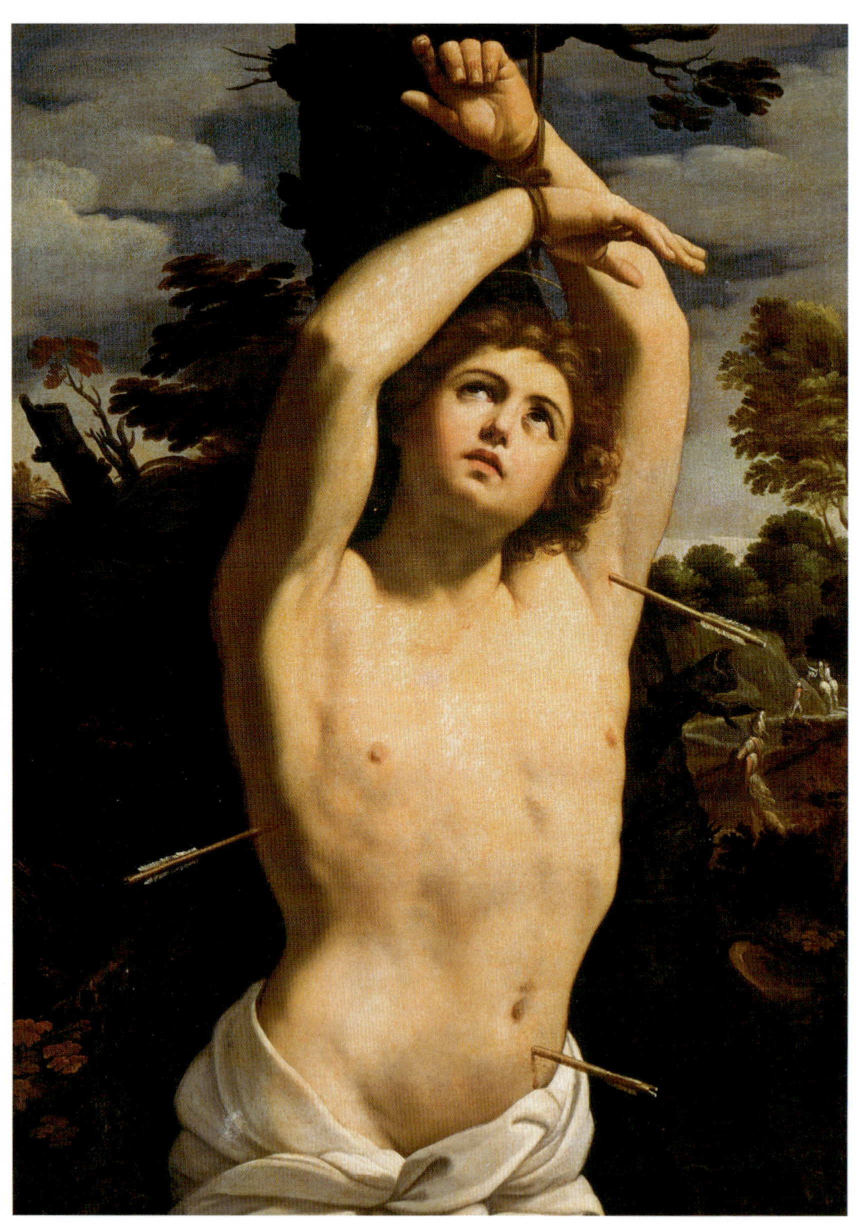

Guido Reni *Saint Sebastian, c.* 1615. Oil on canvas, 128 x 98 cm. Rome, Pinacoteca Capitolina

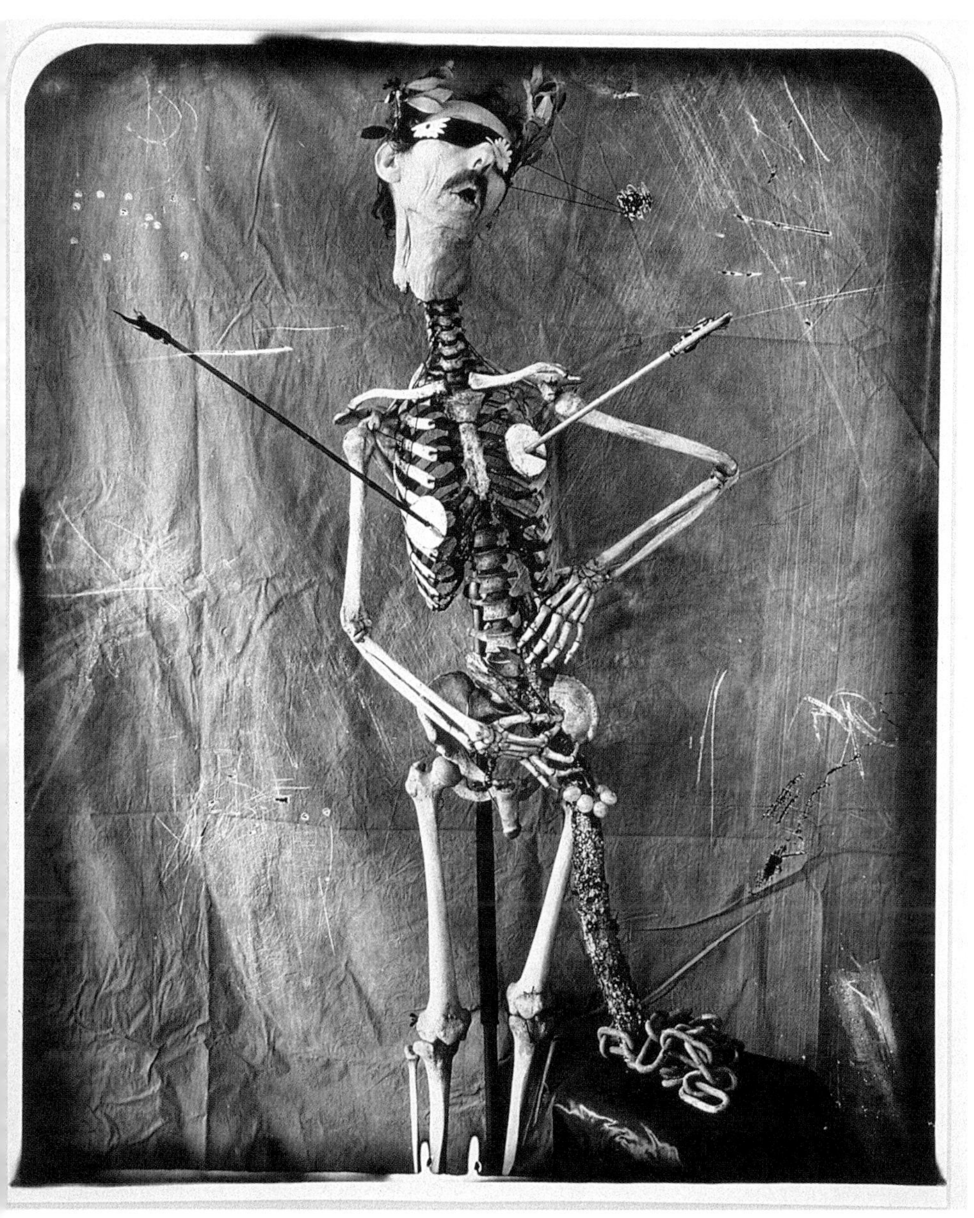

el-Peter Witkin *Queer Saint*, 1999. Toned silver gelatine print, 40.5 x 32 cm

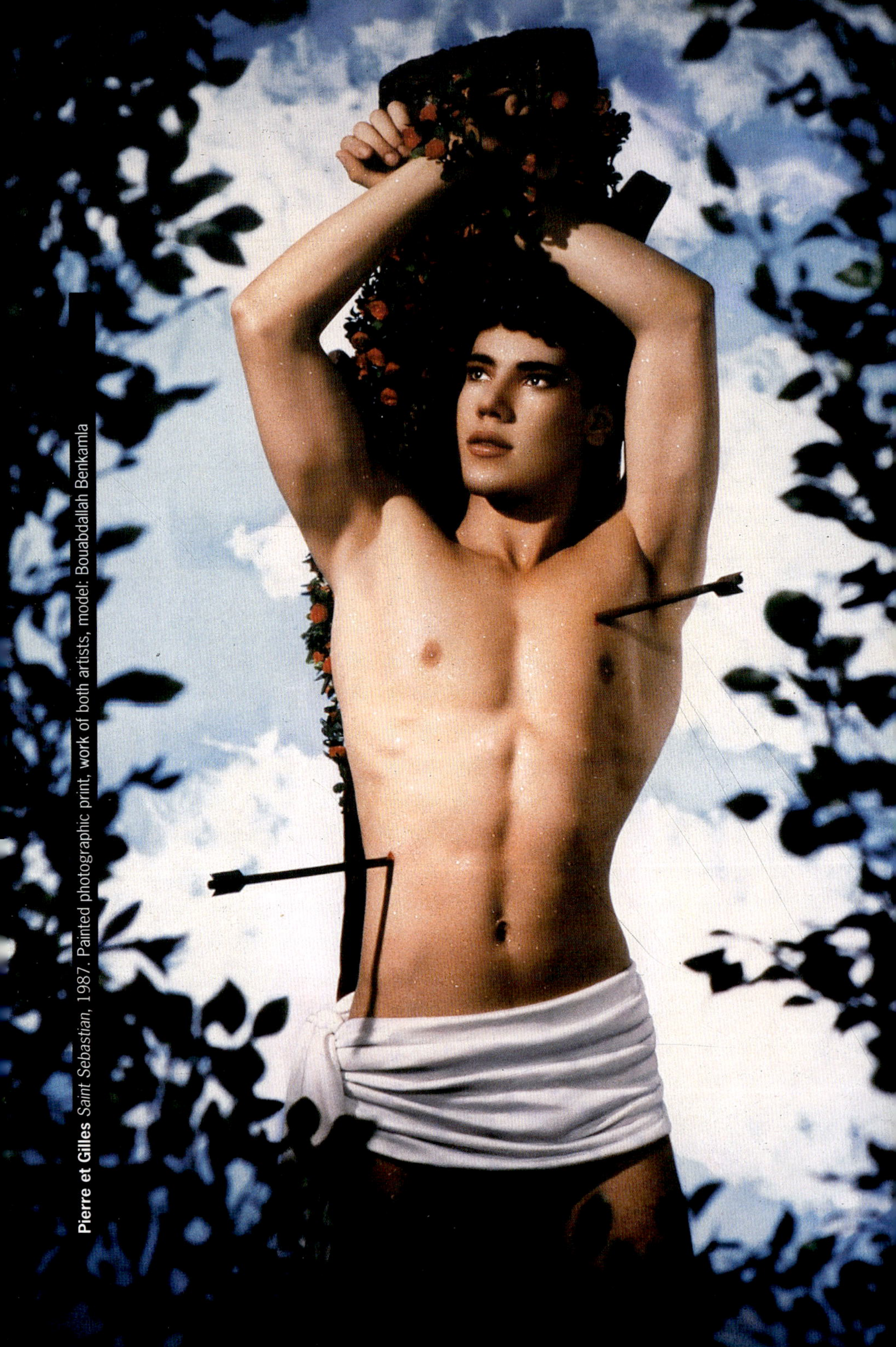

Pierre et Gilles *Saint Sebastian*, 1987. Painted photographic print, work of both artists, model: Bouabdallah Benkamla

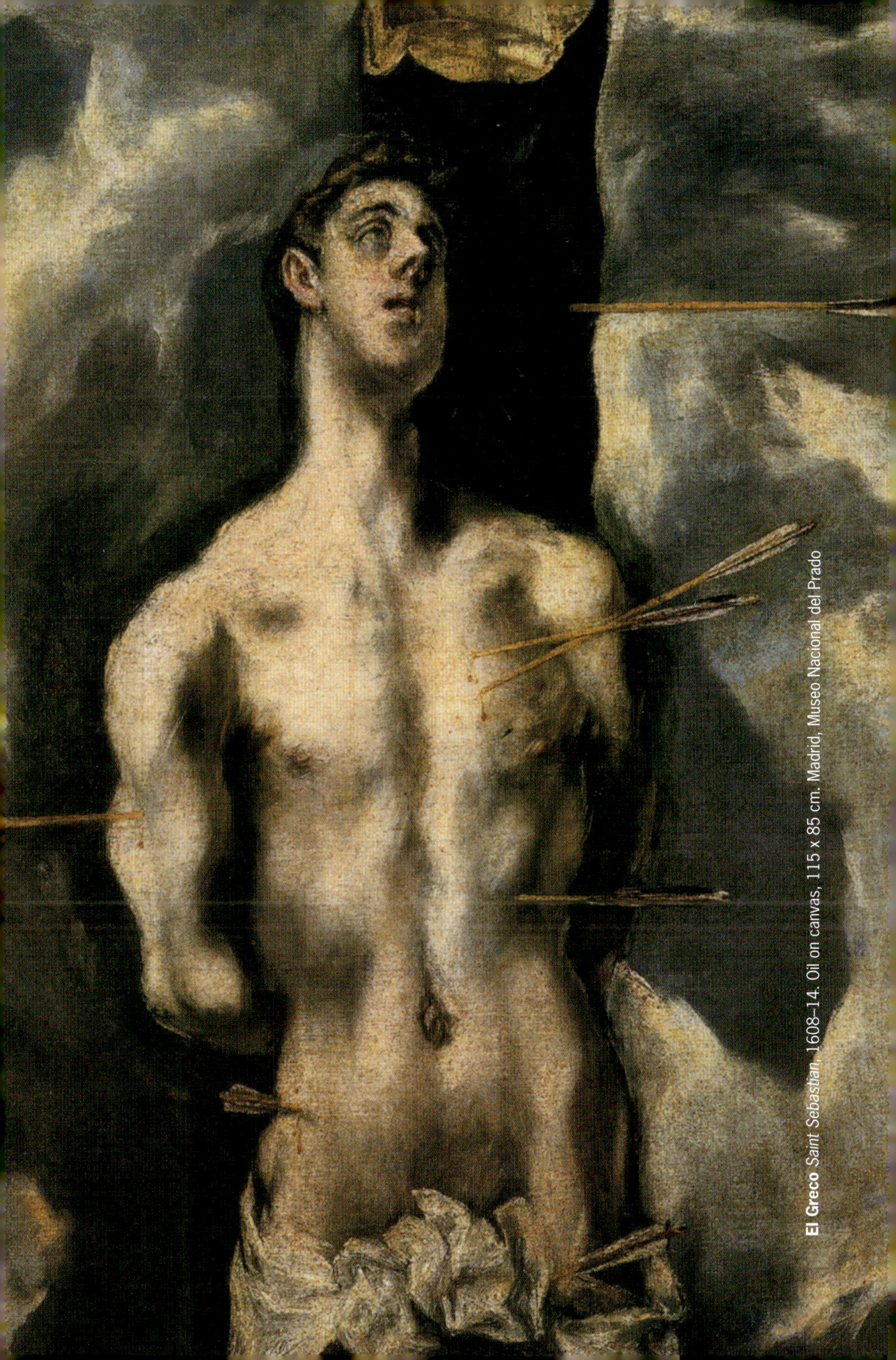

El Greco *Saint Sebastian*, 1608–14. Oil on canvas, 115 x 85 cm. Madrid, Museo Nacional del Prado

The Evolution of Allure

Christians were urged to imitate, to be, and, via art, even to look like images of the saints. Above all they were urged to imitate images of the Virgin and of Christ, the latter being the incarnate image of both man and God, and both of them fully susceptible to, and capable even of eliciting, human sexual urges (though on their part without sin). Often, representations of such holy persons were in turn modeled on selected men and women of the community. The process was mutually reinforcing: certain types were holy because they looked like preexisting holy pictures, and those pictures had in turn been based on local selectables.

George L. Hersey

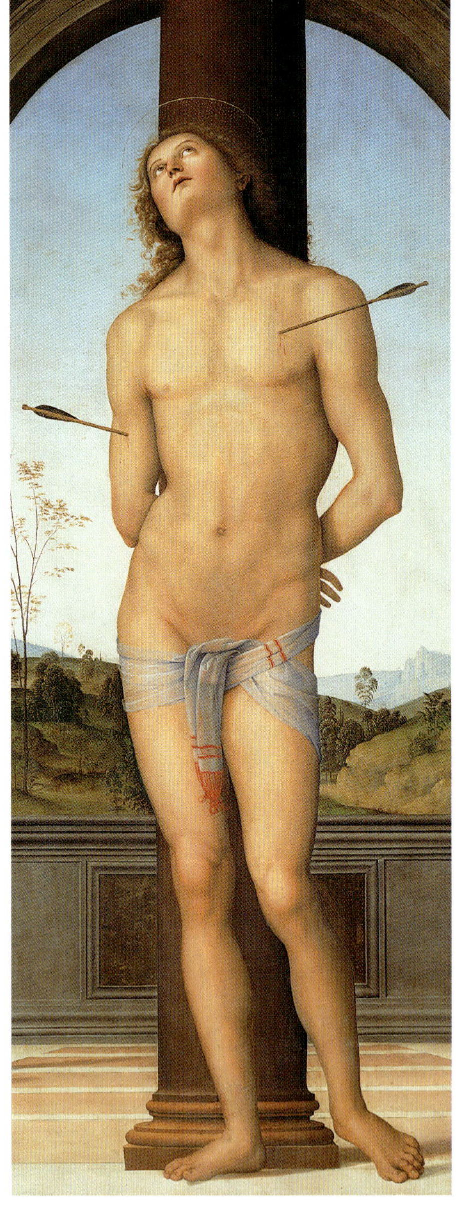

Perugino *Saint Sebastian* (detail), c. 1490
Oil on wood, 176 x 116 cm
Paris, Musée du Louvre

George L. Hersey, *The Evolution of Allure. Sexual Selection from the Medici Venus to the Incredible Hulk*, Cambridge, MA: MIT Press, 1996.

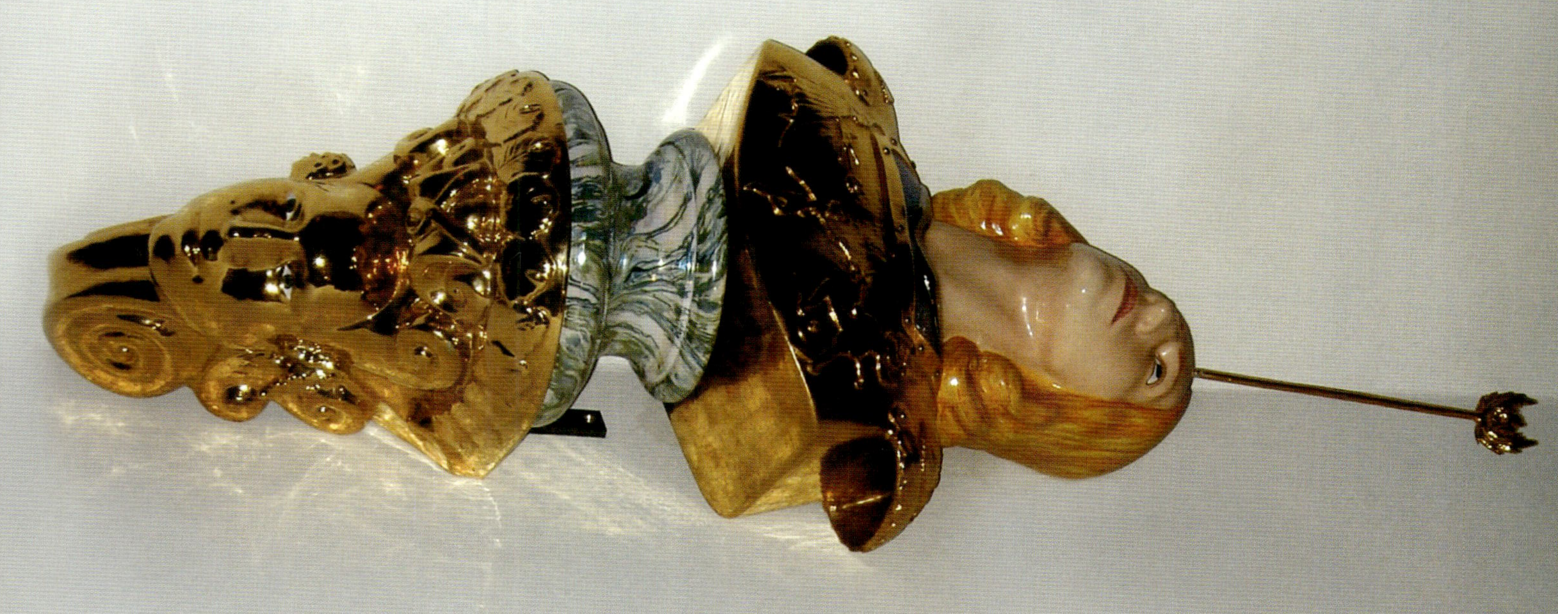

Luigi Ontani *BELLIn/mBUSTI = SanSebastianONTÀ*, 1996. Polychrome ceramic with third-fired finish in fine gold

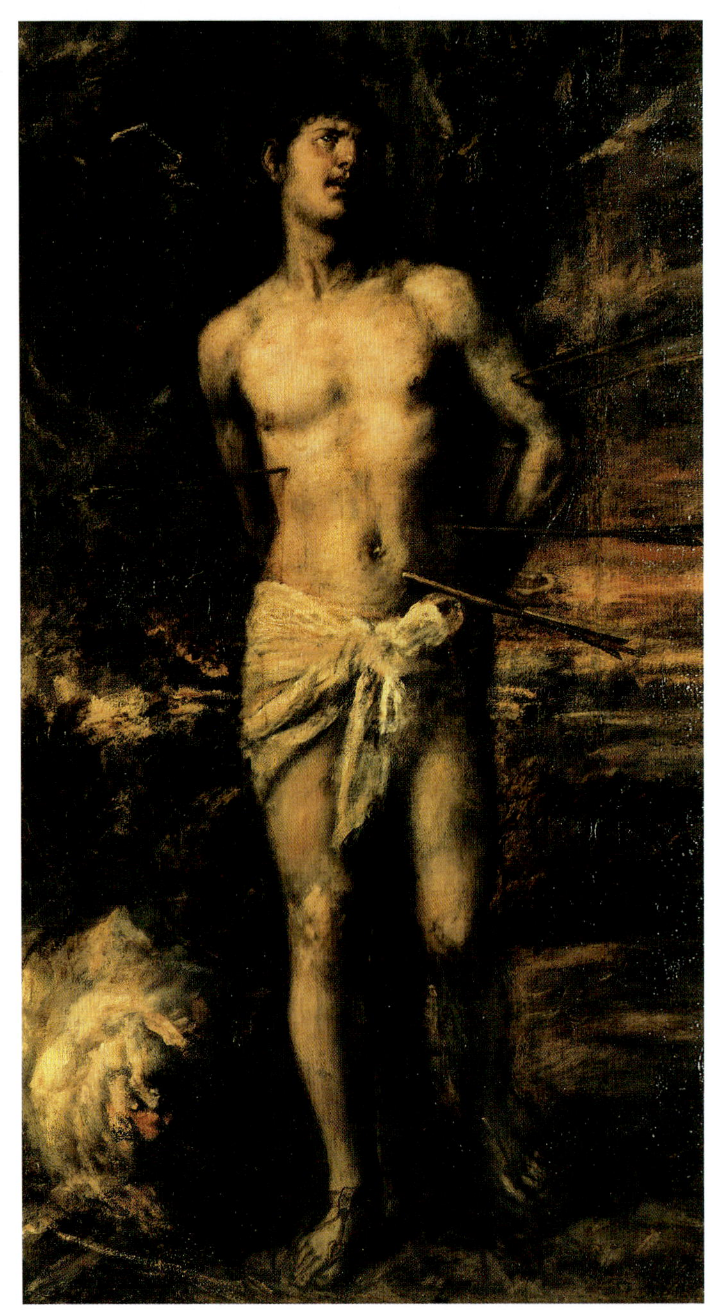

Titian *Saint Sebastian*, c. 1570. Oil on canvas, 210 x 111.5 cm. St Petersburg, State Hermitage Museum

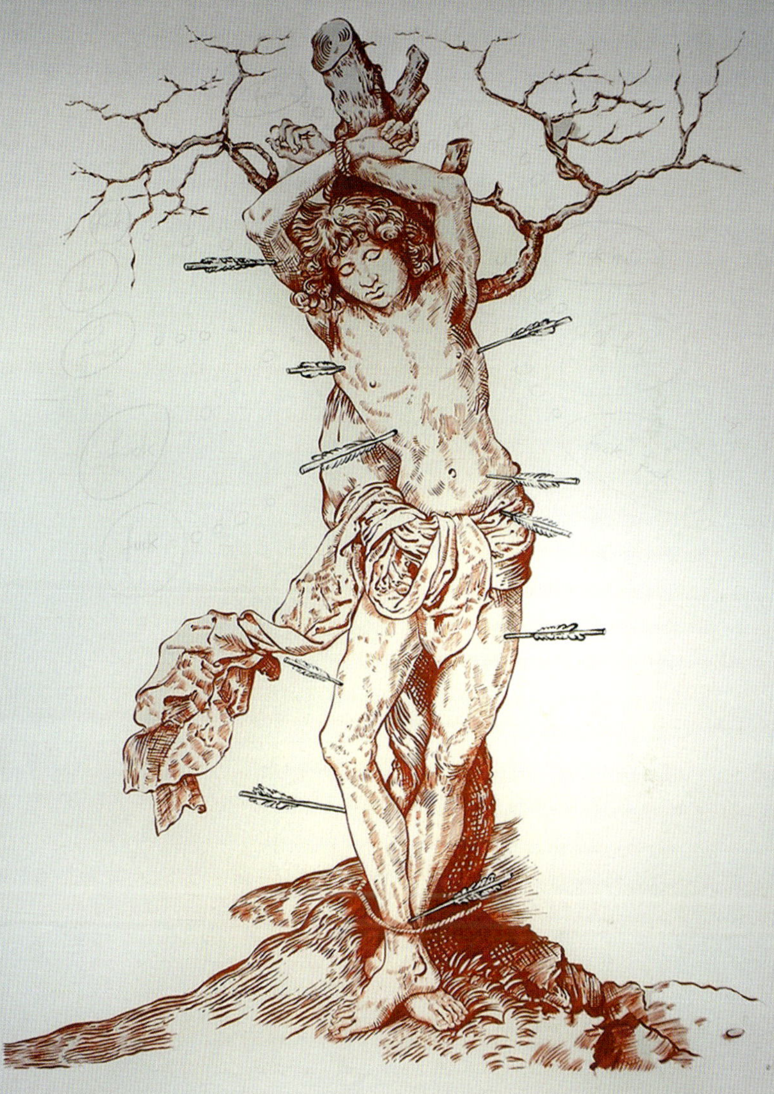

David Godbold *Popes & Bears*, 2006. Painting on wall and vinyl texts, variable dimensions

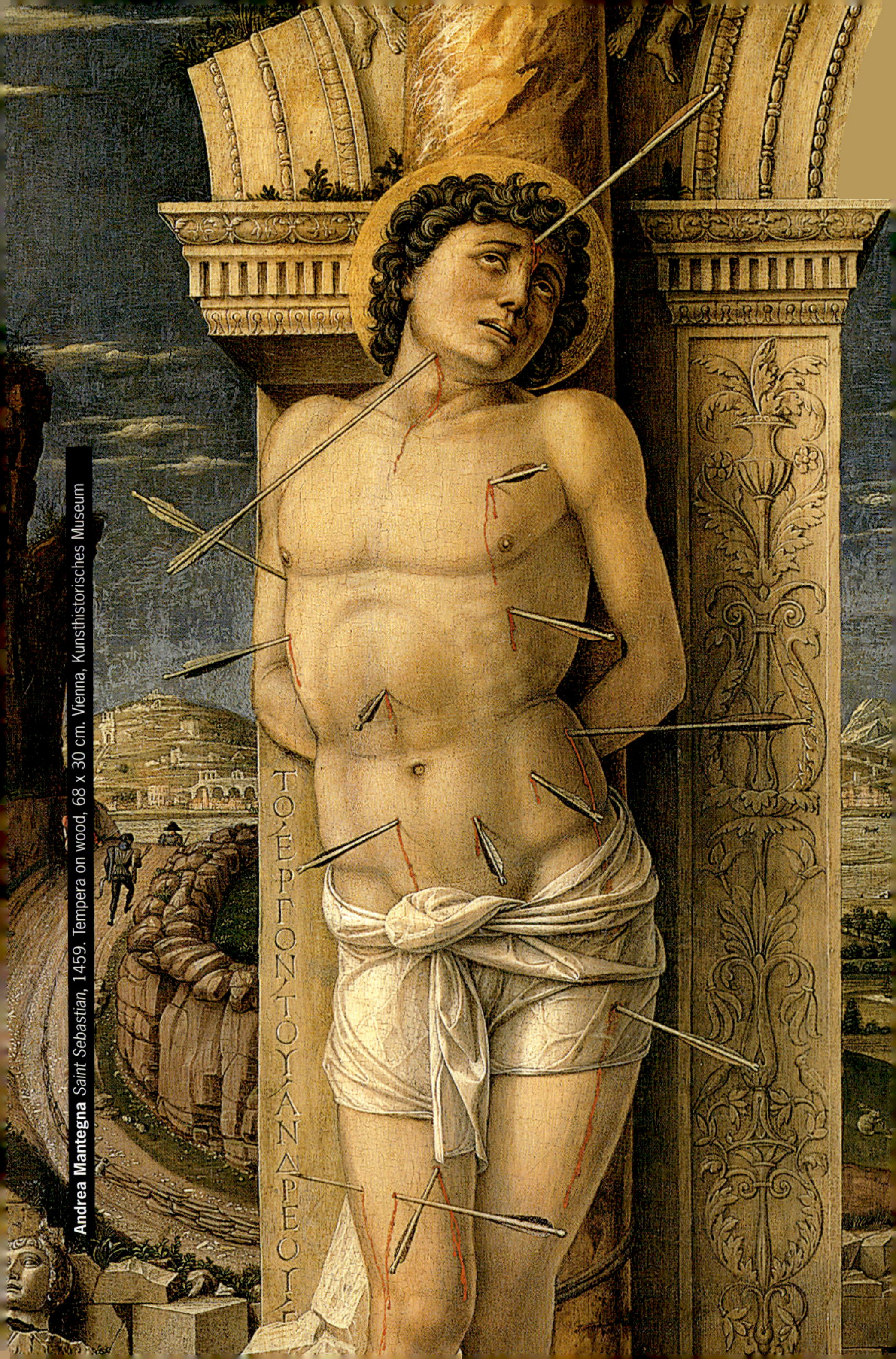

Andrea Mantegna *Saint Sebastian*, 1459. Tempera on wood, 68 x 30 cm. Vienna, Kunsthistorisches Museum

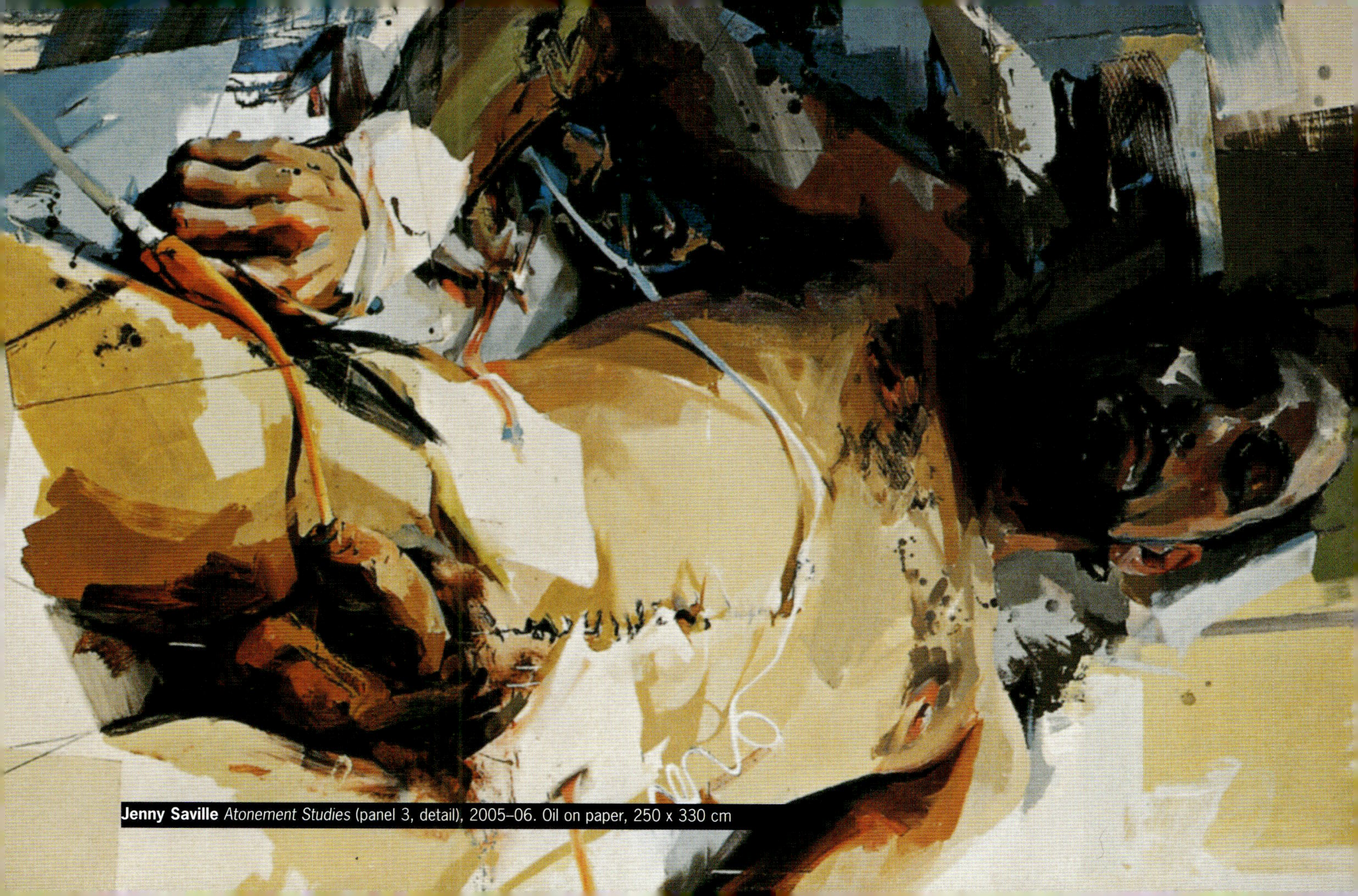

Jenny Saville *Atonement Studies* (panel 3, detail), 2005–06. Oil on paper, 250 x 330 cm

Spaces of Prayer

Popular religious pictures survive church renovations and migrate from demolished buildings to modern ones despite the architects, clergy, and liturgy committees who would rather eliminate them. The persistence of these pictures is not a matter of leisurely nostalgia. People find it difficult, even impossible, to worship comfortably without them. This persistence is, rather, an index of visual piety. The image creates a devotional space, a place to encounter or interact with the sacred. Many say that the picture corresponds to the mental image of Jesus that is present in prayer. Both homes and worship spaces are transformed by the images displayed therein. Images are the means by which a space becomes familiar and personal. People take their Sallman pictures from house to house as they move through life, hang them among the photographs of their relatives, place them in their children's bedrooms, and admire them in religious classrooms and the sanctuary. Such images have the power to make a place home by installing there a sacred presence, an icon that listens to believers and watches over them.

David Morgan

David Morgan (©), *Visual Piety. A History and Theory of Popular Religious Images*, Berkeley, Los Angeles & London: The Regents of the University of California, University of California Press, 1997.

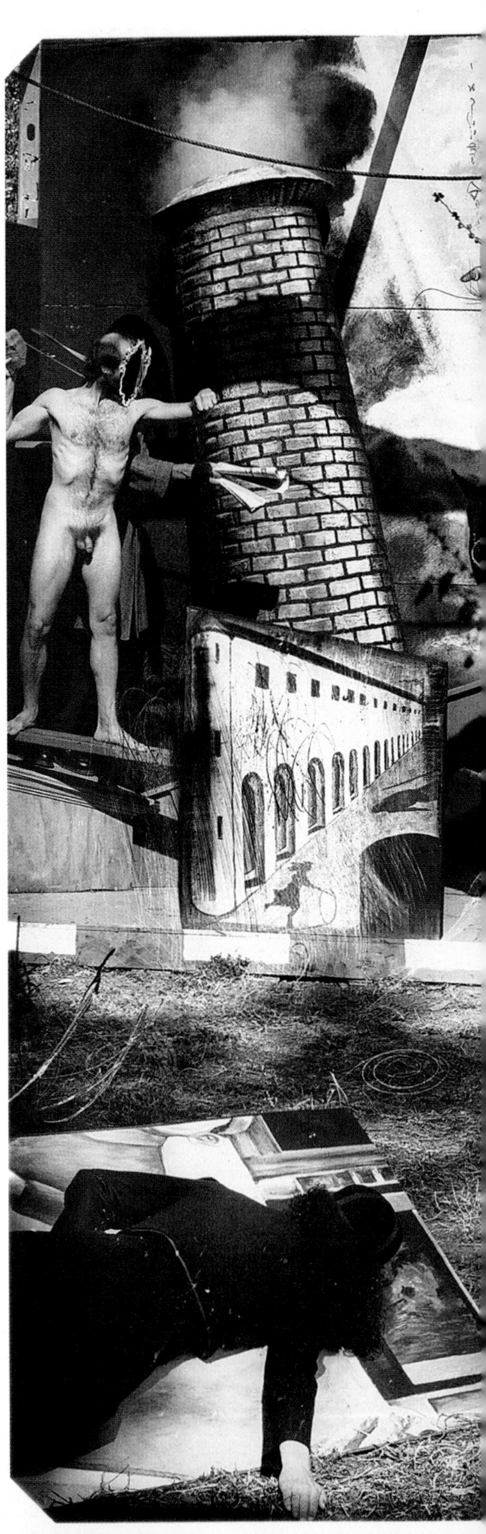

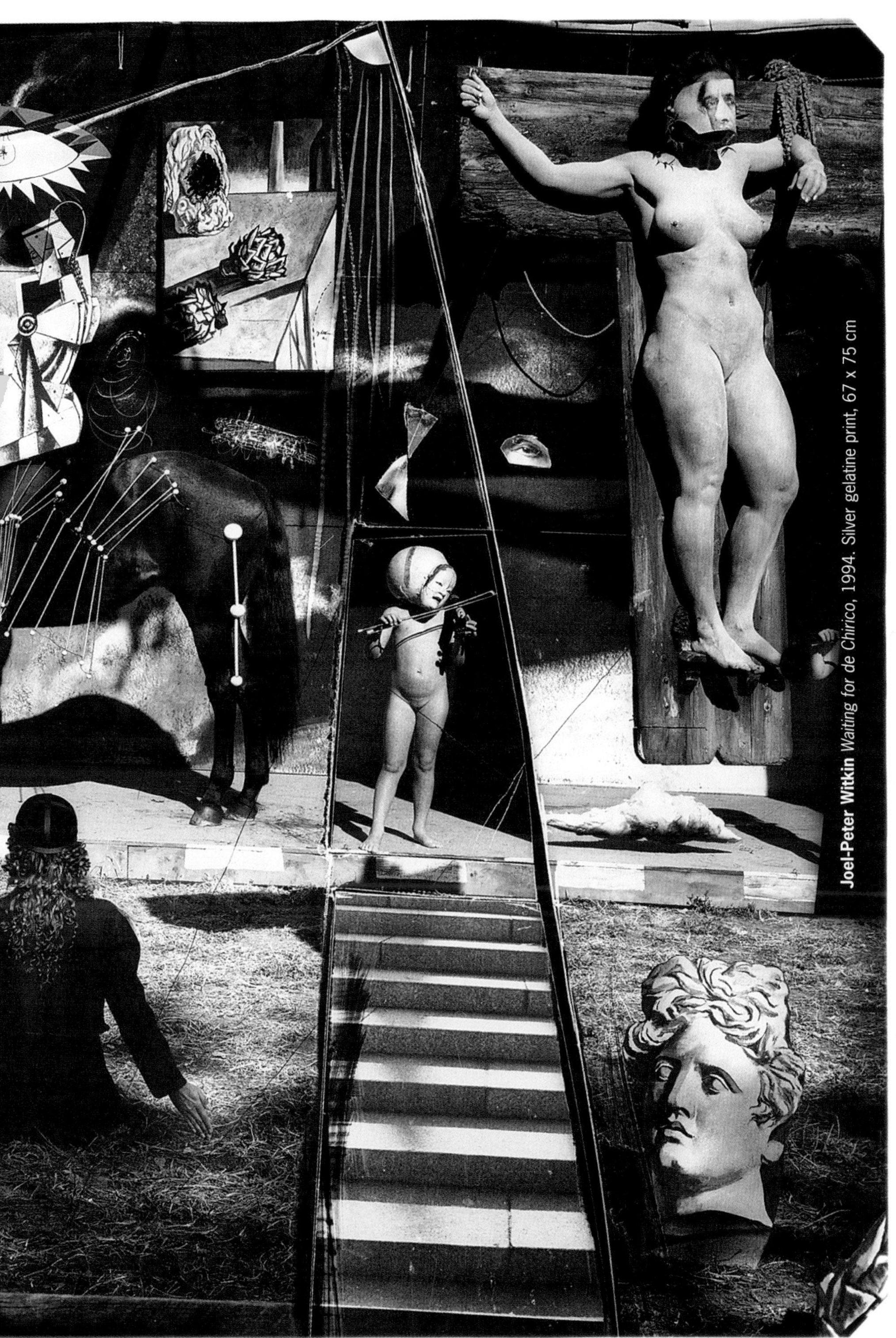

Joel-Peter Witkin *Waiting for de Chirico*, 1994. Silver gelatine print, 67 x 75 cm

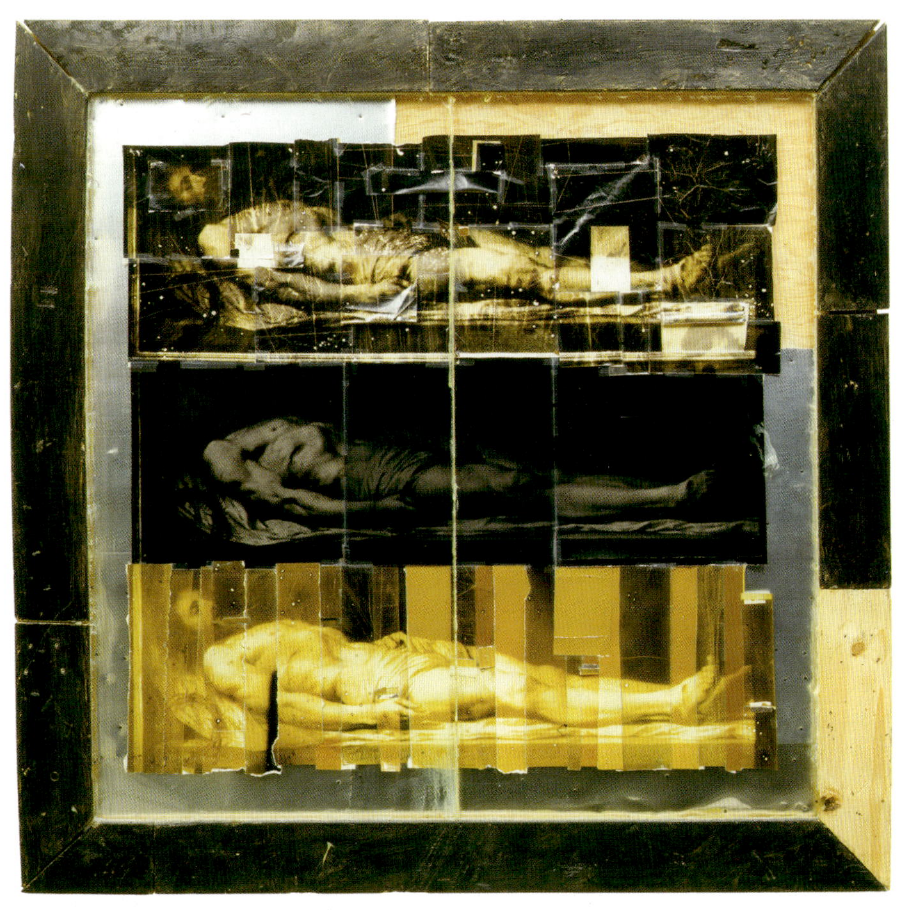

Doug and Mike Starn *Triple Christ*, 1986. Toned silver gelatine print, wood, glue, glass and aluminium, 165.1 x 165.1 cm

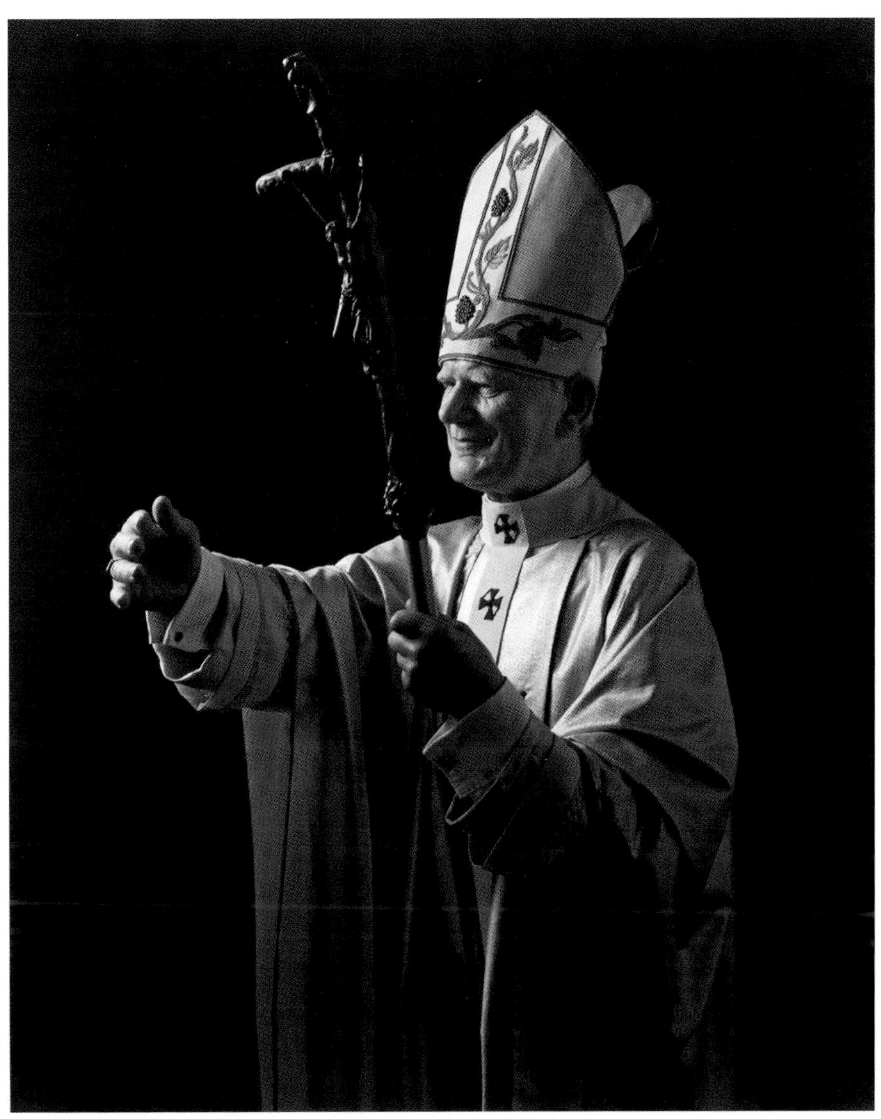

Hiroshi Sugimoto *Pope John Paul II*, 1999. Photographic print, 149 x 119 cm

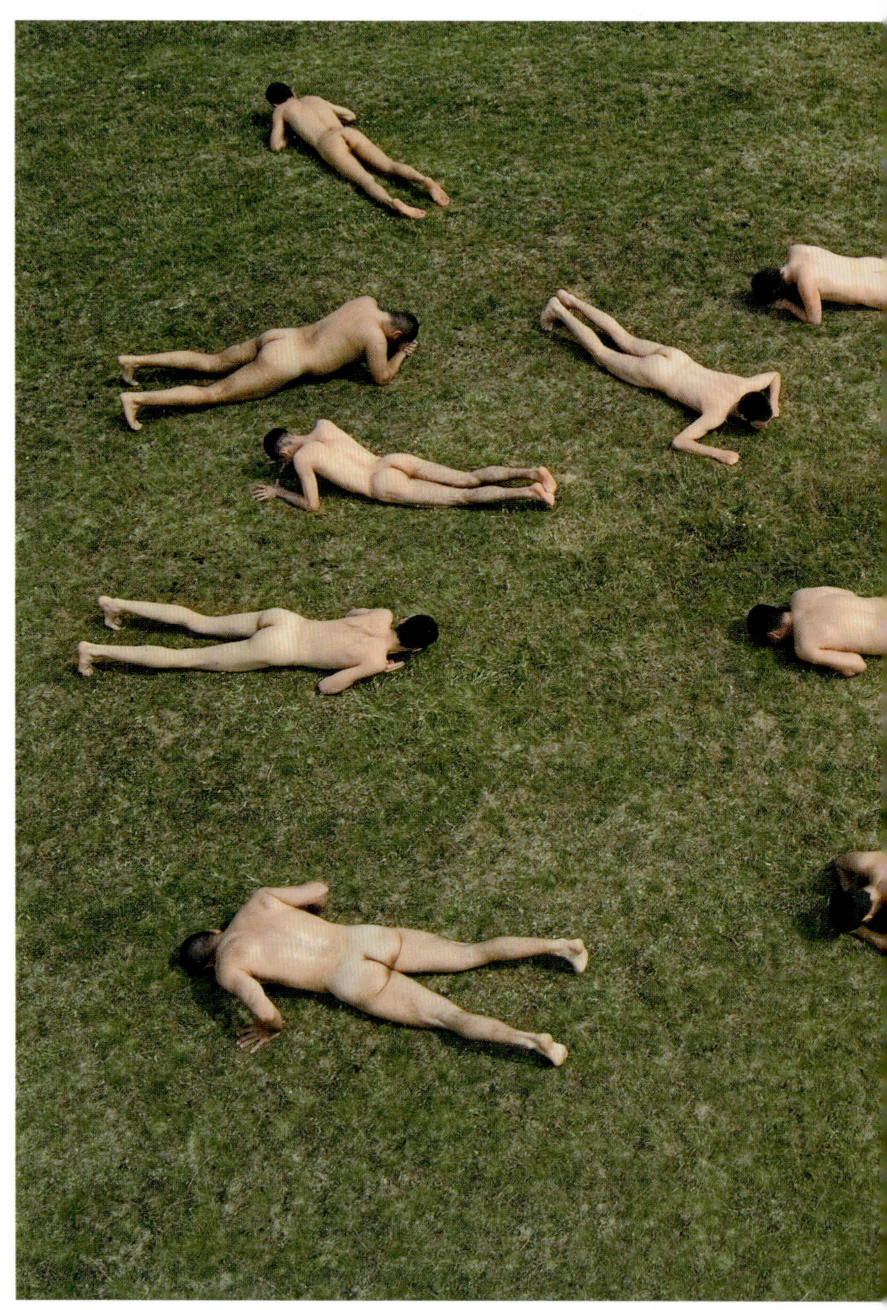

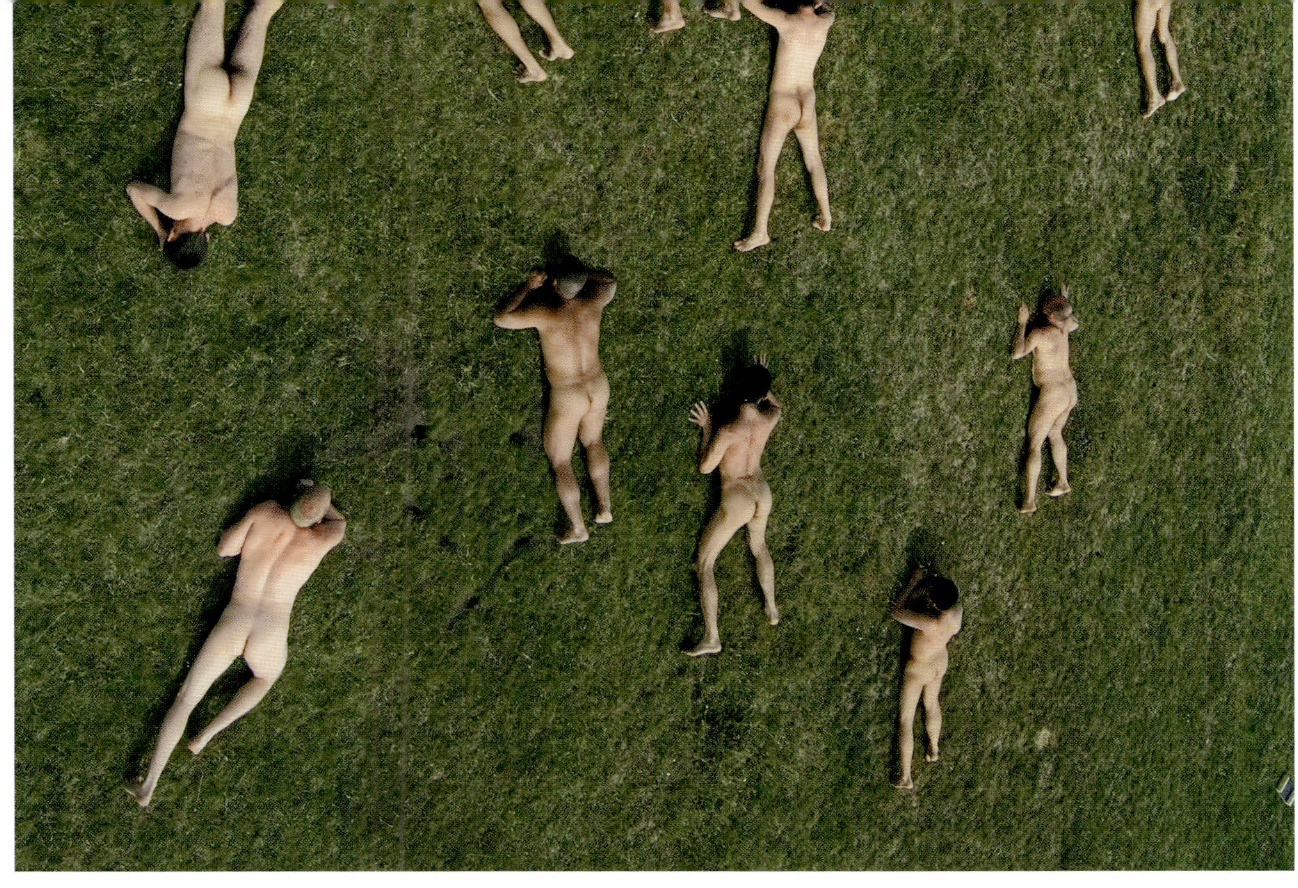

Marina Abramović *Balkan Erotic Epic: Group of Men Copulating with the Earth*, 2005 (still from the video *Belgrade*)

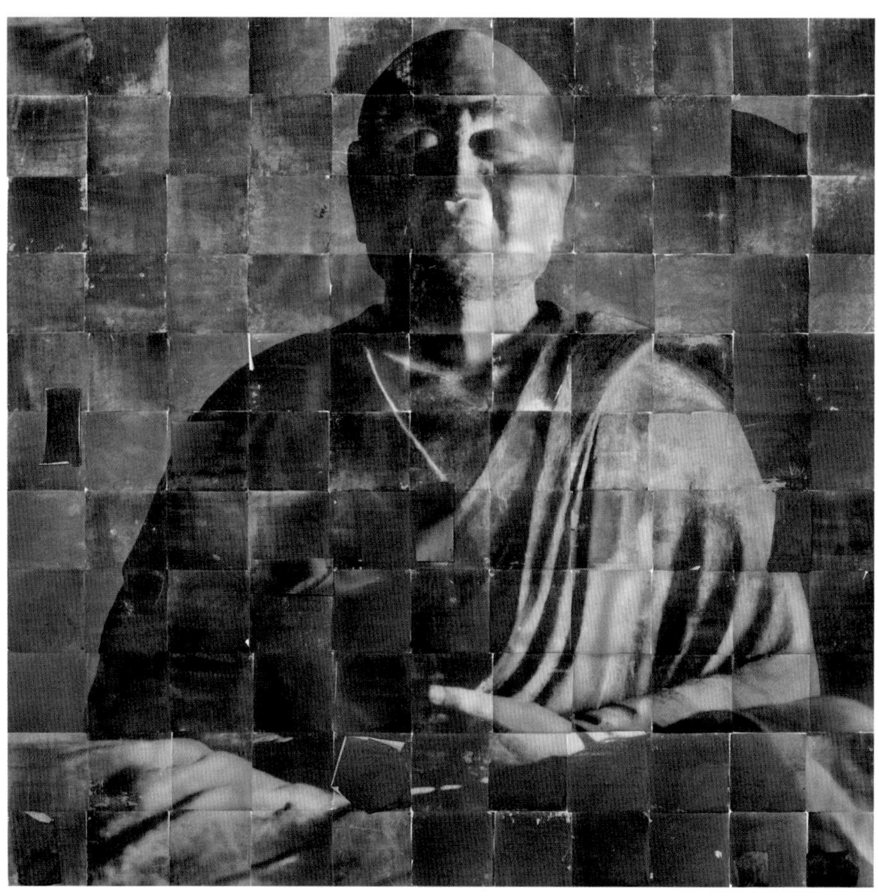

Doug and Mike Starn *Ganjin Head*, 2000–04. Sulphur-toned silver print with tea stains on Thai mulberry paper, 304.8 x 304.8 cm

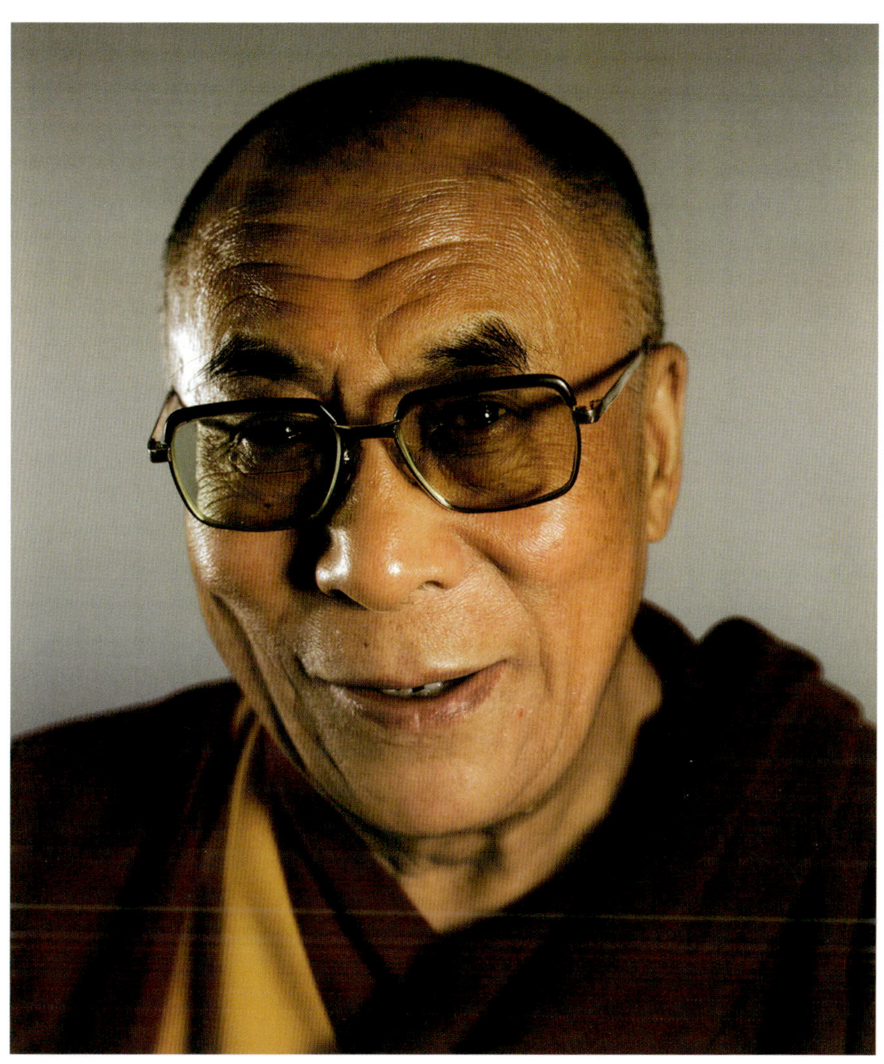

Chuck Close *Dalai Lama*, 2005. Photographic print, 127 x 101.6 cm

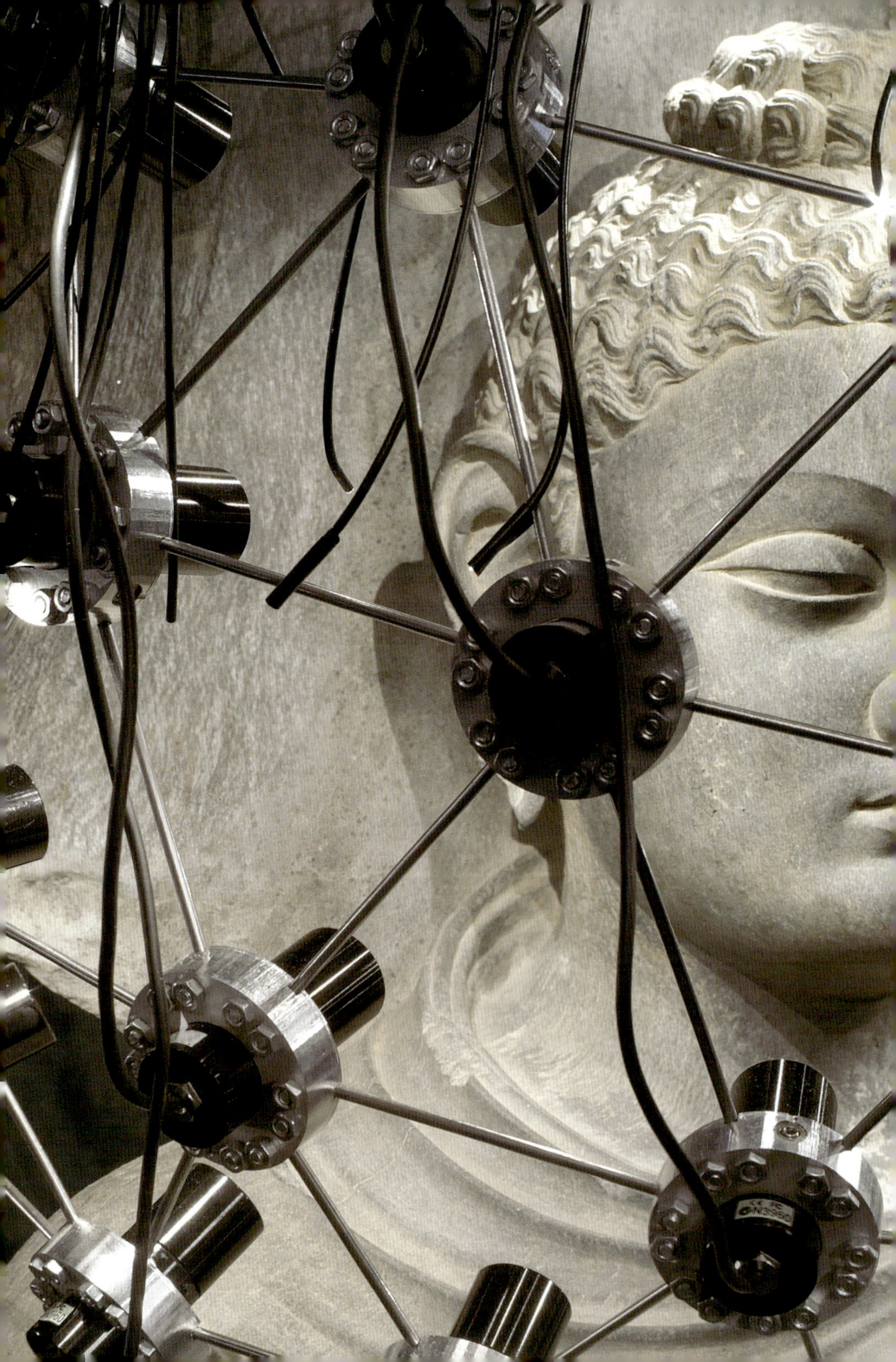

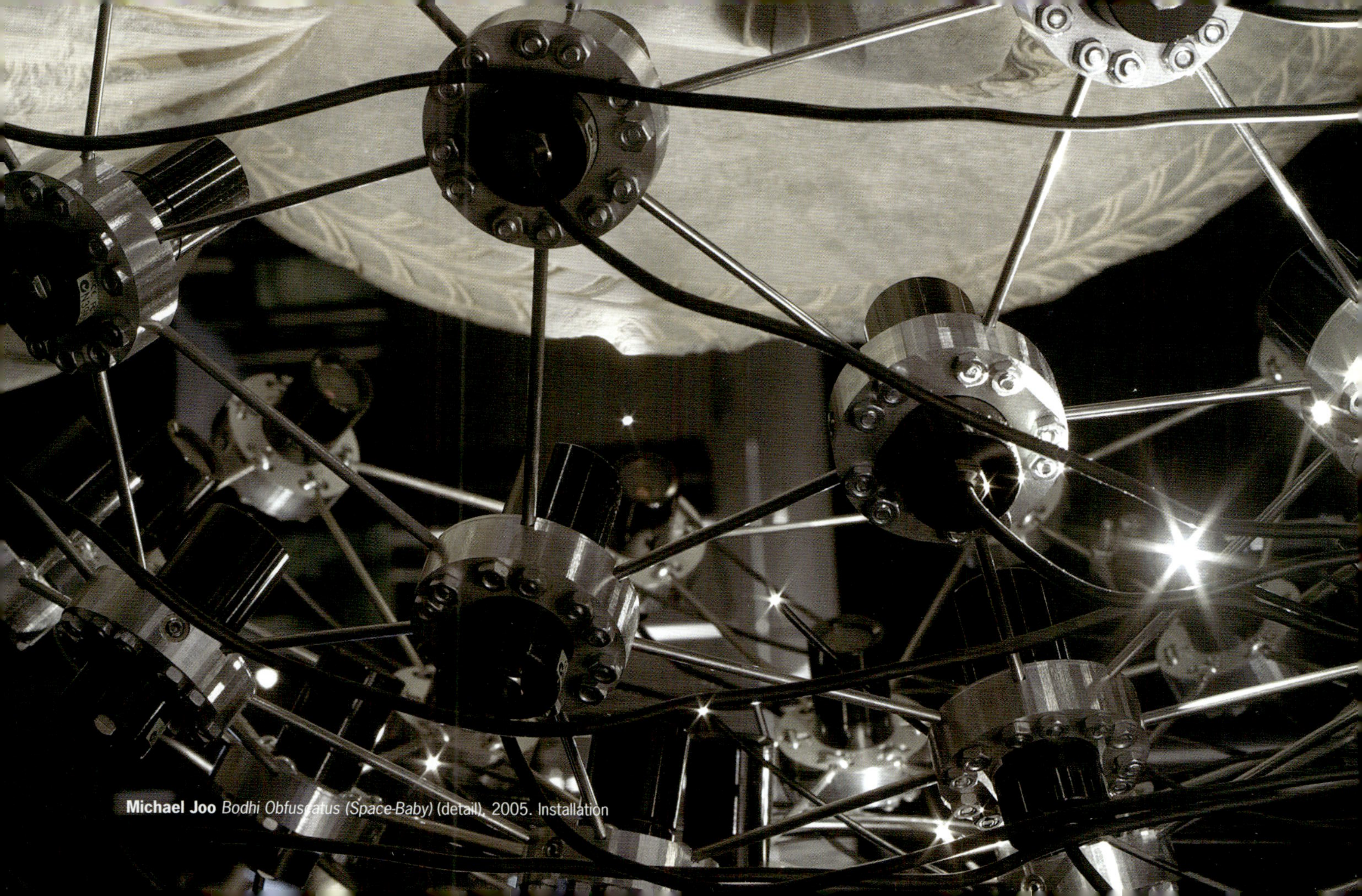

Michael Joo *Bodhi Obfuscatus (Space-Baby)* (detail), 2005. Installation

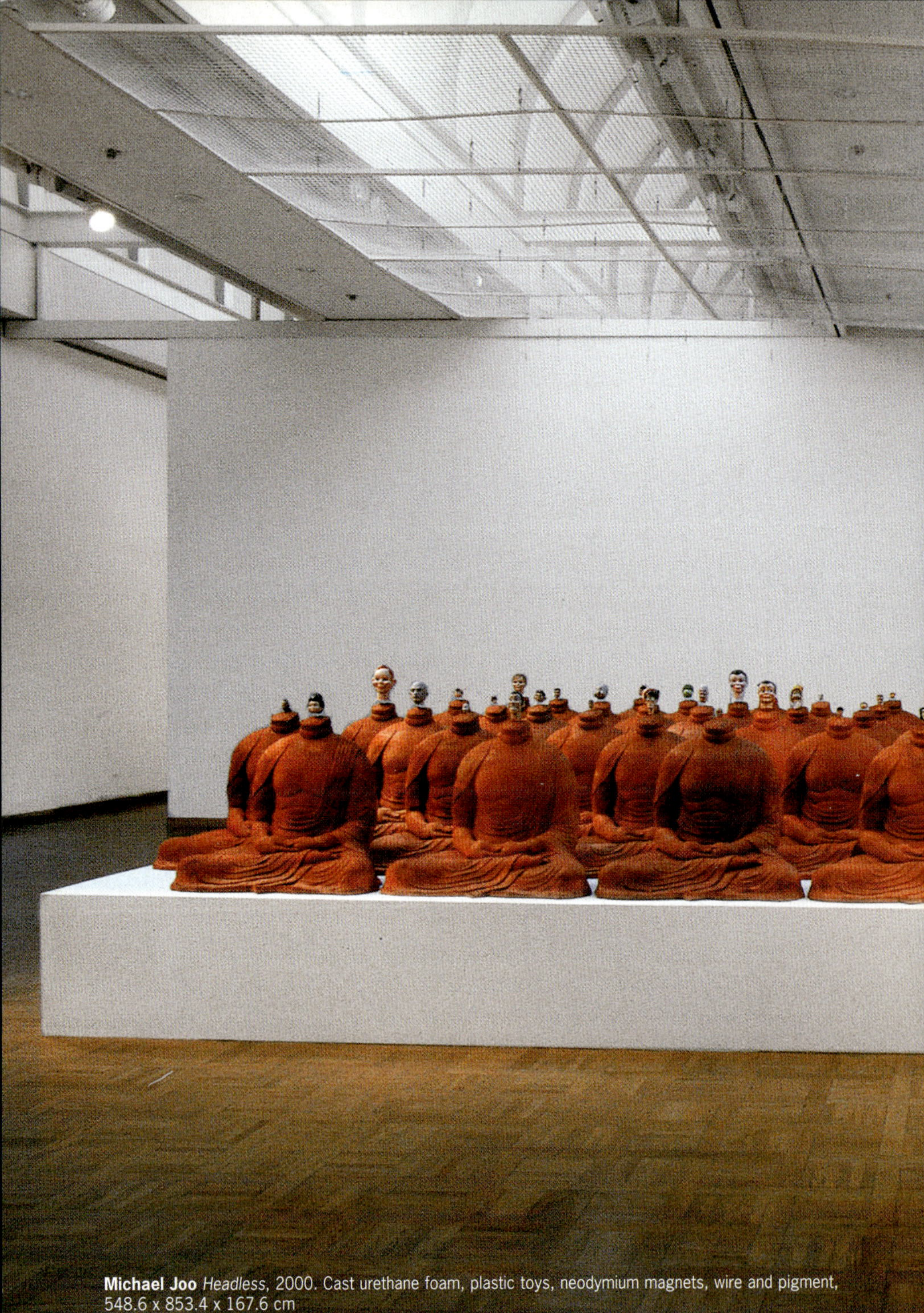

Michael Joo *Headless*, 2000. Cast urethane foam, plastic toys, neodymium magnets, wire and pigment, 548.6 x 853.4 x 167.6 cm

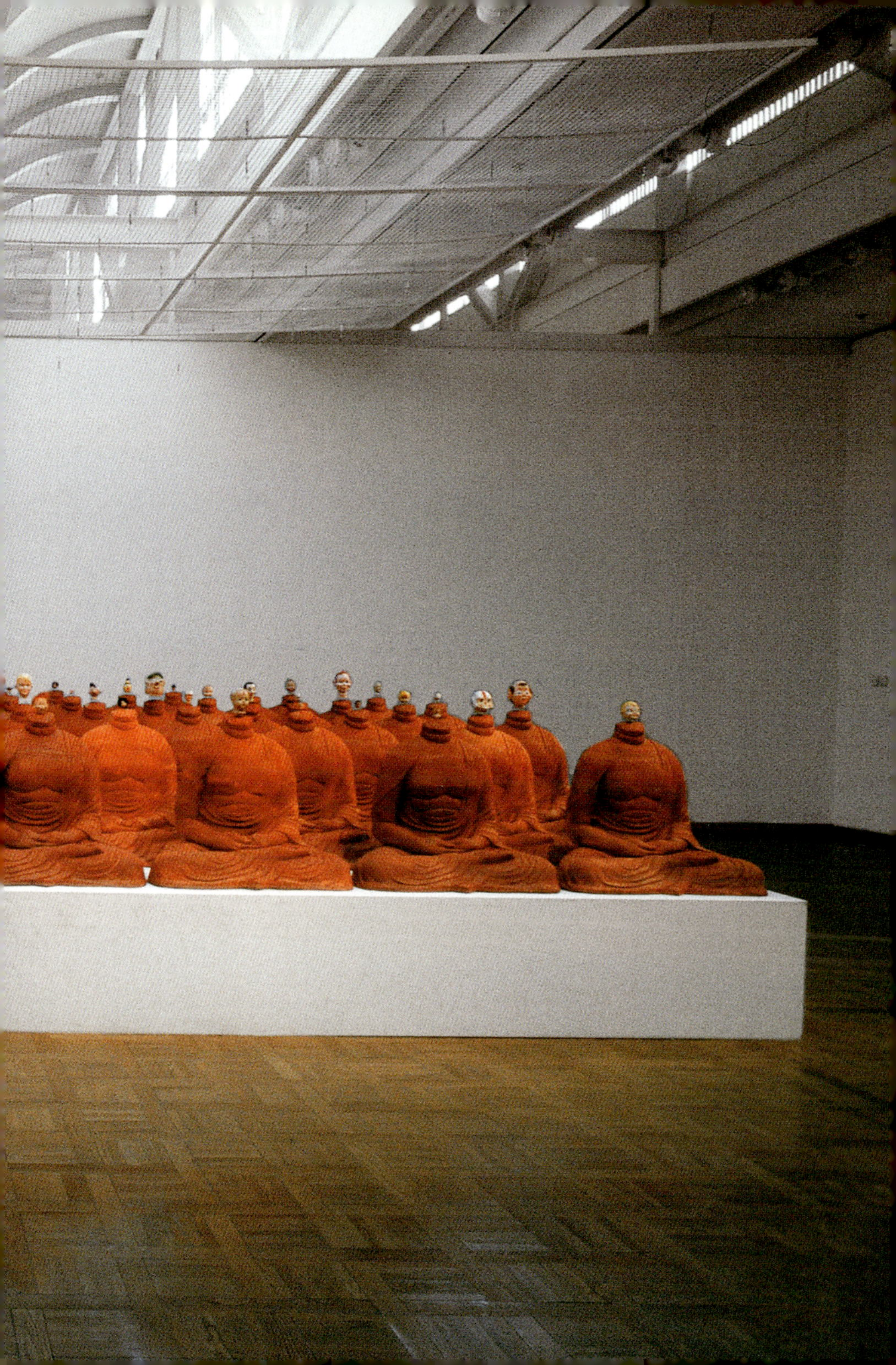

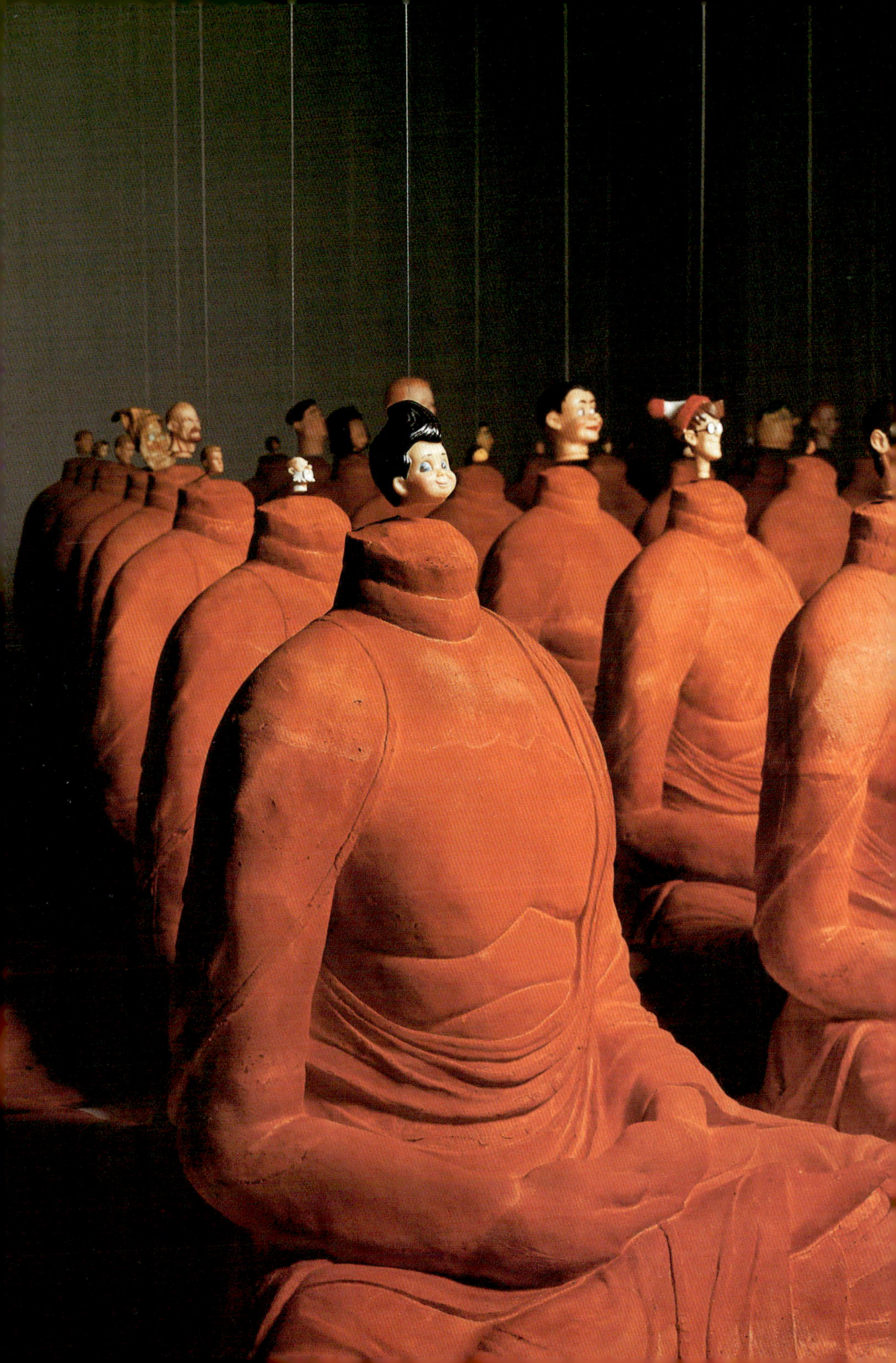

The Question of the Sacred

Julien Ries

The Sociological Option

Research into the sacred began at the end of the nineteenth century. At the dawn of the twentieth, the French school of sociology, strongly influenced by positivism and evolutionism, saw in the sacred a conceptual category whose origin should be sought in society. Identified with the *mana* of primitive man discovered by some ethnologists, the sacred was considered a category of the collective consciousness. Thus, it was in the totem of primitive peoples that Émile Durkheim looked for the origin of religion and religions. Going beyond this doctrine of the identity of *mana* and the sacred, Henri Hubert and Marcel Mauss did not hesitate to assert the identity of the sacred and the social. In the sacred they saw an idea-force around which myths and rituals are interlinked.

A philosopher of the Durkheimian school, Lucine Lévy-Bruhl, transposed sociological doctrines into the sphere of primitive thought, which he called pre-logical thought. He established a dichotomy in the thinking of humanity, which did away with the concept of the spiritual unity of the human race. In view of the political use which Nazi ideology made of this argument, Lévy-Bruhl later reconsidered and amended his ideas.

The sociological positions have been systematized by Roger Caillois. In his eyes, the sacred is a stable and transient property, introduced in addition to the real. It is a mysterious and dangerous energy, hard to handle but highly effective. In his sociology of the sacred, Caillois placed the accent on the efforts made by humanity to avoid the ageing of society. He

Michael Joo *Headless* (detail), 2000. Cast urethane foam, plastic toys, neodymium magnets, wire and pigment, 548.6 x 853.4 x 167.6 cm

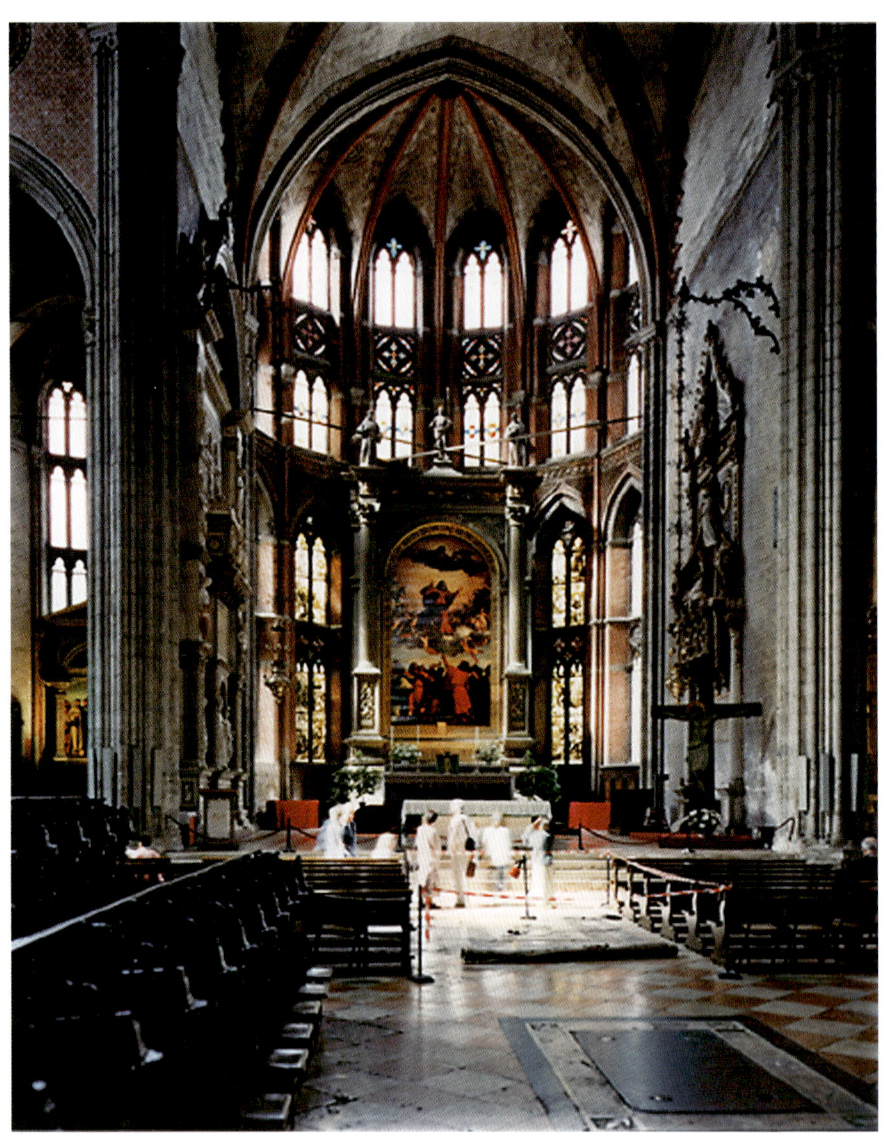

Thomas Struth *Church of I Frari, Venice*, 1995. Photographic print, 232 x 184 cm

attempted to highlight the dialectics between sacred and profane: the sacred of respect, the sacred of transgression, the sacred of dependence, the sacred of violation and the sacred of regulation alternate with the profane and ensure the equilibrium and the smooth functioning of the social group. In his work *La Violence et le sacré*, René Girare remained in the Durkheimian tradition. He tried to develop a theory on the identity of violence and the sacred. Through his theory of basic violence he thought he could rediscover the foundations of primitive religion. Girare's work constitutes an attempt at interpretation of the founding rites and myths of our civilization.

The Phenomenological Option

A new approach very soon emerged that attempted to understand the specific phenomenon of the sacred. Nathan Söderblom was interested in the psychological origin of the concept of sacred, which he sought in the reaction of the human mind to the presence of what appeared surprising in a supernatural sense. Rudolf Otto uncovered three faces of the sacred: the sacred as luminous, the sacred as value, the sacred as a priori category of the spirit. Taking a course that goes through four stages — *Kreaturgefühl*, *tremendum*, *mysterium*, *fascinans* — the human being draws nearer to the mystery and discovers the divine majesty. Thanks to his interpretations of the signs of the sacred, the religious man can perceive and discover the luminous that is made manifest in the unfolding of history. Thus, alongside the inner and individual revelation of the sacred, there is a historical revelation. In Otto's eyes, it is on this dual manifestation of the sacred that personal religion and the various religions are founded respectively. The prophets and the founders of religions are interpreters of the sacred; the Son of God is an example of this.

Continuing along the path opened by Otto, Gerardus van der Leeuw sought to gain a better understanding of the two faces of every religion: on the one hand, the face of the mystery; on the other, the face of human experience. The author put himself in the situation of an observer of *Homo religiosus* before the manifestation of the sacred; a position that allowed him to outline the religious human being.

The Anthropological and Hermeneutic Option

Continuation of this phenomenological research allowed Mircea Eliade to show that the sacred is manifested as a power of a totally different order with respect to the order of natural forces. The human being senses the sacred because it manifests itself. Eliade considered this manifestation to

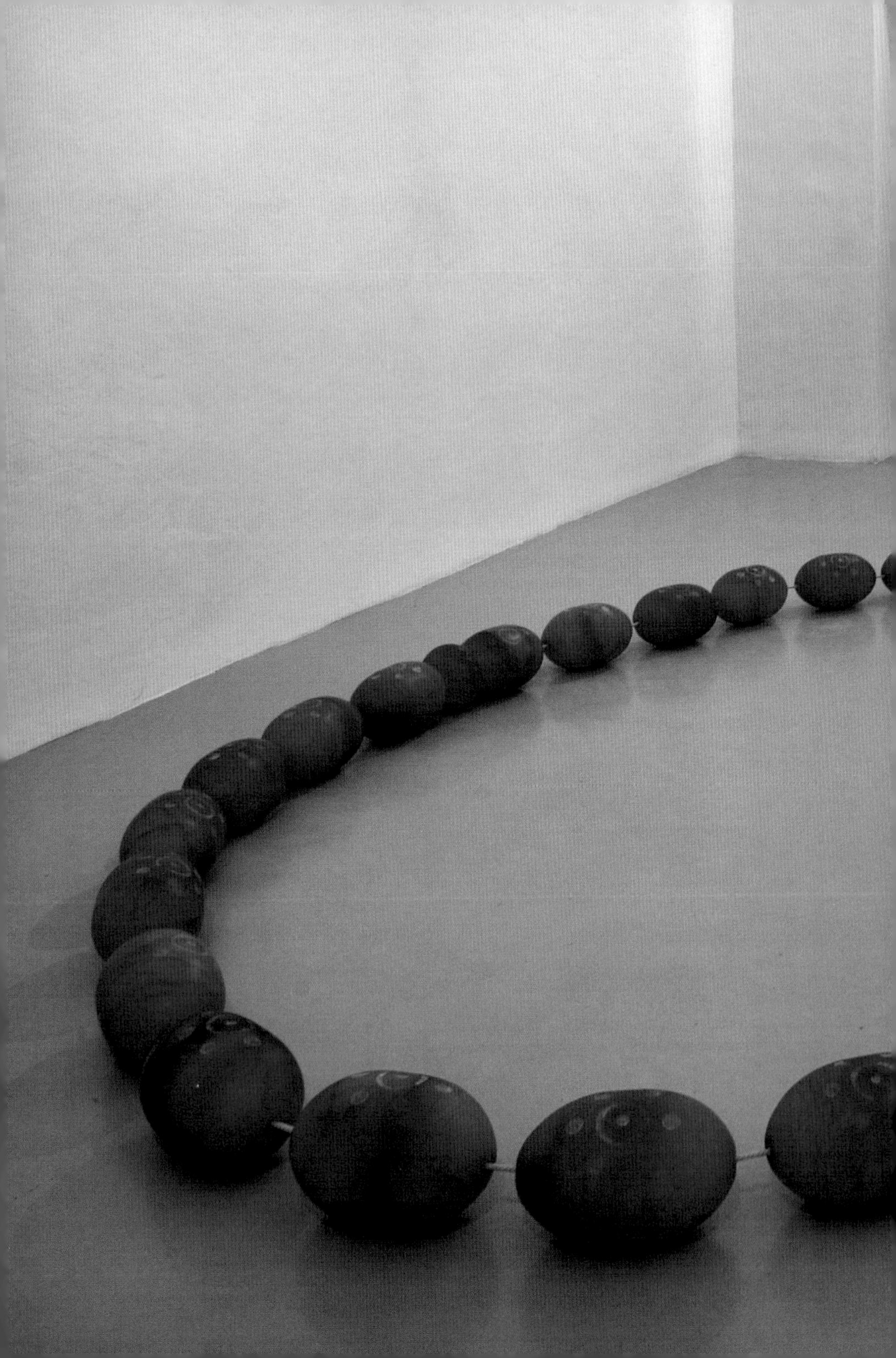

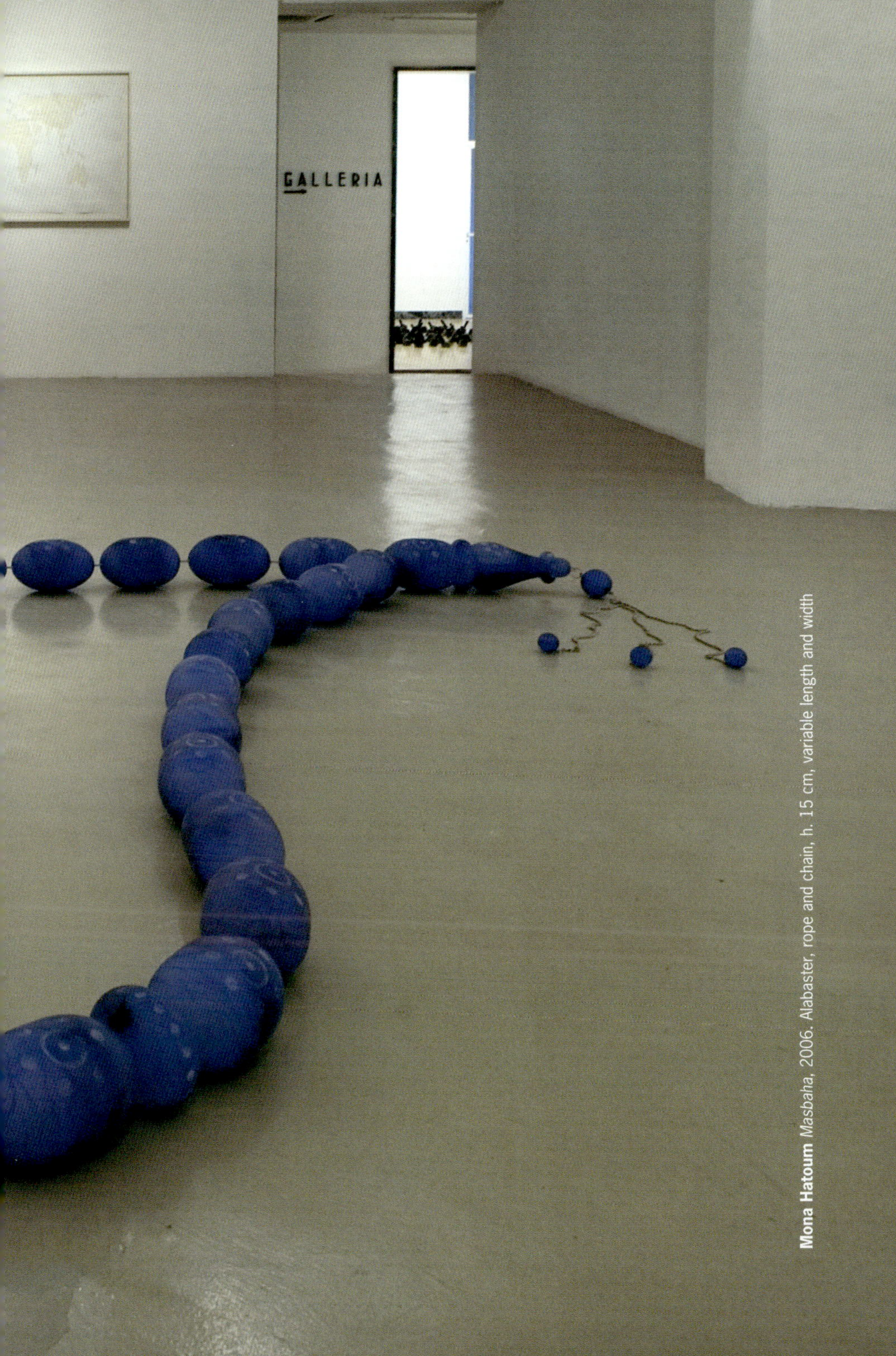

Mona Hatoum *Masbaha*, 2006. Alabaster, rope and chain, h. 15 cm, variable length and width

be an essential element, as it is what makes it possible to describe it. He proposed a term to indicate the act of the manifestation of the sacred: hierophany. The historian of religions found himself in the presence of numerous hierophanies, which allowed him to grasp on the one hand the uniformity of the nature of the sacred, and on the other the considerable variety of its forms. Each hierophany is inseparable from religious experience. Analysis of the different hierophanies makes it possible to discern three elements present in all manifestations of the sacred: the natural object through which the manifestation takes place, the invisible reality that is made manifest and which R. Otto called the 'numinous', the divine; and the element of mediation or natural object cloaked in sacredness, and for this reason separated from its natural context.

Eliade's analysis allowed a new stage to be reached in the discovery of the sacred by the historian of religions. It was through the phenomenology of its manifestation that the historian grasped the nature of the sacred: it is a power of a different order from the natural order. Thus, the sacred reveals to the human being a transcendent power that has its source in the deity. On the other hand, his analysis of the notion of hierophany showed that the sacred plays a fundamental role as mediator between transcendent reality and *Homo religiosus*. It is at the level of the mediation that the mystery expressed by a symbolic body of myths and rituals is situated. Thanks to the work of Eliade, corroborated and explained by the researches of Dumézil and Ricœur, the historian of religions has an invaluable range of tools at his disposal, which allows him to understand better that central figure in human history, the *Homo religiosus*, and to grasp the historical and trans-historical message of which he is the bearer. We can speak of an anthropology of the sacred and a hermeneutics of the sacred.

The Question of the Sacred

Immediately after the Second World War, the West saw the beginning of a discussion of the sacred, better known as the 'question of the sacred'. At the origin of this discussion lay a theological movement that found part of its inspiration in the prison writings of Dietrich Bonhoeffer, a German Lutheran theologian, disciple of Karl Barth and fierce opponent of Hitler's National Socialism — something which cost him his life.

According to Bonhoeffer, humanity was headed for a non-religious era. And so theology had to stop counting on a religious a priori of the human being. Religion and *Homo religiosus* corresponded to an age of humanity that would soon come to an end.

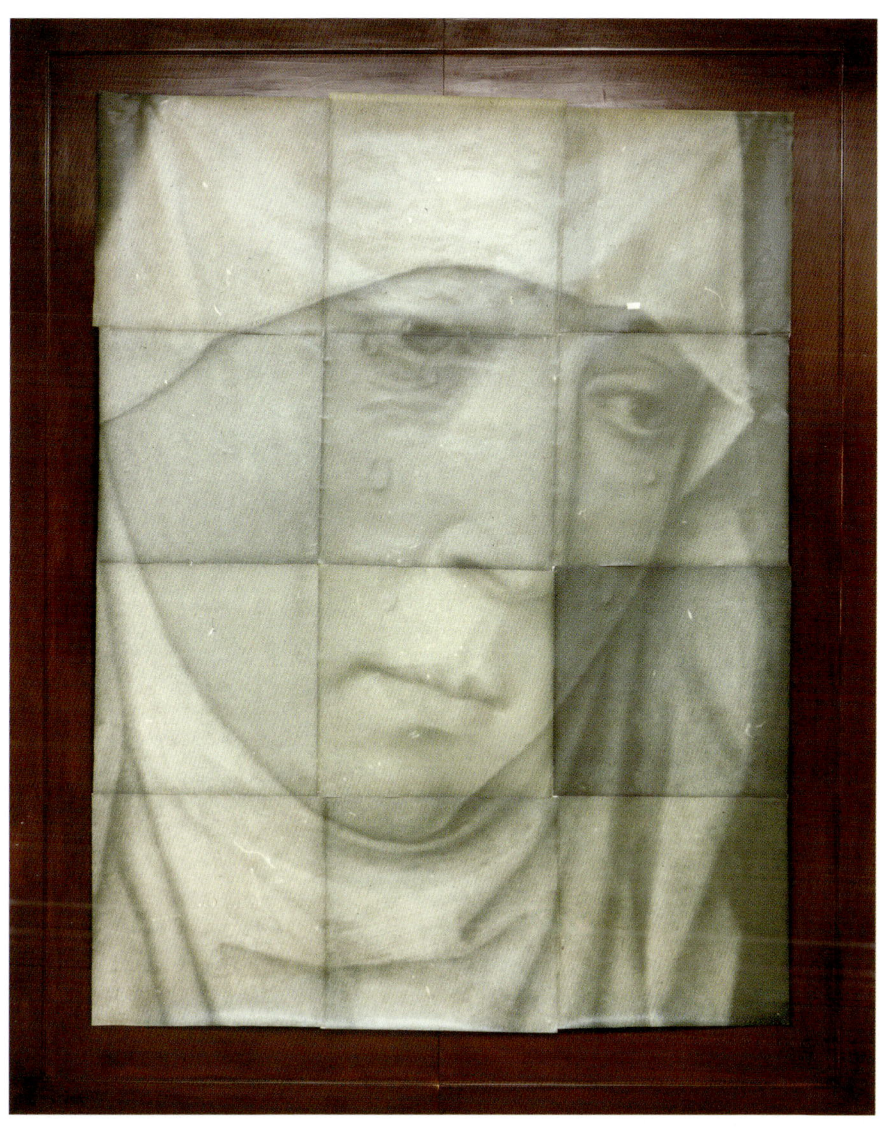

Doug and Mike Starn *Green Mater Dolorosa*, 1987. Coloured silver print, 238.76 x 187.96 cm

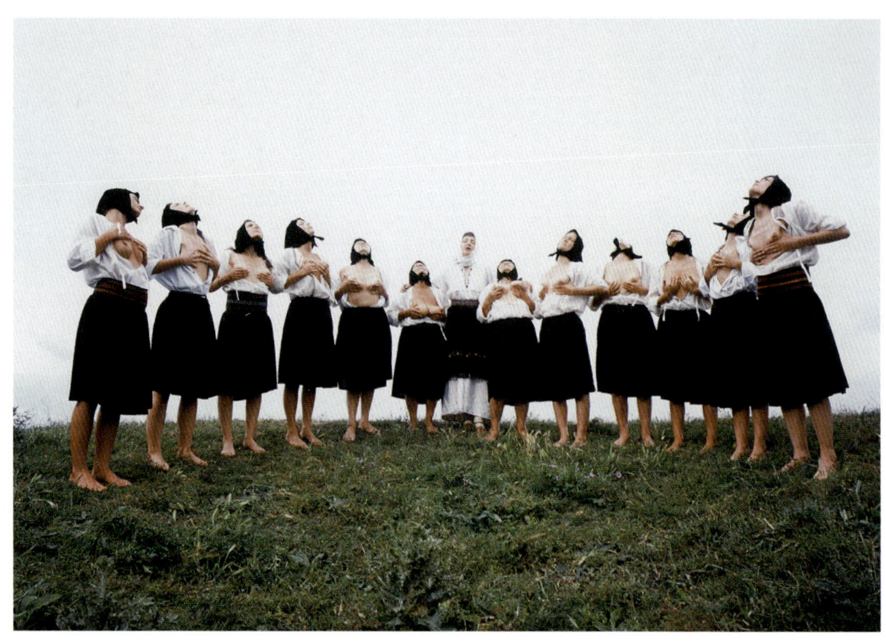

Marina Abramović *Balkan Erotic Epic*, 2005 (still from the video *Belgrade*)

The road down which Bonhoeffer had gone was taken further by the theology of the death of God. This theology has striven to separate faith and religion, even to put them on opposite sides. Faith is the relationship of the believer with the living God. Religion bears the mark of the sacred. The theology of the death of God seeks to show that secularization, the fruit of industrial civilization, represents a chance for the development of a truly purified faith. As can be seen, these theological arguments have given rise to a discussion of the sacred from a perspective limited to the ambit of Christianity. Numerous Christian theologians have reacted, and over the course of three decades we have seen a debate over the sacred conducted by authors who had practically no knowledge of the vast realm of the sacred investigated by the historian of religions.

In parallel to this theological controversy is situated the reductionist position of some psychologists of religion, convinced that 'the fable of the sacred' had been manufactured by the science of religions at the beginning of the twentieth century. In this science they see a 'left wing' headed by Durkheim and a 'right wing' with R. Otto as its leader. In the eyes of these psychologists of religion, the left and the right have one

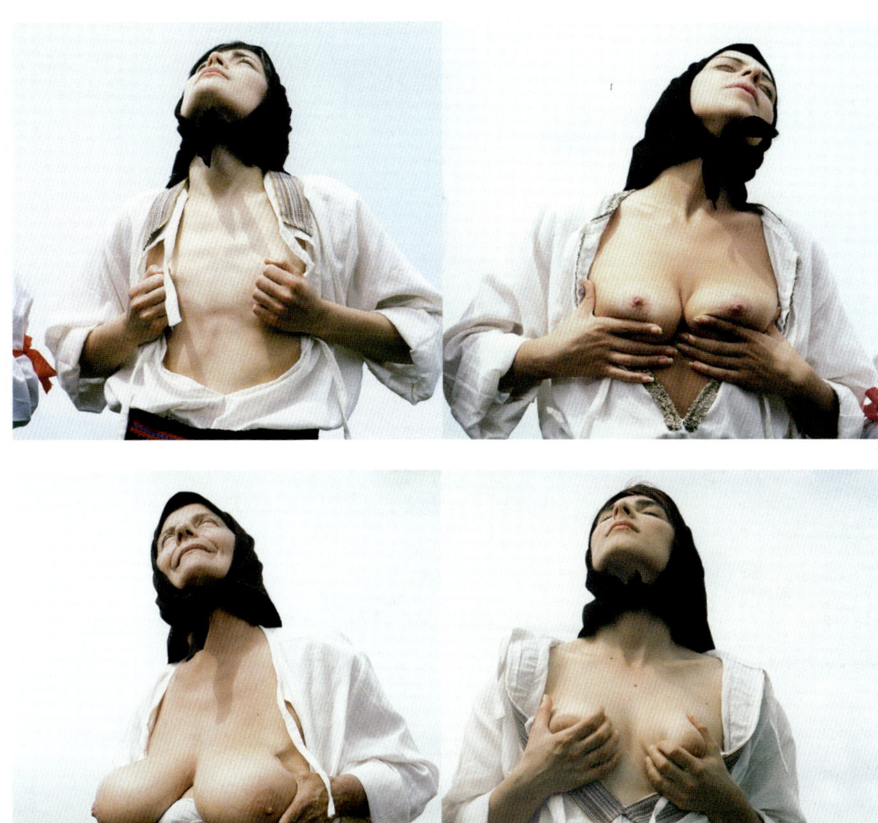

Marina Abramović *Balkan Erotic Epic*, 2005 (stills from the video *Belgrade*)

thing in common: they both seek in the affective experience of the sacred the mother of religions. They hold that this 'fable of the sacred' lies at the origin of a comfortable and popularized psychology, which marries the concept of sacred to that of need. So that rituals would have a need for sacralization as their origin.

Objective Sin and Subjective Sin

The rule of the day of abstinence, i.e. the ban on eating meat on Fridays, is a very old ecclesiastic law, of both the Catholic and, with a few variants, the Orthodox Church. Like every exclusively church law, it is binding only

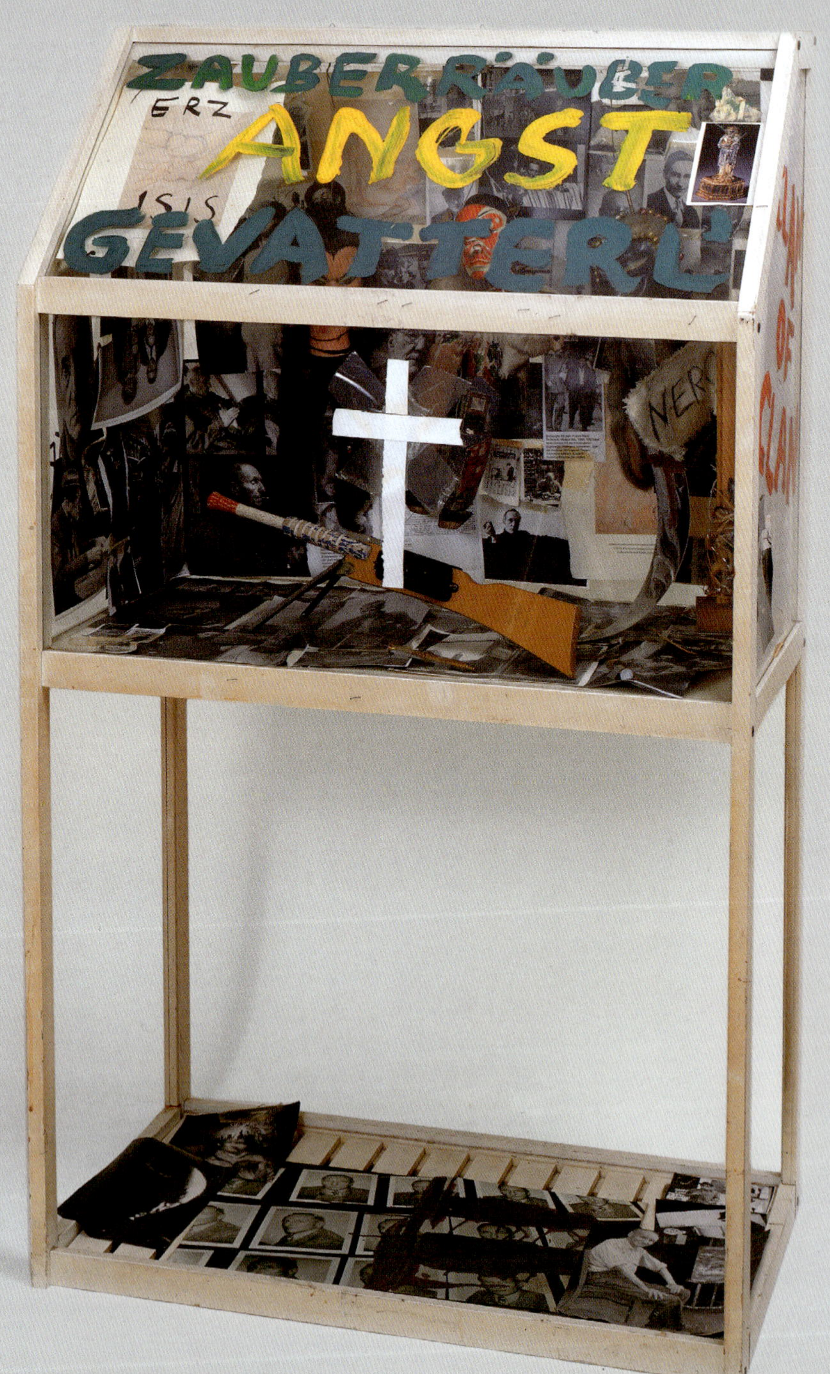

Jonathan Meese *Burroughs-box*, 1998–99. Mixed media, 140 x 80 x 45 cm

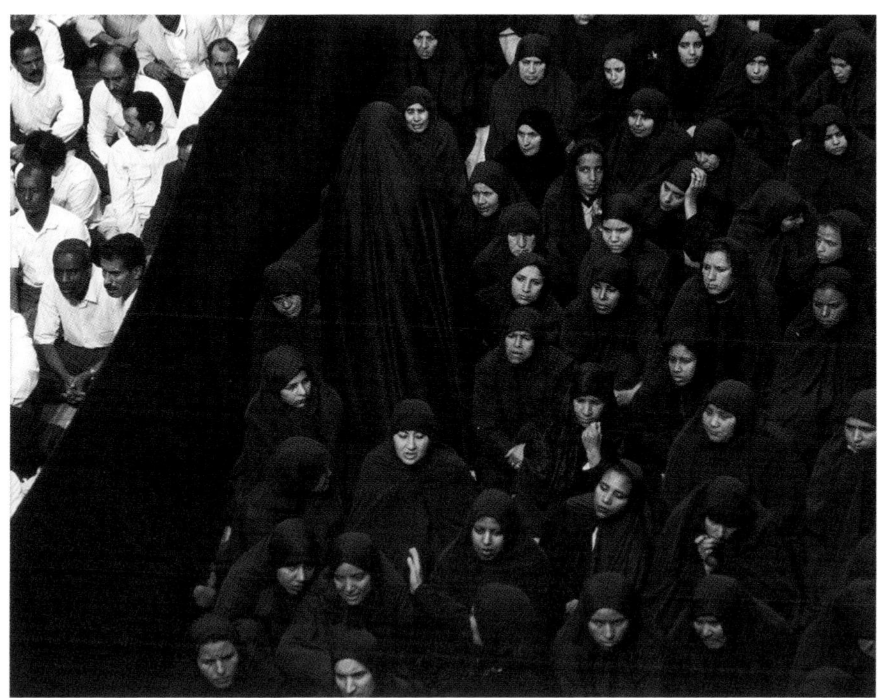

Shirin Neshat *Fervour Series (crowd from front, woman leaving)*, 2000. Silver gelatine print, 45.4 x 56.5 cm

when it can be obeyed without damage to yourself or to others. I use this law to illustrate the difference between objective sin and subjective sin, as it lends itself very well to this purpose.

It is Lent, I know that it's Friday, and I eat meat even though I can easily do without. In that case I am sinning both objectively and subjectively. I think that it's Thursday, but actually it's Friday: I eat meat; I am sinning objectively, but not subjectively. It's Thursday, but I think it's Friday: I eat meat; I am sinning subjectively, but not objectively.

Only subjective sins need to be confessed. Objective ones, however grave, are really just errors as far as the individual is concerned.

Julien Ries, *Il Senso del Sacro nelle Culture e nelle Religioni*, Milan: Jaca Book, 2006.

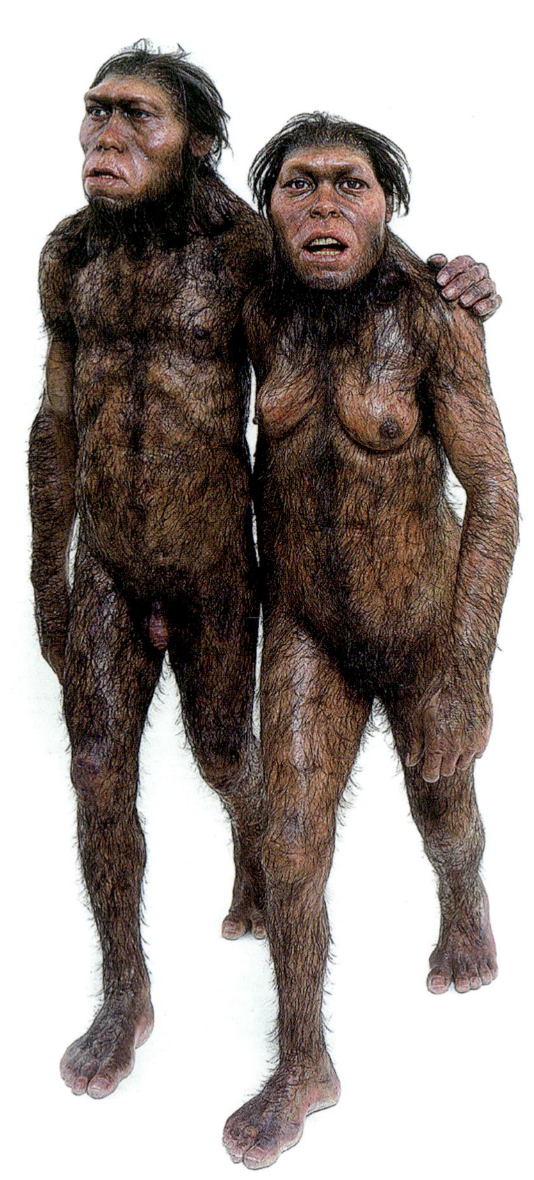

Tim Noble & Sue Webster *Masters of the Universe*, 1998–2000. Translucent resin, fibreglass, plastic and human hair, 137.1 x 68.5 x 78.7 cm

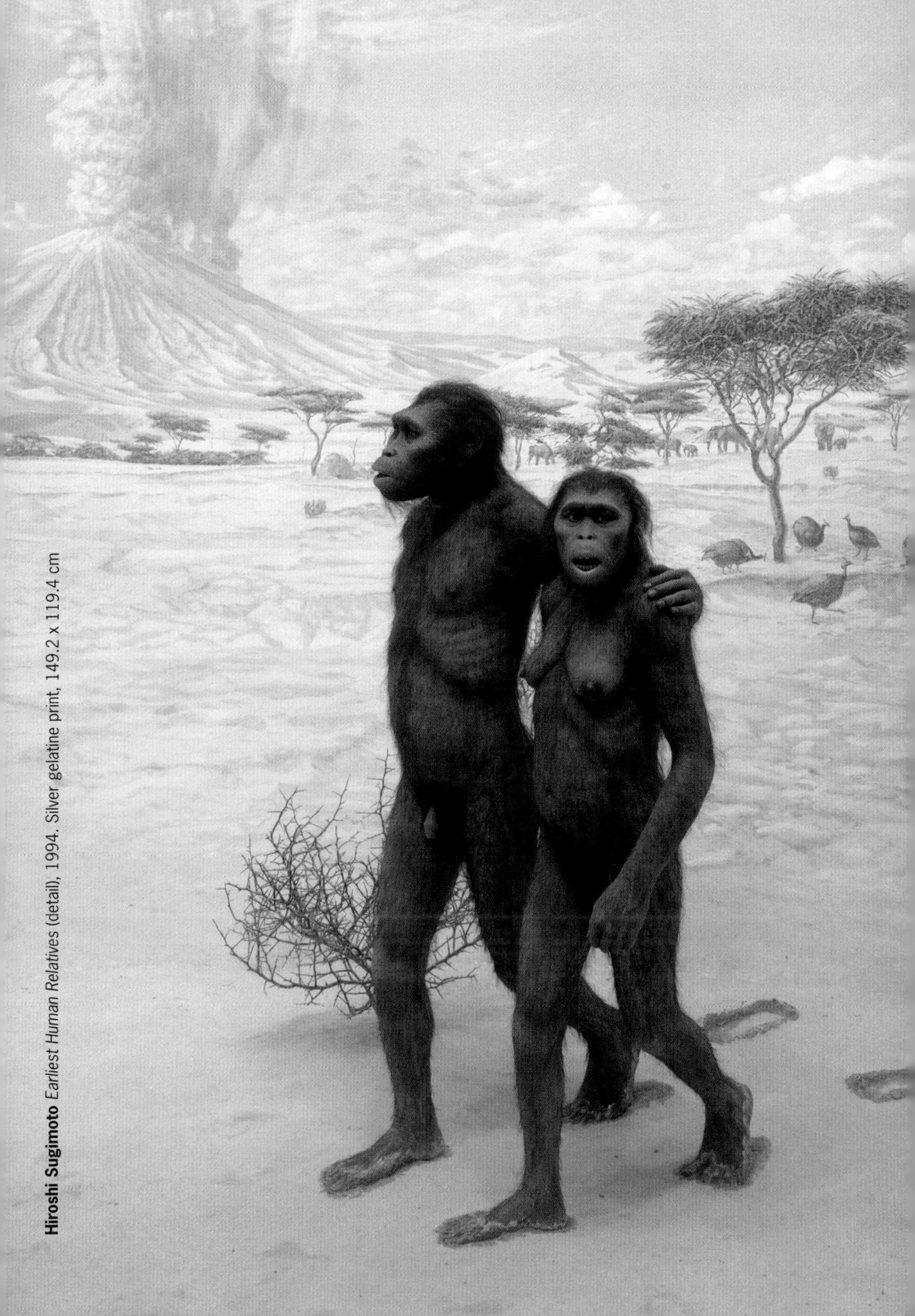

Hiroshi Sugimoto *Earliest Human Relatives* (detail), 1994. Silver gelatine print, 149.2 x 119.4 cm

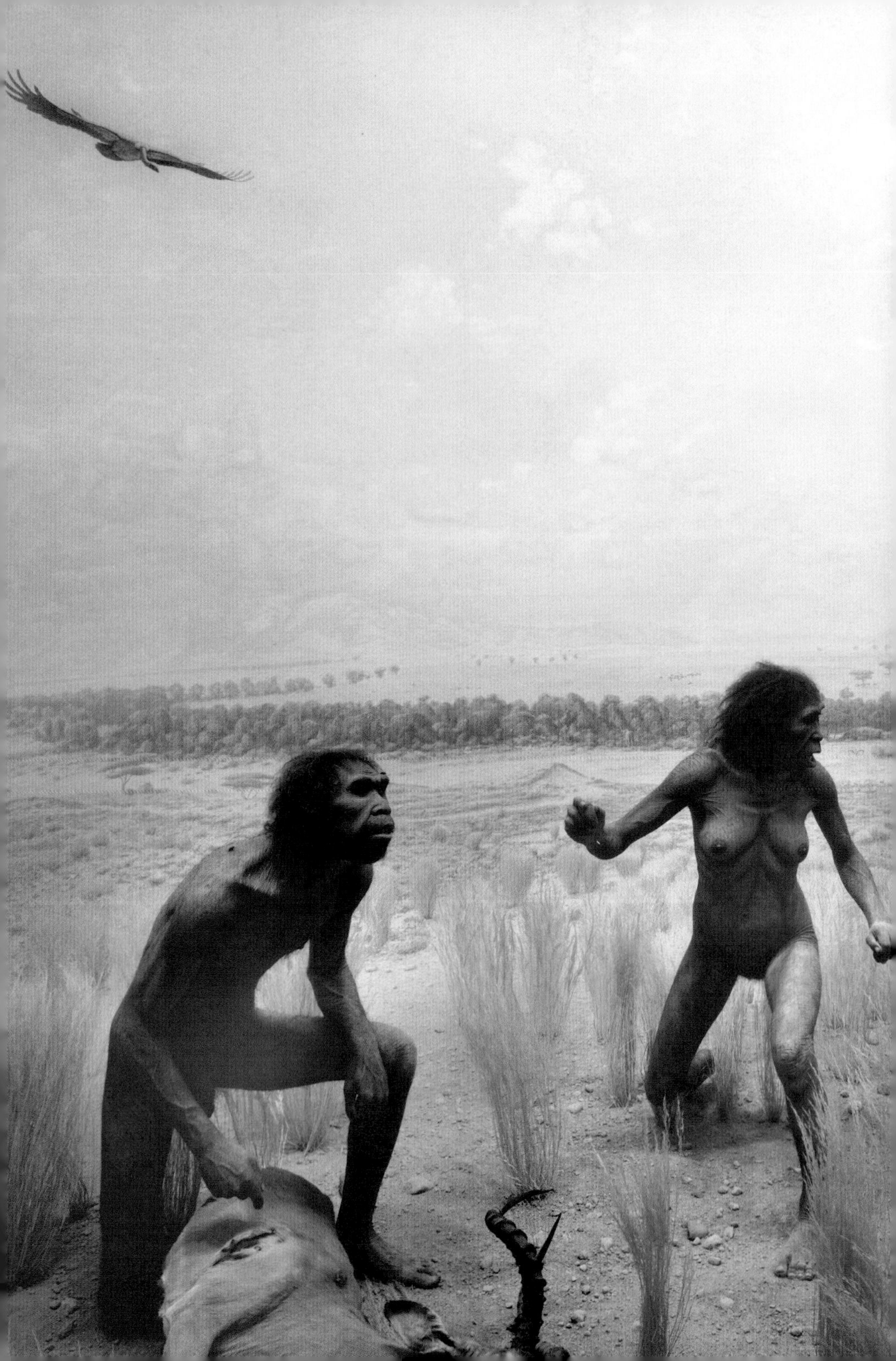

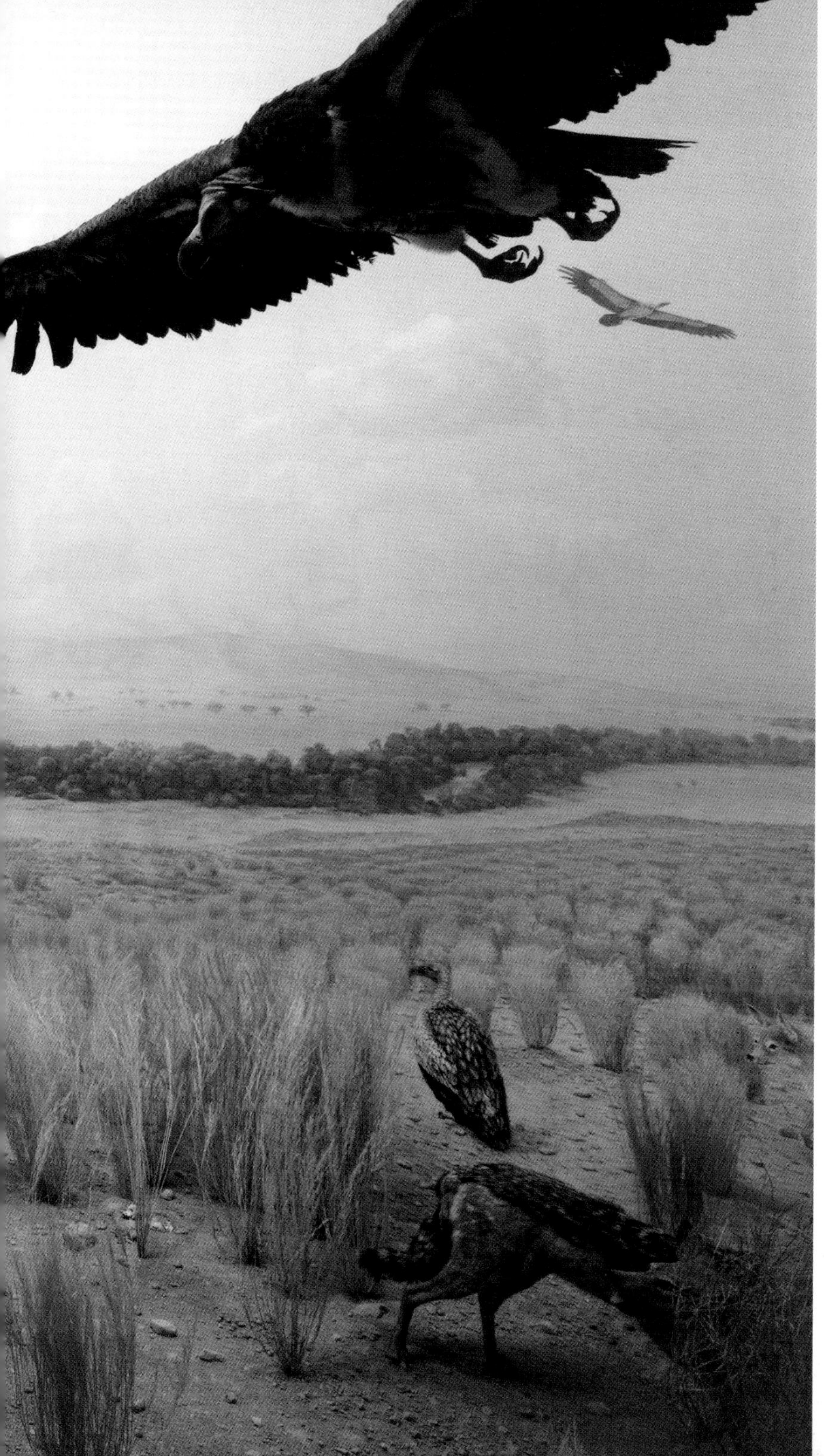

Hiroshi Sugimoto *Homo ergaster*, 1997. Silver gelatine print, 42.4 x 54.2 cm

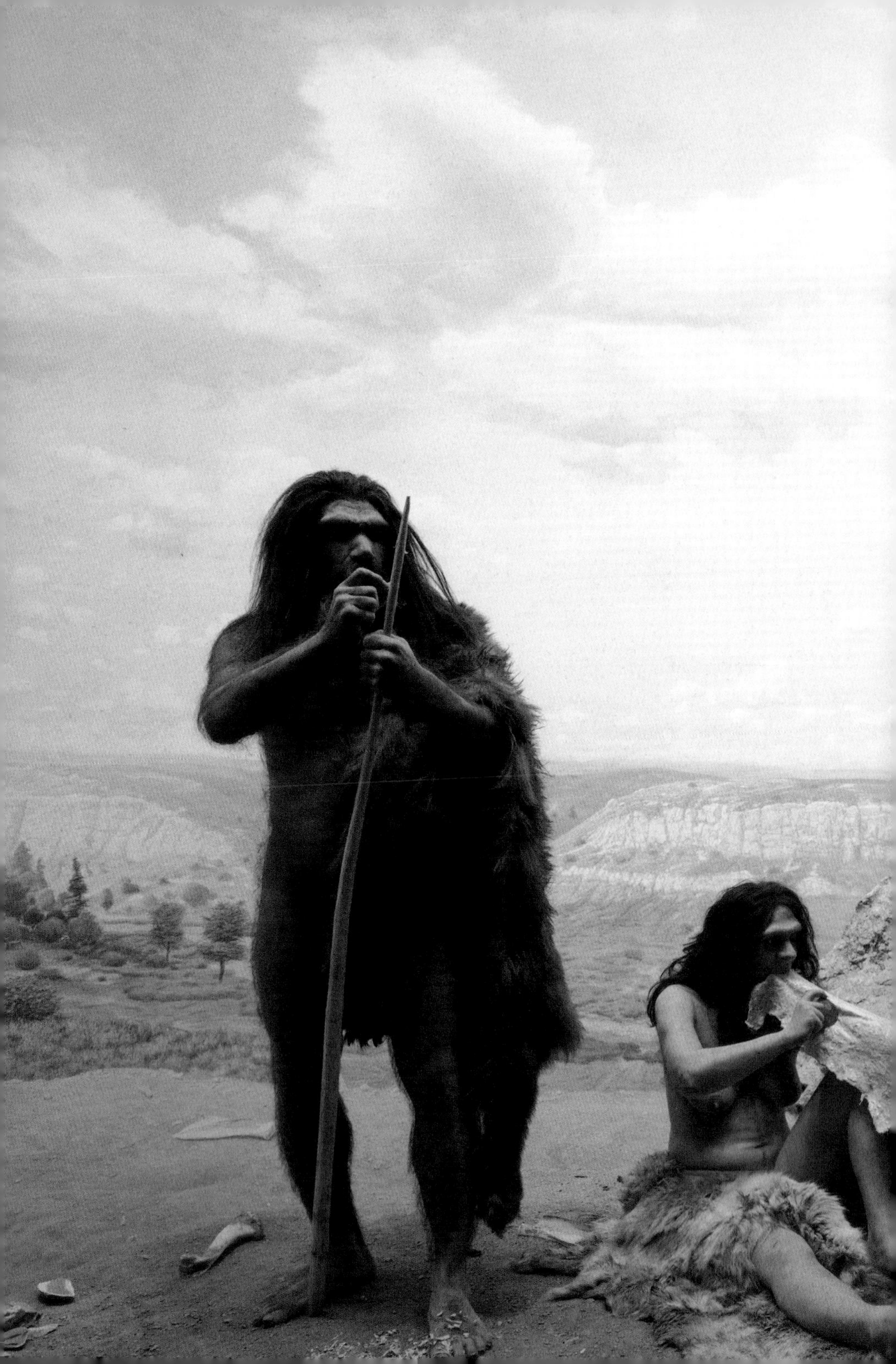

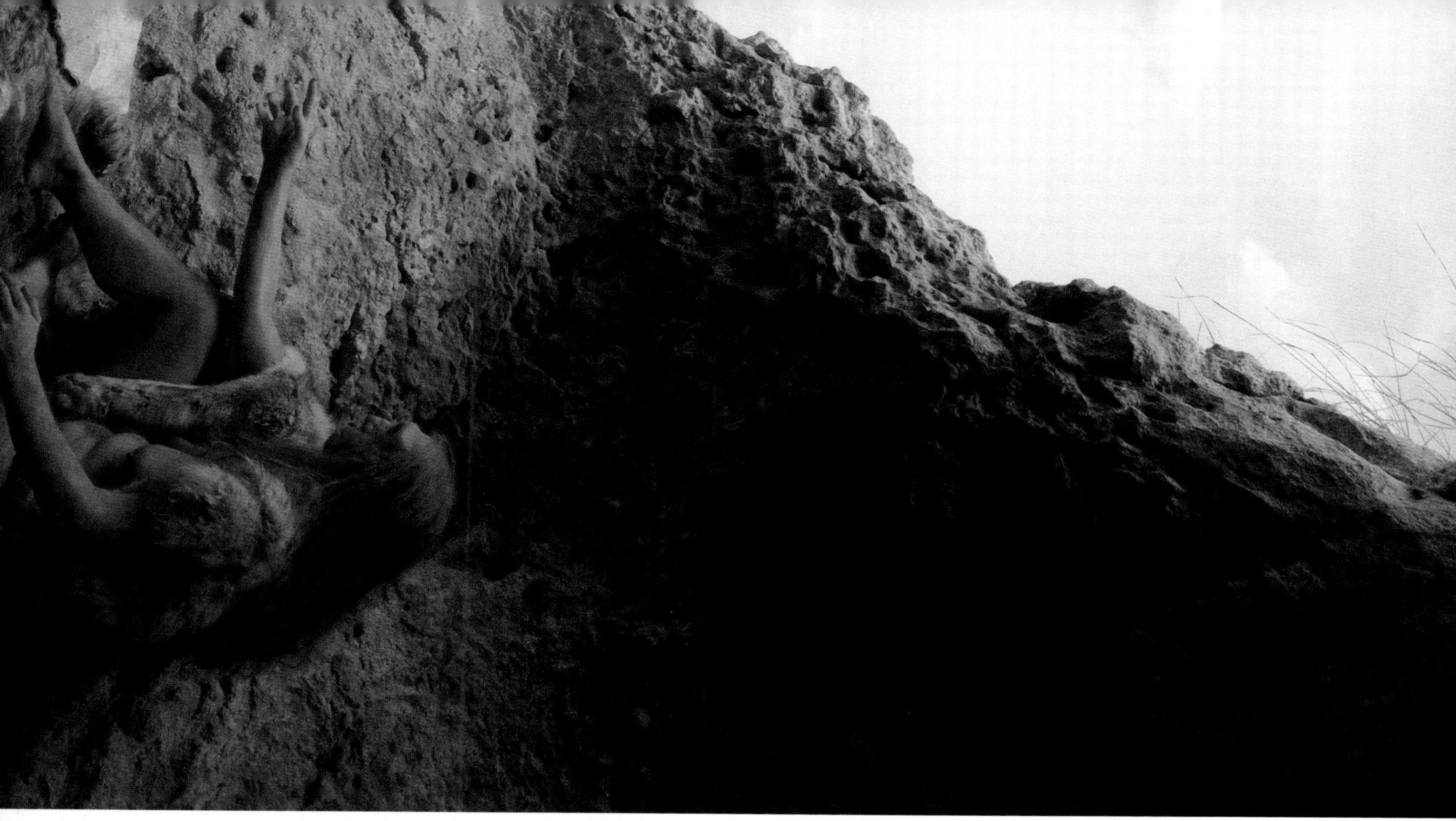

 Hiroshi Sugimoto *Neanderthal*, 1994. Silver gelatine print, 119.4 x 149.2 cm

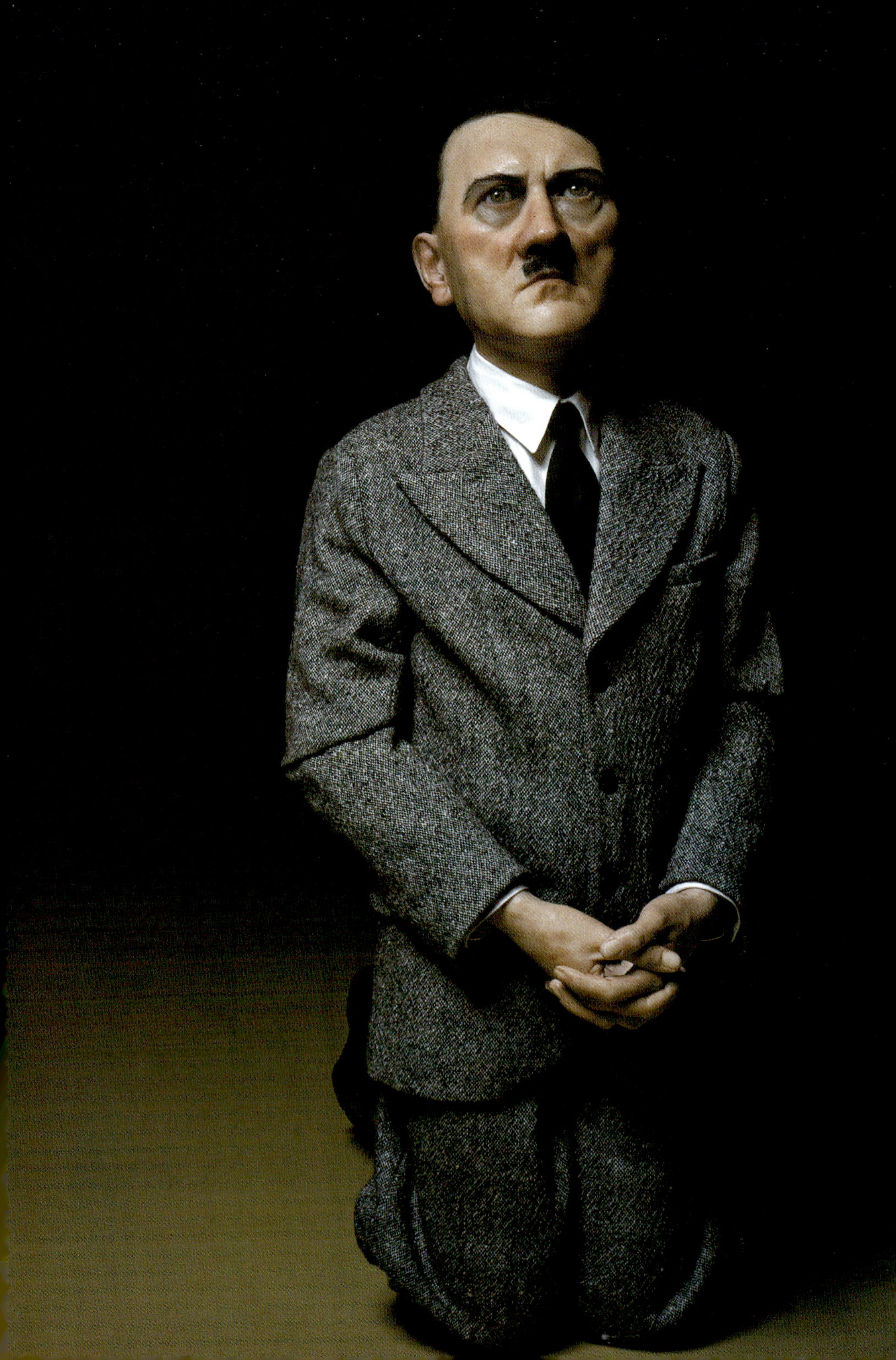

The Fall of Satan

Pierre Riches

The mythical description of the fall of Satan is of great help in understanding the concepts of original sin, pride and independence. It could also be studied through the great literary versions of the story of Faust, those of Marlowe, Goethe, Valéry, Mann, etc., where Faust does not so much want power in order to raise himself above all the rest (there can even be a perverse humility in pride), but wishes to be himself the source of what affects him; he wants to be his own master, he wants to be independent.

Tradition has it that Satan's battle cry was *non serviam*, 'I will not serve'. For those who do not love, dependence is service in the sense of servitude.

An old French Dominican once described the sin of Satan — Lucifer, the most beautiful of all the angels — to me in this way: he looked in the mirror and did not want to see anything else, and said: 'Moi', Me. And so it was.

Asserting our independence, we impoverish ourselves, since being in non-truth we cannot be in love — love and truth, the good and the true are interchangeable.

So what can be done? It is certain that desiring one's own freedom, one's own independence, is a legitimate and perhaps even dignified goal; in itself there is nothing wrong in wanting to be like God.

Quite the contrary.

The solution offered by God — by love — is simple: you gain your independence by giving yourself up trustingly to love (this is the foundation of the act of faith).

Maurizio Cattelan *Him*, 2001. Wax, fibreglass, hair and fabric, 101 x 41 x 53 cm

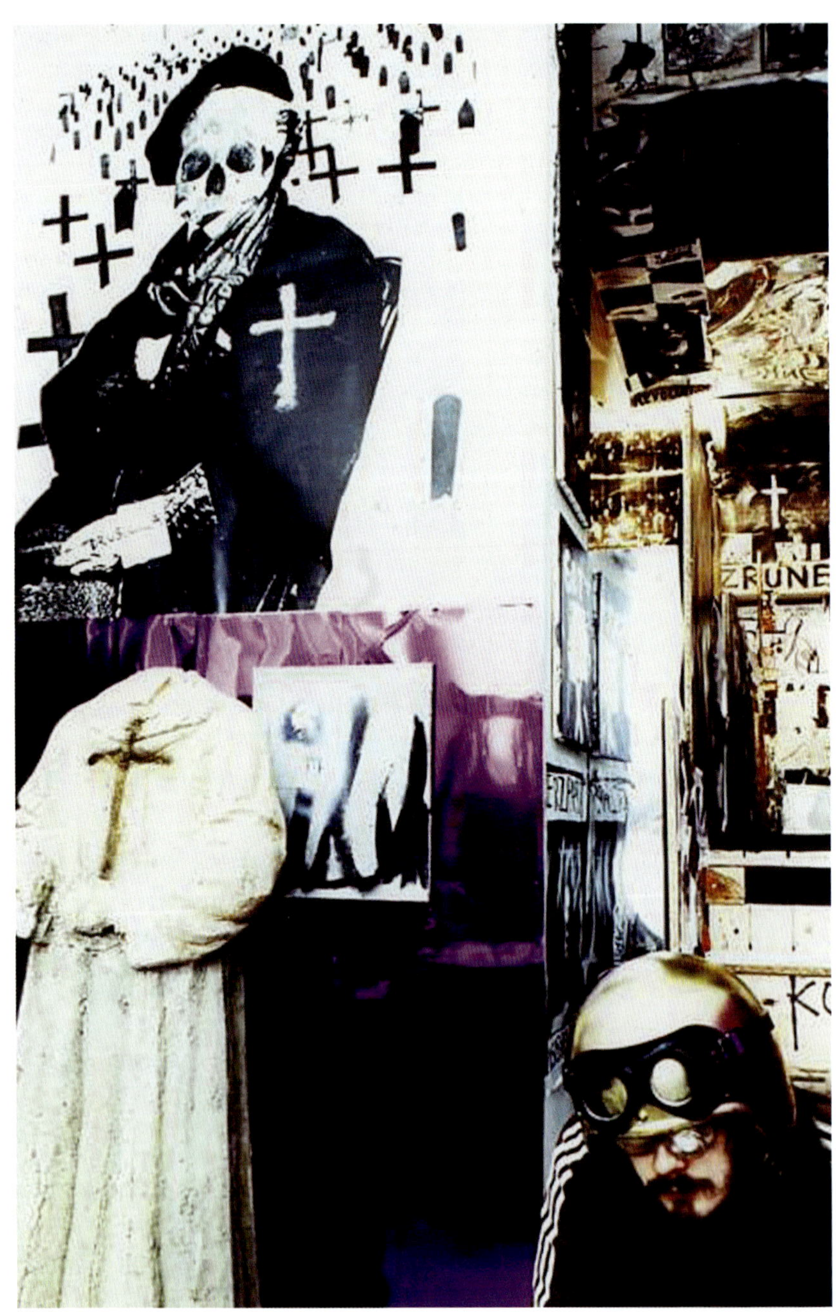

Jonathan Meese *Dr Cyclops*, 2000. Performance

Having faith in God is reasonable and perfectly in keeping with our psychology: if God is how we have described him, he knows us better than we know ourselves and loves us more than we can love ourselves. So we can in all wisdom have complete trust in him. He desires our 'completeness', our full development, which means our freedom too.

Let us remember that the Christian God is not an omnipotent God in the absolute sense (I am speaking in human terms), but has to submit to his own 'laws', i.e. to the laws of love. So he can only give us freedom to the extent of our faith in him; to the extent that we accept the truth, we accept him. We go along with his will, which is the highest good and good for us. We submit to him.

Our free submission in the relationship of love is the assertion and affirmation of our desire for independence. Whereas liberty, independence and individualism impoverish, sterilize and kill, the giving of the self, dependence and union liberate, nourish and give life.

Another word for this submission is obedience.

Sin

A note on sin — even a rather lengthy one — seems necessary.

Many Catholics I have known have had their lives haunted, rendered dark and difficult, by the education they received on the question of sin; and many who have ceased to be practising Catholics have done so because they have — rightly — rejected a religion that was presented to them as little more than a series of rules and precepts, which were then almost bound to be transgressed.

Childhoods and adolescences poisoned by a huge sense of guilt — you only have to look around you to see the results.

Believers still suffer psychologically, and therefore existentially, from what they now recognize intellectually as an aberration in their religious education; unbelievers are no longer able to recognize Christ in the Church because of the education they received, or have enormous difficulty in becoming reconciled with it.

Here I shall try to present not a minimalist but, on the contrary, almost a maximalist vision of sin that, I hope, will be easier to accept.

God is not someone who hides behind the pillar to spy on you, with his gun levelled to shoot you if you do wrong, nor does he keep an account book. God is not an accuser. Indeed 'the accuser' is a name traditionally given to Satan. It is we who, in order to come close to God, have to accept the truth: we have to recognize that we are limited, and therefore prone to sin (just as Adam and Eve were).

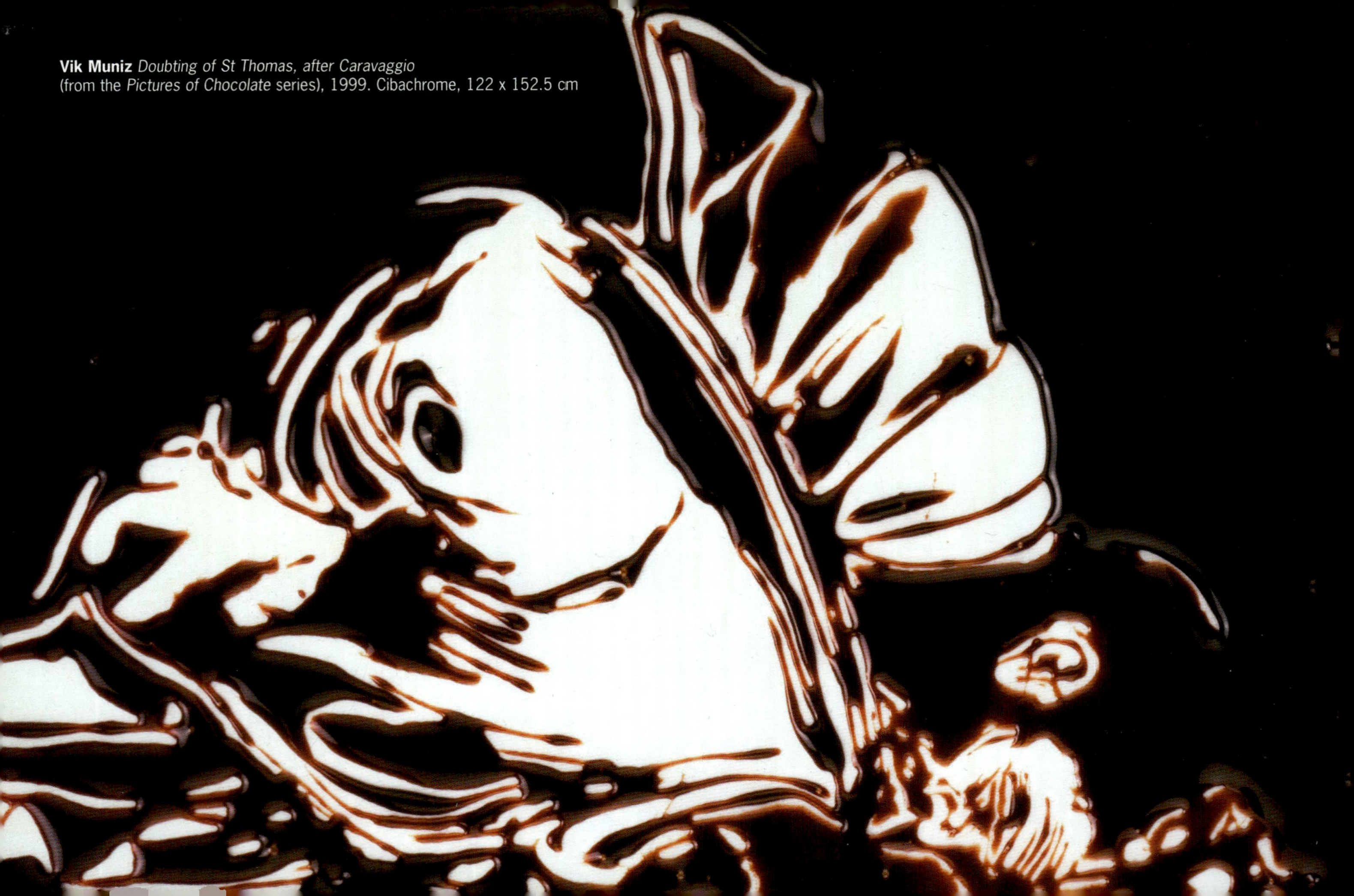

Vik Muniz *Doubting of St Thomas, after Caravaggio*
(from the *Pictures of Chocolate* series), 1999. Cibachrome, 122 x 152.5 cm

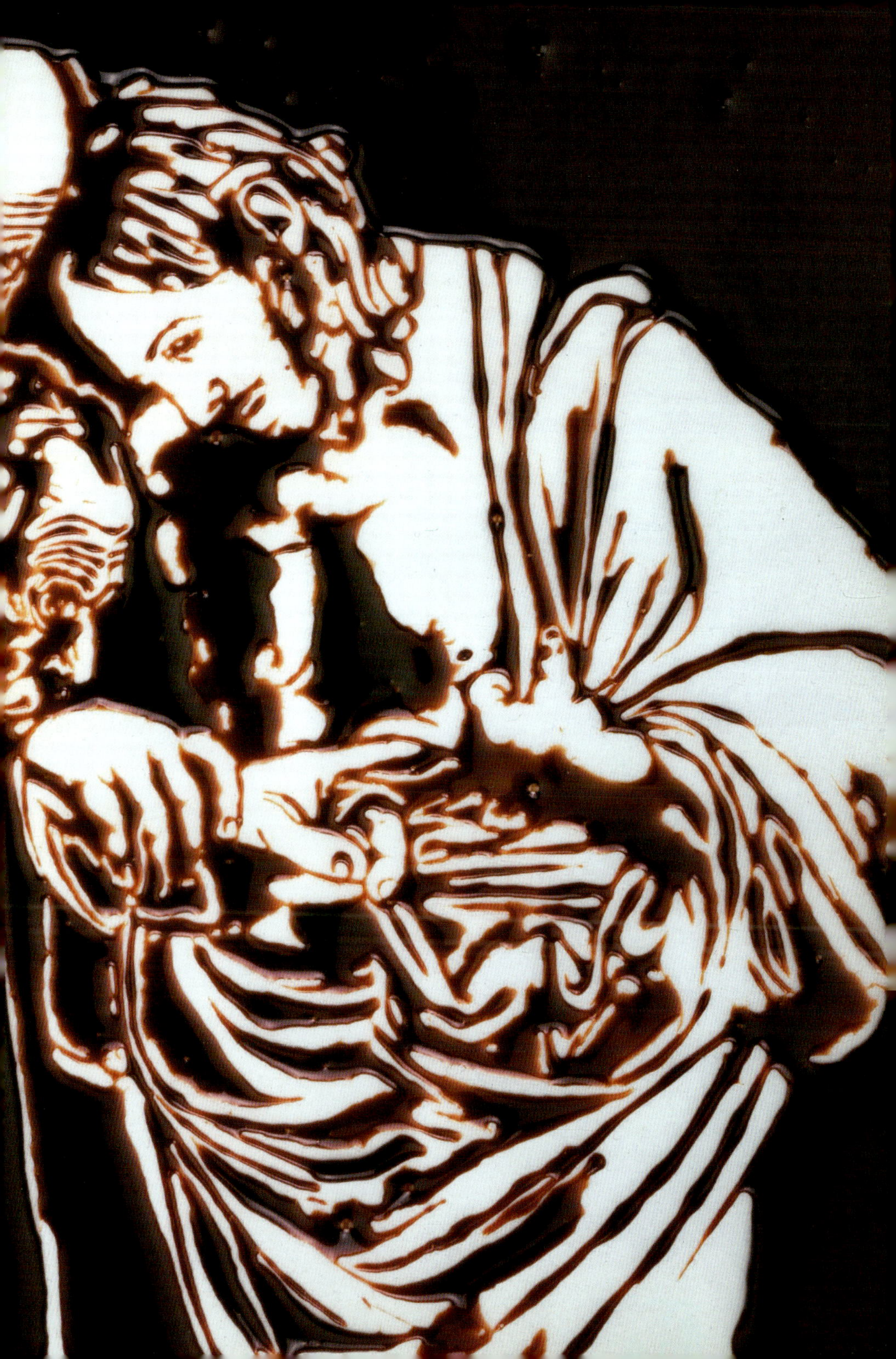

This is what the liturgy at the beginning of every Mass says: 'to prepare ourselves to celebrate the Sacred Mysteries, let us call to mind our sins'. This 'calling to mind' of the truth does not accuse us but sets us free. It redeems us (to use St Paul's term), makes us at peace with ourselves, prepares us to receive God.

Choosing truth puts us on God's side: and then we may indeed sin, we may fail, but we will be forgiven, not seven times, 'but until seventy times seven' (Matthew 18:22). We will be weak, sinners, but not sinful, unworthy, damned.

Let us remember however — and this is not a threat but part of the truth that is humility — let us remember that we are creatures of time, in time, and hence that we can betray this choice. We are not 'confirmed in Grace', our choices cannot yet be 'eternal'. Whence the necessity of the sacraments, of receiving Holy Communion and going to confession 'at least once a year'. Our choice has to be renewed, confirmed.

Sin is any act of non-love, of indifference, of culpable disregard for or even hatred of God, of our neighbour, of ourselves.

In so far as we do not love, we sin. You can list as many sins as you like, but they are only sins if they are acts of non-love.

And this is why only subjective sins are really sins as far as our relationship with God is concerned (for instance, the sacrament of confession, where those are the sins that are confessed).

Of course there is a gradation in this not loving that translates into venial sins or great sins.

If there is just one banana in the fruit bowl, and I know that the person next to me really likes bananas, and I take it, then I sin, but only venially. But if I know that my neighbour has lost all his money and has no food to give his children, and I do not help him, even though I can, that is a grave sin.

Sin, like love, is not fixed in each of us, but always changing.

I like the expression 'hardening of the heart' that is used so often in the Bible.

Each time that we love God, our neighbour or ourselves, each time we carry out an act of love, our hearts grow softer. Each time we carry out an act of non-love, our hearts grow harder. The heart is a continual pulsation, soft-hard-soft. Great sins make it very hard (and blind us too).

Acts of love, of repentance, soften it.

'Mortal' sin is nothing but a grave act that hardens the heart. The word 'mortal' presupposes that an individual persists in this 'hardening' until his death, without repentance: it means that he prefers non-love to love, death

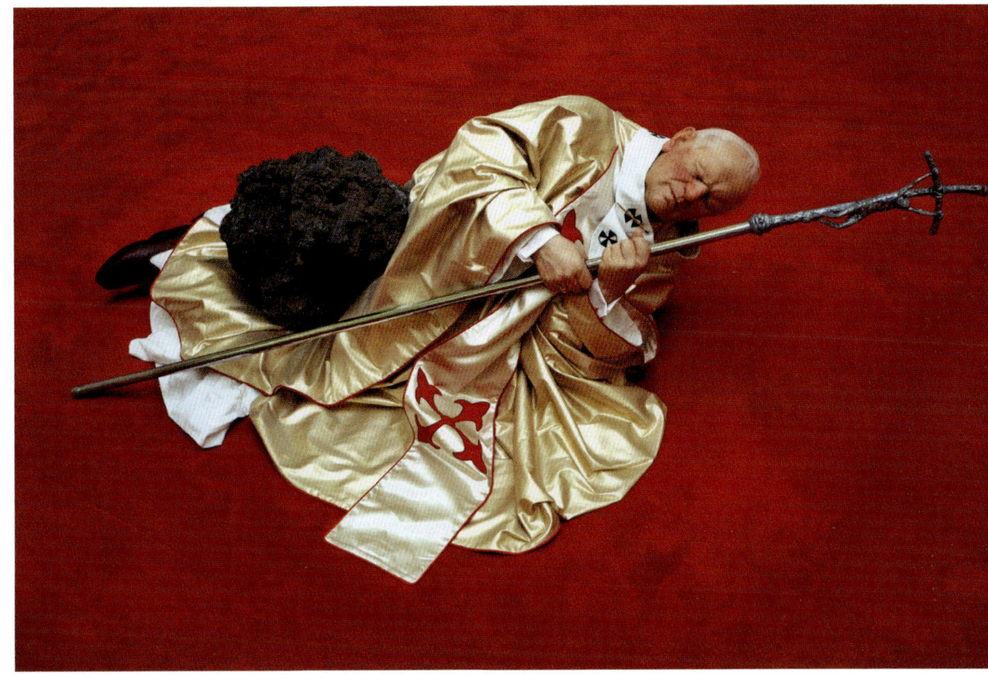

Maurizio Cattelan *La nona ora* (*The Ninth Hour*), 1999. Wax, fibreglass, hair, fabric, stone and carpet, variable measurements

to life. To me it seems wrong to say that an individual is in a state of 'mortal sin'. At the most it can be said that he has objectively committed a mortal sin. It seems wrong because we can never know if in the individual there are or have been all the elements that, according to the Church itself, are required to commit a mortal sin. There are four of these elements:

1. That the act has really been committed (or not committed in the case of sins of omission).

2. That it is really something grave (and not just considered so by the individual or by a group).

3. That there was full premeditation at the moment it was committed.

4. That there was express consent.

But who — apart from God who sees into our hearts — can judge if there was full premeditation or express consent ? Someone knows when he has sinned gravely, even if he is not certain that the consent or intention were full. It is for precisely this reason that the Christian should never despair, but also why he must confess. The year before my baptism, a

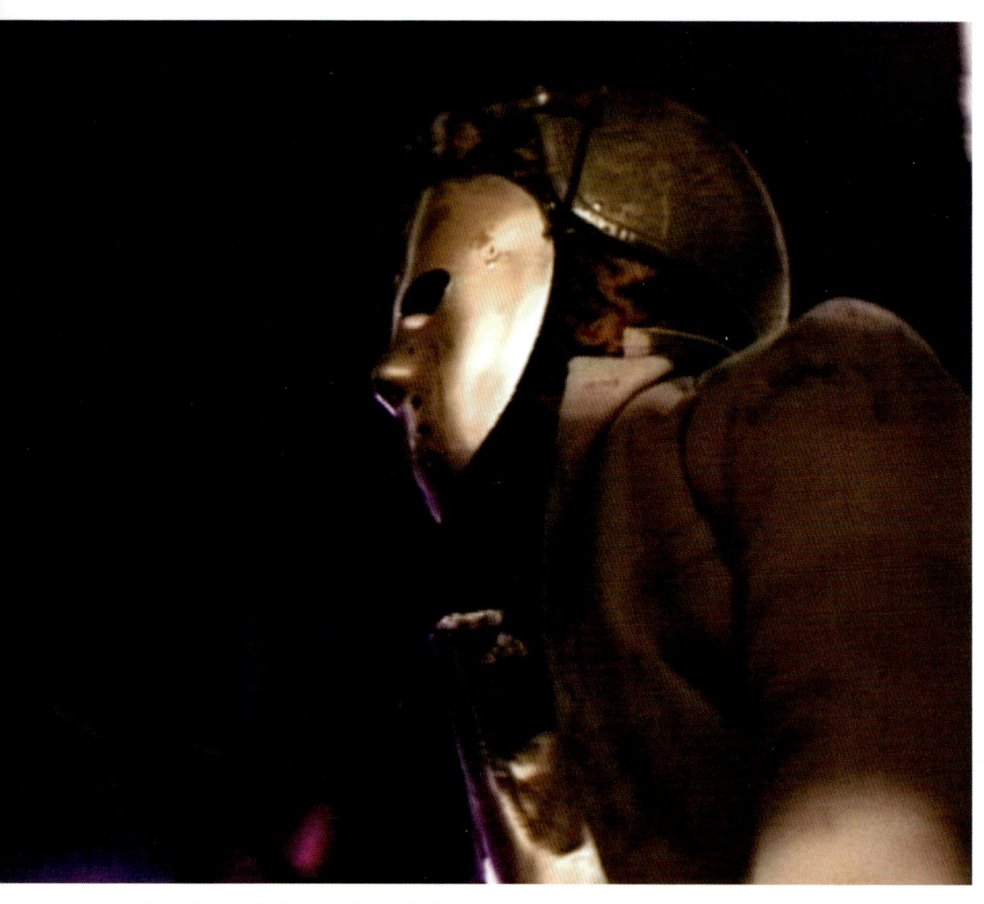

Jonathan Meese *Dr Cyclops*, 2000. Performance

friend told me: 'After all, sin is wasting time, your own, God's, other people's'. Seen from another perspective, it could be said that sinning, we remain in Time, we remain slaves of Time, we do not grow.

Sin and Error

A theologian whom I think highly of, Monsignor Carlo Colombo, once put forward this concept in class — expressing some doubts, I seem to recall, but proposing it all the same: every error is a kind of sin. This made me think a great deal. It implies that every error comes from sin; not necessarily from the sin of an individual, but from the sins of the whole of society, in time and in space. Sins snowball, they pollute the atmosphere. This ought to include — but here we would be going too far — original sin and the sins of the angels. Then we are struck by this malign snowball — or fragments of it — and we get things 'wrong'.

As if there were an enormous, universal war between good and evil, between God and Satan (a war that still rages in time, but that has already been won by Christ outside of time), and we, blind and caught up in this war, often err even when we do not sin.

While it is certain that there is responsibility for subjective sin, there is not necessarily responsibility for objective sin, which can often be called error. But, strange to tell, certain 'errors' also take on the flavour of sin and are punished: one thinks of the crime of manslaughter — in a road accident for example – where there is still a certain degree of culpability.

From this point of view, every mistake becomes more serious; we will have to be much more 'careful', more aware of our actions (paradoxically 'error' can then become 'sin'), and perhaps our whole burden of sin grows lighter — all this should make us more humble in the recognition of our frailty.

Pierre Riches, *Note di catechismo per ignoranti colti*, Milan: Arnoldo Mondadori Editore, 1997, by kind permission of the Author.

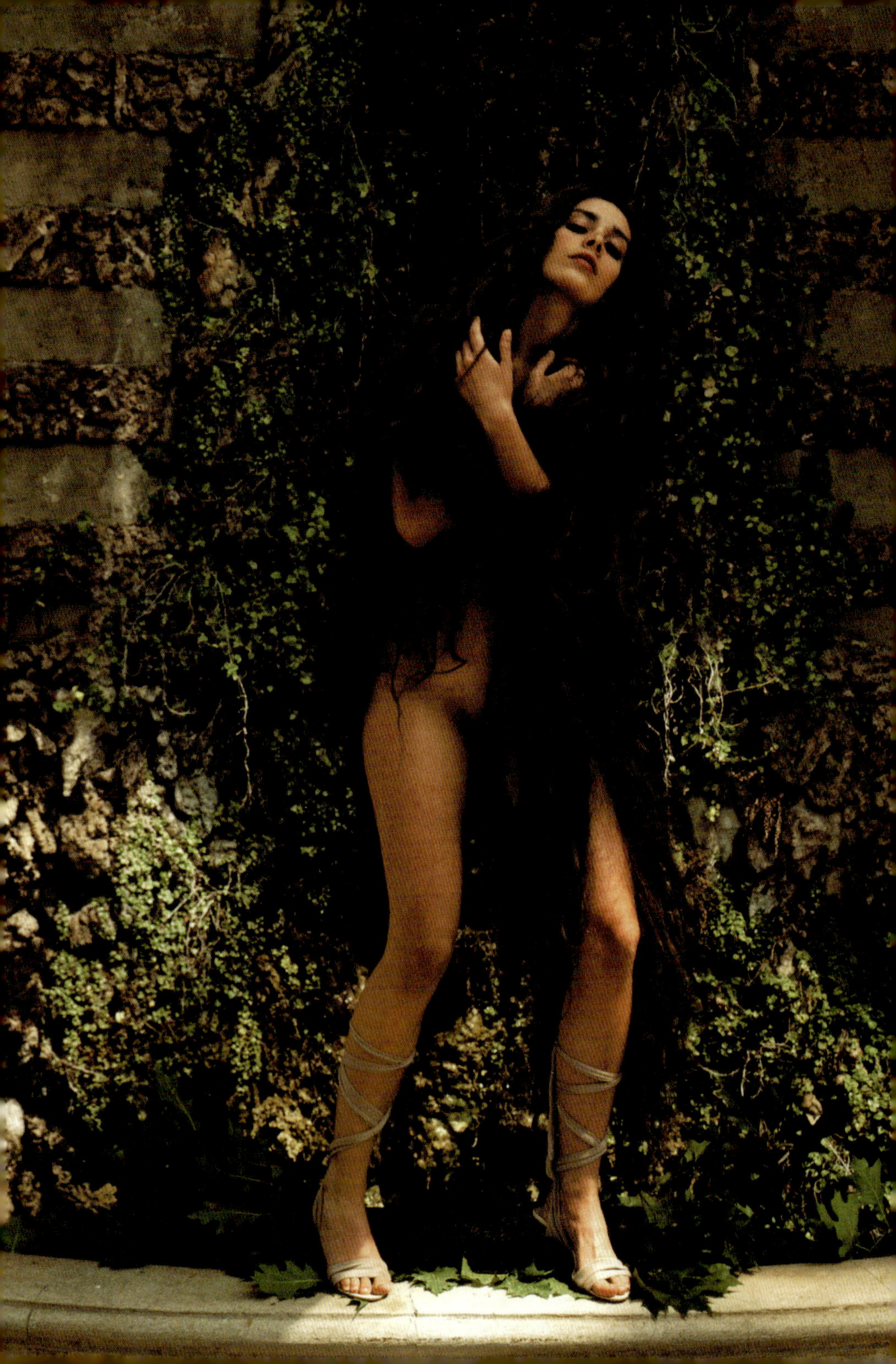

The Concept of the Body in Judaism

Arturo Schwarz

Jewish theology agrees with the Talmudic, Midrashic and Kabbalistic literature on three fundamental concepts: the sanctity of the body, the sacrality of sexual relations and the non-duality of body and spirit. The same arguments are addressed in the philosophical system of Baruch Spinoza, while the third — the non-duality of body and spirit — finds further confirmation in neuropsychology and in the theories of Freud and Jung.

The sanctity of the body is affirmed in the sacred texts of Judaism starting with the first chapter of Genesis, where a verse reads: 'God created man in His image; [...] male and female He created them'. By the sanctity of the body, Judaism intends that the body has no impure parts, nor are the body's sexual and physiological functions considered shameful. These concepts are a recurring leitmotiv in the Bible and the exegetical literature on the sacred texts, and are reiterated over time. In illustrating them, I will limit myself to the views of four of the key thinkers of the early centuries of the Common Era, all of whom lived in my own native city, Alexandria, Egypt.

The first is Philo of Alexandria, the greatest philosopher of Hellenistic Judaism, active in the first century AD, who praised the sensory organs as 'guardians and friends of the soul'.[1] Saadia Gaon (ninth century), the most illustrious philosopher and theologian of his time, considered 'the human body entirely pure'.[2] The noted philosopher and medical doctor Maimonides, born in Spain in the twelfth century and later lived in Egypt, maintained that the body is a divine gift and had a character of 'noble and

Vanessa Beecroft *VB53 – 031NT*, 2004 (printed in 2005). Digital C-print, 253 x 180 cm

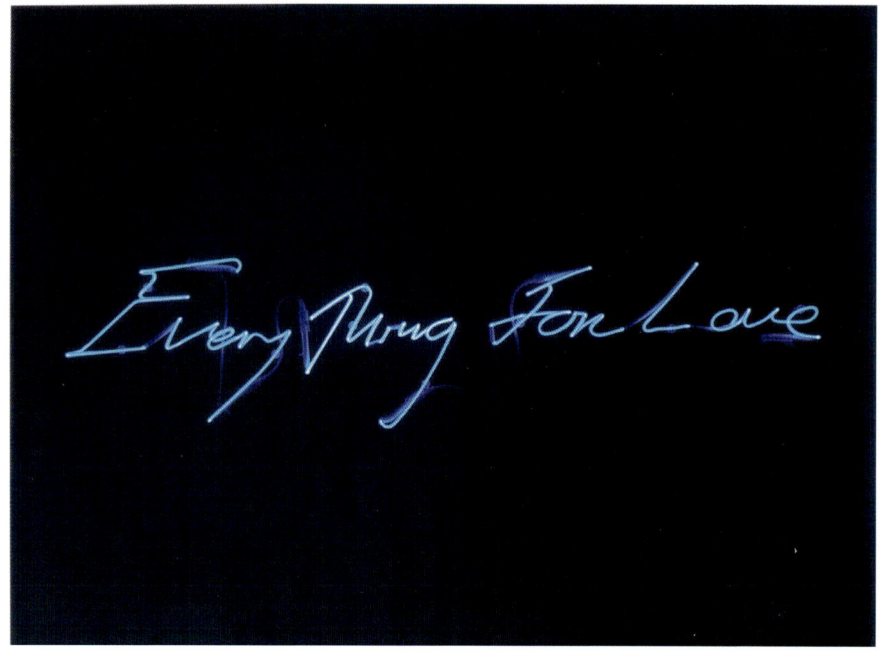

Tracey Emin *Everything For Love*, 2005. Neon

ultimate perfection'.[3] The great scholar Anatoli ben Joseph, contemporary and fellow-countryman of the other three, was likewise explicit: 'A God that loves the soul cannot disdain the body, important as it is for the preservation of the individual and the species'.[4]

The Gnostic concept whereby the body is a prison of the soul is foreign to Judaism, which is in turn contrary to the view of Christian morality, which sees the body instead as a source of sin. The Jewish vision of the body is best summarized in the definition of Baruch Spinoza, according to whom the body is the expression of the divine essence itself.[5]

The sanctity of the body is coextensive with the sacrality of sexual relations, seen not only as a means of preserving and perpetuating the species in accordance with the biblical injunction to 'go forth and multiply', but as a source of pleasure and happiness. The Bible emphasizes the right to happiness, if only because, as Spinoza explained, 'Happiness (*lætitia*) is the passion by which the mind passes from a lesser to a greater perfection'.[6]

Many passages of the Qohelet (the Hebrew name for the Book of Ecclesiastes) celebrate and exalt pleasure.[7] The ardent desire to express one's thankfulness to God is selfsame as the ambition to be happy, since it

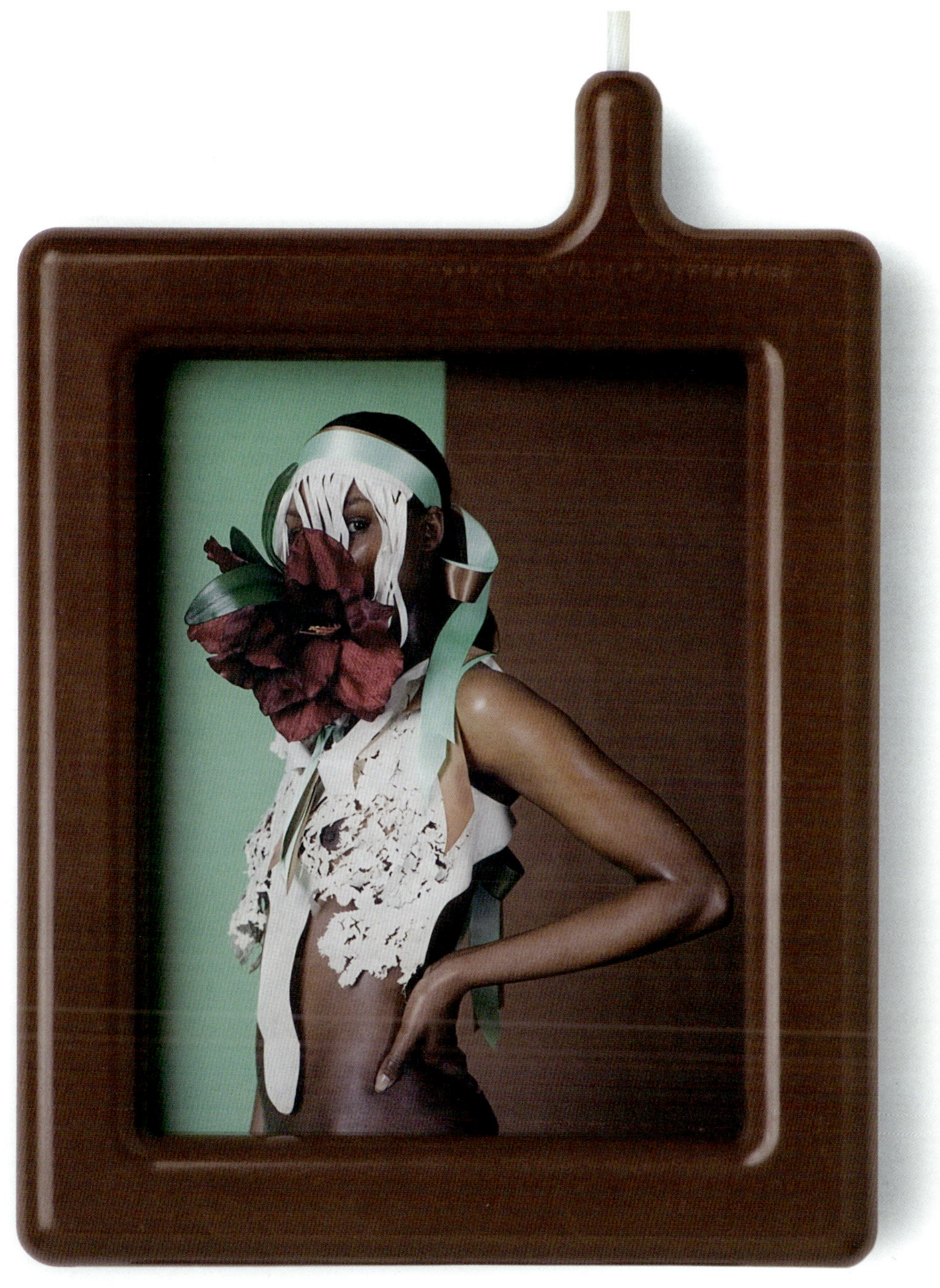

Matthew Barney *A Pele da Lâmina*, 2004. High-density photographic print and polyethylene, 73.7 x 49.5 x 5.1 cm

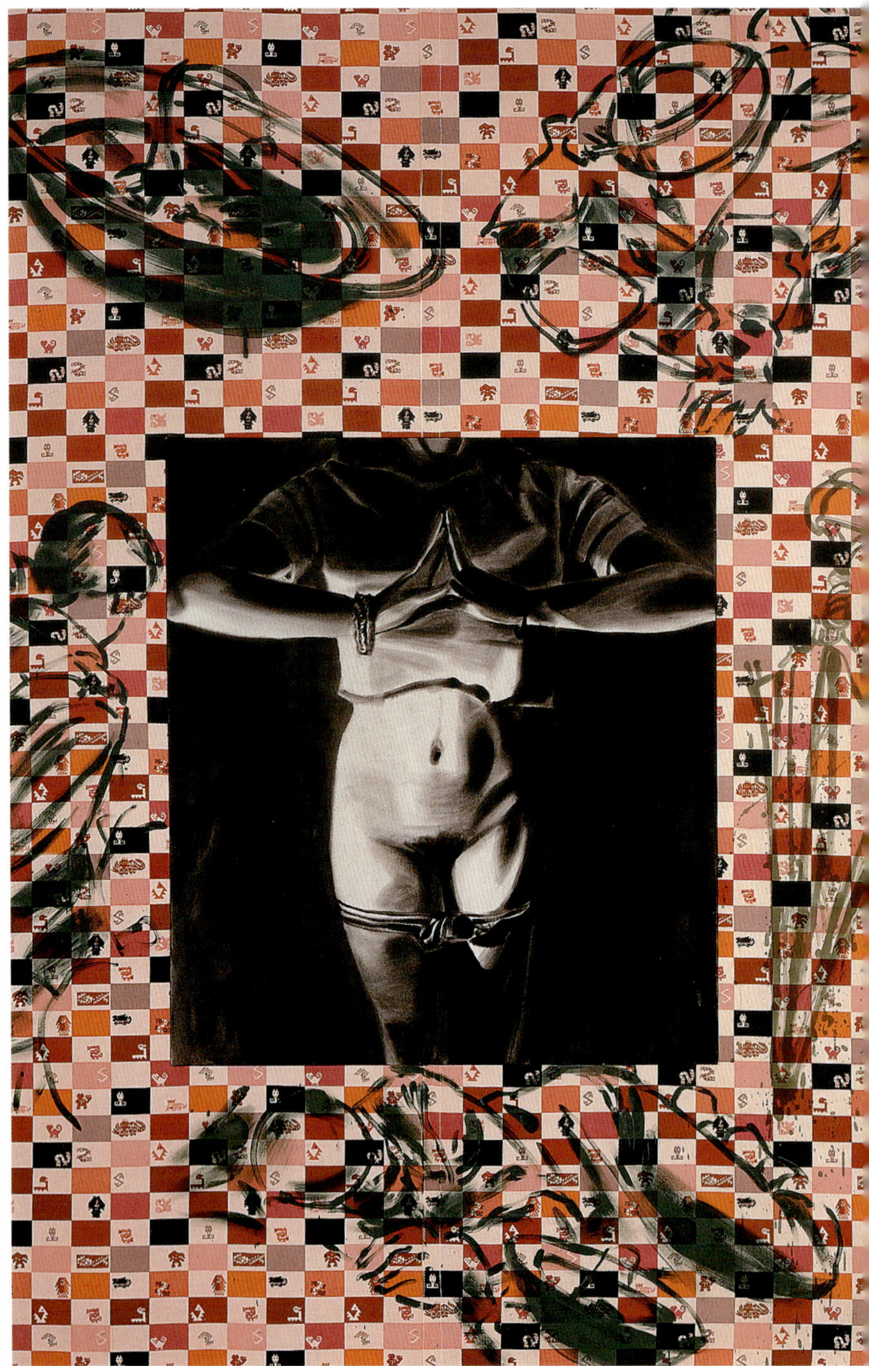

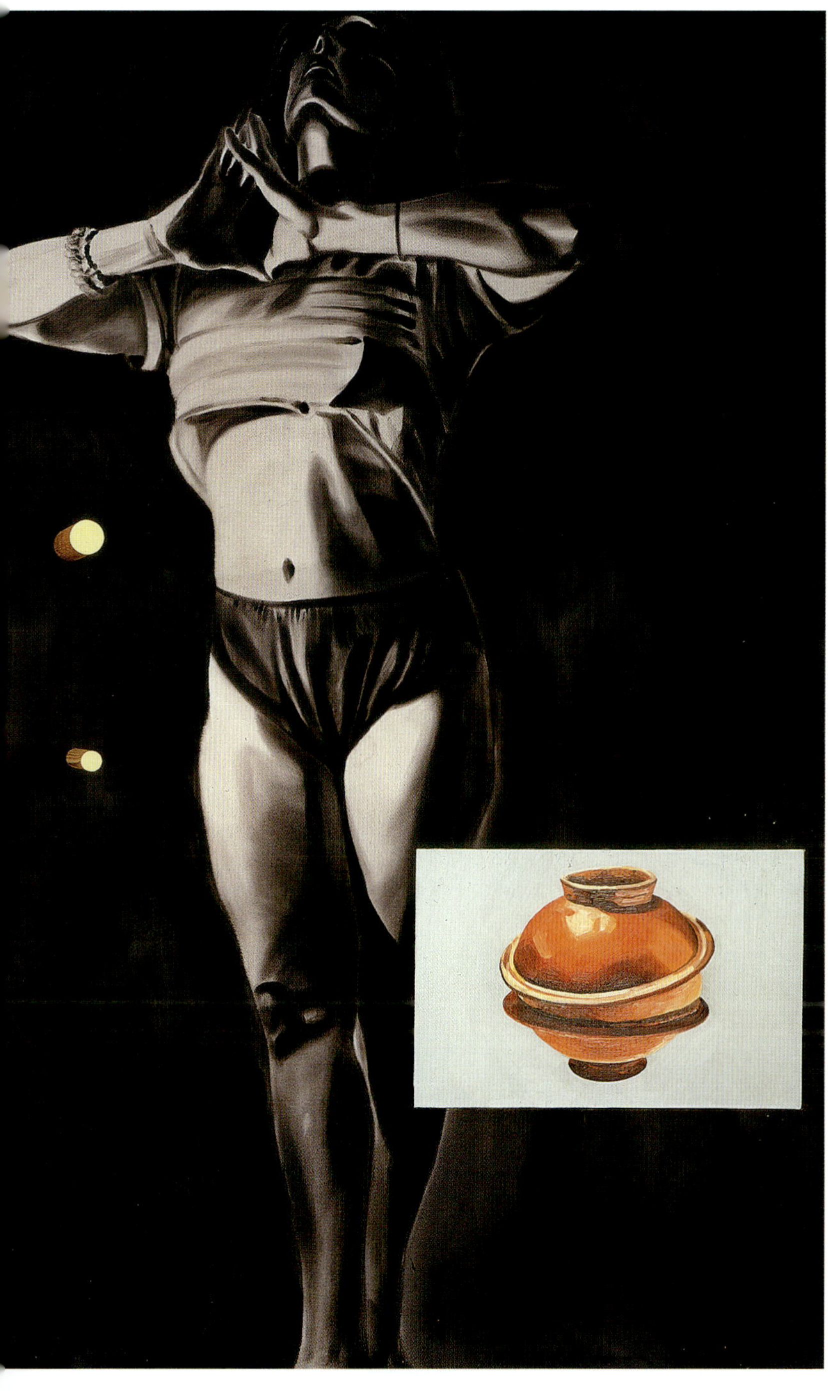

David Salle *Maid of Germany*, 1988. Oil on canvas, 274 x 375 cm

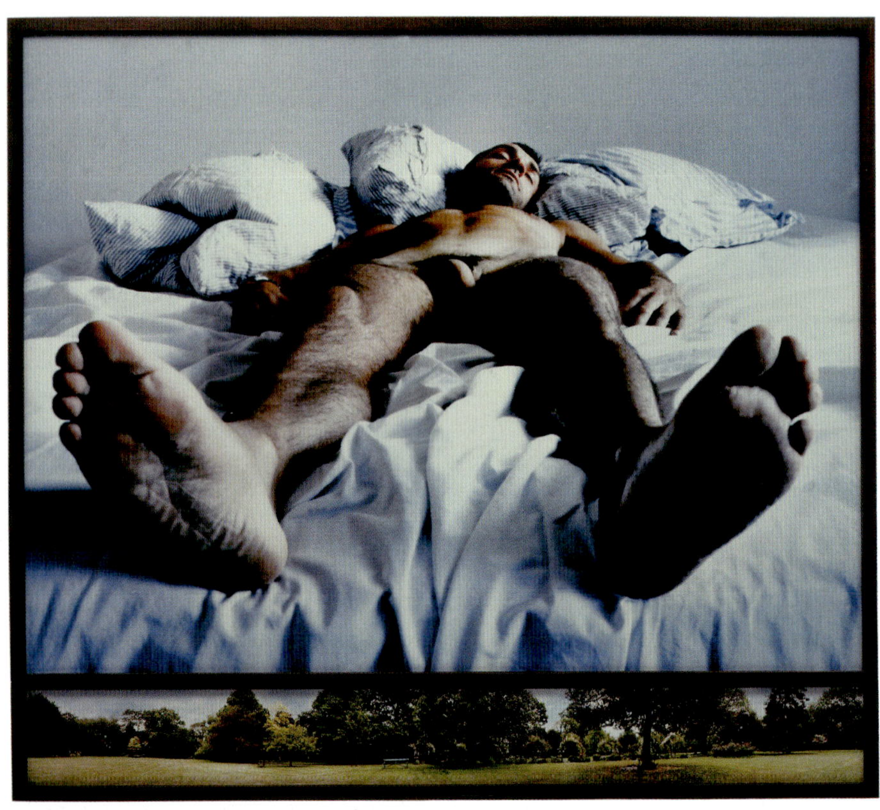

Sam Taylor-Wood *Soliloquy VII*, 1999. C-type print, bipartite frame, 222 x 242 cm

is only from happiness that love and thankfulness can come. The Palestinian Talmud teaches that the divine Presence dwells only in a joyful heart,[8] and condemns those who abstain from the pleasures and joys of this world.[9]

As for conjugal happiness, Isaiah ben Mali di Trani, a thirteenth-century Talmudist, points out that 'the quest for pleasure is a legitimate reason for conjugal relations'[10]; Judah Leon Abravanel, in his turn, explains that the aim of love is not possession but 'the delectation of the lover in the beauty of the beloved'.[11] This view defines another of the fundamental differences between the Jewish and Christian ethics: the Christian notion of original sin has no counterpart in the sacred or exegetic literature of Judaism. A Hebrew term corresponding to 'original sin' was coined only in the thirteenth century, with the onset of the great debates between

Jewish and Christian theologians. Adam and Eve were not banished from Eden for having realized their nakedness, or for having sexual relations or for eating from the tree of knowledge — which, by the way, was planted expressly for them — but for having picked this fruit before it was ripe, and before they themselves, having just been differentiated as male and female, were ready to receive the gift of knowledge. This reading is confirmed by the masters of the Kabbalah. Rav Yosef Gikatilla, in his *Sha'are Orah* (Gates of Light), writes 'God did not stop Adam from eating from the Tree of Life, which he was free to do'.[12] Indeed, God 'commanded Adam to wait a bit [...] if Adam had waited to eat the fruit until it had reached the time and place of the essence of that which is called the "fifth" [alluding to the "fifth essence", i.e. the quintessence: the pure highly concentrated essence of living which corresponds to the fifth stage of the alchemical process], he never would have been drawn into the abyss'.[13]

The moral of this Biblical tale anticipates an idea of Spinoza's. Premature knowledge in an unprepared individual will blind rather than illuminate. As such, Spinoza writes in a letter of February 1663 to Simon de Vries, 'knowledge can be harmful for people who have not reached a more mature age'.[14]

Let us return to the sacred dimension of carnal love. The Italian doctor Shabbatai Donnolo (913–982) attributed it to God himself: 'With his vital spirit, he instilled in man the spark of desire to copulate'.[15] A text by an anonymous Spanish Kabbalist of the thirteenth century entitled *Iggeret ha-qodesh* (Letter on Sanctity) clarifies not only the sacredness of sexual union, but its initiatic value as well: 'The sexual relationship between a man and his woman is a clean and holy thing when conducted the right way [...] because a proper sexual relationship is called "knowledge" [*daat*]'.[16] In the same chapter the complementary aspects of male wisdom and female intelligence are underscored, a symbiosis that is necessary for the union that will enable the lovers to arrive at transcendent truth: 'Know that man is the secret of wisdom, and woman the secret of intelligence; and the pure sexual relationship between them is the secret of knowledge'.[17]

Abravanel, basing himself on a widely diffused Kabbalistic idea, maintained that love elevates us to the summit of knowledge, and also believed that it was love that sustained the entire cosmos, from the furthest planet to the rock at the core of the earth: 'there is nothing that unifies the universe and all its many things if not love, for love is what made the world and all its parts come to be [...] love is a vitalizing spirit that permeates the whole world, and is the bond that unifies the entire universe'.[18]

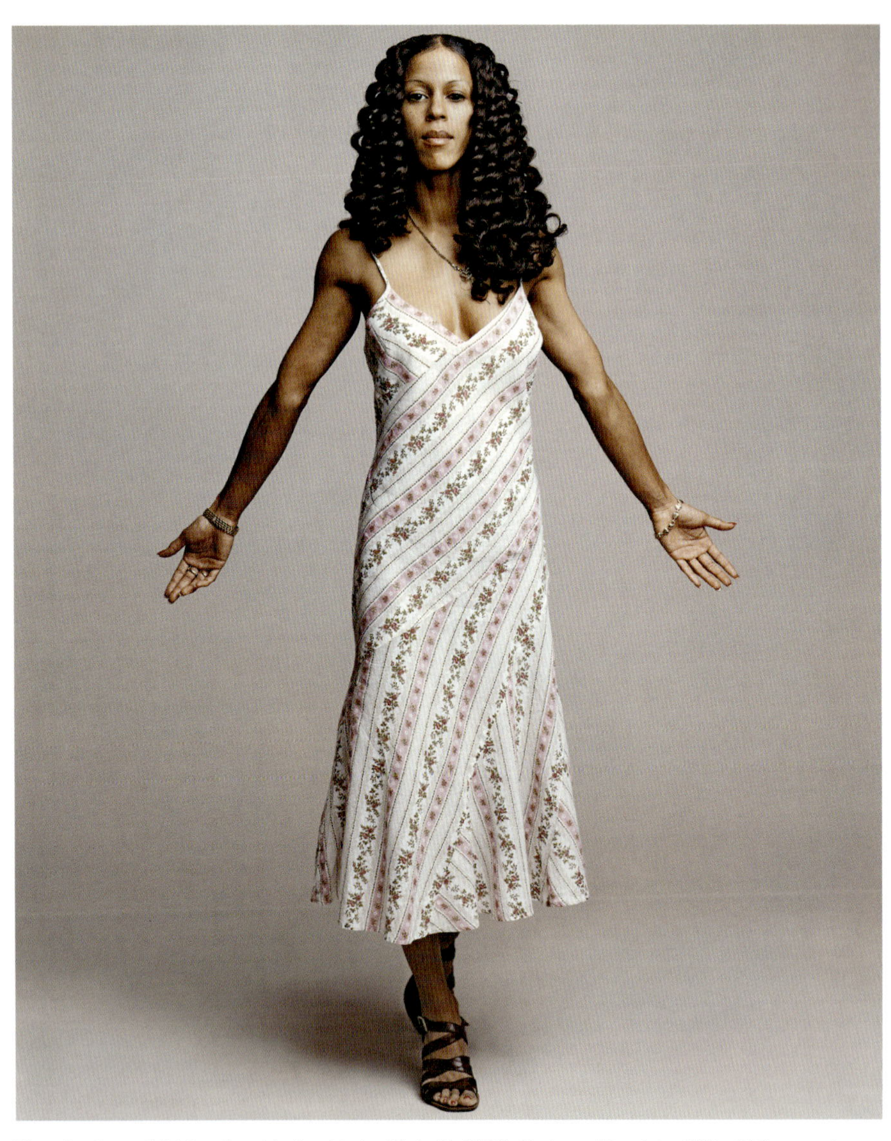

Timothy Greenfield-Sanders *Heather Hunter* (diptych), 2003. Photographic prints, 153 x 122 cm each

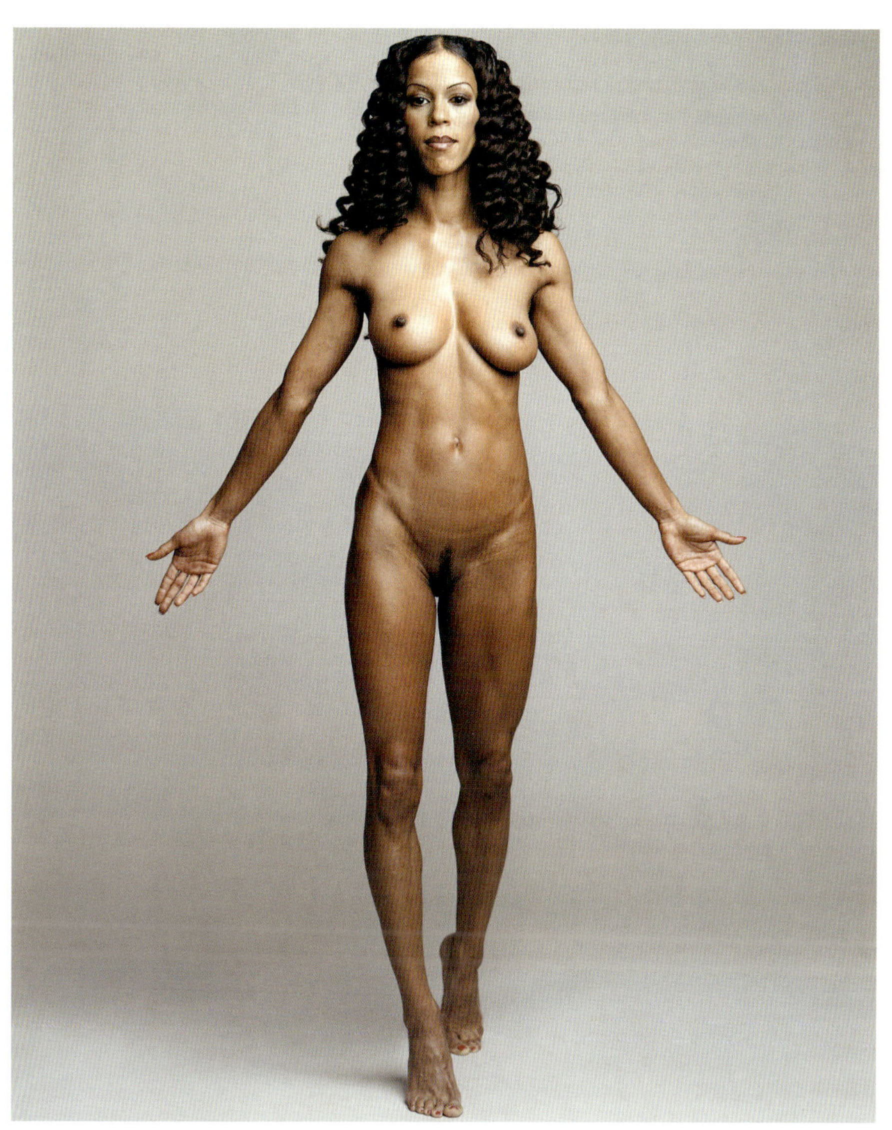

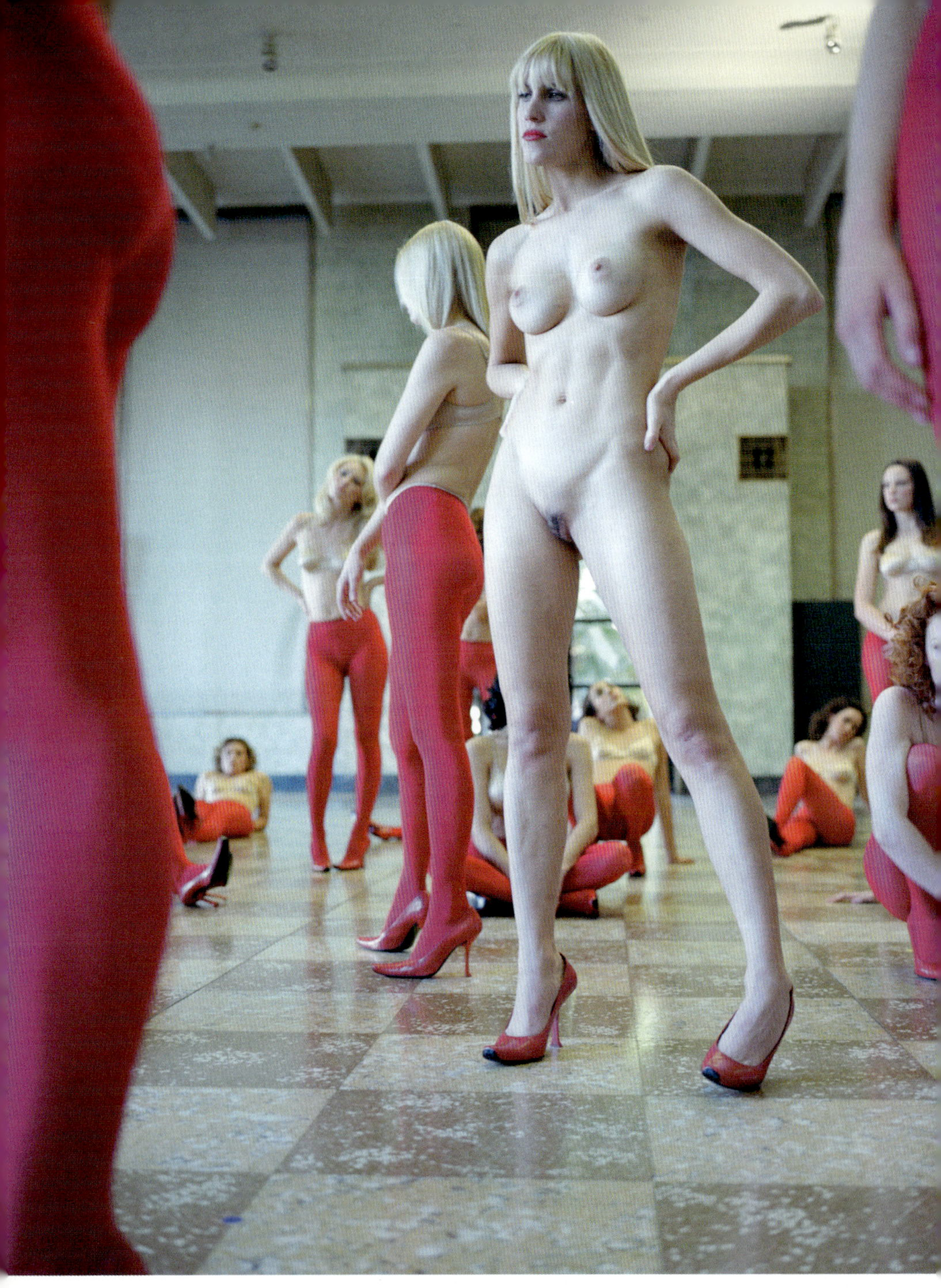

Vanessa Beecroft *VB40*, 1999. Museum of Contemporary Art, Sydney

As a consequence of the divine nature of the body, the concept of a hierarchical relationship between body (*basar*) and spirit (*ruach*), or much less their dissociation, is utterly foreign to Judaism. There is a Talmudic parable that illustrates this well. A man wished to protect the fruit of his garden from thieves, so he hired a crippled man and a blind man to guard it. But the crippled man was able to steal the fruit by sitting on the shoulders of the blind man, thereby demonstrating how the body and spirit share the same responsibility for our actions.[19] Analogously, the qualitative difference between spiritual love and carnal love is rejected. In the Zohar, the relationship between these two sentiments is seen as that of the flame and the candle, wherein one cannot exist without the other.[20]

[1] Philo of Alexandria, *Le Origini del male*, Milan: Rusconi, 1984, p. 236 (Deter X:33).
[2] Saadiah Gaon, *Emunot ve Deot*, English translation by S. Rosenblatt, Yale University Press, 1948, 933, 6.4 (6.17).
[3] Maimonides, *La Guida dei perplessi*, Turin: UTET, 2003, pp. 614–16 (III:27).
[4] Anatoli ben Joseph, *Malmad ha Talmidim*, Lyck 1866, 79b.
[5] B. Spinoza, *Etica*, II, Def. 1; also I:14, cor. and I:25 cor.
[6] Ibid., III, Def. II.
[7] *Qohelet* 2:24; 5:17–19; 8:15; 9:7–10; 11:7–9.
[8] ySukkà 5:1.
[9] yQiddushin 4:12.
[10] Tosafot Rid, Yevamot 12b.
[11] Abravanel 1535, p. 369.
[12] Giqatilla 1561, English translation p. 219.
[13] Ibid., p. 368.
[14] B. Spinoza, *Epistolario*, letter no. 9, p. 69.
[15] Quoted in C. Mopsik, *Lettre sur la Sainteté*, Paris: Éditions Verdier, 1993, p. 46.
[16] *Iggeret ha-qodesh* 2, Italian translation p. 421.
[17] Ibid., p. 423.
[18] Abravanel 1535, p. 165.
[19] Sanhedrin, 91 a–b.
[20] Zohar, I:83b.

Published here for the first time by kind permission of the Author.

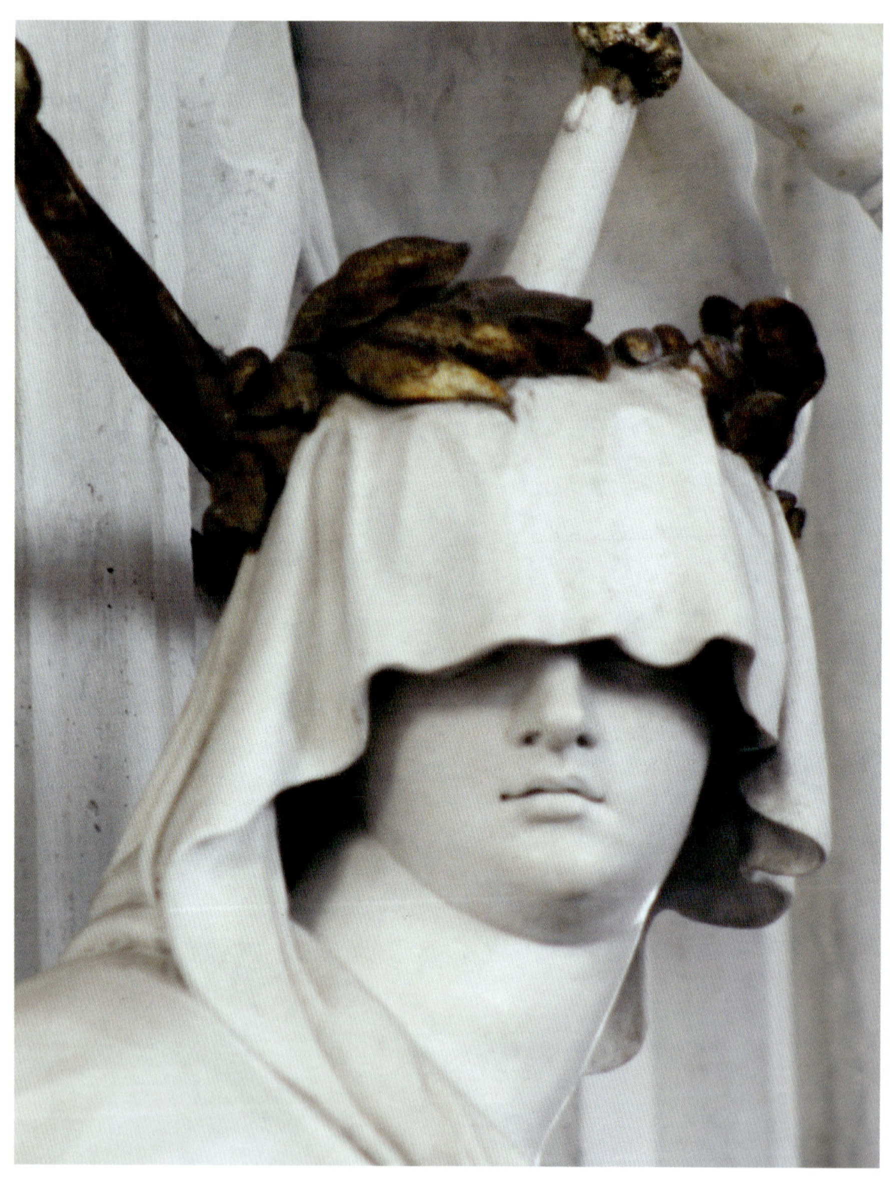

Giacomo Serpotta *Elemosina*, 1701. Marble. Palermo, Oratorio di San Lorenzo

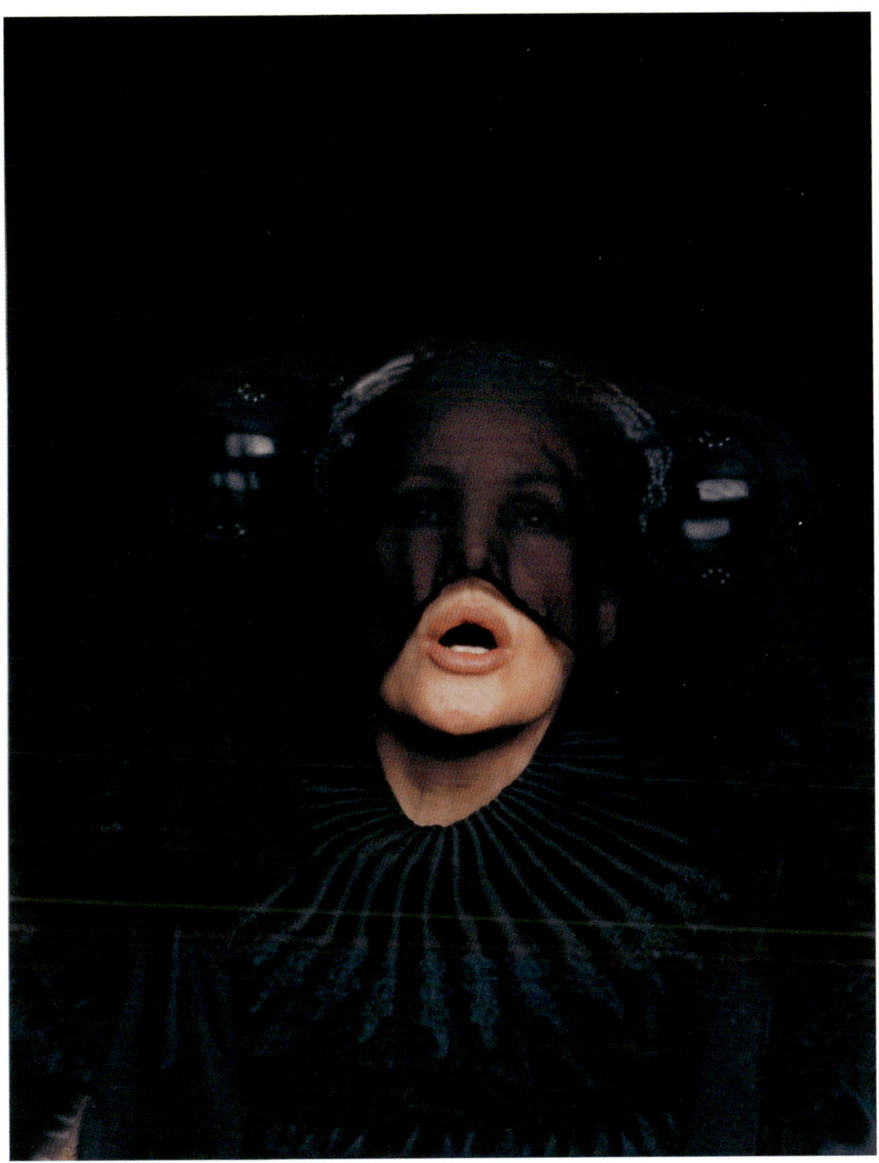

Matthew Barney *The Queen of Chain* (from *Cremaster 5*), 1997. Silver gelatine print, acrylic frame (published without frame)

Size of Hell

Philosophers have been speculating about the size of hell for centuries. Using passages from the Bible, ancient legends and simple guesswork, scholars have sought to determine the exact dimensions of the realm of the damned.

In *Christ and Satan*, a Christian poem dating back to the 1100s, determining the area of hell is a major plot point. After Satan fails to tempt Christ in the desert, the Devil is ordered to measure his kingdom. The Savior demands that Satan go back to the underworld and crawl hell's length and breadth on his hands and knees through the foul-smelling darkness, then report on its size. Satan does so and declares that the underworld extends for 100,000 miles. Though an imaginative piece of prose, the measurement from *Christ and Satan* has been universally dismissed as a 'colorful' but baseless concept. But the work attests to humanity's fascination with the subject of hell's perimeters.

[The matter] received serious treatment from noteworthy Christian intellectuals as well. The most prominent preacher of the fourteenth century, Berthold of Regensburg, claimed that only one person in 100,000 would be saved. The rest would bake in an unquenchable fire for all eternity. This assertion has been largely condemned, however; not only for its pessimism but because it would necessitate an enormous place for the damned to reside.

Influenced both by the frivolous and somber estimations of the devil's kingdom, sixteenth-century scientist Galileo took up the concept during his early studies. He used specifications from Dante's *Divine Comedy: The Inferno* to calculate the distance between earth, heaven, and hell as well as the dimensions of the underworld itself.

And though his treatise was simply musing, his theories about mortality, the afterlife and humanity's place in the universe are believed to have influenced numerous artists, including Milton (author of *Paradise Lost*) who visited Galileo in Italy before writing his masterpiece.

Today, most people consider determining the exact size of hell a moot issue. Since hell is a spiritual dimension, physical measurements are meaningless and do nothing to amplify or ease the suffering of the damned.

Miriam Van Scott

Miriam Van Scott, *Encyclopedia of Hell*, New York: Thomas Dunne Books / St. Martin's Griffin, 1998.

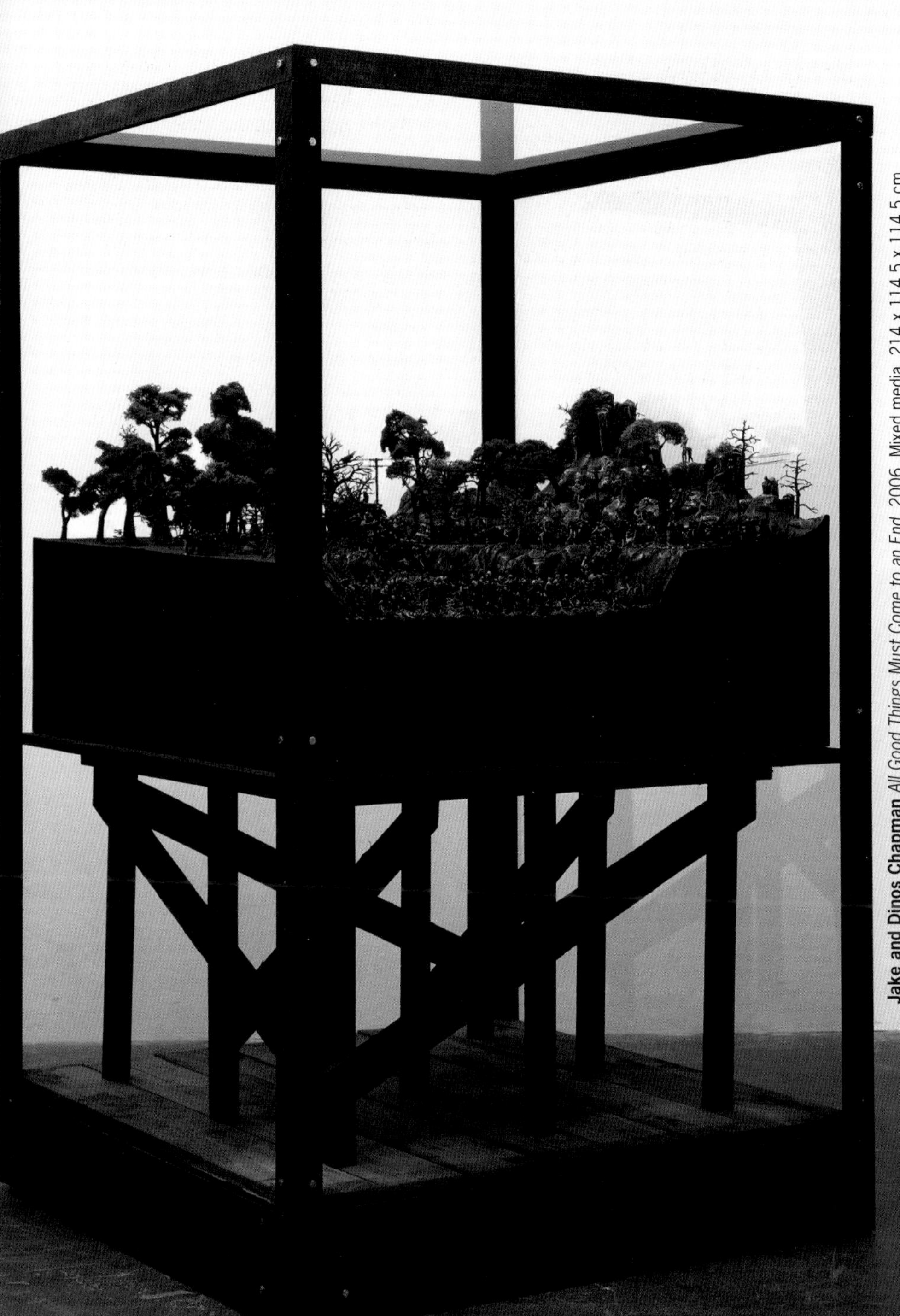

Jake and Dinos Chapman *All Good Things Must Come to an End*, 2006. Mixed media, 214 x 114.5 x 114.5 cm

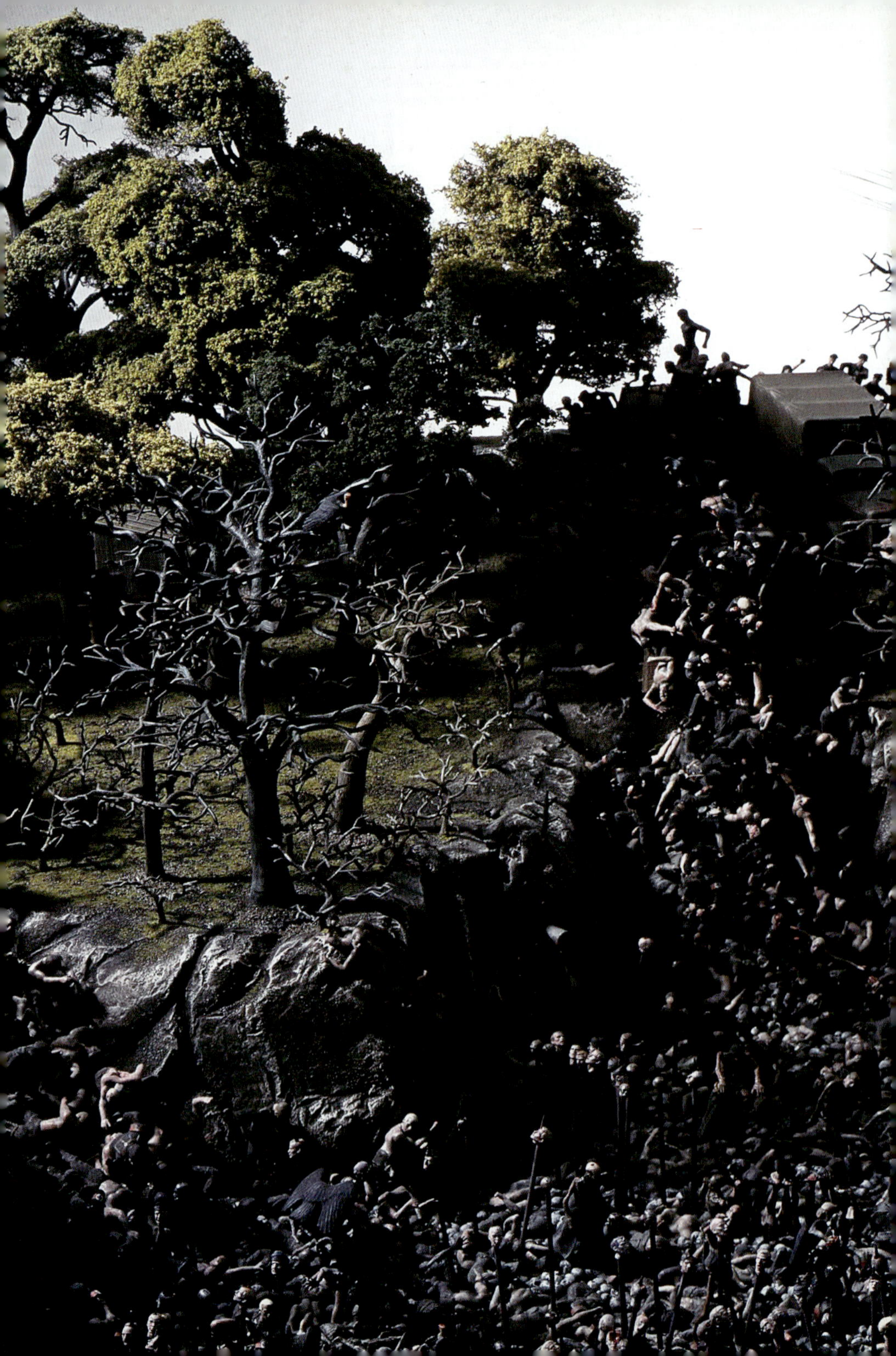

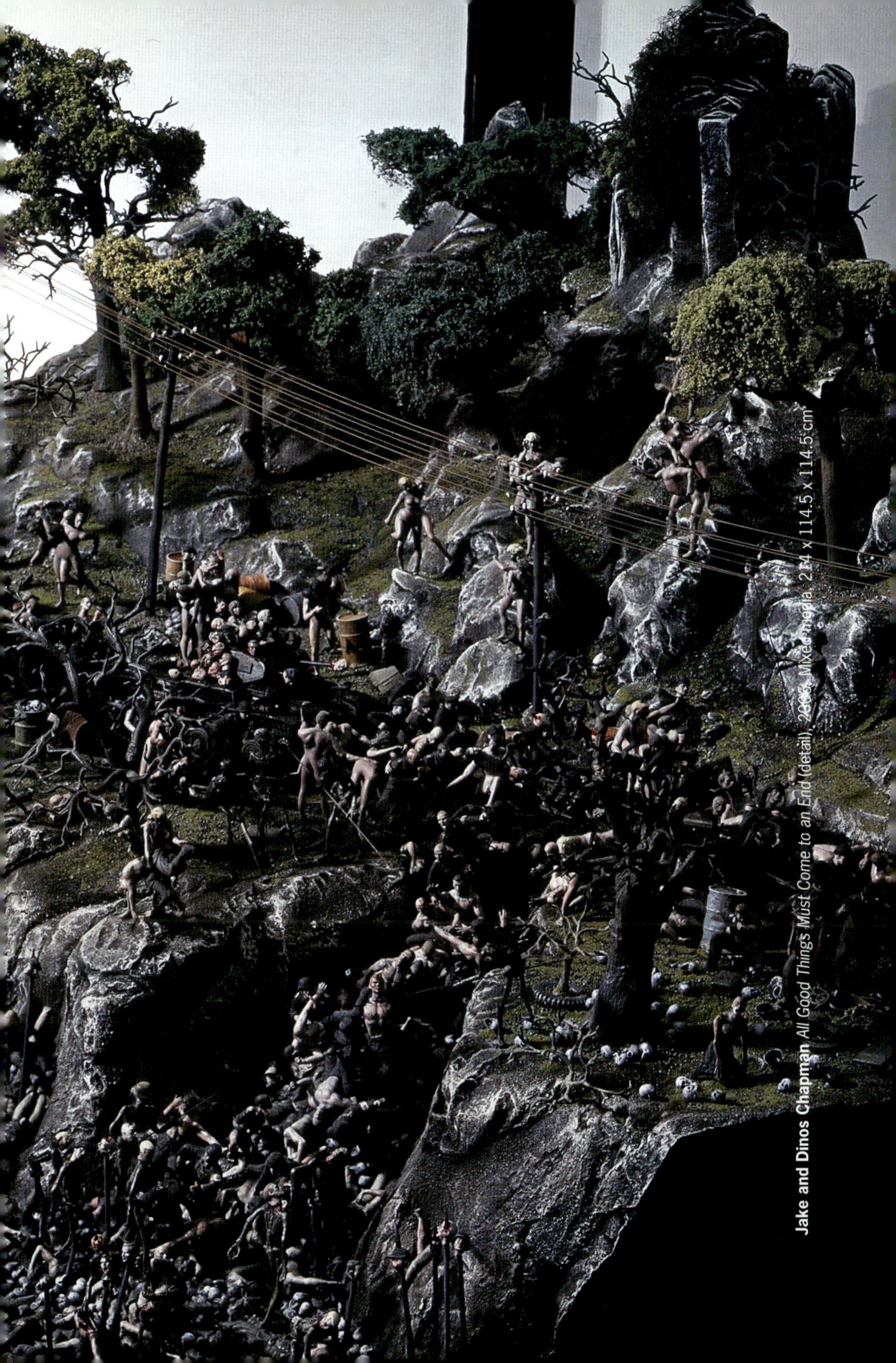

Jake and Dinos Chapman *All Good Things Must Come to an End* (detail), 2006, Mixed media, 214 x 114.5 x 114.5 cm

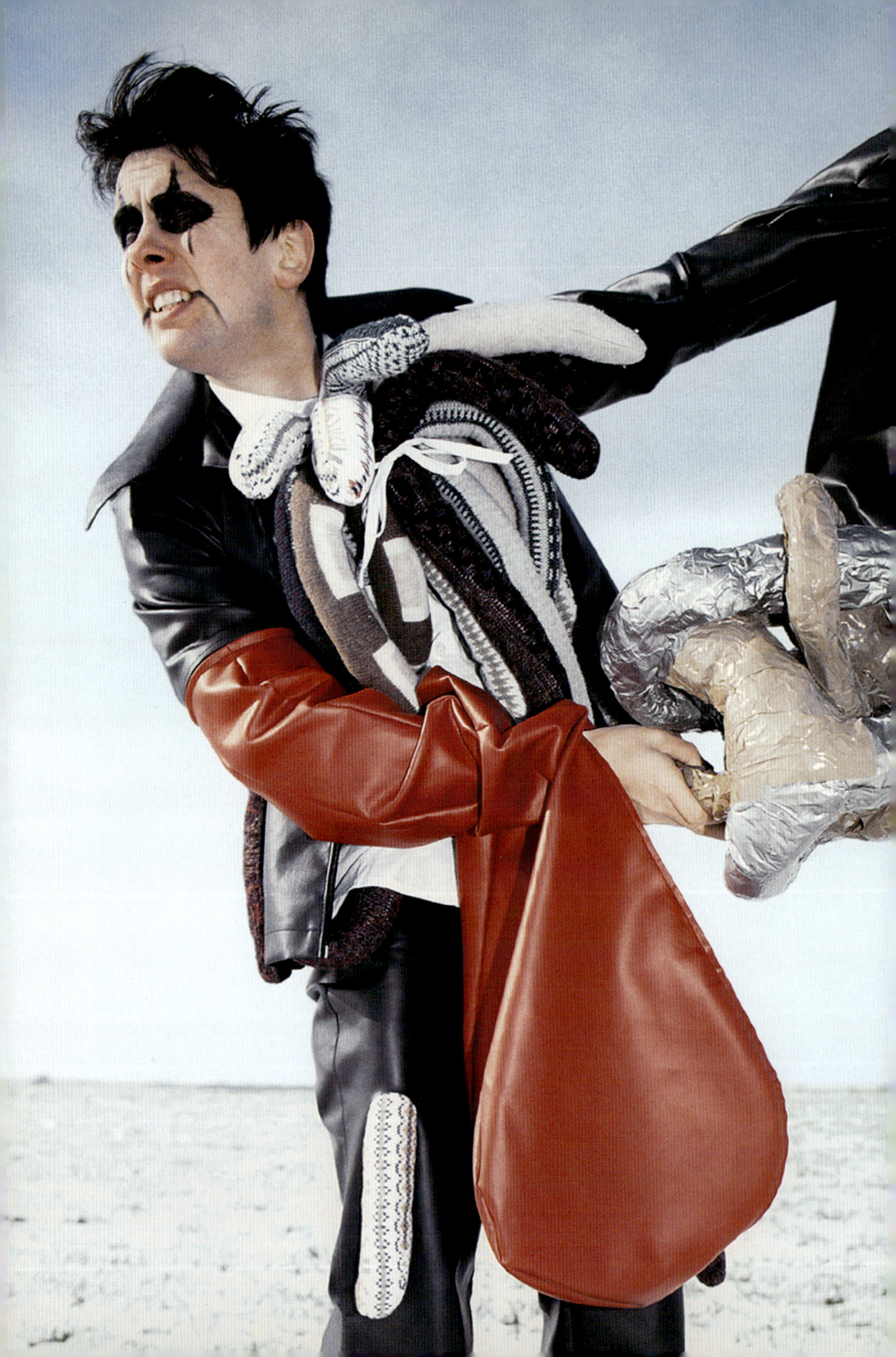

Who is the Serpent?

Vito Mancuso

Destruction and Reconstruction of Original Sin

Who is the serpent? To grasp the profound teaching contained in the dogma of original sin, one must try to understand who the serpent really is. For he, after all, is the winner: his campaign of temptation has succeeded perfectly; indeed, it succeeds more every day.

The Serpent is not the Devil

Traditional literature has always identified the symbol of the serpent as the quintessential representation of the Tempter with a capital 'T', the figure of Satan. This is of course an ancient reading, a biblical one, and stands as an unassailable theological dictum.

However, while this is not necessarily a forced reading, it is certainly a gloss on the original text, which never states and does not even suggest that the serpent is Satan (thus the recurring discord between bibleists compelled to defend the Hebrew text and systematic theologians whose aim is to defend Church dogma).[1] The ancient Jewish tradition from which the story of Genesis 3 derives does not contain a figure that could be even hypostatically identified with the Devil, who would only appear many centuries later, on the threshold of the Christian era in the Book of Wisdom, written in Greek and as such not inspired by and not included in the Hebrew biblical canon, according to which 'God did not make death' (1:13), 'but by the envy of the Devil, death entered the world' (2:24). This interpretation of Genesis 3 that identifies the serpent with the Devil was made by the New Testament, and from there it became an irrefutable cornerstone of 2,000

John Bock *Alice Cooper*, 2001. Video

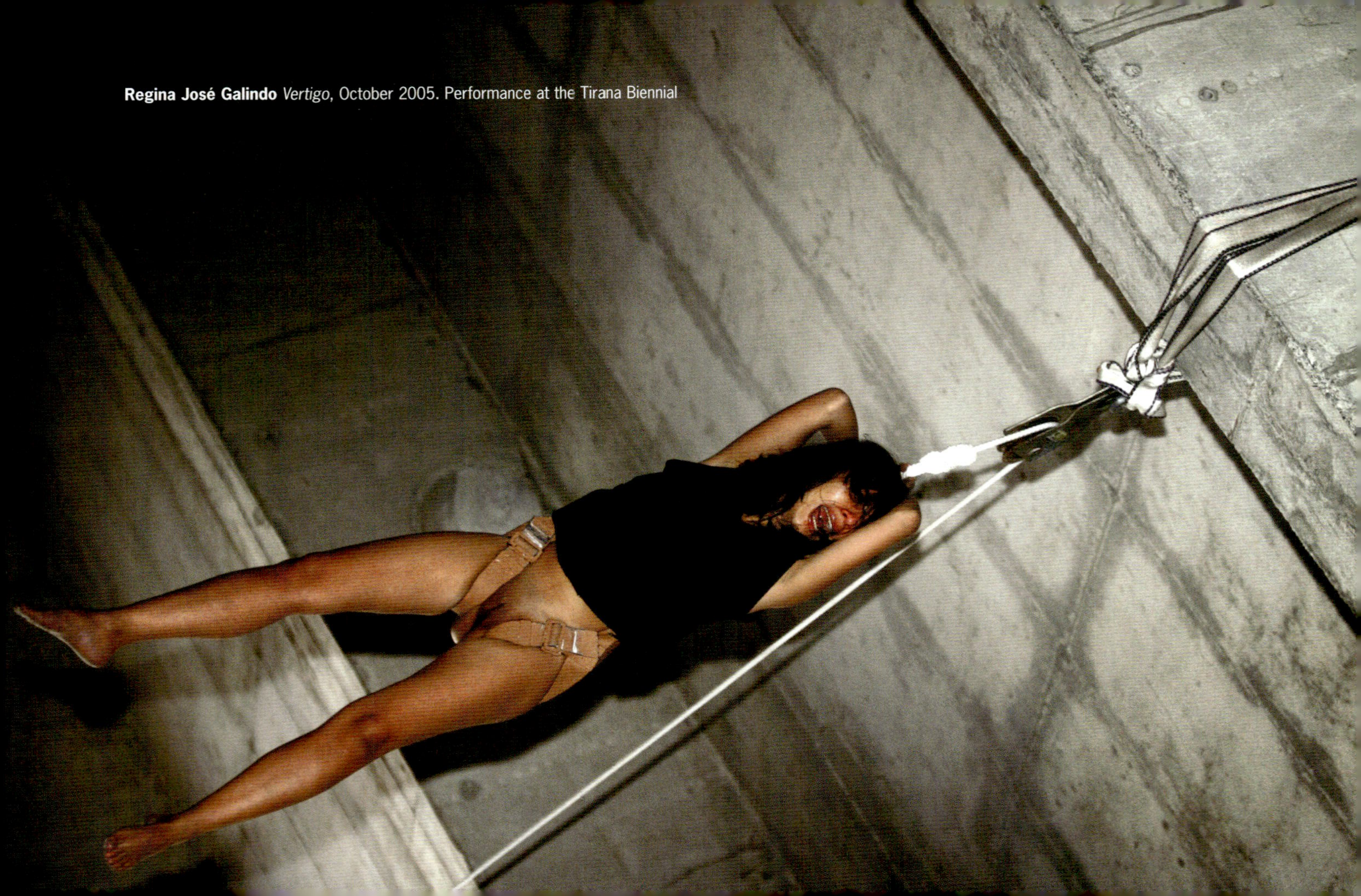

Regina José Galindo *Vertigo*, October 2005. Performance at the Tirana Biennial

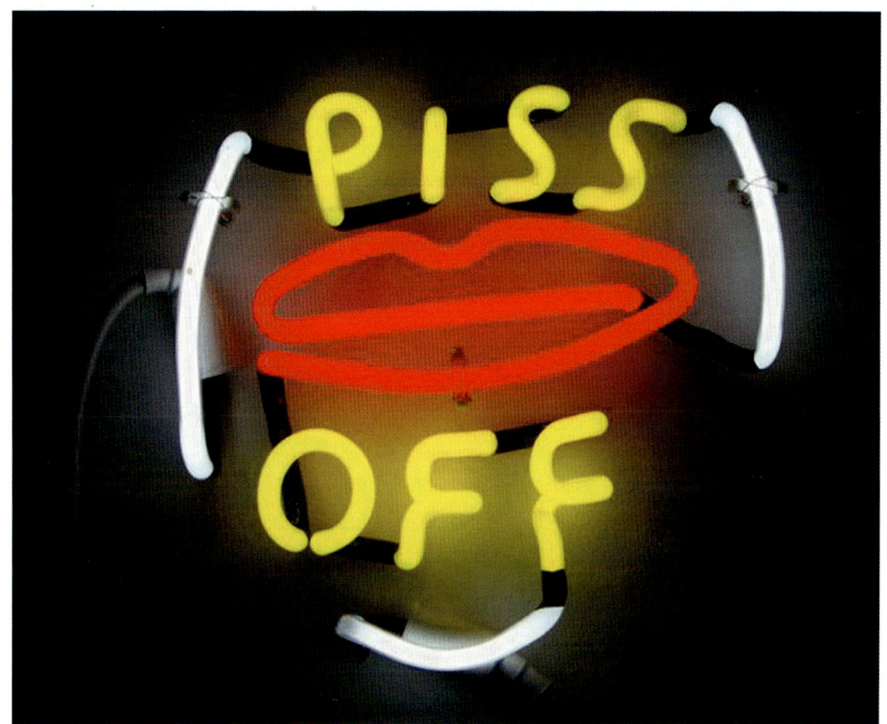

Tim Noble & Sue Webster *Piss Off*, 2004. Neon, 26 x 27 x 3 cm

years of Christian thought. But it is precisely here that all the difficulties surrounding the dogma of original sin are concentrated, creating unresolved and perhaps irresolvable questions, foremost among which is the destiny of those who die unbaptised (the vast majority of the human race, naturally, if one takes into account the 100,000 years that *homo sapiens* has been around), and thus guilty in the eyes of God, which excludes them from salvation [...]. That being said, the problem remains: who is the serpent? And if the serpent is not the Devil, when does the Devil enter the scene, and with him the origin of evil? [...]

The Serpent is Life

... The serpent is the quintessential symbol of the ambiguity of life. [...] The divine sphere, the demonic sphere, the cosmic sphere, the sapiential sphere — in reality they are nothing but the broader sphere of life that envelops humankind from all sides and confuses us, denying us any fixed point whatsoever when we try to keep our eyes open to the epiphany of life rather than close ourselves in the blindness of ideology. And in fact this life seems just like a serpent, one that slithers malevolently who knows where,

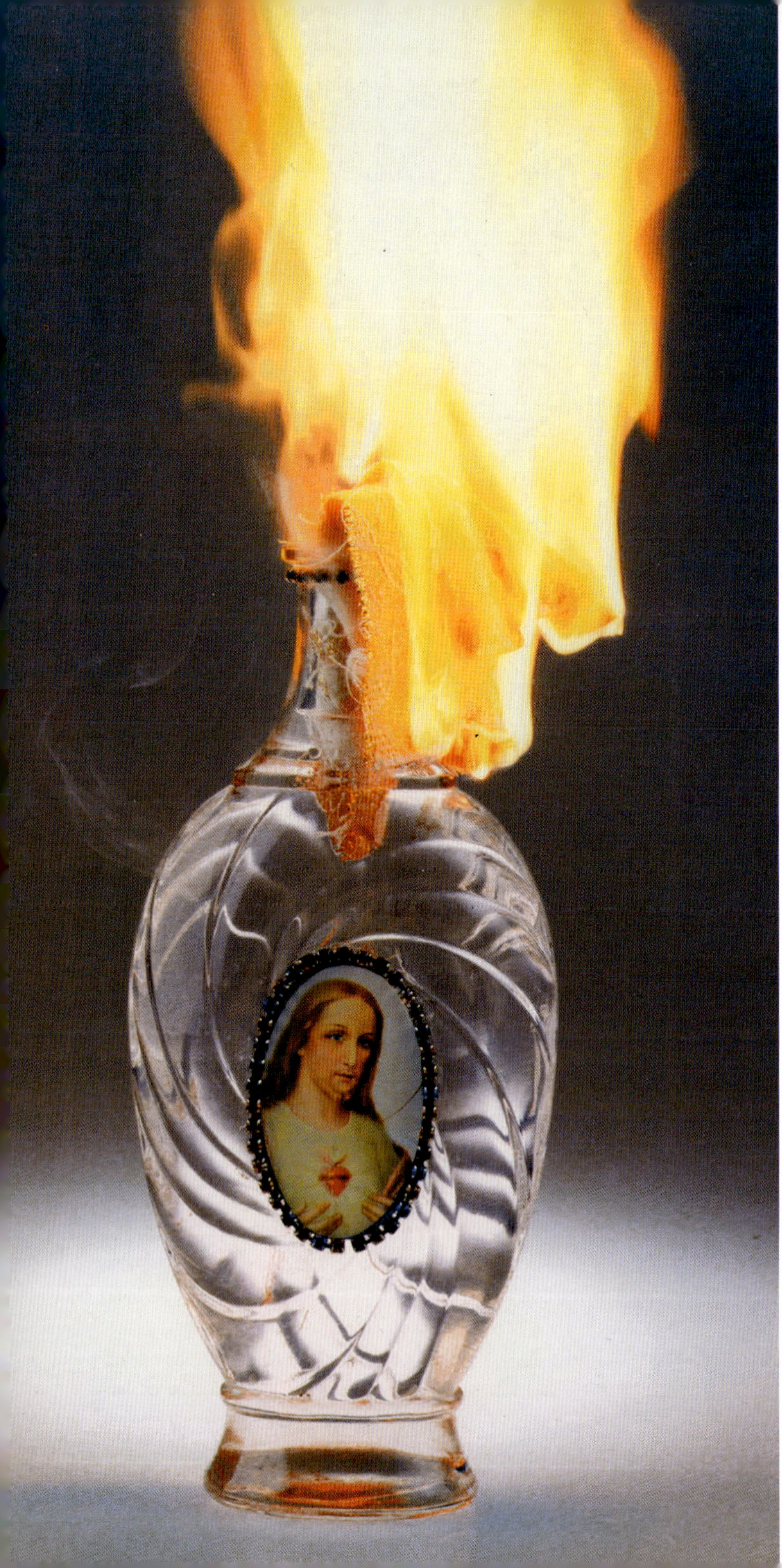

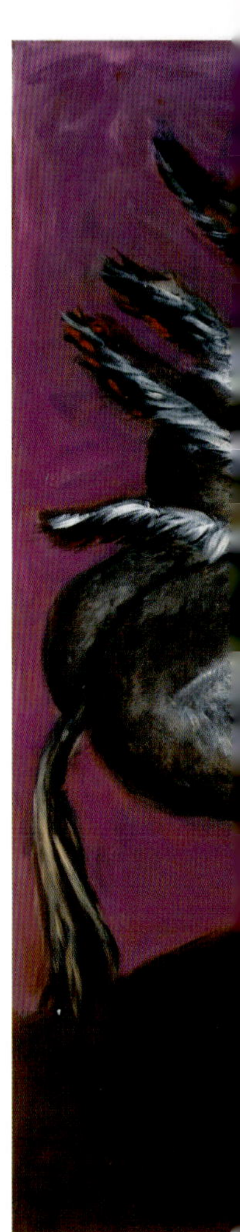

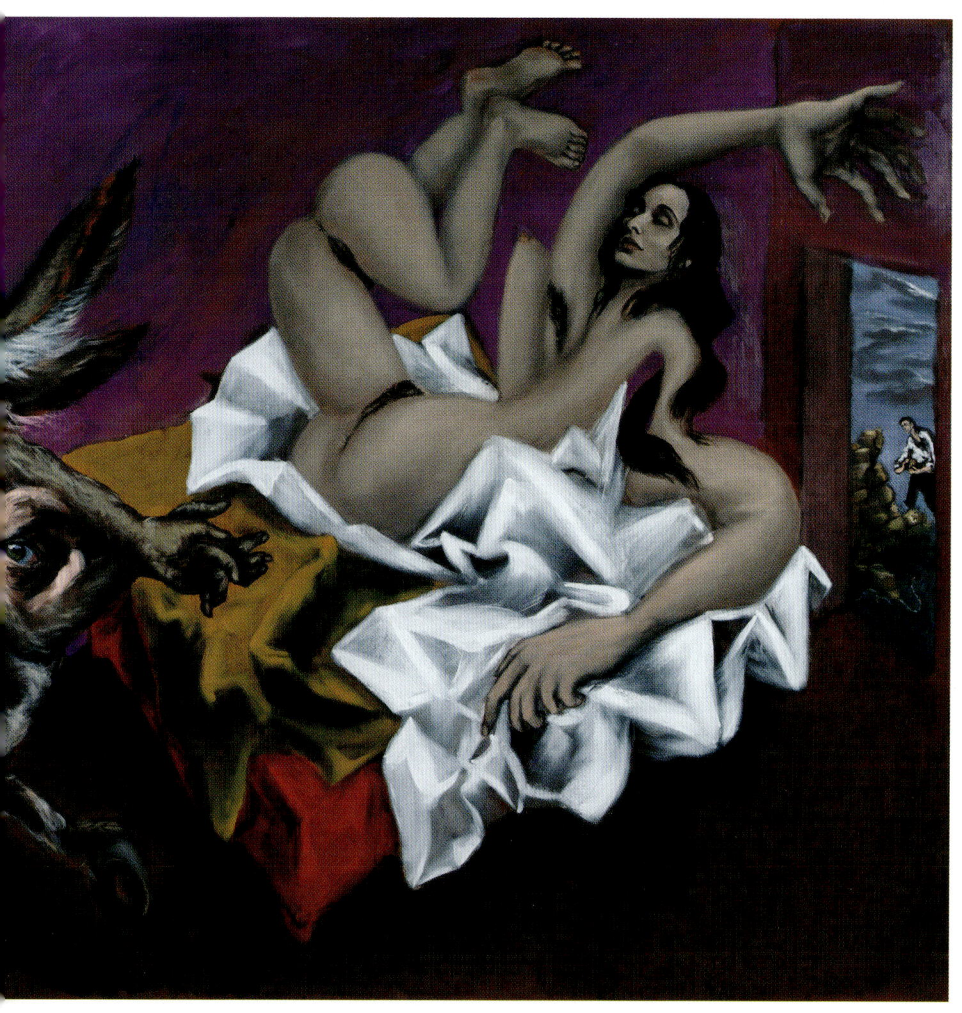

Gérard Garouste *Dina*, 2005. Oil on canvas, 205 x 260 cm

Opposite
Antonio Riello *Christian Molotov*, 2002. Glass bottle and gasoline, 40 x 15 x 5 cm

such that once we see it and wish to grab hold of it we need to exercise maximum caution, for that life-serpent can also lead us to death. If we give ourselves over excessively to life, to its joys and amusements, if we abandon ourselves heedlessly to its seductions, its poison quickly enters our body and leads us towards death.

Alongside the symbology of life is the symbology of death, for life and death form an inextricable nexus, are indeed one and the same: life nourishes itself on the death of others, and will in turn become nourishment for

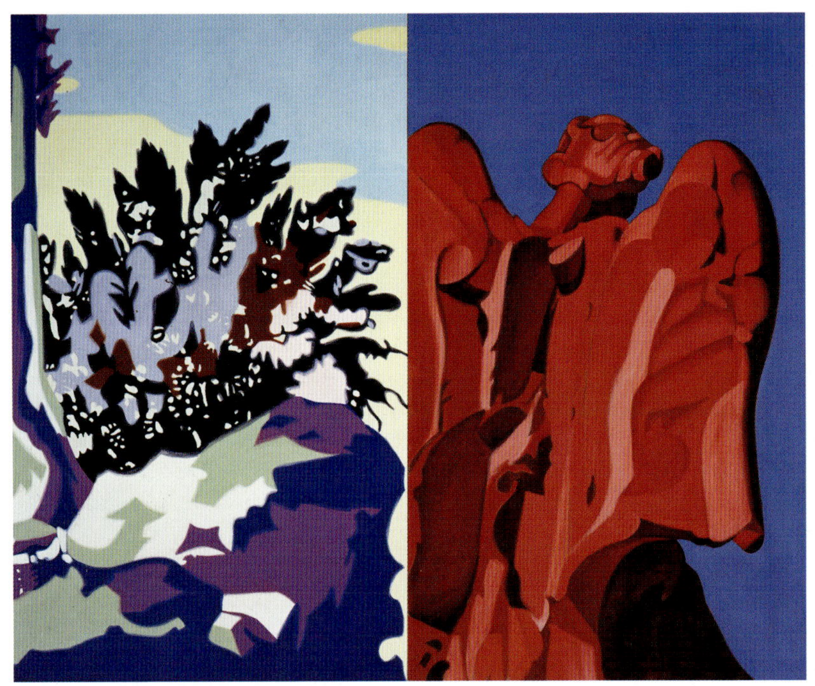

David Salle *Red Angel*, 2001. Oil and acrylic on canvas, 145 x 173 cm

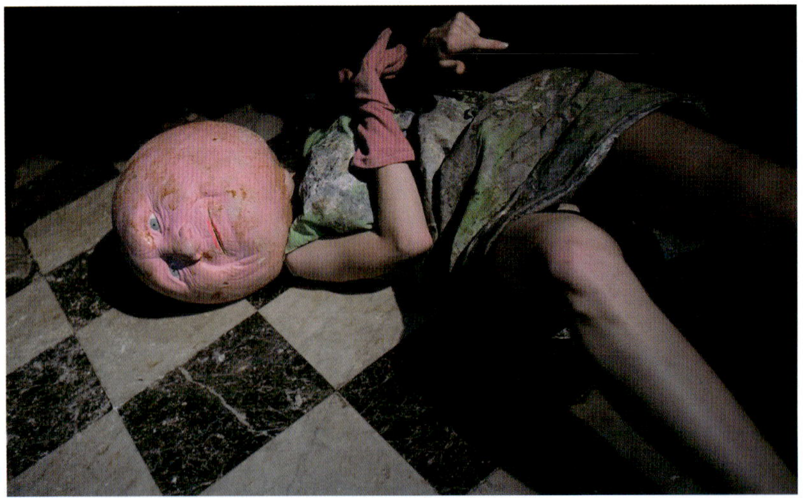

Paul McCarthy *Piccadilly Circus (Green Queen on Marble Floor)*, 2003. Print on aluminium, 122 x 183 cm

the lives of others still on the perpetual carousel of the world and its multiple manifestations. Temptation comes from no other place than the ambiguous and contradictory nature of life, as well as from the nature, equally ambiguous and contradictory, of the realm of knowledge and spirit.

So the serpent is life. But denying that the serpent is the Devil does not make the question any less dramatic, nor does it imply the negation of the Devil's existence [...].

Sheep Without a Shepherd

This would mean that Genesis 3 has nothing to do with the birth of evil. If the serpent is not Satan, this is not an account of the origins of evil. If anything is born here it is sin understood as transgression of a prohibition, but not evil in the objective sense. Evil could not have been born here because there was not yet good, and evil is only the corruption of the good, ontologically parasitic with respect to the good. But before their transgression Adam and Eve did not know the good. They are in a state of paradisiacal innocence, without freedom. They're not yet fully human. Their eyes, as the text recounts, are not yet open. They don't know that they're naked. They don't know each other. They have no self-awareness. How is it possible to postulate the corruption of such an ingenuous condition?

A distinction needs to be made between the temptation exercised by life and the temptation that comes instead from the spirit of evil, or the unclean spirit, as Jesus called it. It is only when we enter into this second and much deeper dimension that we can commit a truly mortal sin, one that leads to death. And this is the only true dimension of sin.

Let us consider how we are born and raised, the multiple positive and negative conditionings we receive: we did not choose our mothers and fathers or how they think and behave, yet our lives depend heavily on them, in a good way when we're good, bad when we're bad, just as our lives also depend on other adult figures and friends who influence our lives without our having chosen them.

Psychoanalysis has something to teach us in this regard, for it knows that behind every aberrant behaviour there are corresponding aberrant behaviours to which the person in question was subjected as a child. And while it's true that not everything about us can be ascribed to childhood influences, and that free will exists, allowing us to build our own stories, who would presume to draw a clean line to define the boundary between the spontaneous dimension of free will and the cloudier one of conditioning? Who will cast the first stone?

Poor humankind, one mustn't assign to them such a crystalline and organized freedom right from the start. The majority of them know nothing

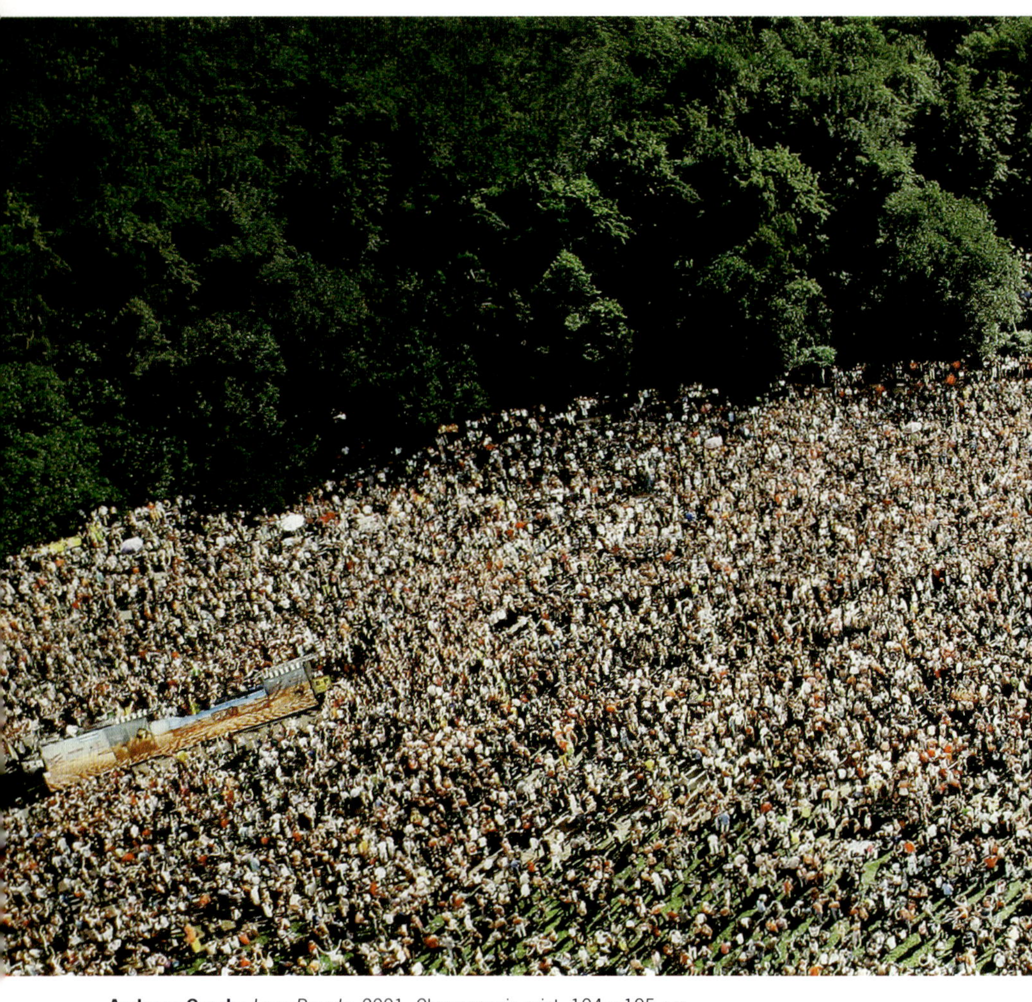

Andreas Gursky *Love Parade*, 2001. Chromogenic print, 104 x 195 cm

of the sort. And the dogma of original sin speaks exactly of this natural absence of a free will oriented towards the good, or to use the traditional terminology, this absence of grace. Humanity should be thought of as 'sheep without a shepherd' (Mark 6:34), just as the merciful eye of the master sees them, significantly different from the pitiless attitude of Augustine and other men of the Church who see them as a 'damned mass'.[2] The lack of a shepherd is the lack of guided freedom, of direction, of a determined will. It is being under the spell of mercenaries, charlatans, snake oil salesmen and

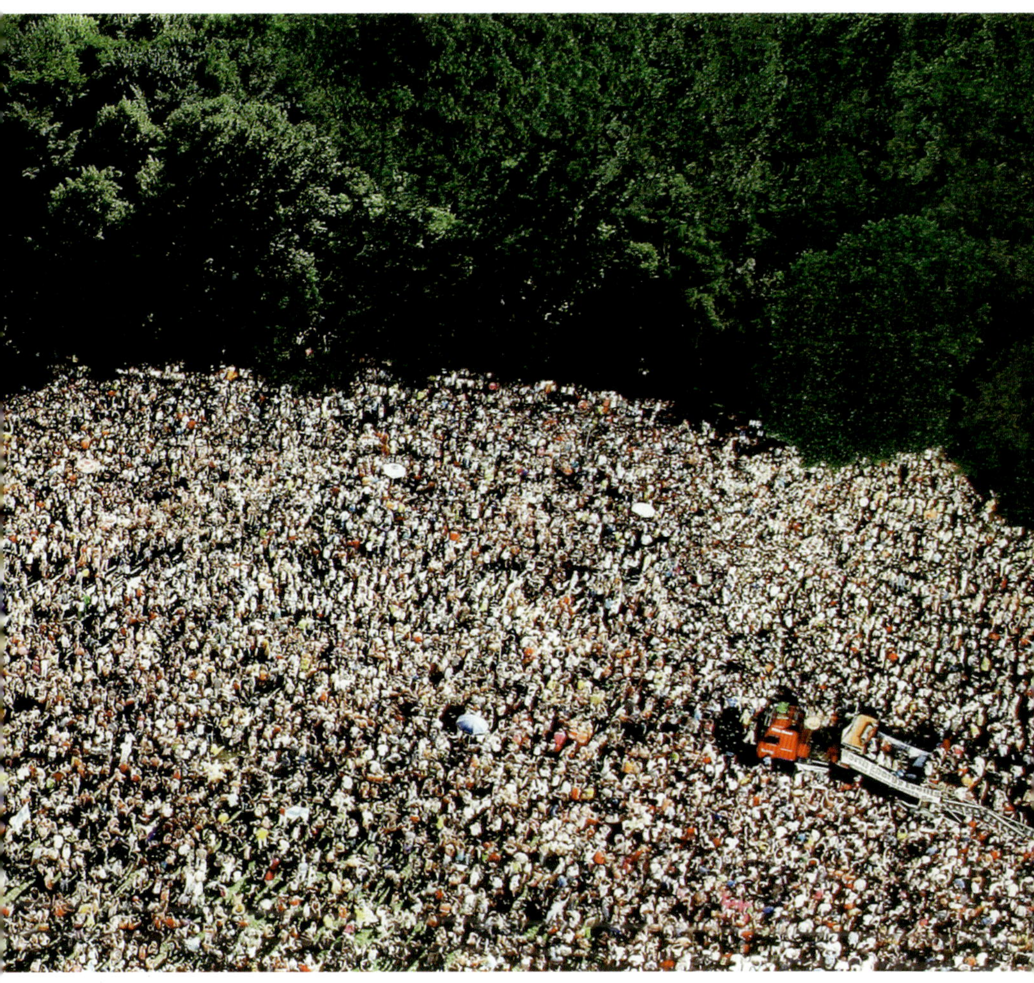

populists of every stripe, of those who shout the loudest, who prove themselves strongest. Because people naturally do not follow those who tell them the truth, but those who appear to be the strongest. People are seduced by strength, not by truth. Try staging an election campaign on a platform of service to the truth and you will see how miserably few votes you receive. This negligence with which people treat the truth, this condition of being without a shepherd, without direction, enslaved to the base desires with which they are born, is original sin. And Satan has nothing at all to do

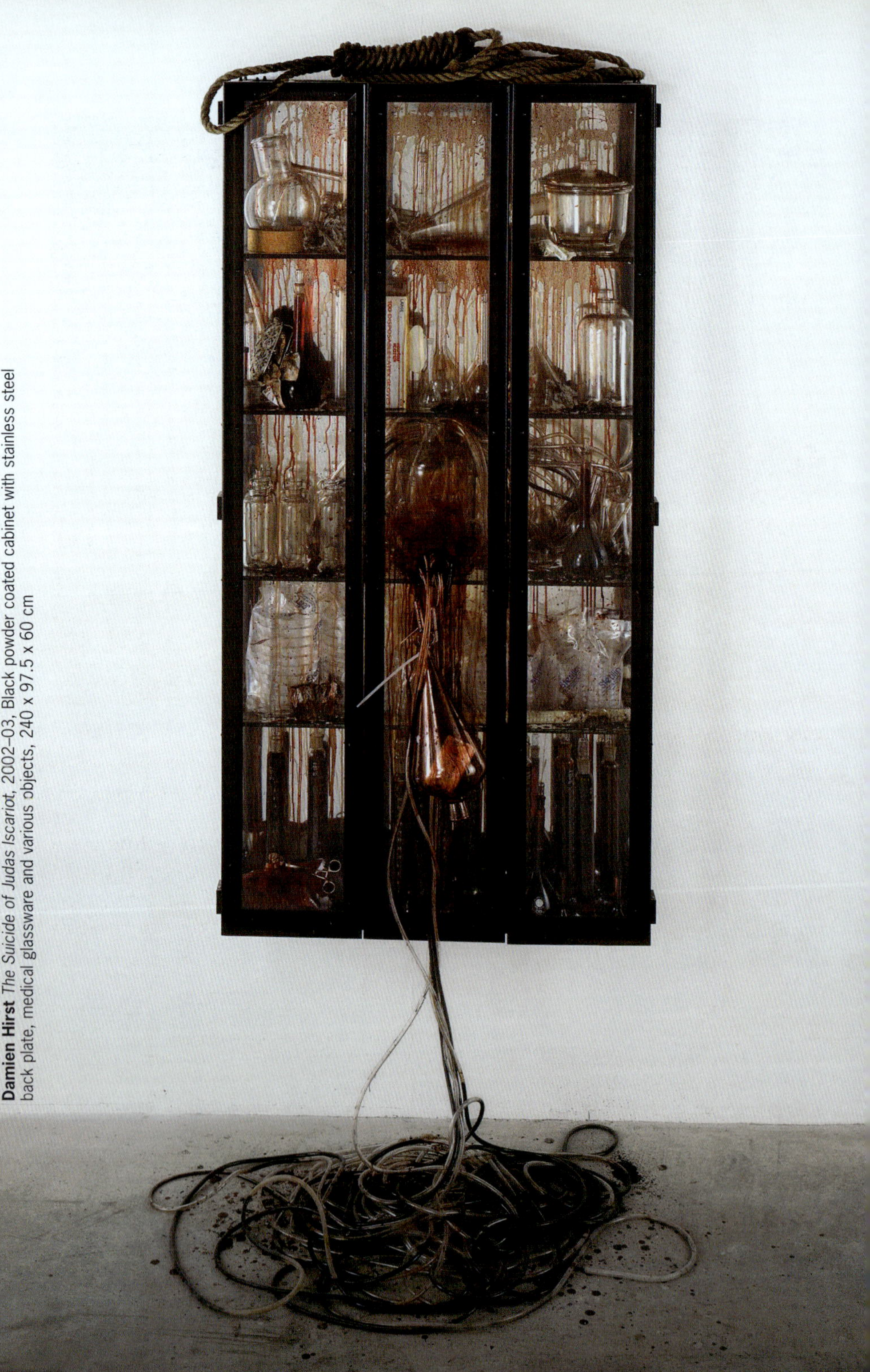

Damien Hirst *The Suicide of Judas Iscariot*, 2002–03, Black powder coated cabinet with stainless steel back plate, medical glassware and various objects, 240 x 97.5 x 60 cm

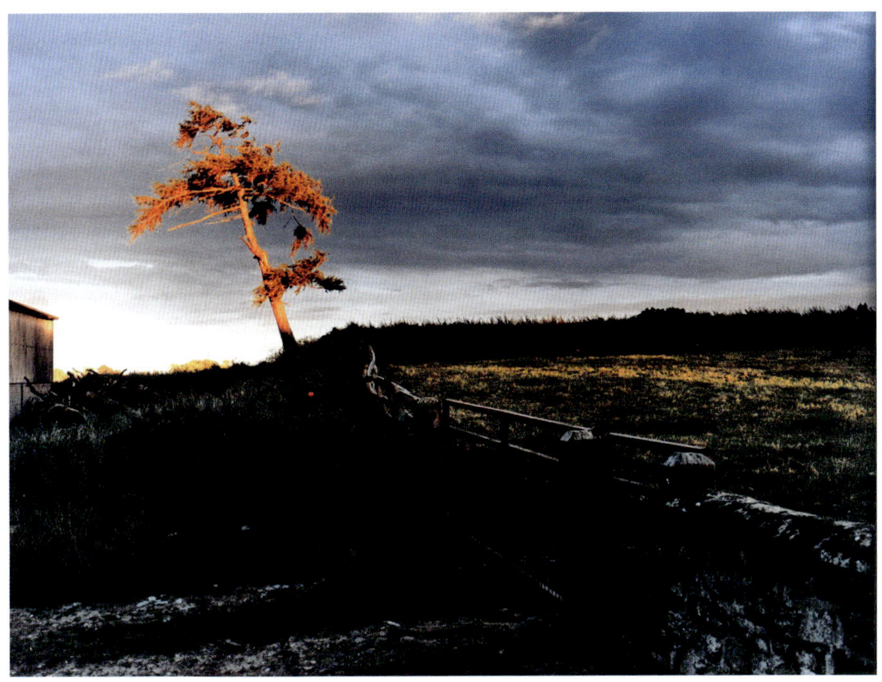

Sam Taylor-Wood *Self Portrait as a Tree*, 2000. C-type print, 75.6 x 91 cm

with it. We mustn't attribute original sin to Satan. It is a theological error, and it needs correction [...].

Original sin has many valid things to say. The error lies in calling it sin and making it the fault of every child that is born. There is no sin there, only the human condition, whose liberty is necessitated, imperfect, corrupt, if you will. And to whom can we trace the responsibility for this imperfection? To the serpent, obviously. To life.

[1] A noted bibleist begins an article about Adam's guilt by underscoring how it is no longer necessary to 'bring up yet again the reciprocal unease of the bibleist and the systematic theologian when dealing with biblical texts concerning the sin of Adam'. G. Borgonovo, in *Scuola Cattolica*, 126, 1998, p. 337.
[2] Augustine, *De Civitate Dei*, XV, 1, 2. This passage is paradigmatic of many others made by Augustine in this regard.

Vito Mancuso, *Per amore. Rifondazione della fede*, Milan: Mondadori, 2005 (II ed. 2006), by kind permission of the Author.

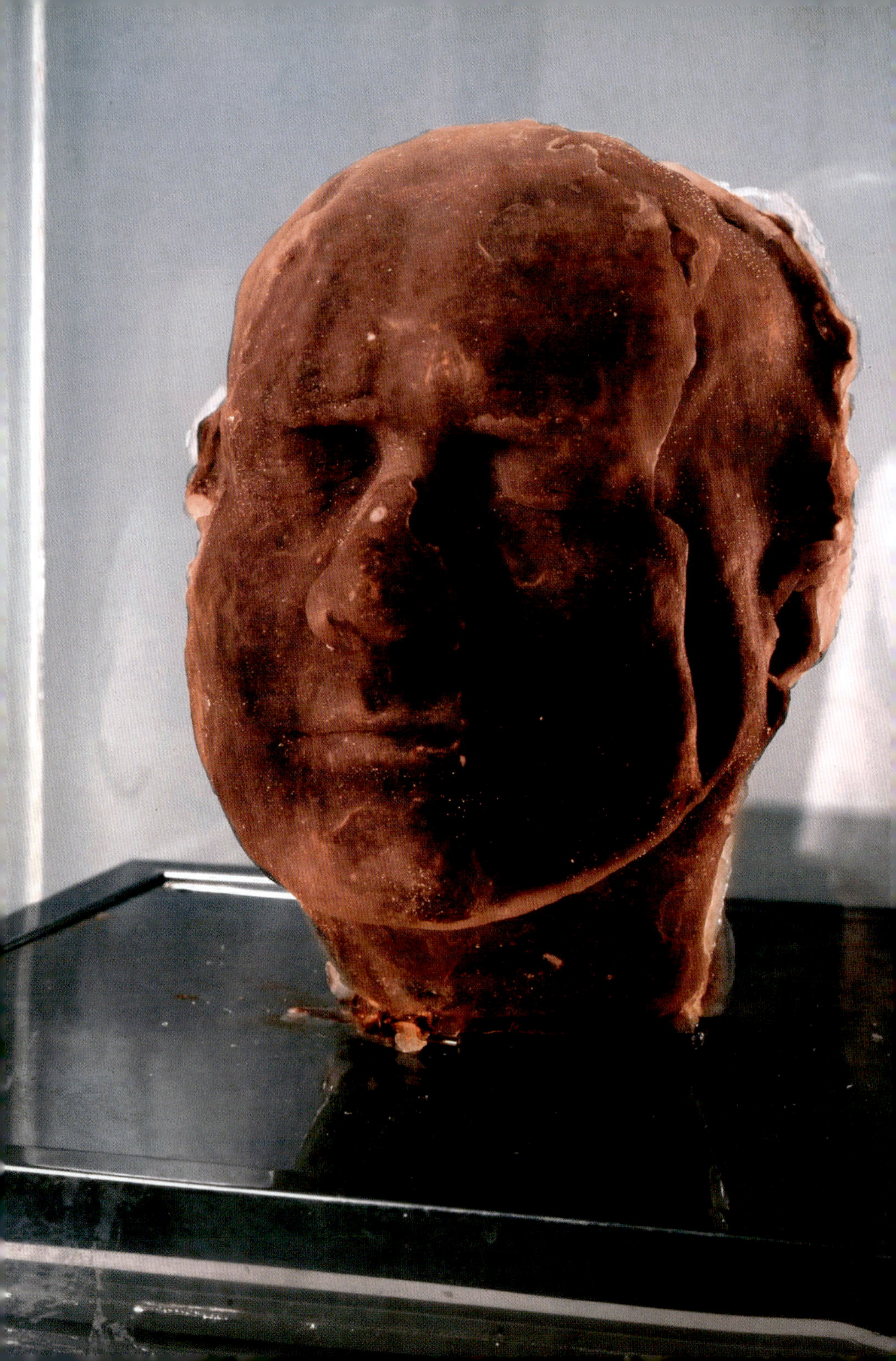

Dangerous Art

Arthur C. Danto

In the days before *glasnost* cast its first pale and tentative light over what was once referred to as the Evil Empire, authors from the West who went there as cultural emissaries found it bracing — 'inspiriting' was the term used by Hortense Calisher — to be in a world where writing was considered dangerous. The sense of having one's words suddenly mean something might — almost — have been a fair exchange for the freedom one might have to surrender, if the latter were purchased at the cost of no one especially caring how it was exercised in art: as it might suddenly enter a feminist's mind that it was deeply moving to be in a culture where it meant something 'to be a woman', even if at the cost of a freedom and independence she had fought to achieve. I dare say very few would strike the bargain, freedom perhaps trumping significance in one's schedule of values, an ordering to be reckoned with when we sentimentalize organic communities by contrast with individualistic liberal societies, where the intervention into single lives by the aggregate social order is marginal and limited. And in any case, the intoxication of being thought of as dangerous is somewhat diminished by the reflection that it is not art alone but personal correspondence and even mere conversation that will have been considered dangerous enough to justify monitoring by the state, functioning as a literal, suspicious, humorless, and largely arbitrary referee.

When the censor functions as a third party at every interchange of discourse, at whatever level of communication, the remaining two parties will inevitably resort to intricate and oblique strategies of concealment

Marc Quinn *Self*, 1991. Artist's blood, stainless steel, plexiglass and cooling system, 208 x 63 x 63 cm

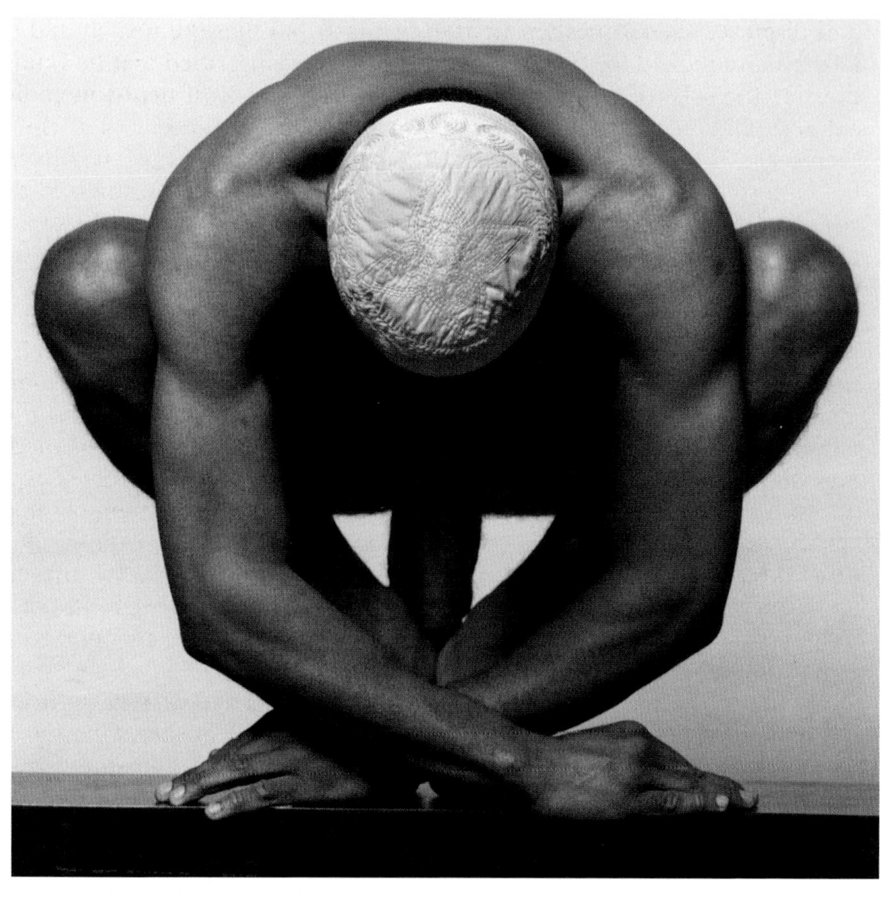

Robert Mapplethorpe *Jimmy Freeman*, 1981. Silver gelatine print, 39.2 x 49.2 cm

and disguise, where lines are written primarily so that the text should be located and looked for between them, and the uninscribed text be finally that for the sake of which the written one exists — as if heard melodies exhausted their role in making unheard melodies audible to a third, secret ear. I have been with Poles whose every utterance is filtered through so many strata of irony that no one who has not internalized the complex sequence of bureaucracies under which they mastered Aesopean concealment can hope to understand them fully or participate in anything save a cursory interchange. I am, in such colloquies, reminded of Proust's description of the narrator's great-aunts in the Combray section of *Remembrance of Things Past*, as 'women who had brought to such a fine art the concealment of a personal allusion in a wealth of ingenious circumlocution, that it would often pass unnoticed even by the person to whom it was addressed'. Once a labyrinth of tertiary significations mediates between author and reader, writing as such, even when frivolous, is not to be taken at face value, and everything is dangerous even, or especially, when it seems most ingenuous. Paranoia becomes a rational posture when 'Jack and Jill went up the hill' is under cryptographic surveillance and the censor is desperate not to let anything get through. Its being hidden is what makes it dangerous, even if it would not be recognized as especially dangerous if openly said.

In January 1986, the PEN organization hosted in New York an international conference of writers to ponder the topic 'The Imagination of the Writer and the Imagination of the State'. It was an uninspired title, or at least did little to enlist the imagination of the writers invited to address one another beyond the obvious sort of remark, predictably made the first morning: 'The State has no Imagination' (ha ha), a piety that wore rapidly thinner as it was repeated from session to session. But it seems to me an argument can be made that the imagination of a writer is very much a product of what the imagination of bureaucrats concerned with writers imagines writing to be, since the writer's consciousness has internalized the schedule of permissibilities and prohibitions that defines the political morality of expression. The imagination of the state may then just be the imagination of the writer writ large. That the system of political legitimacy and the structures of artistic expression should be reciprocals of one another is after all a deep thesis of Historical Materialism — the view that art and politics are surface manifestations of the same deep structure that defines a social order. But I am proposing a less ponderous thesis in the social psychology of art, that our art and our political reality are made for one another; that each, one might say, is the same set of symbolic forms differently embodied — in the media of artistic administration and artistic expression respectively. If one were to construct an architectural model of artistic consciousness under a system of censorship, it would look like one of Piranesi's prisons: stairways leading nowhere, doors opening onto blank walls, dead ends masked as infinite vistas, causeways ending in abrupt emptiness, unsuspected shafts, circuitous corridors leading insidiously back to the point at which one enters them, where the inhabitants bump into themselves rounding corners and the victim recognizes in the blackness of the torture chamber that the executioner is himself. If, as has been insisted since Plato, the soul is an isomorph of the state, then the objectification of the soul in literature is the best picture of the state we can have, providing we can learn to read it. But naturally, if this is true, writing can be translated from one political culture to another only at the most superficial level. How are we to replace the texts that haunt the interlinear emptinesses, the eloquent blankness of margins, if even the use of a semicolon may carry the semiological density of poetry?

When *glasnost* comes, it is, accordingly, a mixed blessing to the artist who had counted on the hermeneutic mentality that guaranteed subtleties and depths that simply wash away when there is no presumption of hiddenness. 'For Soviet Rock Musicians, Glasnost Is Angst' was the headline of a *New York Times* article. Rock music was itself defined as hidden, its form reflecting the standing attitude toward artistic content in general, and hence necessarily an underground activity: it was, the reporter says, 'a subterranean world of illicit clubs and black market tapes, subject to police raids and regular condemnations in the official press'. To legitimize rock is therefore to rob it of its form and hence of its meaning: an officially condoned rock is precisely rock that the state has conquered, so that poor Boris Grebenshchikov is damned by his acceptance to fear he will lose his edge by virtue of official acceptance, as did his friend Andrei Makhareivich, the leader of a group called Time Machine. 'Nobody can believe that the system has changed', Boris complained. 'They think we must have changed'. The only way to remain artistically honest is to continue to conceal, or at least for one's audience to continue to believe the bland lyrics cover dark messages intended specifically for them, much as the youth of twenty years ago believed *Sergeant Pepper's Lonely Hearts Club Band* transmitted a code underneath the resented approbation of parents, and that the Beatles remained subversive after all. So the indelible structures of what I have elsewhere called deep interpretation — interpretation which asks what is really being said in what in fact is said

— was carried forward, and remained as a precondition of artistic significance, into the era of *glasnost.*

Deep readers will have noticed, a paragraph back, a distorted echo of a famous phrase of Wittgenstein's: The human body is the best picture we have of the human soul. His point, infinitely contestable as everything he wrote is, is that we can have no picture of the human mind save as embodied, and so in speaking of it we are ultimately speaking of the bodily gestures and expressions which give mental states their form and mental language its criteria. I want to say something parallel, that the artwork of a state embodies the state, or that the state is embodied in the set of artworks it enfranchises, so that writing is never not the inscription of the political order in which it is done, and that all art is political in consequence, even if politics should not be its immediate content. Political art, that is, is a species of art that is political in the way I am suggesting, so that even the least political of writing celebrates, in the structure through which its readers address it, the order of politics in which those readers themselves have their form, and their literary imagination embodies the same politics as the works to which they respond. And of course that raises the problems alluded to in the remark about translation: for works that embody distinct political orders are in some deep way as incommensurable as those political orders themselves are.

This is so even when art is most free, as in our own political order, though one of the points I want to make is that the only freedom we are likely to accord is the maximal degree of freedom. Consider the defenses advanced on behalf of *Ulysses* or *Lady Chatterley's Lover.* The argument was not that the words and phrases that occurred in these works and which raised the question of censorship did not, in themselves and as such, merit censorship: they really were scatological or offensive; the authors would not have used them if they were not; but since they occurred integrally in what experts agreed were works of art — works in fact of high literary art — they could be allowed — as if, understood as forming parts of artistic wholes, the words or phrases could not affect the reader, who was, by this fact alone, immunized against what would have been their toxin if written or uttered in a non-artistic context. It was as if its being art neutralized content much as being officially acceptable in another part of the world neutralizes art. And it is this that enables art to be free. It is true that there remains the danger that those insensitive to the concept of art might search out the books for the thrill of seeing dirty words in print — as we all did, when young and nasty, with our parents' dictionaries. But the concept of art interposes between life and literature

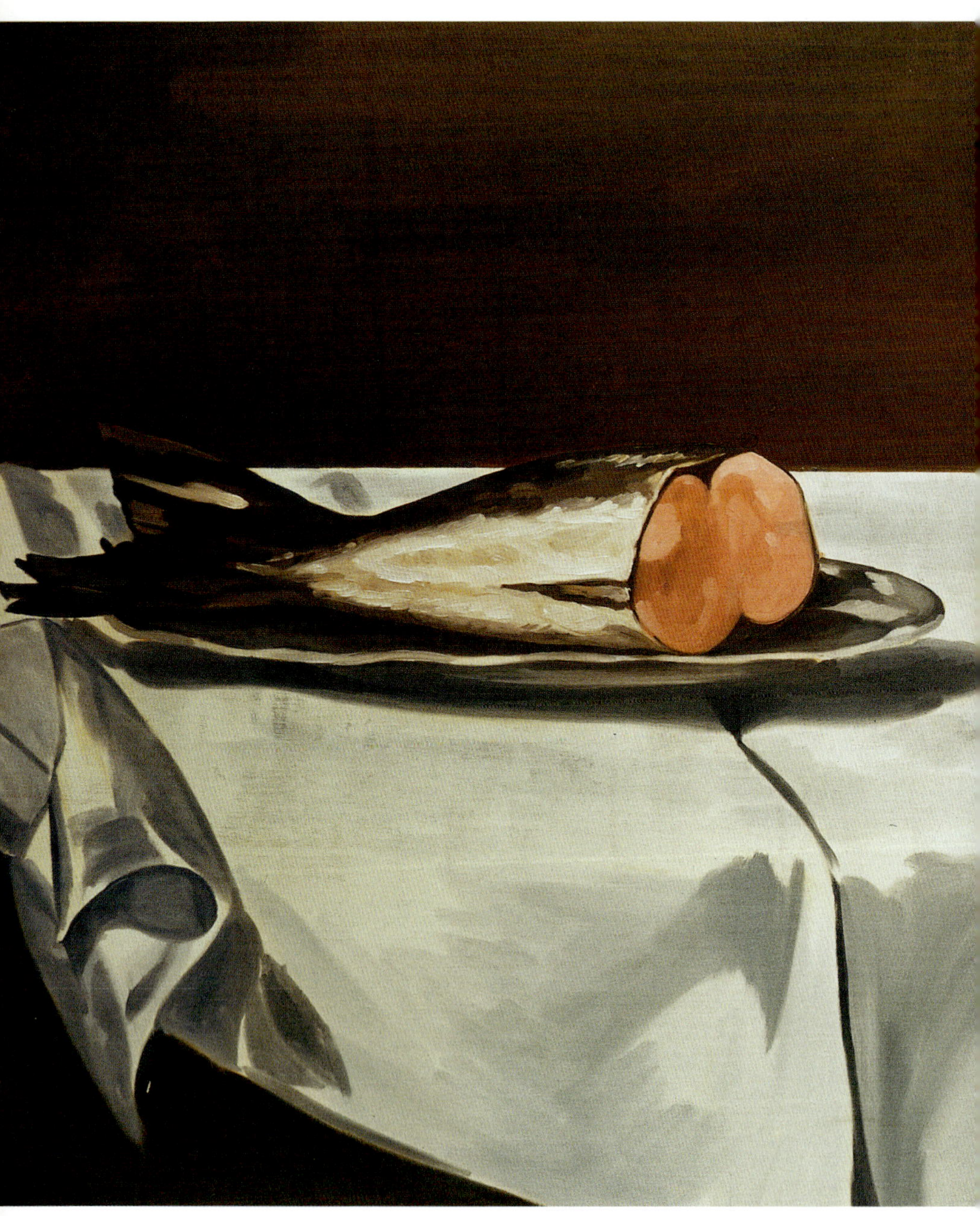

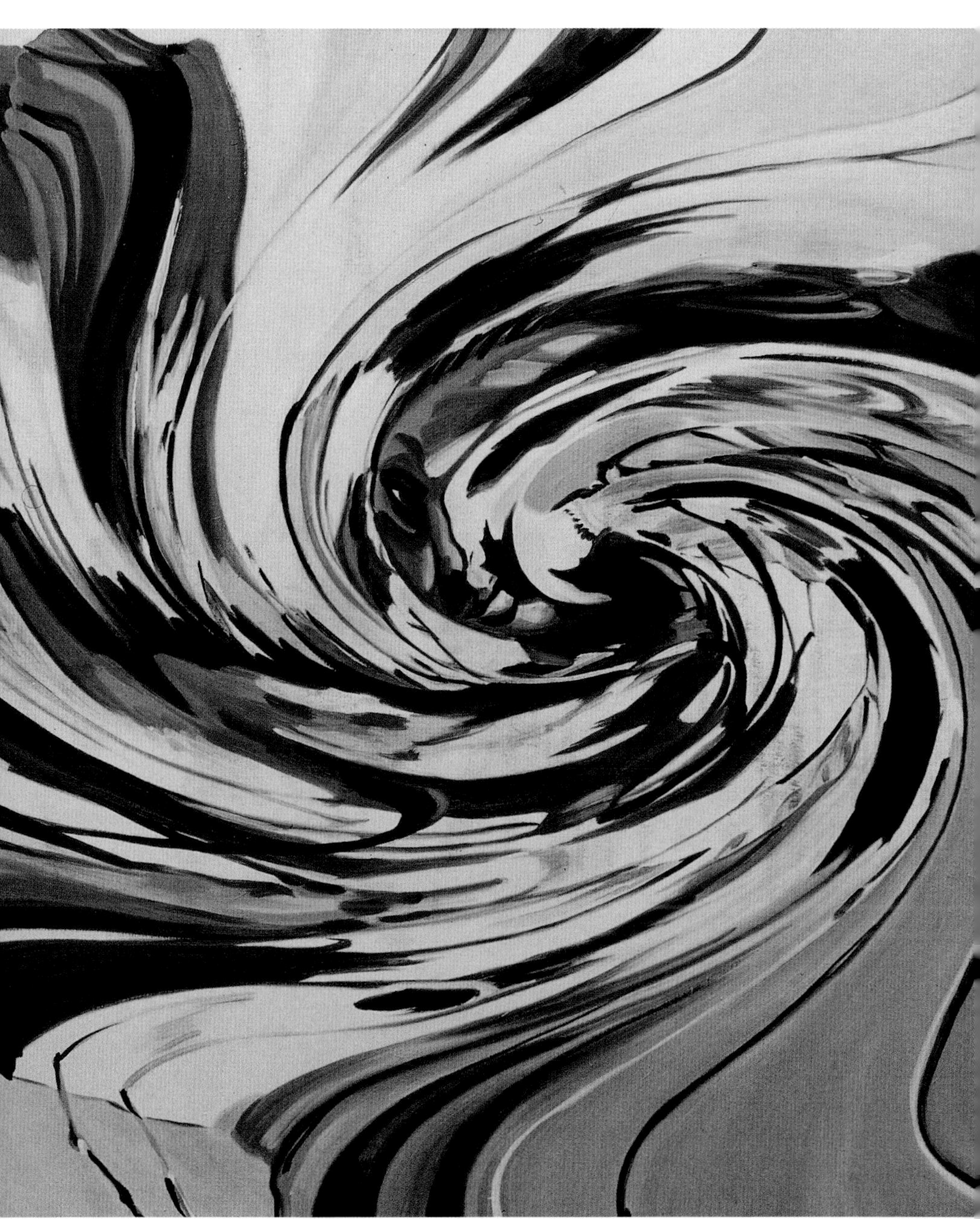

David Salle *Still Life with Vortex* (diptych), 2006. Oil on canvas, 92 x 200 cm

a very tough membrane, which ensures the incapacity of the artist to inflict moral harm so long as it is recognized that what he is doing is art. And this leads to the nightmare of impotency that accounts in some measure for the relief our writers felt in the political world where art was acknowledged as dangerous. What more tormenting dream could a playwright have than imagining putting the deepest and most unsettling challenges to the values of an audience, only to receive a standing ovation from those he intended to portray as hypocrites, villains, Tartuffes, Iagos, corrupters, transgressors, rogues, and swine? It would be as though Hamlet, meaning to trap the conscience of the King in the mirror of art, were instead to please the King, who likes the way he is shown and tips a wink of complicity to his wayward stepson, for whom there is now an inkling after all of hope. But it is even worse here, for the question of like or not like does not arise, it being art. Nietzsche once wrote as an aphorism of desperation: 'I listened for an echo and heard only applause'. So those writers excited by the vision of art as dangerous when abroad have failed to recognize how dangerous art must be perceived to be at home if our way of dealing with it is to ensure, by conceptual repression, that it cannot but be innocuous if art. That is why the freedom in question is total. If there were degrees and distinctions, we would be treating it as other than art. You can say whatever you like, since it has no real meaning, providing it is art. So it is not really freedom either.

I have never fully understood the thesis that art is dangerous, and particularly that it is politically dangerous, but certainly it is a very ancient thesis and is part of what I have elsewhere designated the philosophical disenfranchisement of art — for the first philosophical responses to art were in effect theories, the political purpose of which was to extrude art, somehow, from the possibility of efficacy, and lodge it, metaphysically or institutionally, where it could do us no harm. Nietzsche held a theory of the birth of tragedy that could go some distance in accounting for this fear and hence this need. His thought was that ancient tragedy evolved out of Dionysian rites, which were perceived as especially dangerous to the moral order because participation in them consisted of orgiastic frenzy, the dissolution of restraints of every sort, the creation of hallucination so extreme that, as represented in *The Bacchae*, a mother could participate in the dismemberment and cannibalization of her own son. In an odd way, art was a way of taming these barbaric practices, putting them at a kind of distance so that instead of participants there was an audience, segregated by the conventions of theatricality from a spectacle that reenact-

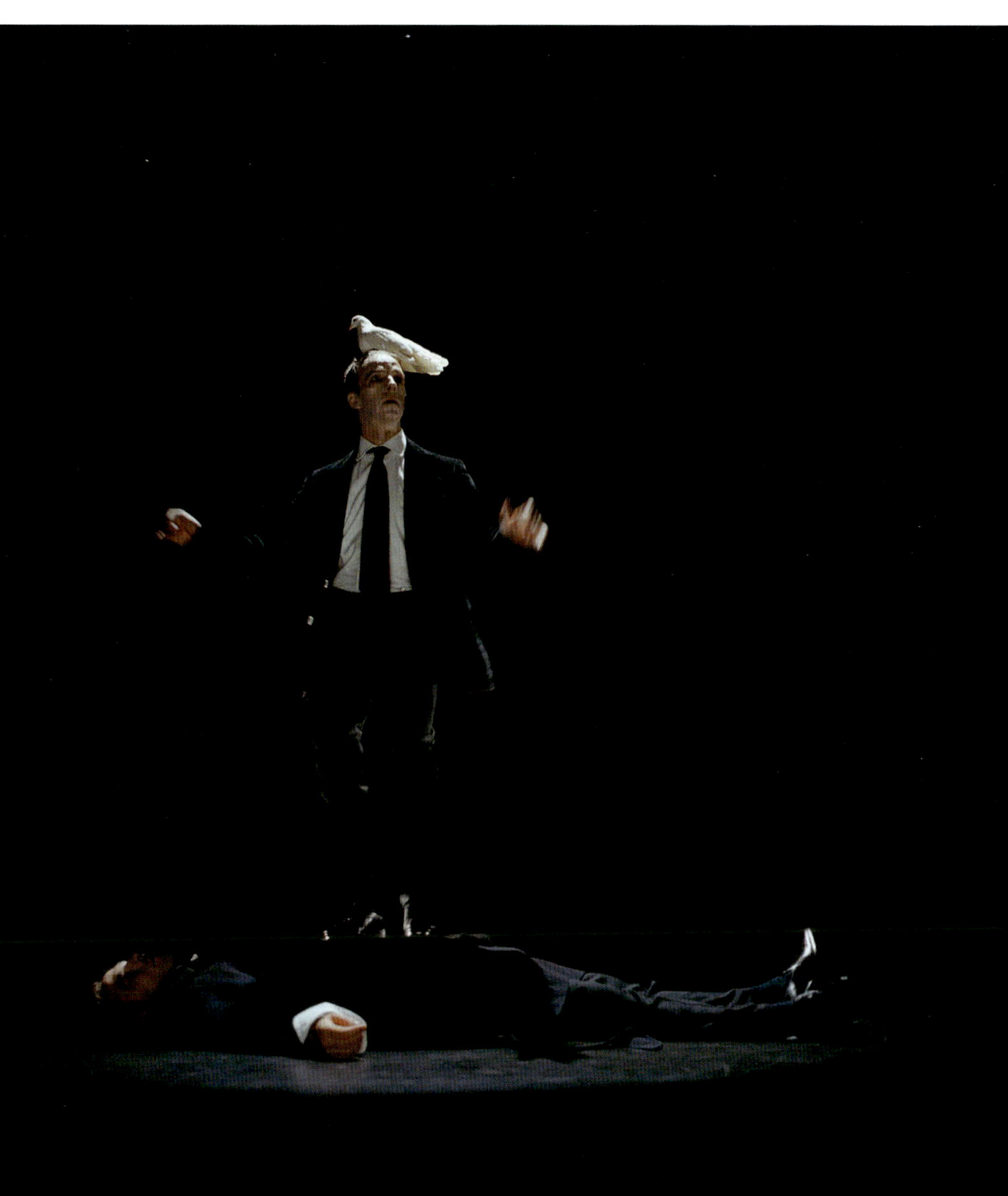

Sam Taylor-Wood *Ascension*, 2003. 35 mm film, 4' 15"

ed, in some symbolic way, practices the smoking memory of which remained in the Greek unconscious as a threat to order, value, stability. Perhaps the tacit recognition of suppressed danger energized the spectacle, and the work of art was like Pandora's box, concealing in itself the dark, destructive energies the threat of whose release meant chaos. But, once the conventions were in place, they could then be used as a kind of transparent shield by artists or poets who then could say or do whatever they wished under the protection of the institution, something like the fool of the medieval court, who had an effect on his viewers because he was a poet, without, for exactly that reason, being exposed to any adverse effect on himself. I have in mind especially the Old Comedy (470–300 BC), the wounding exaggerations of which, at the hands of Aristophanes, knew no limit and respected no person. Behind the shield of poetry, Aristophanes moralized, agitated, wounded, maligned, slandered, lied, lobbied, and pleaded on behalf of values that had not a chance any longer, in the name of an order that had long vanished, but in language that was magnificent and moving — and dangerous for that reason. He was not an intellectual, however, and as Plato undertook to show, no artist really was, none of them knowing anything and hence none of them to be trusted in circumstances, like politics, where knowledge was essential. And bit by bit Plato, himself wounded through the treatment by Aristophanes of Socrates in *The Clouds*, dismantled the conventions of the theater and reconstituted them as a metaphysics of art which guaranteed that art could have no effect whatever, making it impossible for it any longer to be dangerous. And in the process of giving a systematic definition of art, Plato defined philosophy — which may in fact before then have been the somewhat untrammeled and dissystematic enterprise Aristophanes depicted it as in *The Clouds*.

Consider, for example, just the theory that art is imitation. It has been insufficiently appreciated how political the theory is, for it has the effect, if credited, of paralyzing the artist: if audiences appreciate that art is illusion, sufficiently like reality to be mistaken for it but logically situated outside reality, so that it could have neither the causes nor the effects of reality itself — an idle epiphenomenon — then art is metaphysically ephemeralized. It can tell us nothing we do not already know, and the artist is reduced to a mere simulator, with knowledge of nothing save how to imitate. So he cannot have the authority of someone who works in reality — like a carpenter, or a navigator or a doctor — or who understands how to know reality, like the philosopher, rather than, as a mirror, someone who knows only how to register the appearances. Mimesis was, then, less a theory of art than a philosophical aggression against art (one which, by the way, makes Aristophanes impossible), vaporizing art by situating it in a plane where it can do no harm because of how dangerous it was when not in that plane and interacting effectively with political reality. How deeply this theory of ephemerality has been internalized by artists themselves is testified to by Auden's thought that 'poetry makes nothing happen'. And yet Auden felt, in the same poem, that there is compensation for ineffectuality, namely, a kind of immortality because of Time's worship of language. Time worships language 'and forgives everyone by whom it lives'. And so it allows us to remember Aristophanes for what one authority calls 'the true glories' of his art: his praise of country life in *The Peace*, the serenade in the *Ecclesiazusae*, the maiden song from *Lysistrata*, the chant of the Initiated in *The Frogs.* In brief, ephemeralization is compensated for by aestheticization, and Aristophanes is redeemed for art by being reduced to an anthology of literary gems.

We no longer accept the mimetic theory, which has to be in any case distorted if it is to capture works of art much more complex than those that satisfy themselves by mere resemblance — and we begin to see the first serious effort to transform it from an aggression to an analysis in the *Poetics* — but it does not greatly matter, politically, since in aestheticization we have the supreme disenfranchisement, for the work of art is reduced by its means to something that exists for gratification. There exists a contrast, almost canonical, between the 'aesthetic point of view' and 'the practical point of view', the latter being the perspective under which the question of what to do arises, where the consideration of what difference or effect something has comes into play, and where we are engaged with reality. And this contrast is enshrined in one of the masterpieces of disenfranchising philosophy, Kant's *Critique of Judgment*, where in the first instance art is something we judge and where the judgment is aesthetic, that is, with reference finally to taste. It is there that Kant defines beauty in terms of having no purpose though appearing to be purposive — 'Beauty is the form of the purposiveness of an object, so far as this is perceived in it without any representation of a purpose'. Kant's theory of art is somewhat more complex, but beauty is an essential part of it. In the first instance, an artwork is beautiful only on condition that it seems like nature, and hence beautiful in the way in which nature is (in a sense this is a disguised form of the theory of mimesis, for the artist seeks to imitate nature by seeming free from all artifice). And in the second instance, art deserves to be called beautiful on the basis of taste, hence aesthetic judgment. So in the end, Kant's theory of art is this:

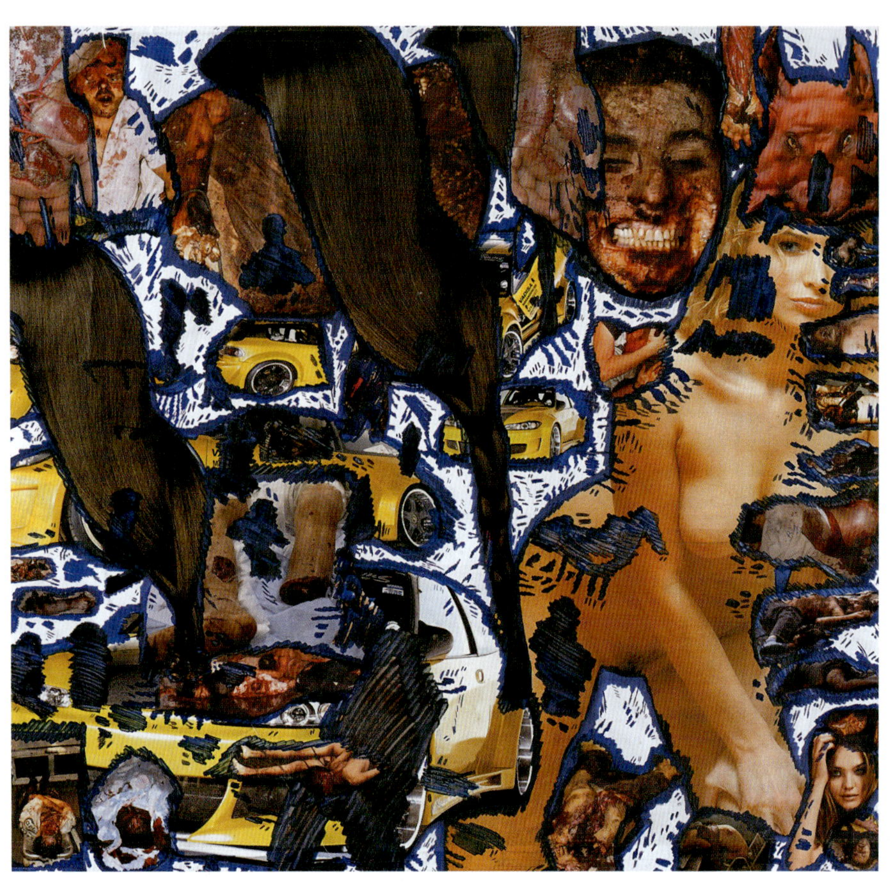

Thomas Hirschhorn *Dessin Jaloux (Civic)*, 2006. Paper, plastic film, adhesive tape, pen and felt-tip pen, 84 x 89 cm

Artworks please without subserving any interest (hence he opposes a theory of art as having any use). They please 'without concepts' — or they awaken the sense that there is a concept without any specific concept being implied, so they as it were awaken thought without allowing thought any substance, which restates in effect his 'purposiveness without any specific purpose' theme; and that aesthetic judgment is essentially universal and so outside politics just because politics is the sphere of conflict, and especially of conflicting interests. An imitation appears to show something with a purpose, but can have no purpose of its own, since it fails if we don't know the original and is useless if we do. So let the artist be free since it does not matter what he does. We have built a logical pedestal which in fact is an ingenious form of prison, and I have often remarked on the resemblance between the use of the pedestal here and in the extrusion of women from the practical affairs of life: Plato, too, was prepared to honor the artists by exile, until he hit upon the theories that were a better form of exile, kicking art upstairs.

Aesthetics was invented as a discipline in the eighteenth century, a period when nature was sufficiently under human domination that one could address it from without, see it as an object less of threat than for pleasure, as in landscape gardening, which, according to Kant, 'gives only the appearance of utility and availability for other purposes than the mere play of the imagination in the contemplation of its forms'. In brief, nature and art seemed together the object of a single kind of disinterested judgment, abstracted from all questions of use and practice. And I think it not coincidental that the age of aesthetics, as we may call it, was coeval with the rise of the political values of the liberal state, with its great emphasis on the apparatus of natural rights and inalienable freedoms. In the sixteenth and seventeenth centuries, the history of English literature was pretty much the history of censorship. In large measure, I believe, literature seemed to open up ways of saying things that could not be said directly, which meant already that literature was a mechanism of repression, standing to the writer's true beliefs and attitudes in something like the relationship in which Freud supposes the manifest content of a dream stands to the latent pathogens of the repressed unconscious. What Freud explicitly calls 'the censor' allows the latent thought to be expressed (or 'discharged'), but in highly disguised forms, so much so that it is said to demand immense hermeneutical skill on the part of the therapist to find out what is really meant. The extraordinary political contribution of the aesthetic attitude in the eighteenth century was to render obsolete the mechanisms of indirection between writer and reader. Remember, we are

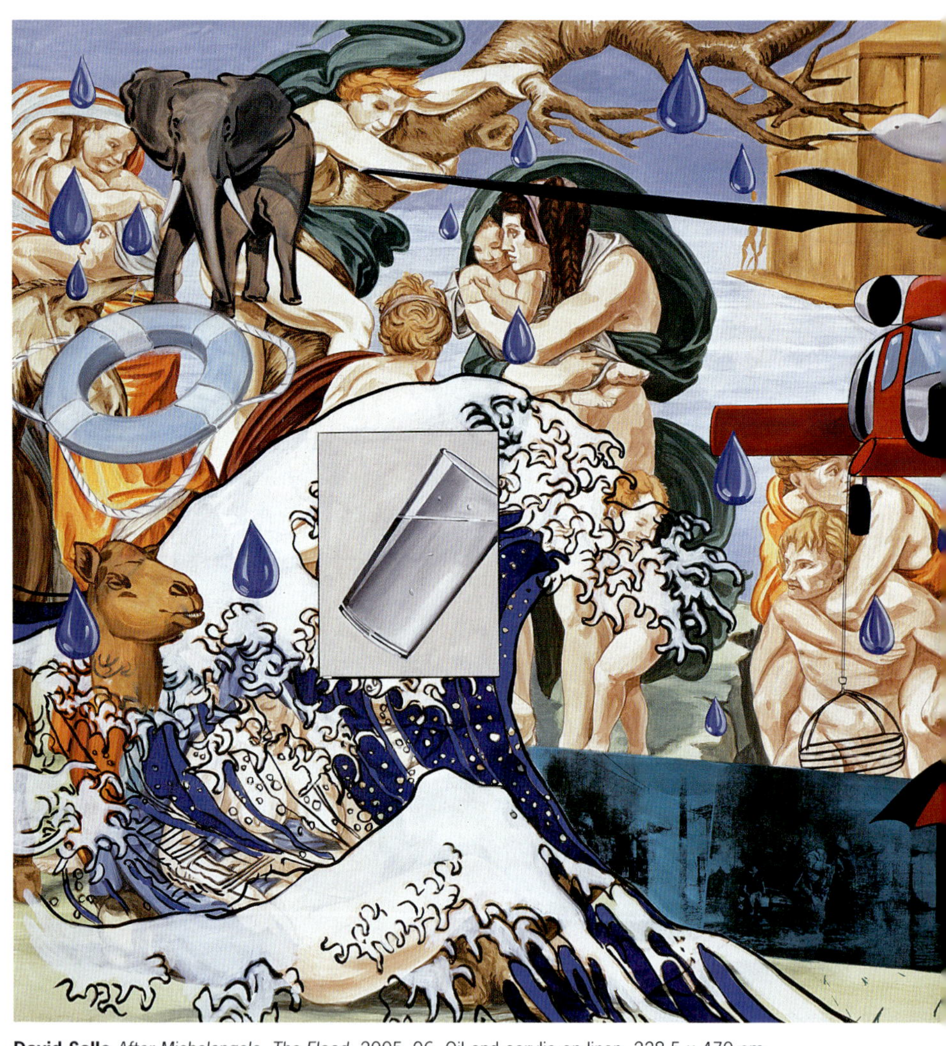

David Salle *After Michelangelo, The Flood*, 2005–06. Oil and acrylic on linen, 228.5 x 470 cm

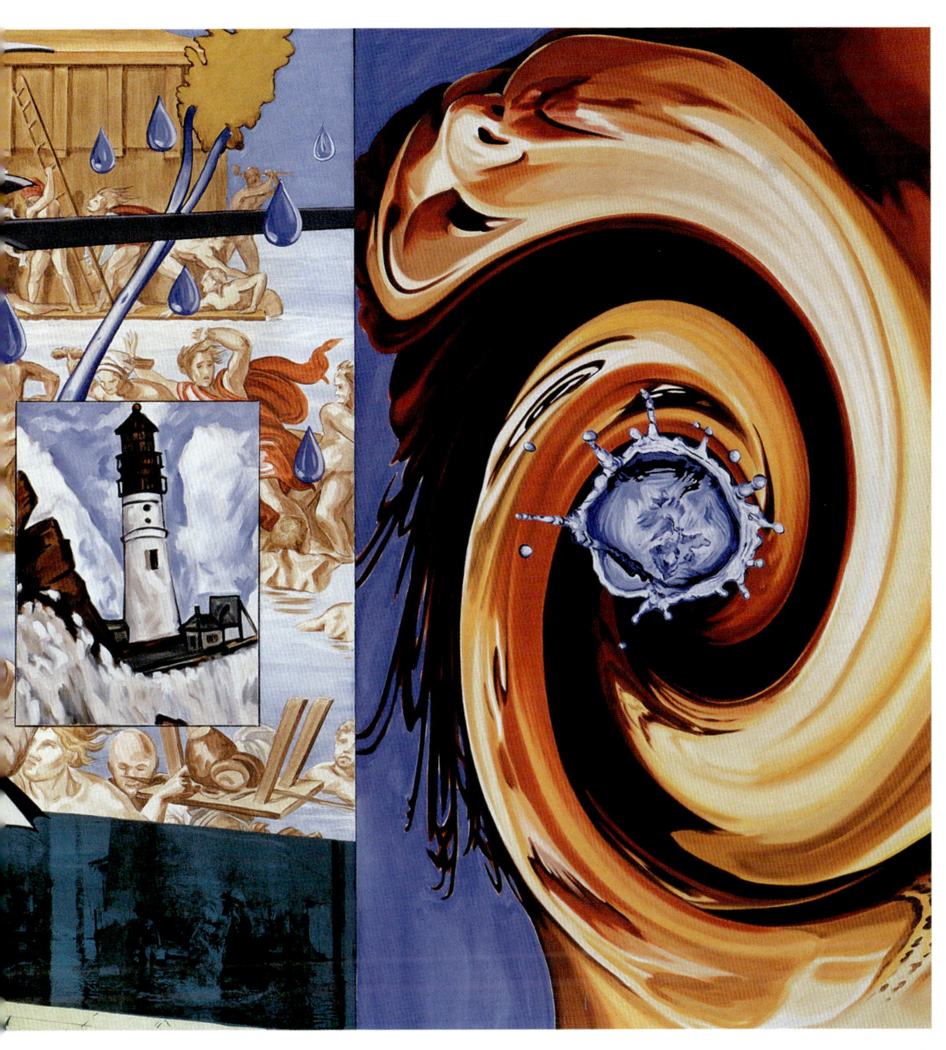

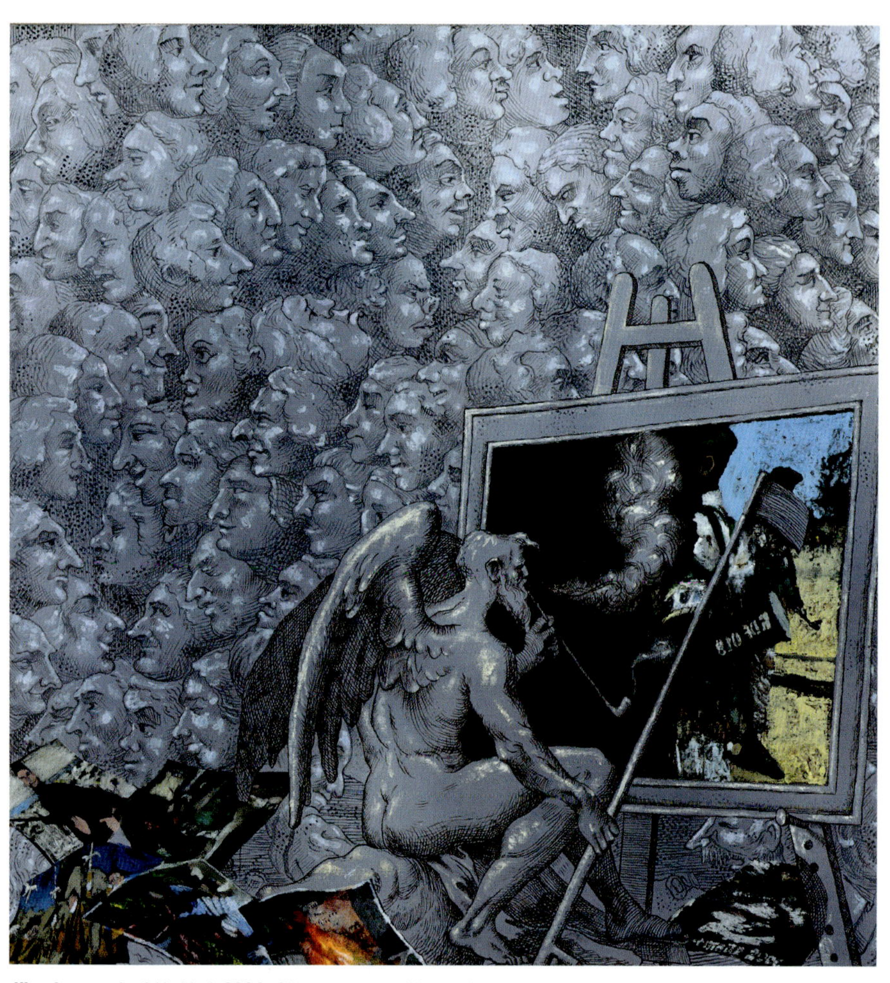

Jörg Immendorf *Untitled*, 2006. Oil on canvas, 160 x 150 cm

discussing literature, not prose as such. There was no press censorship in England after 1695. Milton's *Areopagitica* had its effect only after the Revolution, and thus it was possible to tell the news (except in wartime) and express editorial opinion freely, and so there was no need to have recourse to literary concealment. In literature, too, there was freedom to say anything, as directly as one wished (of course, there was drama censorship in England until very nearly the present, and film censorship in America), without suffering any of the consequences to which one would be liable were one to have said the same thing without the immunities the concept of art introduces. These in effect protect everybody in a way that would be impossible if the same message was transmitted outside the category of the artwork.

Treating a text as an aesthetic object, viewing it through the protective lenses of the new concept of art, audiences were able to contemplate the most incendiary gestures and declarations across an irreducible distance — 'aesthetic distance' it got to be called in a celebrated essay by Edward Bullough — without any effect at all. It allowed the artist perfect freedom, but at the cost of total and logically guaranteed harmlessness. And surely the transformations of poetic style from the seventeenth to the eighteenth century and beyond in English writing have to be explained as due to the acceptance of the new aesthetic point of view. The richly involuted structures of metaphysical poetry have to be understood as correlative with the heavy penalties attached to making a religious or political misstep: Donne's parents were Catholics, in a time when being a Catholic in England was fraught with danger. His mother was descended from Sir Thomas More, who met a martyr's death; his father wrote epigrams. It is as though the densely mazed architectures of such writing, in which reading was an exercise in decoding, were a perfect adaptation under the most severe constraints of artistic, let alone personal, survival.

(I would like at this point to insert a kind of digression. Modern criticism, I think it will be conceded, begins with Eliot, whose paradigms were such writers as Donne and Crashaw, for whom interpretation was required even in their own day as a condition for determining what was being said by means of what in fact was said, and hence *deep* interpretation was the standard way of reading. But criticism then began to assume the form of other systems of deep interpretation — psychoanalysis and Marxism — and under this pressure, *all* texts became concealments and deconstruction an inevitability. This gives the critic a great power, virtually the power of the priest, since only he or she knows what truly is being transmitted, and so constitutes the true reader. The rest of us either have

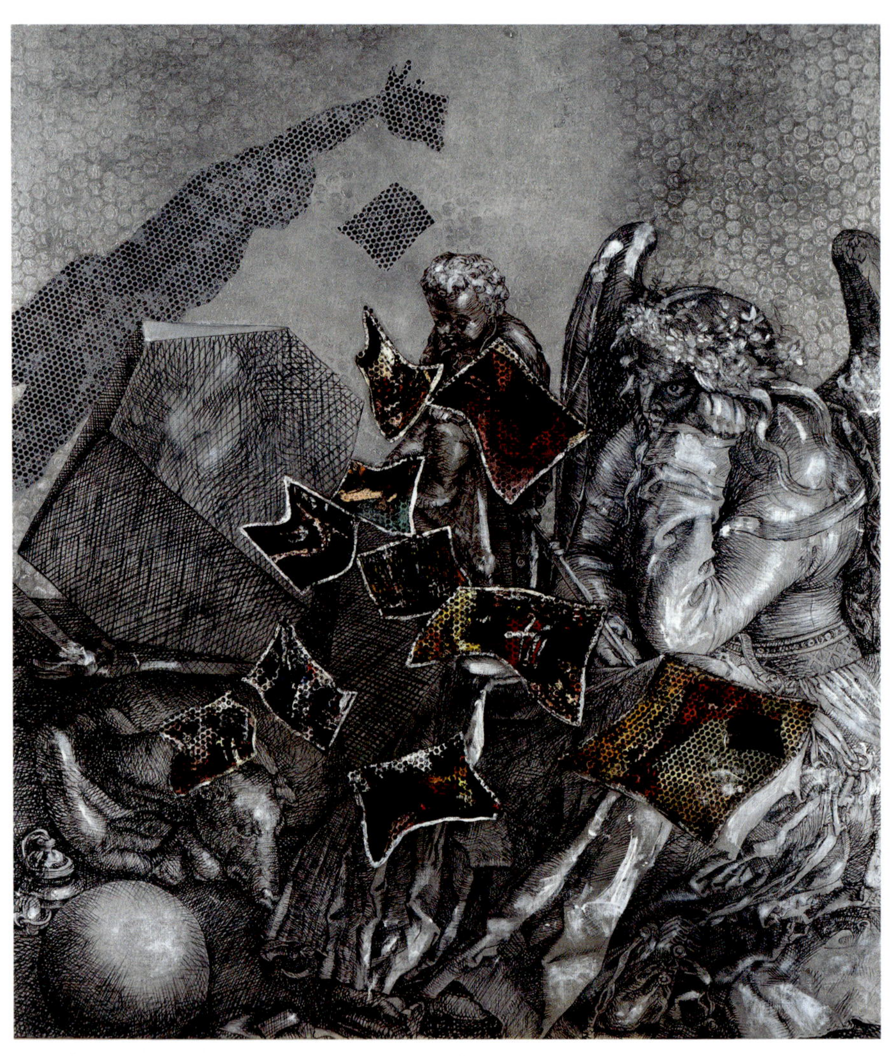

Jörg Immendorf *Untitled*, 2006. Oil on canvas, 160 x 150 cm

to be taught to read or take the critic as the authority. This has had two immediate corollaries. In the first instance, there developed in response a style of writing made to order for the critic, who came to serve the role of the censor in political systems which drive the writer to acts of increasingly complex concealment, where every letter is in effect the purloined letter. And of course the other corollary was the inevitable impact on critical writing itself, which becomes increasingly obscure, to the point that only other critics can read it, and their interpretations are uncertain and obscure, and set forth in any case in texts that in turn require criticism — to the point where criticism exemplifies the literary ideal and a critic like Geoffrey Hartman can claim that the critic is the true artist of our time — or that literature itself is justified to the degree that it makes literary criticism possible.)

When the new schedules of rights and freedoms emerged as politically urgent, forming the political foundation of the great enabling documents in the history of human rights, making persecution for beliefs and feelings a violation of human dignity, aesthetics was ready to hand to ensure that what artists said would have no adverse political effect. Increasingly, direct utterance, with a collateral mistrust of ornamentation and allusion, followed as a matter of course. By the time of Wordsworth, poets could even use the vernacular speech of plain men and women. To be sure, it took some time before the artistic use of coarse speech was essayed, but such was the genius of philosophical aesthetics that the salty locutions of barracks and locker rooms could find their way innocuously onto the printed page.

In the eighteenth century, this would not have been tried. The counterpart of taste as an aesthetic sense — a sense very like what in that period they designated as a moral sense — was taste as an *artistic* constraint. 'Taste', Kant wrote, 'like the judgment in general, is the discipline (or training) of genius; it clips its wings, it makes it cultured and polished; but at the same time it gives guidance as to where and how far it may extend itself if it is to remain purposive. And while it brings clearness and order into the multitude of thoughts, it makes the ideas susceptible of being permanently and, at the same time, universally assented to, and capable of being followed by others, and of an ever progressive culture.' So coarse speech would have been excluded on grounds of taste — but once the artifice imposed by the imperatives of Aesopism abated, and writers could use increasingly direct language and syntax, the concept of aesthetic distance, at first not especially required in the name of artistic freedom, came to serve a function much like the bell the leper was required to ring, opening up a sanitary path through society. As long as it was accepted as *art*, no one was in danger of contagion.

The limits are naturally always being tested. Recently, a group of Jewish vigilantes prevented the Kammerspiel Theater in Frankfurt from putting on what was an evidently explicit anti-Semitic play by Rainer Werner Fassbinder. It is characteristic that people would be more shocked by the Jews than by Fassbinder: a high school teacher in the audience was reported by *The New York Times* as having said that she would be unable to explain all this to her students, since 'I have always told them that art was one thing that could never be touched or prevented'. What I am seeking to explain is how the high school teacher ever could have acquired that view. The case justifies a moment of serious reflection.

Kant made a remarkable observation in connection with the concept of beautiful art; namely, that it was able to treat, as beautiful, things that in reality are ugly or displeasing. It was as though its being art meant that it could not be ugly, unless it failed on grounds that have nothing to do with subject matter: 'The furies, diseases, the devastations of war even when regarded as calamitous may be described as very beautiful, as they are represented in a picture'. Kant meant, I think, that something can be a beautiful representation of an ugly thing, the aesthetics of the subject not penetrating the representation itself. Think of how beautiful Rembrandt's depictions of quite ugly and unpleasing things can be. But Kant, with his marvelous genius for distinctions, made an exception:

'There is only one kind of ugliness which cannot be represented in accordance with nature without destroying all aesthetic satisfaction, and consequently artificial beauty — that which excites *disgust*. For in this singular sensation, which rests on mere imagination, the object is represented as if it were obtruding itself for our enjoyment, while we strive against it with all our might. And the artistic representation of the object is no longer distinguished from the nature of the object itself in our sensation, and thus it is impossible that it can be regarded as beautiful.'

It would be interesting to have an example of what Kant meant, though he interestingly went on to show how sculpture tended to represent things ugly in themselves via symbols and allegories, and hence through art, where the senses alone would not suffice for appreciation, since they were symbolic and required interpretation — as if, for these, the mere fact of aesthetic distance would not suffice and the mechanisms of disguise and concealment which the aesthetic attitude otherwise made obsolete were required. But Fassbinder appears to have been flat-out anti-Semitic in this play, and it is useful to consider this in the light of Kant's position on disgust.

There was a time when, under law, the quotation of obscenity was itself obscene, so that for a certain class of utterances, the distinction between what logicians term 'use' and 'mention' is dissolved. That you cannot mention certain words without being perceived as using them is in some measure testified to by the fact that the Meese Report on pornography was one of the hottest publications on the market (there was a celebrated lingerie catalogue from Bloomingdale's that fell into the same category). In an age, such as ours, of what is termed image appropriation, where painters as it were quote images without being thought any the less original as artists for doing so, the appropriation of pornographic images is perceived as pornographic in its own right. Feminists, in my view rightly, object to the paintings of David Salle for their constant depiction of women in sexually humiliating positions, and perhaps there is an even greater moral stigma that attaches to the appropriation rather than the immediate use of pornography in the manner of David Salle, just because in the latter instance it is being used to arouse males, while in the former case it is being used to outrage and provoke females, so that feminists rightly again sense a degree of overt hostility in the paintings that is a matter of abstract speculation in the originals: the pornographer may be engaged in an entirely different kind of act.

The Jewish protesters in Frankfurt were insisting that the theatrical mimesis of anti-Semitism is in itself already anti-Semitic — that with this discourse, imitation and reality are one. So after two centuries of aestheticism, there are still expressions — racist, sexist, and doubtless others — that act as solvents against the prophylactic shield of art. The teacher was insisting that the concept of art is strong enough to withstand even the idiom of bigotry. The Jews were insisting, with Plato, that something can be art and dangerous, even when mimetic (and here the mimetic theory fails of its purpose); that certain words are hateful even in the mouths of those who do not necessarily mean them, or only pretend that they are being said. It was almost certainly with this in mind that Plato as the architect of an ideal state prohibited young people from imitating certain characters. Whatever the effect on their character, it was true that they would be disgusting in saying or imitiating disgusting things.

The whole of Western philosophy, to judge by its systematic effort to disenfranchise art from any practical role in life, massively confirms this intuition. The art historian Edgar Wind writes as follows in *The Eloquence of Symbols*:

'It is quite customary today, in cases at law, to justify a work of questionable moral value by extolling its artistic merits as if the struggle between the two forces could be settled by a neat differentiation in terms! As if danger to morality ceased where the power of artistic creation begins! As if art merely idealized its object, without intensifying it! Only in an age in which the power of art is unrecognized, an age when the connection between moral and artistic forces has been lost, could one think and judge in that way. For such an age, Plato's demand is bound to read like a riddle.'

Fassbinder said, of *Trash, the City and Death*, his anti-Semitic play: 'It's only a theater piece', going on to insist that its 'possibly reproachable' methods are used, because otherwise 'you get something as dead as everything else in the German theater landscape [...] The play doesn't care about taking certain precautions and I think that's right. I have to be allowed to react to my own reality without regard to anything. If I'm not allowed to do that, then I'm not allowed to do anything at all'. But of course this is false. The Jews who formed a screen so that the audience could not see the actors in Frankfurt were not forbidding Fassbinder's films, just this play — 'reacting to *their* own reality'. Of course, that reality was complicated by the fact of its being Germany, by the fact that the director, Gunther Rühle, had said that the *Schonzeit*, literally the 'no hunting season', for Jews might perhaps be lifted. In New York, the play opened in a Lower East Side storefront theater on Rivington Street, where, according to an extremely negative review by Tom Disch, the director did everything he could to make the performance as revolting as possible — including having the actor who plays 'A, the Rich Jew' urinate into a plastic bucket that remained on the stage until the curtain fell. There were no vigilantes, perhaps because the reality of New York's Jews really can tolerate a lot. Anyway, no one much cared here.

I think Kant's analysis goes some distance toward explaining why art is dangerous. It is dangerous because its methods are open to the representation of dangerous things, but in such a way that it becomes as dangerous as they are. The representation of anti-Semitism is as dangerous as anti-Semitism itself, and possibly more so, because the artist uses his freedom to address the objects of his hatred at their most civilized, namely,

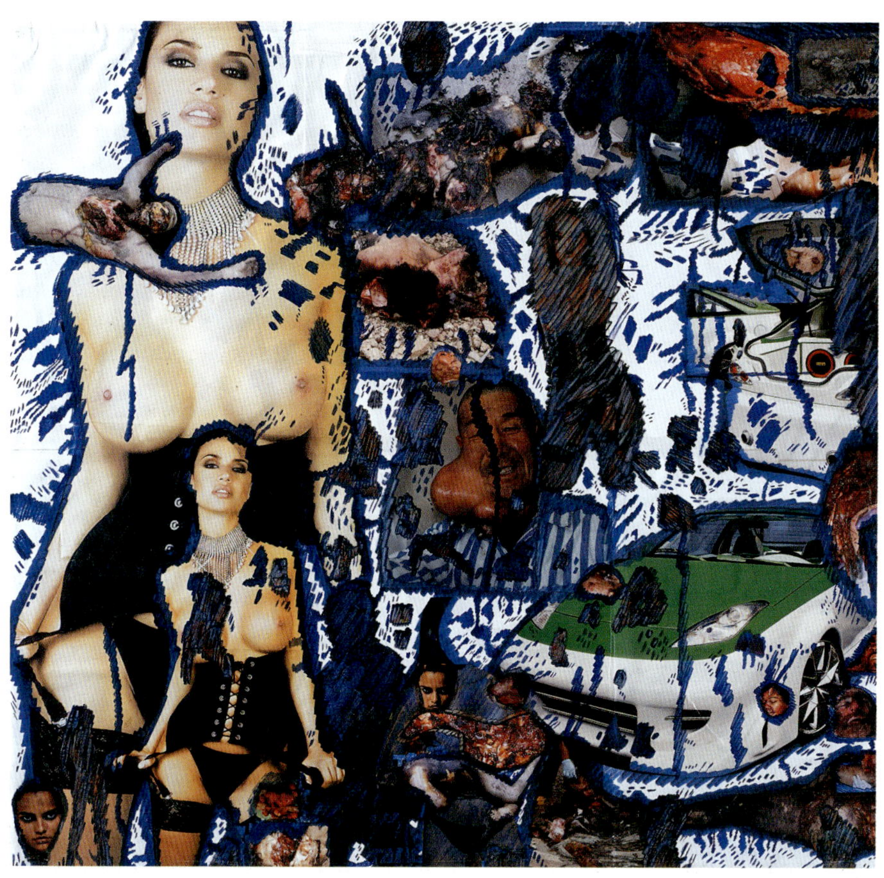

Thomas Hirschhorn *Dessin Jaloux (Crocodile)*, 2006. Paper, plastic film, adhesive tape, pen and felt-tip pen, 84 x 89 cm

as members of a theatrical audience — just as the appropriator of pornographic images attacks women at their most civilized, as members of an art world where the conventions of its being art are supposed to prevent them from striking back while they are being assaulted. This is the obverse of the contradiction Kant identifies in the depiction of the disgusting. We can see this contradiction in both the chief ways of responding to the danger of art. In one part of the world, art is dangerous because a seditious interpretation is possible, even of the most innocent sentence. Ideally, under such a system art should be eliminated in the interests of public safety, but the residual prestige of high culture has so far prevented such a final solution, leaving censorship as an uneasy compromise. In the other part of the world, writing, so long as it is perceived as art, is categorically excluded from the class of dangerous acts, but this because the very concept of art prevents the interpretation that would be natural if we were dealing with real discourse. The task of the writer under the first system is to circumvent the censor, but at the risk of losing his audience, which cannot find the thread. I expect it is this that makes abstract art seem so dangerous under the system of censorship — the censor keeps looking for the code. Or writing becomes, as it is under contemporary strategies of criticism, simply the occasion for canny interpretations, since readers can attribute to it any meaning they choose, on the assumption either that the author is being especially subtle or that things are revealed which he himself is not conscious of. Under the alternative system, the task of the writer is evidently constantly to test the concept, again at the risk of losing his audience, this time by transforming them into vigilantes whom he has the moral luxury of putting down as barbarians or philistines when they take a stand against what is after all ART. The two systems involve two distinct attitudes toward artists, and of artists toward themselves. In the one system, the artist, however conformist, is incipiently a rebel. In the other system, every rebel, however outrageous, is incipiently a conformist. In the one system, the political prison is a standing risk. In the other, a presidential ceremony with a Citation for Excellence is the standing promise.

It is unclear that writers or artists from either sphere are easily interchanged, all the less so if the imagination of the writer and the 'imagination' of the state are in the equilibrium of pre-established harmony that I proposed they are. From the one side, the freedom on the other must be intoxicating until it is appreciated how much that freedom costs. On the other side, the danger must be intoxicating until it is appreciated how innocuous the texts would be if there were freedom.

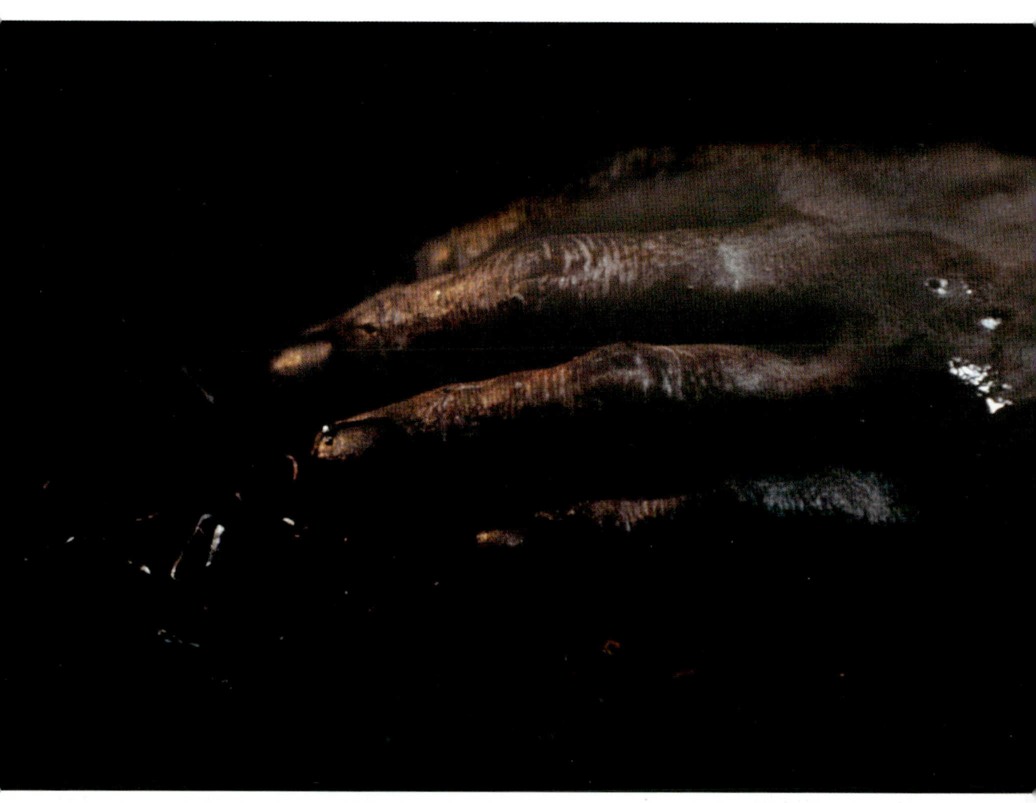

Cindy Sherman *Civil War*, 1991. Photographic print, 120 x 178 cm

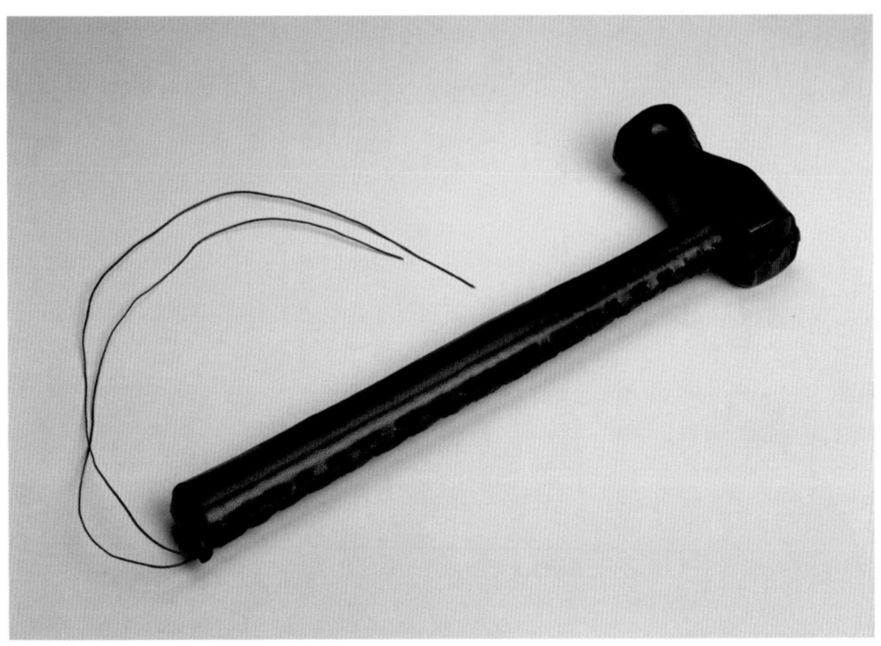

Monica Bonvicini *Leatherhammer 1*, 2004–06. Hammer lined with leather, 30 x 10 cm

Given the abysses which separate the two continents of artistic psychology, it is understandable that representatives from either side should communicate, as at the rather awful meeting of PEN, at the level of slogans. I shall always bear the memory of world-famous writers behaving like windbags at the most portentous level of meeting-hall oratory.

I suppose we should hope for a relaxation of the aesthetic attitude so that our artists really are exposed to real risks, even if it is important now and then to stop them. And on the other side, a relaxation of the forces that make for deviousness, so that not everything one writes is a real risk taken. But even a minor relaxation on either side means a convergence, or the beginning of one, politically, psychologically, morally. Art is internally enough connected with the rest of life that a change in it must mean a change in everything else. Given the value of social stability, there is a question of the political price of re-enfranchising art.

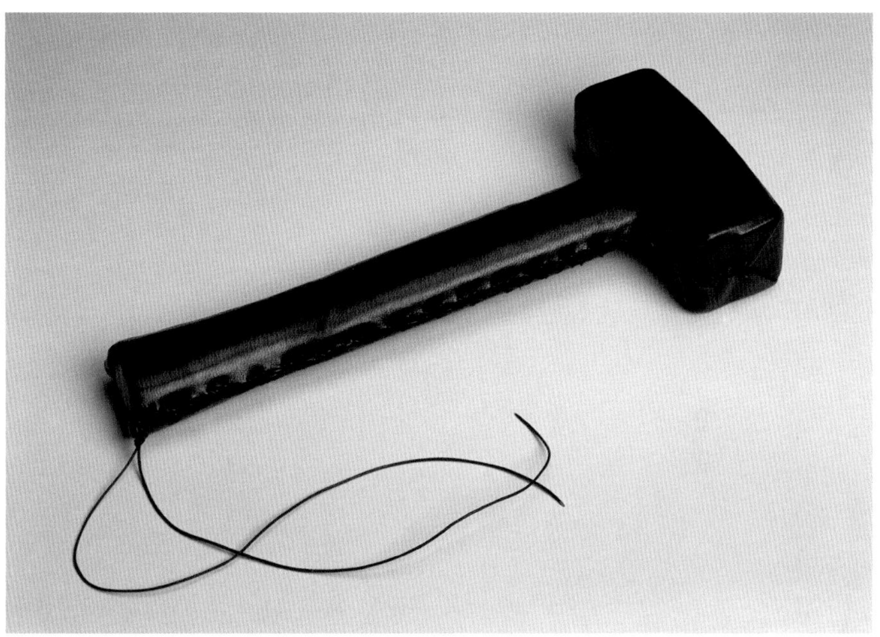

Monica Bonvicini *Leatherhammer 2,* 2004–06. Hammer lined with leather, 35 x 12 cm

My concerns, naturally, are with the philosophical reenfranchisement of art, inasmuch as the disenfranchisement itself is originally philosophical. Here it seems there are two tasks. The first is in a measure archaeological. One has to return to Plato, and to identify what it was, however he characterized it, that he perceived as dangerous in art. And this of course then leads to the difficult question of the correctness of his analysis and the explanation, finally, of where the danger (if there is one) *really* lies. There have been some wrong theories of representation, fascinating but erroneous nevertheless, which have precipitated iconoclastic movements in any number of cultures. These theories are fascinating and fateful in the moral history of art, but they do not explain the dangerousness of art because they are false. My own sense is that the power of art is the power in effect of rhetoric, which I sought to argue in the last pages of *The Transfiguration of the Commonplace*, and rhetoric, aimed at the modification of attitude and belief, can never be innocent and is always real because minds are. The problem with the Platonic theory of art is that it recognized the power but sought to respond to it by offering philosophical theories of art from which it follows that art could not possibly be dangerous because it is too metaphysically ephemeral. This is a form of denial familiar as a kind of psychoanalytic reflex.

Once the power is understood, the next task is a moral one, to remove the merely formal freedom the concept of art has acquired, through which artworks can represent anything in any way without effect 'because it is art'. This is an empty freedom, and we see it colliding with reality in racism and pornography. When Thomas Messer, director of the Guggenheim Museum, refused exhibition of a work by Hans Haacke, he did so on the ground that it was not art, which he clarified by saying that it was not universal, by definition excluding from art the possibility of politics, which is essentially conflictive. This was a double insult to Haacke, the status of whose work as art should be acknowledged. The art world rallied round Haacke, insisting that art should never be censored, the position being the mirror image of Messer's. My sense is that Haacke's work was dangerous only *because* it was art, and that it was intentionally aggressive, using the sanctity of art as a moral shield to infiltrate a politically important space. It was like guerrilla warfare, which uses the morality of the opponent as a defensive weapon. The guerrilla places his artillery, for example, in what is clearly marked as a hospital, and counts on his enemy's reluctance to bomb a hospital as a means of firing at the enemy's plane with impunity. And should the enemy in fact respond by bombing the hospital, the guerrilla can charge barbarism in the court of world opinion. Haacke used the fact that it was art to say things calculated to offend or hurt, and counted on the supposed sanctity of art as a way of securing himself against counterattack.

In truth, Haacke was able to advance his cause through the content of his art — it was a meticulously detailed study in real time of the real-estate dealing by a single company in marginal areas of the city — *and* through the effort to block it. He enjoyed the enviable position of being a revolutionary and a martyr, and so got a great deal more out of the encounter than he would have done had the piece merely been exhibited. This is one of the dangers of opposing art on grounds of content: one runs the risk of raising the artist's prices and turning him into a household word, as happened with Robert Mapplethorpe. So perhaps the most prudent course in dealing with dangerous art is to treat it as if it were after all innocuous, using the sanctity of art as a shield against its toxins, which has always been our tradition. And perhaps when this is at last recognized for what it is, a strategy for disarming art, the artist who means to be dangerous will join with the enemy in secularizing the concept. Both sides have something to gain and something to lose. The artist gains the possibility of direct political action, but has to recognize that this makes counteraction possible and acceptable. The rest of society loses what is perhaps the best weapon it has for dealing with dangerous art, namely, the theory that art in its very nature is innocuous. That theory is our way of acknowledging art's danger.

Arthur C. Danto, *Beyond the Brillo Box. The Visual Arts in Post-historical Perspective*, New York: Farrar, Straus & Giroux, 1992. Courtesy of the Author.

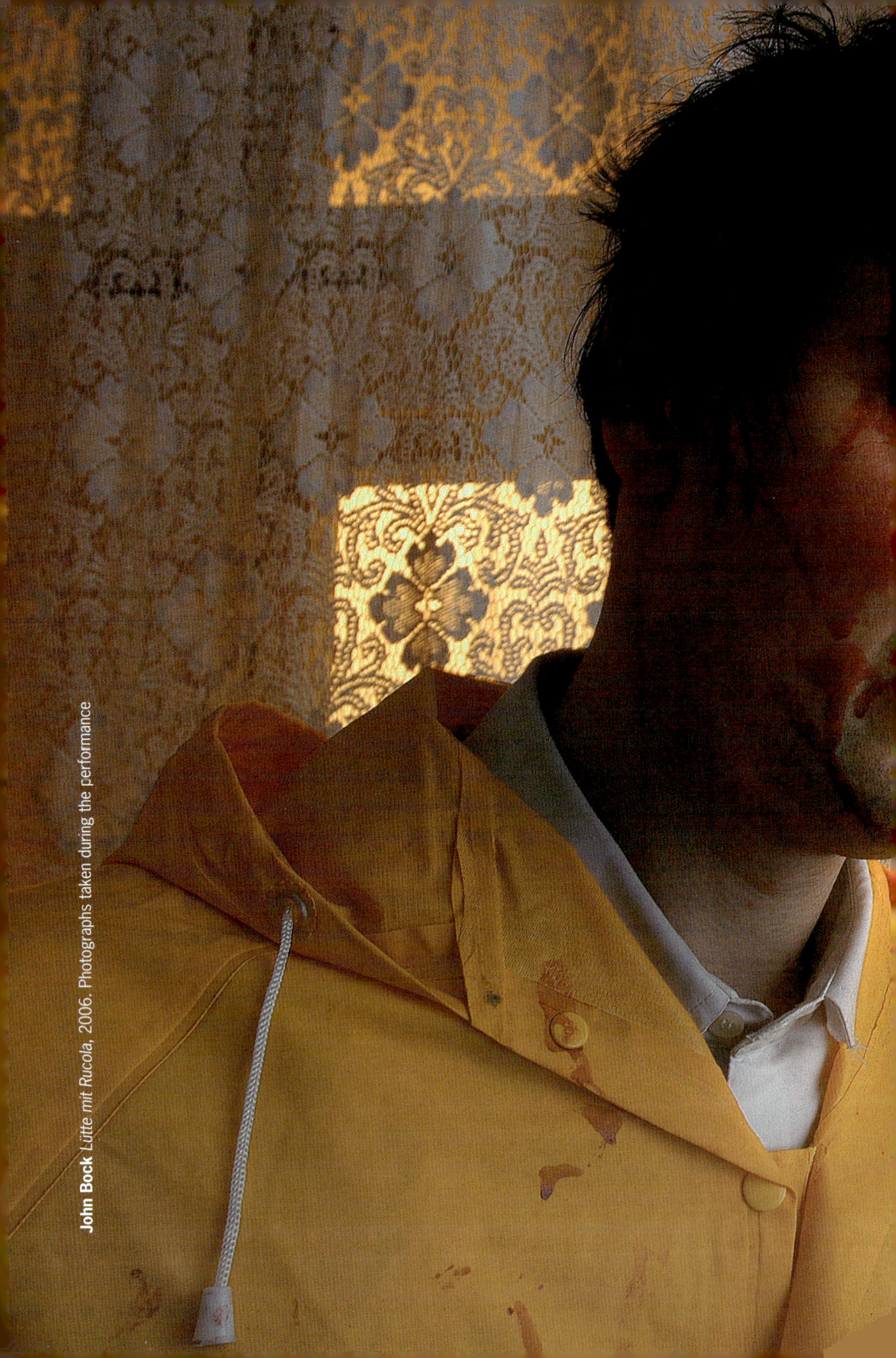

John Bock *Lütte mit Rucola*, 2006. Photographs taken during the performance

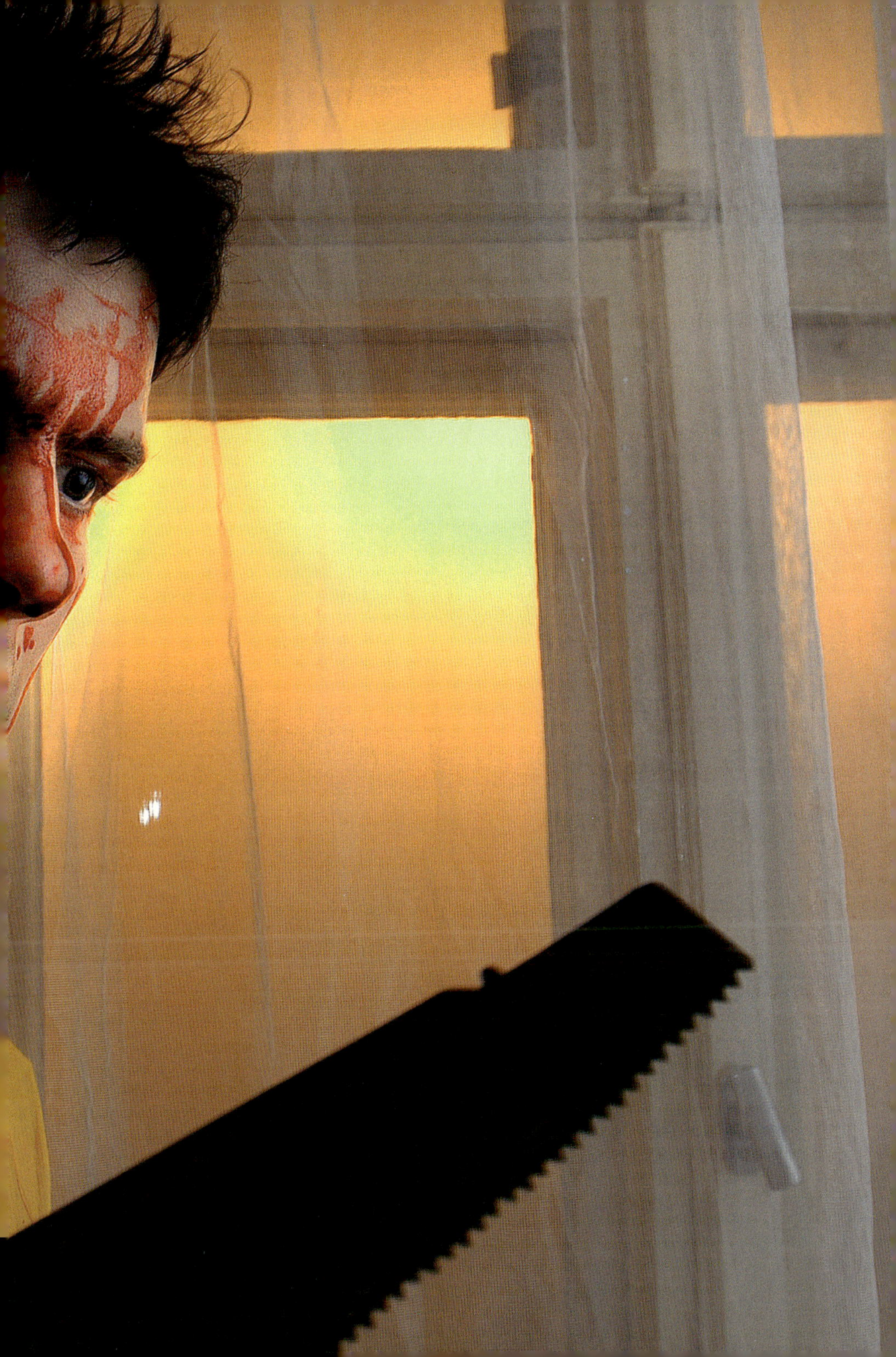

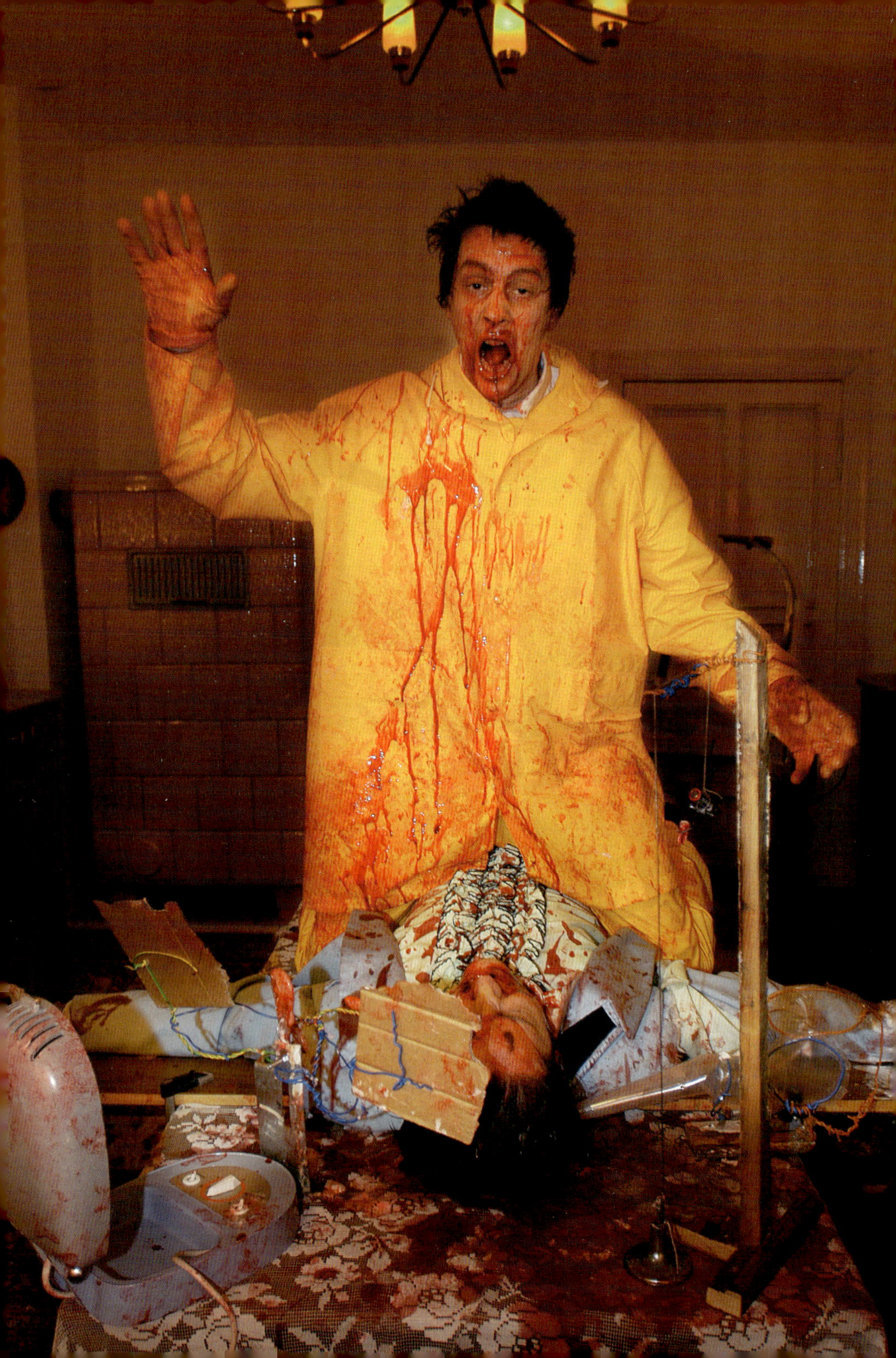

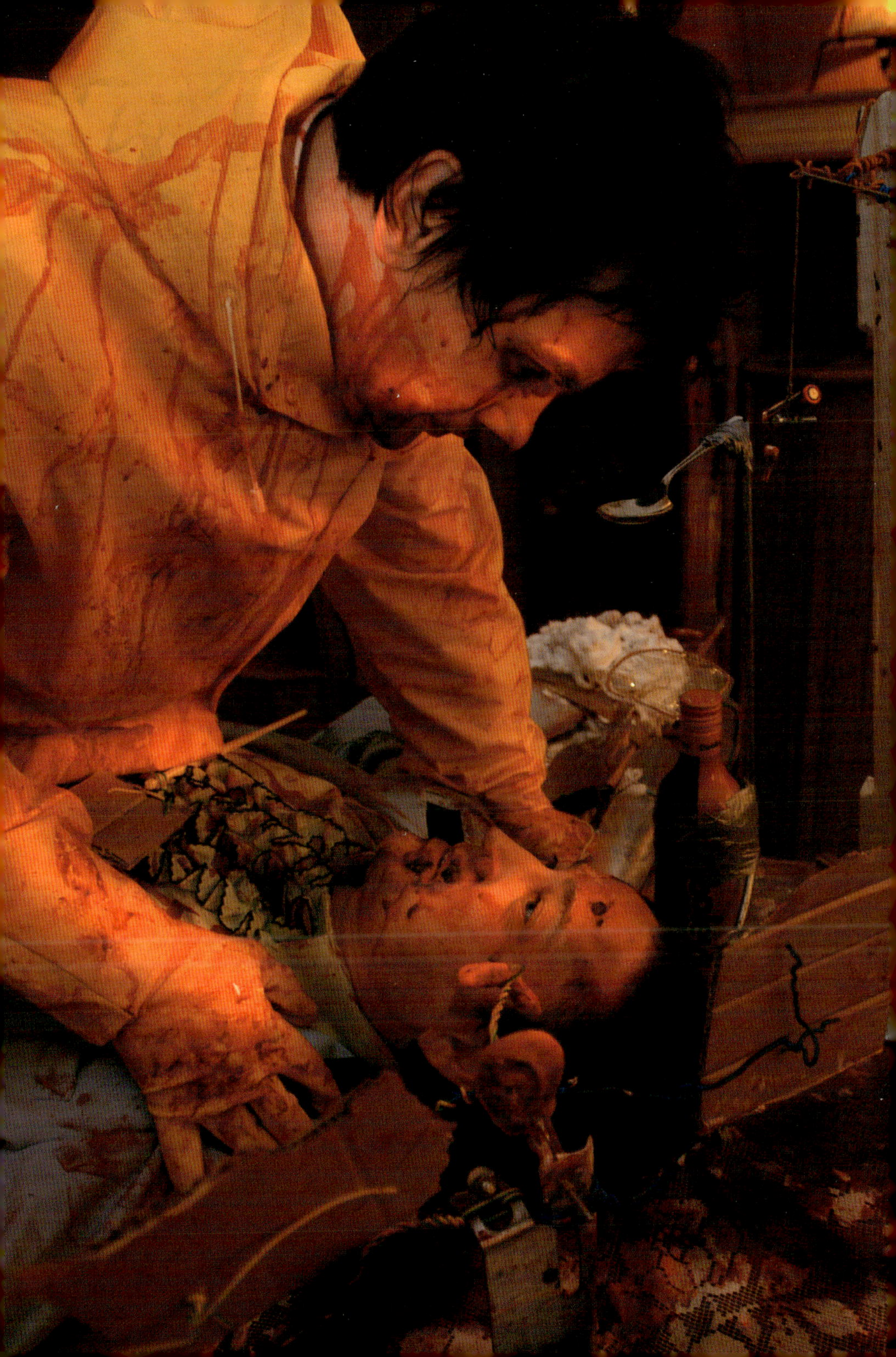

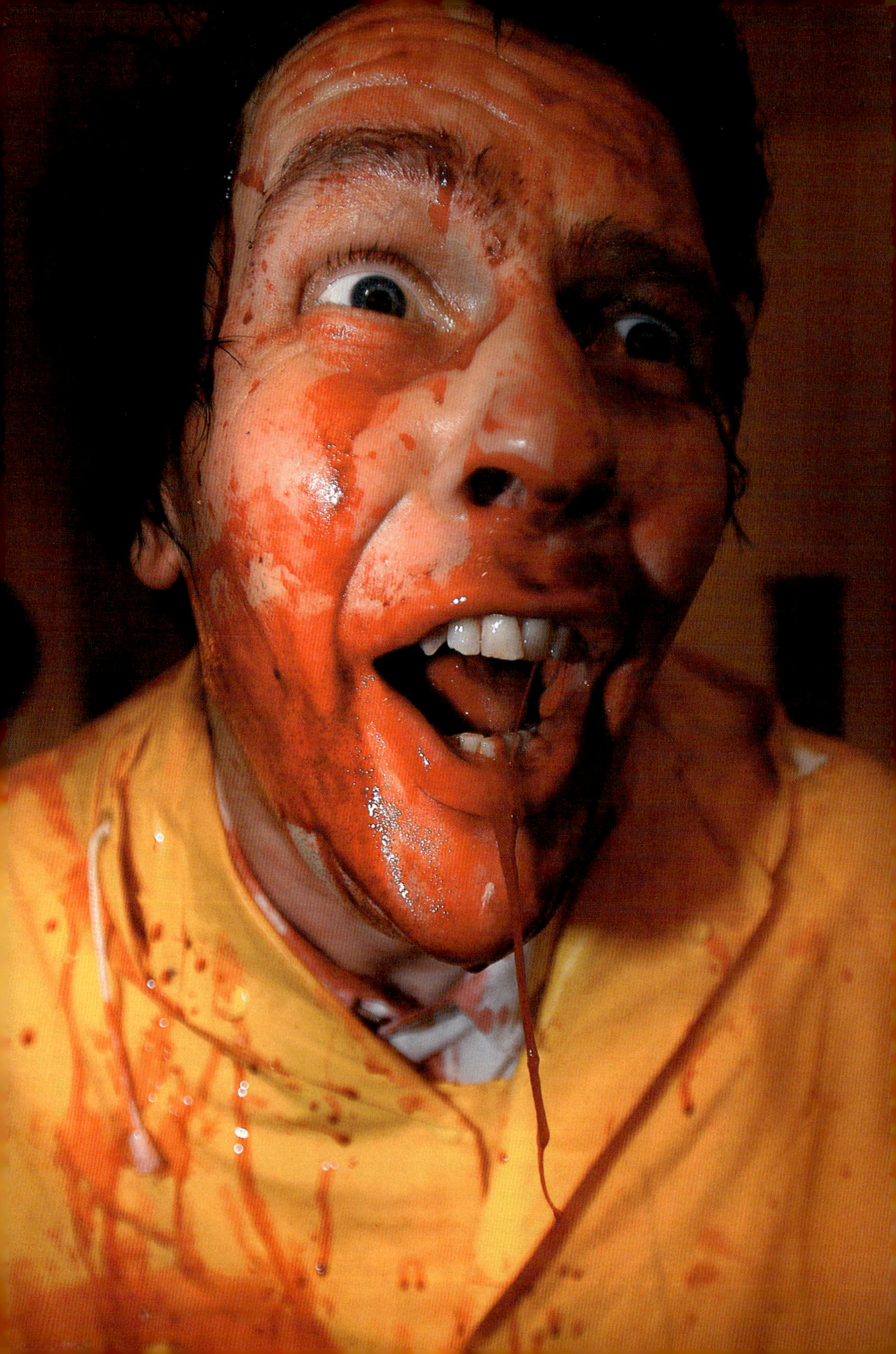

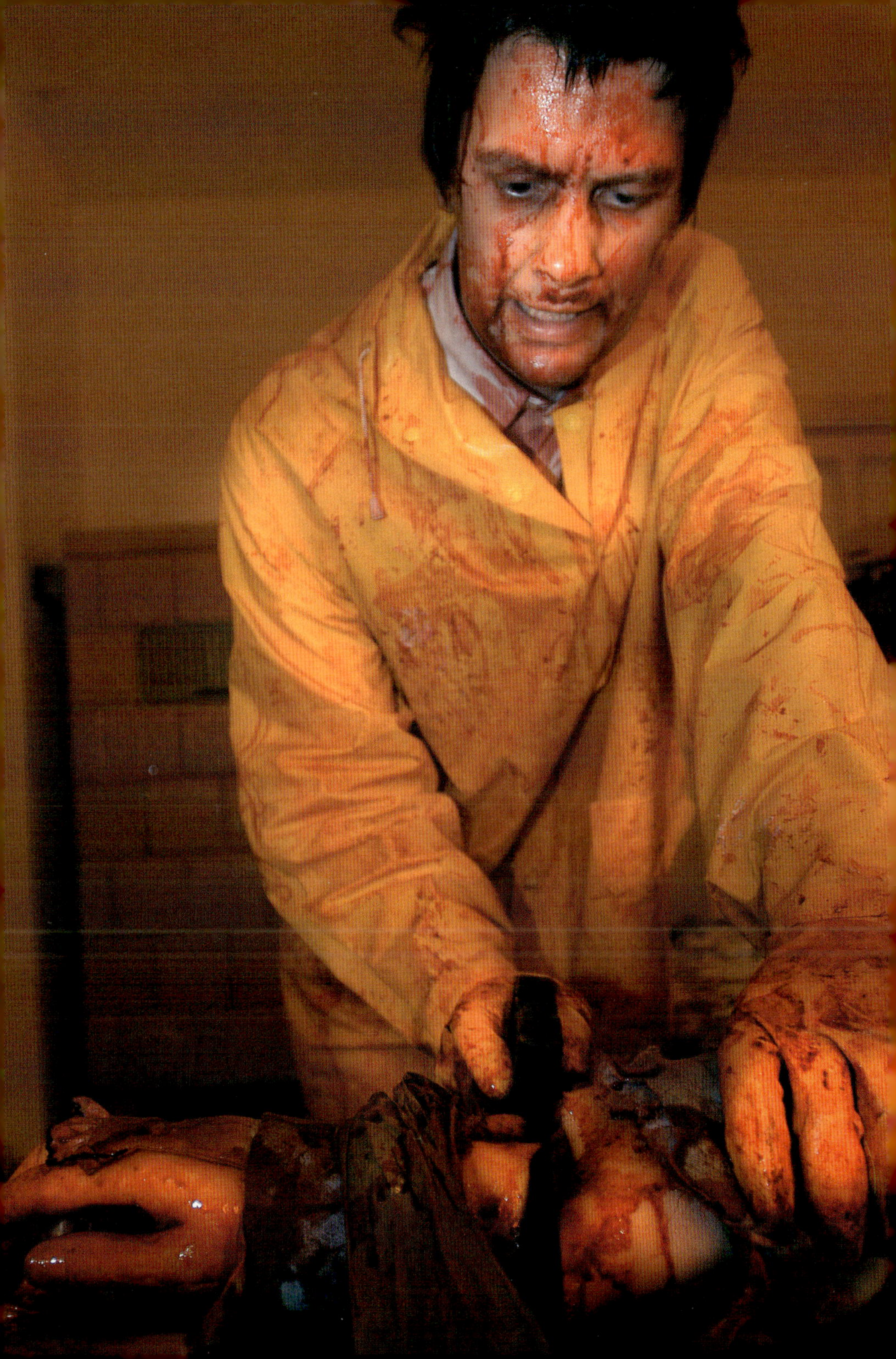

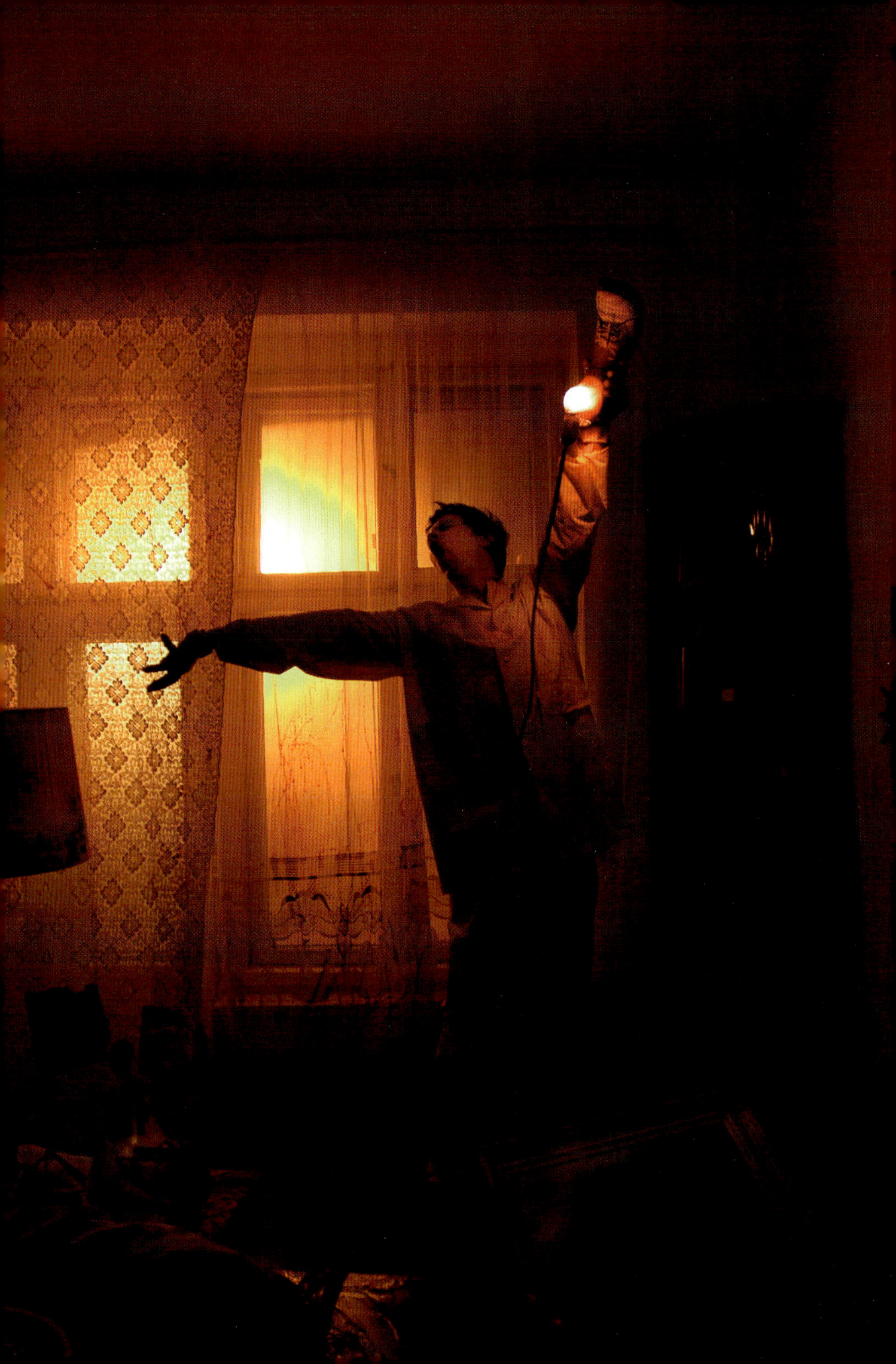

On the Necessity of Evil and Hell

Jean Baudrillard

Irrevocable damnation no longer exists. Hell is no more. While it is true that we still find ourselves immersed in the bastard notion of Purgatory, practically speaking, everything today falls under the category of redemption. This evangelization is clearly the source of all the manifest and marketing signs of well-being and self-realization that are generated by a paradisiacal civilization that adheres to the Eleventh Commandment, the one that cancels out the other ten: 'Be happy and manifest all signs of happiness!' But we can read the same need for salvation and universal retribution in the indictment to which not only all violence and injustice is subject today, but also, retroactively, all the crimes and contrary occurrences of the past… The indictment of the Revolution, of slavery, of original sin, of violence against women, of the hole in the ozone, of sexual harassment. We are, in short, in the middle of the grand jury hearing for the Last Judgment, busily condemning, then absolving and then whitewashing our history, flushing Evil from every nook and cranny to create the image of a radiant universe, ready to pass on to the next world. A colossal, inhuman, superhuman, and all too human undertaking. As Stanislaw Lec puts it: 'There is no doubt that the view we have of humankind is too anthropomorphic'. So why cultivate this perpetual factory of penitence, this chain reaction of remorse? Because everything must be saved. Today we are at this point: everything will be liberated, the entire past rehabilitated, polished until it's transparent… as for the future, it's even better and even worse: everything will be genetically modified to achieve the biological

John Bock *Lütte mit Rucola*, 2006. Photograph taken during the performance

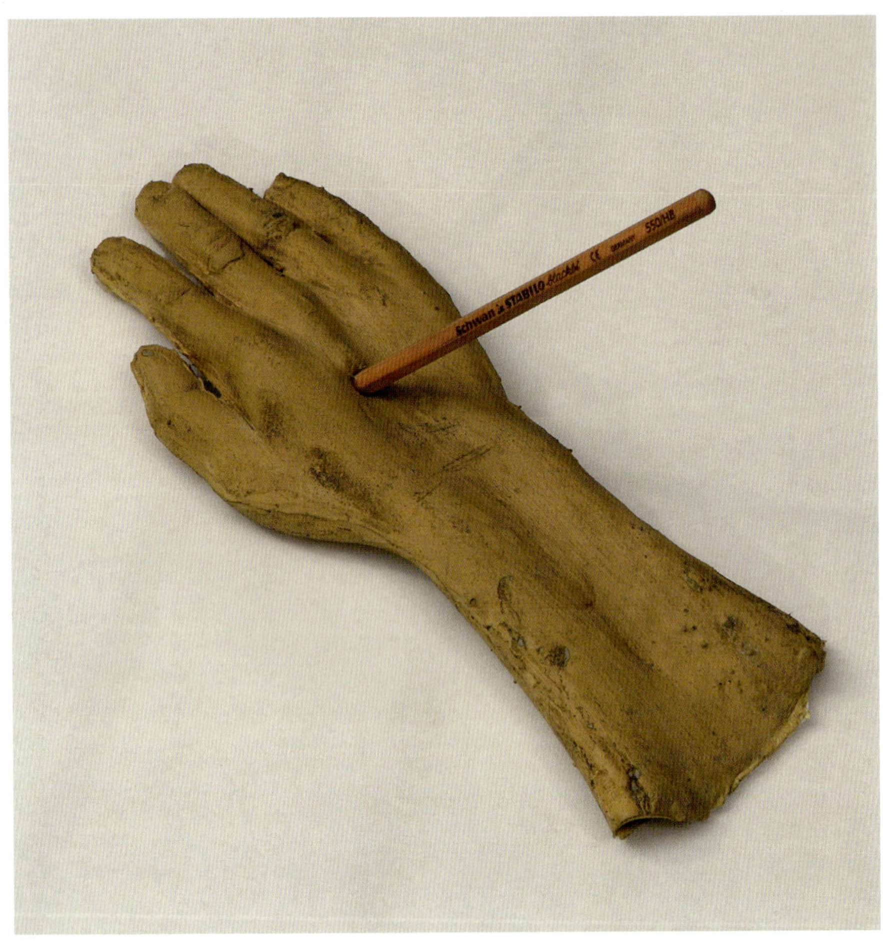

Maurizio Cattelan *Untitled*, 1997. Latex with pencil, 28 x 10 x 18 cm

perfection and democratic perfection of the species. The salvation that used to be defined as an equivalence of merit and grace, once the abscess of Evil and Hell are excised and cleaned up, will be defined as an equivalence of genes and performance.

To tell the truth, once happiness becomes the pure and simple general equivalent of salvation, heaven will no longer need to exist. There is no paradise without the inferno, nor light without darkness. Those who are not damned cannot be saved (by definition, but also by intuition: what would be the elect have then to enjoy, apart from the contemplation of

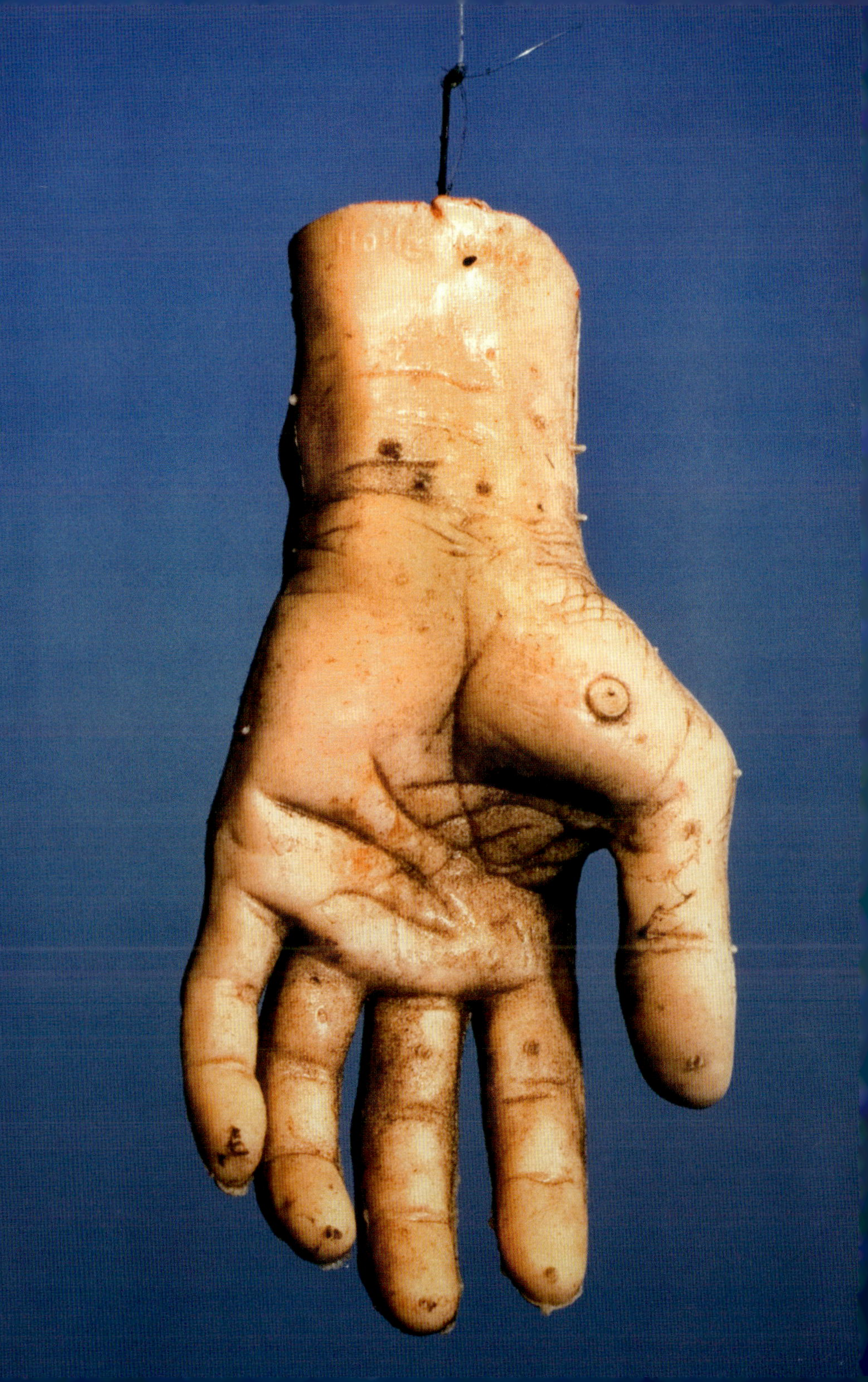

Paul McCarthy *Untitled* (from the *Propo* series), 1999–2000. Cibachrome on aluminium, 183 x 122 cm

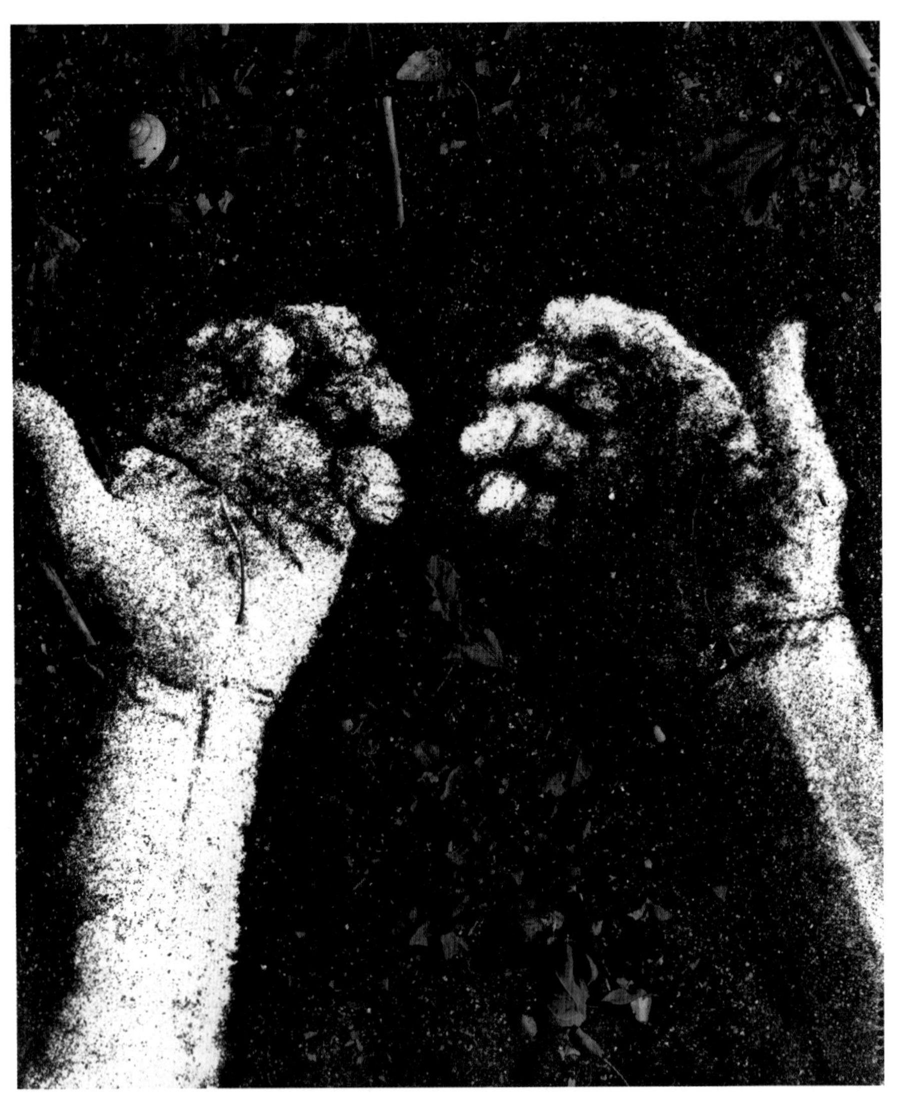

Vik Muniz *Hands* (from the *Pictures of Soil* series), 1997–99. Sepia-toned silver salt print, 61 x 51 cm

God, if not the compelling spectacle of the damned and their torments?). And once the whole world is virtually saved, no one is, for salvation no longer has any meaning. It is the promised destiny of our democratic mission: dead in the egg because it forgets the necessary discrimination, because it banishes Evil. This is why an unequivocal evil presence is essential, an Evil without the possibility of redemption, an irrevocable criterion of discrimination, an eternal dualism between Heaven and Hell, indeed in a certain sense a predestination of Evil, for there can be no destiny without predestination. There is nothing immoral in this. According to the rules of the game, there is nothing immoral in the fact that some win and others lose, not even in the possibility that everyone loses. What would be immoral indeed is if everyone wins, and yet this is the contemporary ideal of our democracy, that everyone is saved. Which is not possible without constantly and forever raising the bar, provoking endless inflation and speculation. Because in the end, happiness consists not so much in an ideal relationship with the world as in a rivalry and eventual victorious relationship with others. And this is good: it means that the hegemony of the Good, of the individual's state of grace will always be subject to defeat brought on by a challenge or a passion, and that any kind of happiness or ecstasies might be sacrificed for something more vital, belonging to the order of will according to Schopenhauer, or of power, or the will to power according to Nietzsche, but in any case linked to Evil which, though it has no definition it can at least be summarised as such: that which is predestined to occur, contrary to any felicitous fate.

Thus the imperative of maximum performance and ideal realization clearly contains within itself, though dissimulated by euphoric exaltation, evil and unhappiness in the form of the profound repudiation of such a glorious prospect, in the form of a secret, pre-announced disappointment. Perhaps it is nothing more than a collective form of sacrifice, human sacrifice but fleshless, distilled into homeopathic doses.

Wherever people are condemned to total freedom or to an ideal self-realization, this subversion insinuates itself, this automatic abreaction from their very goodness and happiness. Compelled to depend on themselves for maximum efficiency and enjoyment, they remain disunited and their existence becomes dissociated. In a strange world where everything is virtually available (body, sex space, money, pleasure), to be taken or rejected as a whole, there's everything, nothing has been lost in a physical sense, but in the metaphysical sense everything is gone. 'As if by magic', one might say, but it is more a question of disenchantment. Individuals, whatever they may be, become what they are. Without transcendence and without image, they manage their lives as a function that is useless with respect to another world, one that is indeed irrelevant with respect to themselves. Whatever they do, they do better insofar as other eventualities do not exist. No instance, no essence, no personal substance worthy expressing itself individually. They have sacrificed their life to their functional existence. In everything they do, they adhere to the precise numerical calculation of their life and their performance levels. An existence, therefore, that is realized but at the same time annulled, unfulfilled, repudiated, with the point of arrival a completely negative countertransfer.

Along parallel lines, the imperative of maximum performance finds itself in an internal contradiction with democratic moral law that prescribes to steadfastly bring everyone towards equality and everything towards zero, in the name of democracy and the equal division of opportunities and advantages. Implicit in this salvation for all, this universal redemption is the denial of any right to distinguish oneself, to seduce. In order for justice to be done, every privilege must necessarily disappear and everyone will be expected to voluntarily renounce all specific traits, risking becoming an elementary particle: if collective happiness is founded on the levelling of differences and on penitence, it must conclude with the advent of the lowest common denominator and fundamental banalities. It is like a backwards *potlatch*,[1] where everyone tries to one-up each other in their minimalism and victimism, nevertheless ferociously guarding the tiniest element of differentiation and devoting themselves to the bricolage of their own multiple identities.

Penitence and recrimination coincide in a single movement: recrimination means returning to the crime to correct its trajectory and consequences. This is what we are doing by revising our history, the criminal history of the human race, in order to make penance for what we've done up to now as we await the Last Judgment. Though God is in fact dead, his judgement remains. From this derives the widespread syndrome of repentance, of the rewriting (historical for now, as we await the genetic and biological rewriting of the species in the future) that dominates the end of this century, always in the perspective of deserving salvation and of presenting, with respect to the final deadline, the image of an ideal victim. Let it be clear that these are not real indictments, nor is the repentance authentic. It is a question of fully enjoying the spectacle of our own unhappiness.

'Mankind, which in Homer's time was an object of contemplation for the Olympian gods, now is one for itself. Its self-alienation has reached such a degree that it can experience its own destruction as an aesthetic pleasure of the first order.' (Walter Benjamin)

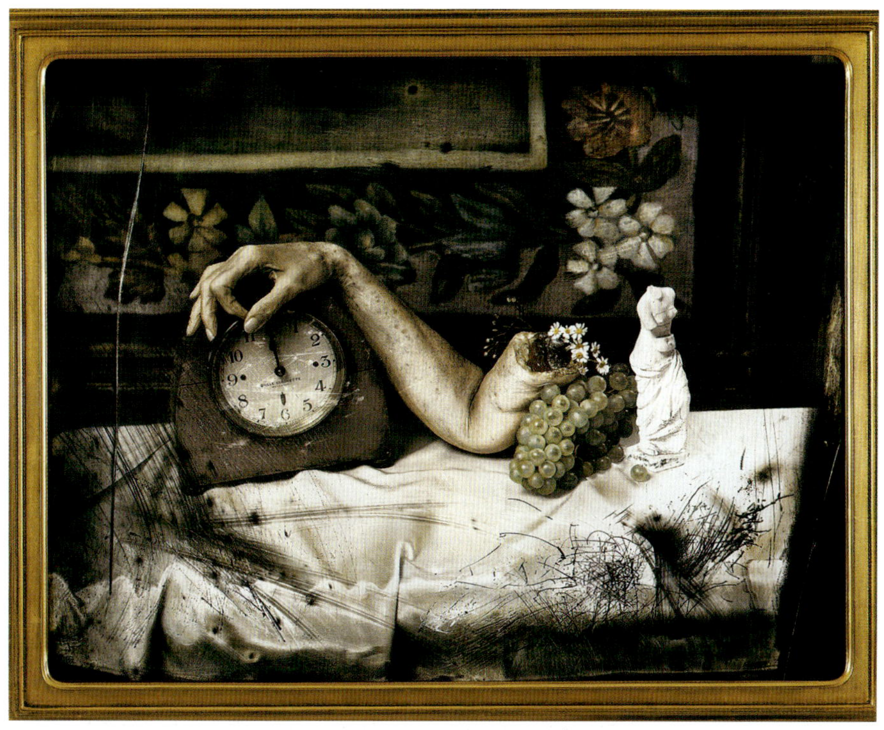

Joel-Peter Witkin *Anna Akhmatova*, 1999. Encaustic, hand-painted on silver salt print, 86.5 x 93.5 cm

Overleaf
Thomas Hirschhorn *Following Higher Law*, 2003. Paper, plastic film, adhesive tape, pen and felt-tip pen, 42 x 60 cm

The latest episode of this devastating revisionism: dismiss not only the history of the twentieth century, but all the violent events of the preceding times, to absorb them all into the jurisdiction of human rights and crimes against humanity (just as every act today is ascribed to the jurisdiction of sexual harassment, moral or political). In the same spirit by virtue of which all works (including the human genome) are inscribed into the ledger of human knowledge, all injustice gets filed in the register of crimes against humanity.

Another recent episode of the revisionist delirium is the proposal to condemn slavery and the treatment of black Africans as a crime against humanity. An absurd attempt to rectify the past in function of our acquired Western humanitarian conscience, once again on the basis of our own criteria, in the purest colonialist tradition: the imperialism of peni-

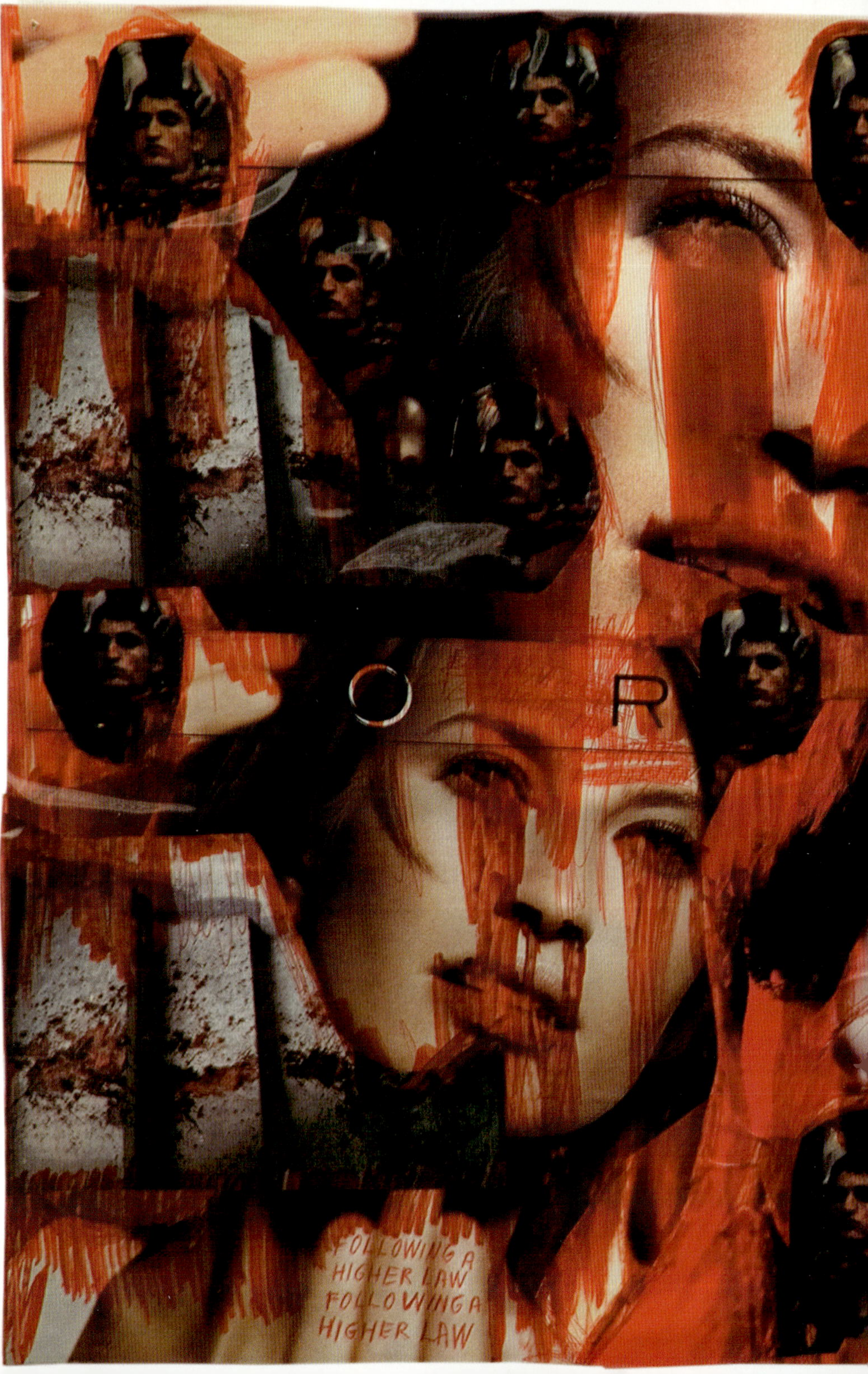
R
FOLLOWING A
HIGHER LAW
FOLLOWINGA
HIGHER LAW

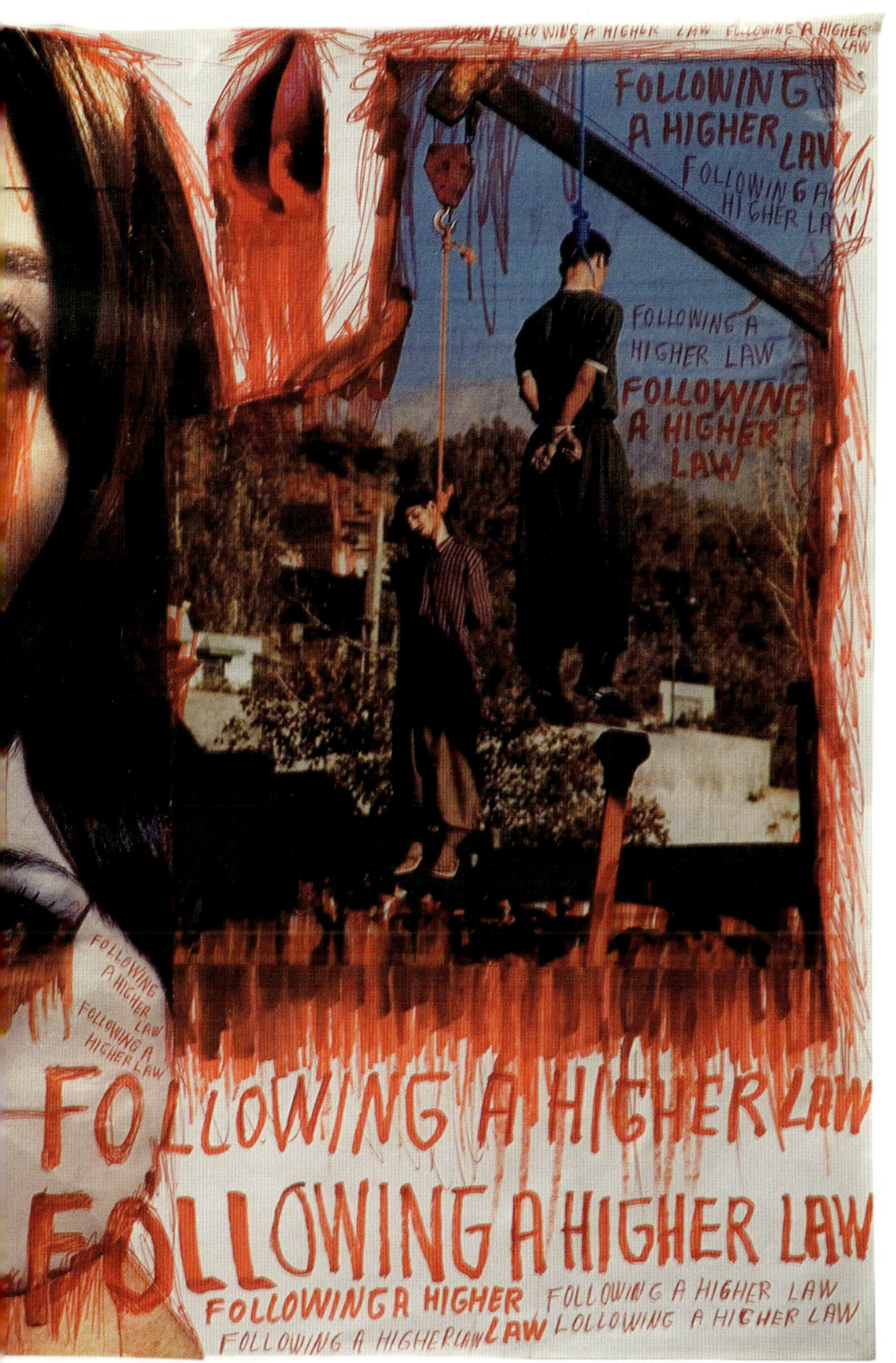
FOLLOWING A HIGHER LAW FOLLOWING A HIGHER LAW
FOLLOWING A HIGHER LAW
FOLLOWING A HIGHER LAW
FOLLOWING A HIGHER LAW
FOLLOWING A HIGHER LAW
FOLLOWING A HIGHER LAW FOLLOWING A HIGHER LAW
FOLLOWING A HIGHER LAW
FOLLOWING A HIGHER LAW
FOLLOWING A HIGHER LAW
FOLLOWING A HIGHER LAW FOLLOWING A HIGHER LAW
FOLLOWING A HIGHERLAW LAW LOLLOWING A HIGHER LAW

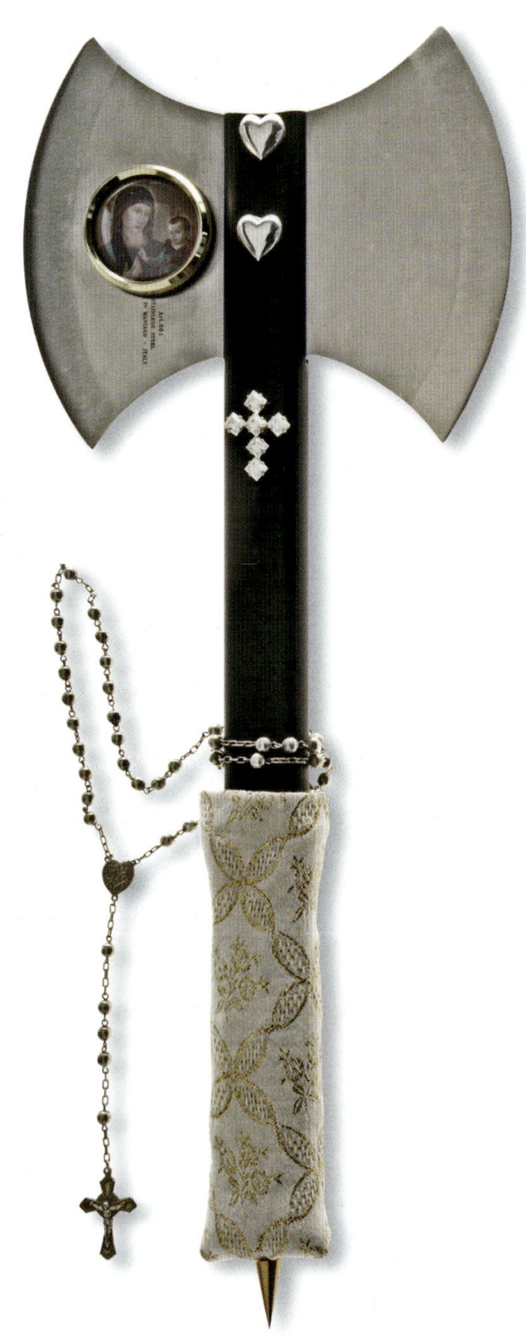

Antonio Riello *Carmela*, 2003. Case and object, 80 x 60 x 6 cm

tence! The idea is that an official indictment would allow 'the peoples concerned' to overcome the tragedy; once their rights were re-established and they were properly acknowledged and celebrated as victims, these peoples could do the necessary work of mourning and archive this page in history once and for all, thereby entering the ranks of modern history as full partners. Almost like an especially effective psychoanalysis. Indeed, perhaps the Africans might even translate this moral acknowledgement into a claim for damages, in keeping with the same monstrous equivalence that made beneficiaries of the Holocaust survivors. If this continues, we will never stop reimbursing, rehabilitating, making reparations, and we will have accomplished nothing except adding the hypocritical absolution of mourning on top of the vicious exploitation of the past, the only result being that evil is transformed, through compassion, into unhappiness.

From the standpoint of our recycled humanism, history is essentially one great crime. Yet without these crimes, history simply would not exist, as Montaigne says: 'If man were to eliminate evil, the fundamental conditions of life would be destroyed'. By the logic of such claims, Cain's murder of Abel would already qualify as a crime against humanity (indeed a genocide, insofar as there were only two of them!), as would original sin.

All this retroactive humanitarian glossing over is absurd. And it all comes from the confusion between evil and unhappiness. Evil is the world as it is and as it has been always, and we can consider it lucidly. Unhappiness is the world as it never should have had to be… but in the name of what? In the name of having to be, in the name of God or a transcendent ideal, of a Good that we have a lot of trouble defining. One can take a criminal view of crime — wherein lies the sense of the tragic — or one can take a recriminatory view, which takes us into the humanitarian realm, a sentimental and saccharine vision that demands constant reparation. It is all the resentment that rises from the heart of a genealogy of morality, demanding from us the reparation of our own lives.

This retrospective compassion, this conversion of evil into unhappiness, is the most splendid industry of the twentieth century. First, as a vindictive mental operation, of which we are all victims, even in our actions, that we can only hope will cause minimum ill (keep a low profile, do everything in a way that everyone else could have done it: decriminalize your existence!). Then, as a fruitful operation and huge added value, insofar as unhappiness (in all its forms, from suffering to insecurity, from oppression to depression) constitutes a symbolic capital whose exploitation, even more than the exploitation of happiness, is inexhaustibly remunerative, for the common thread to be exploited is found within each one of us.

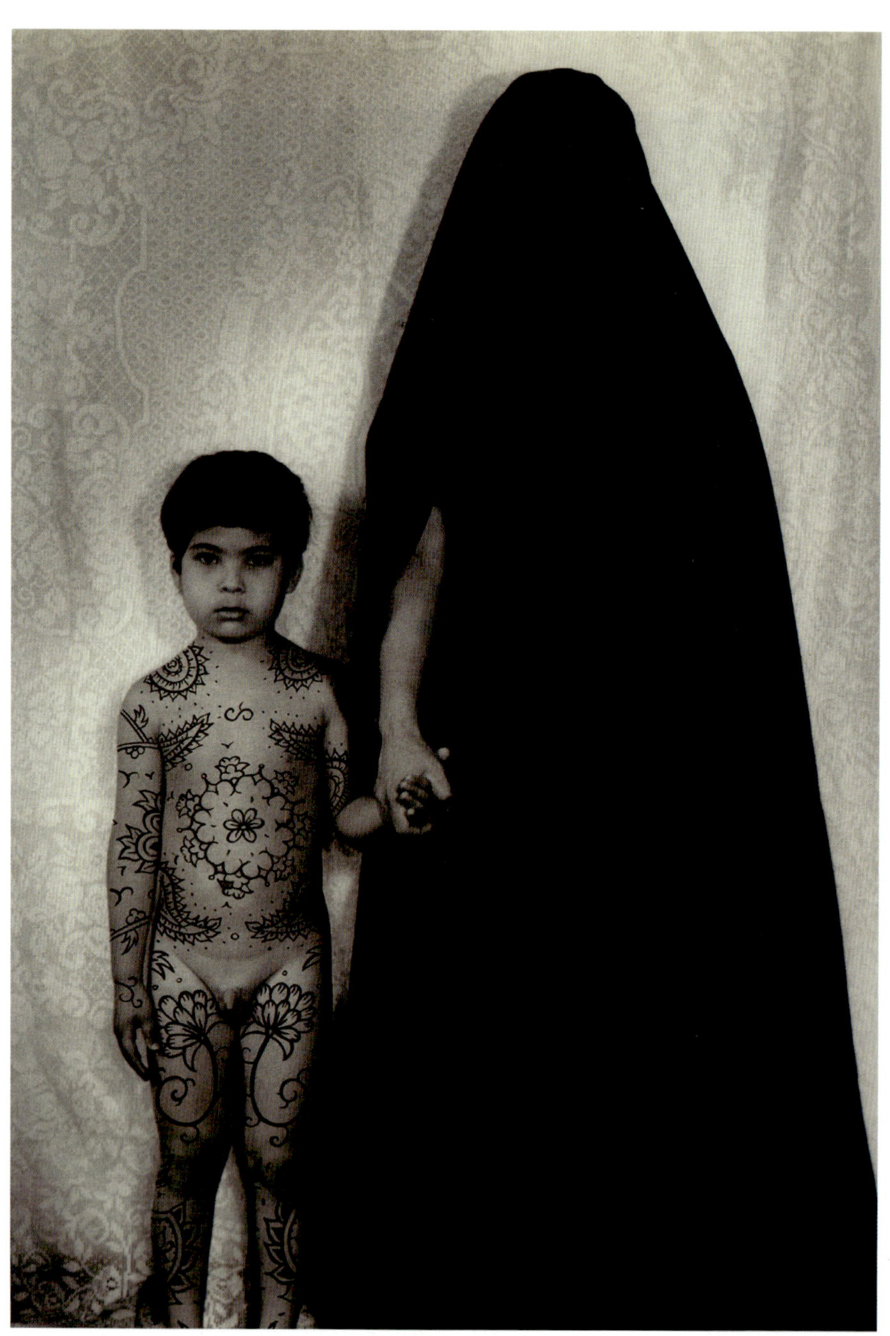

Shirin Neshat *Untitled*, 1996. Silver gelatine print and ink, 149 x 107 cm

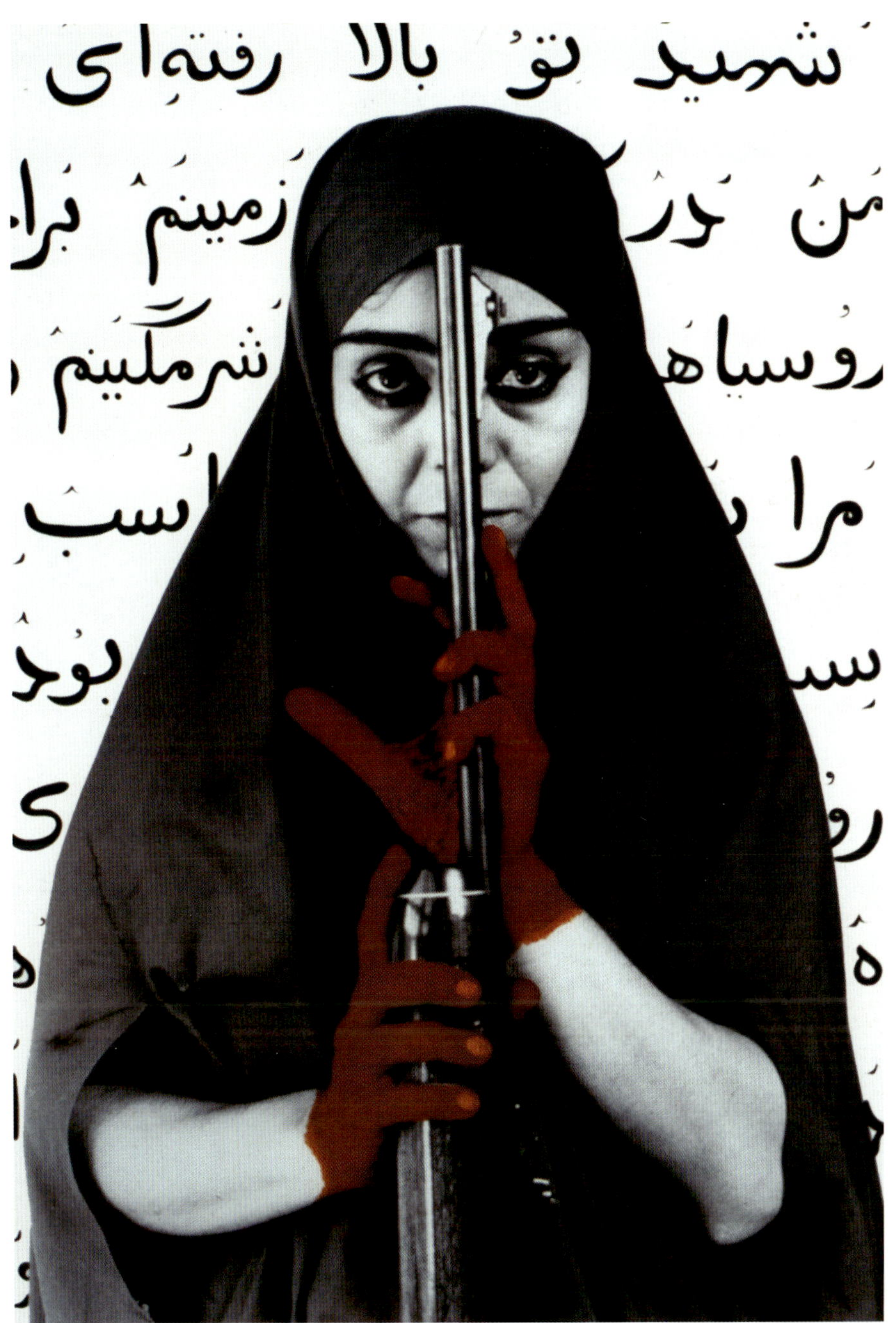

Shirin Neshat *Seeking Martyrdom, Variation No. 1*, 1995. Silver gelatine print and ink, 146 x 102 cm

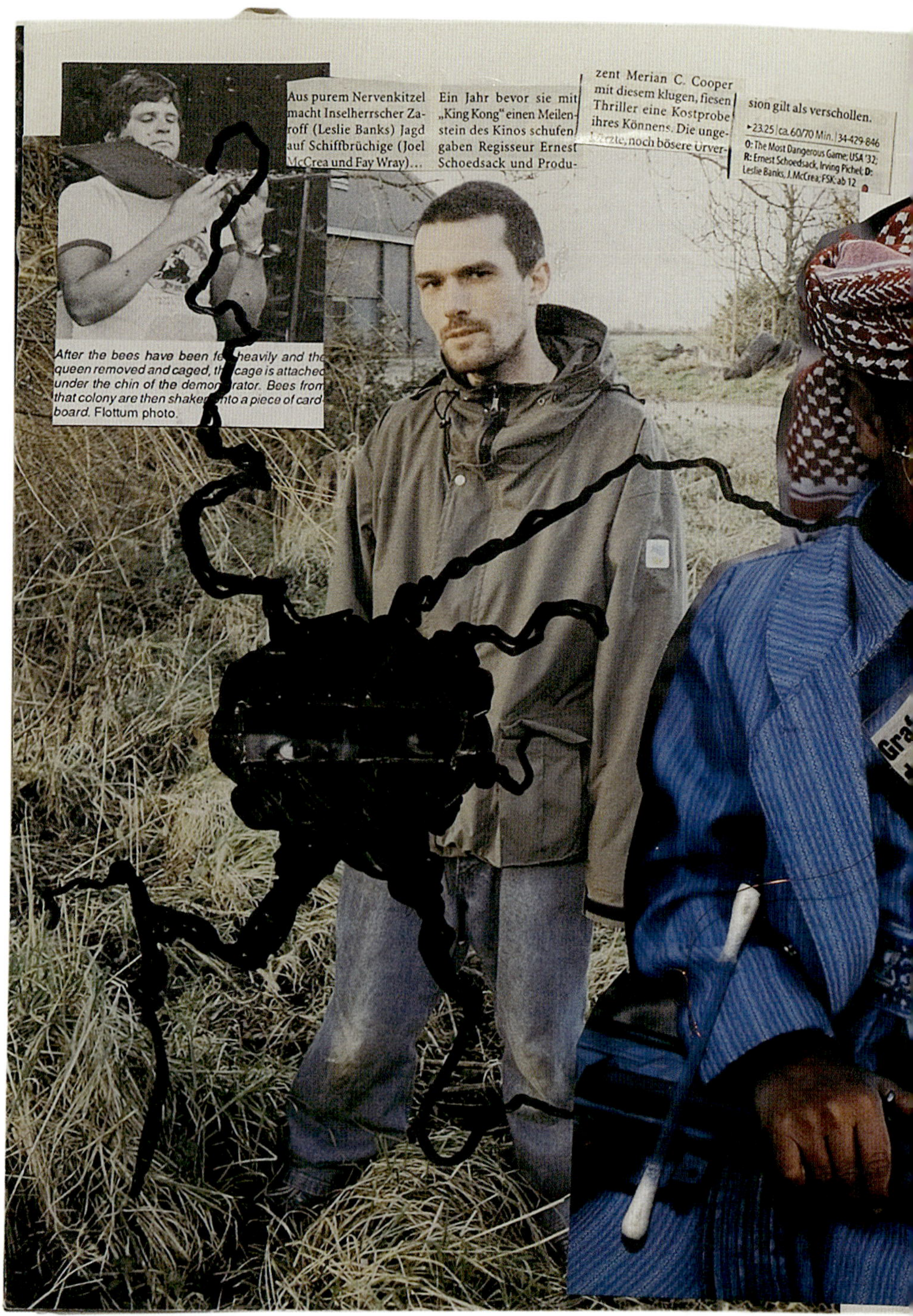

John Bock *Untitled*, 1996–2003. Book, collage of mixed materials and drawings on paper, pizza box, 28 x 21 cm (book); 29 x 31 x 0.5 cm (box)

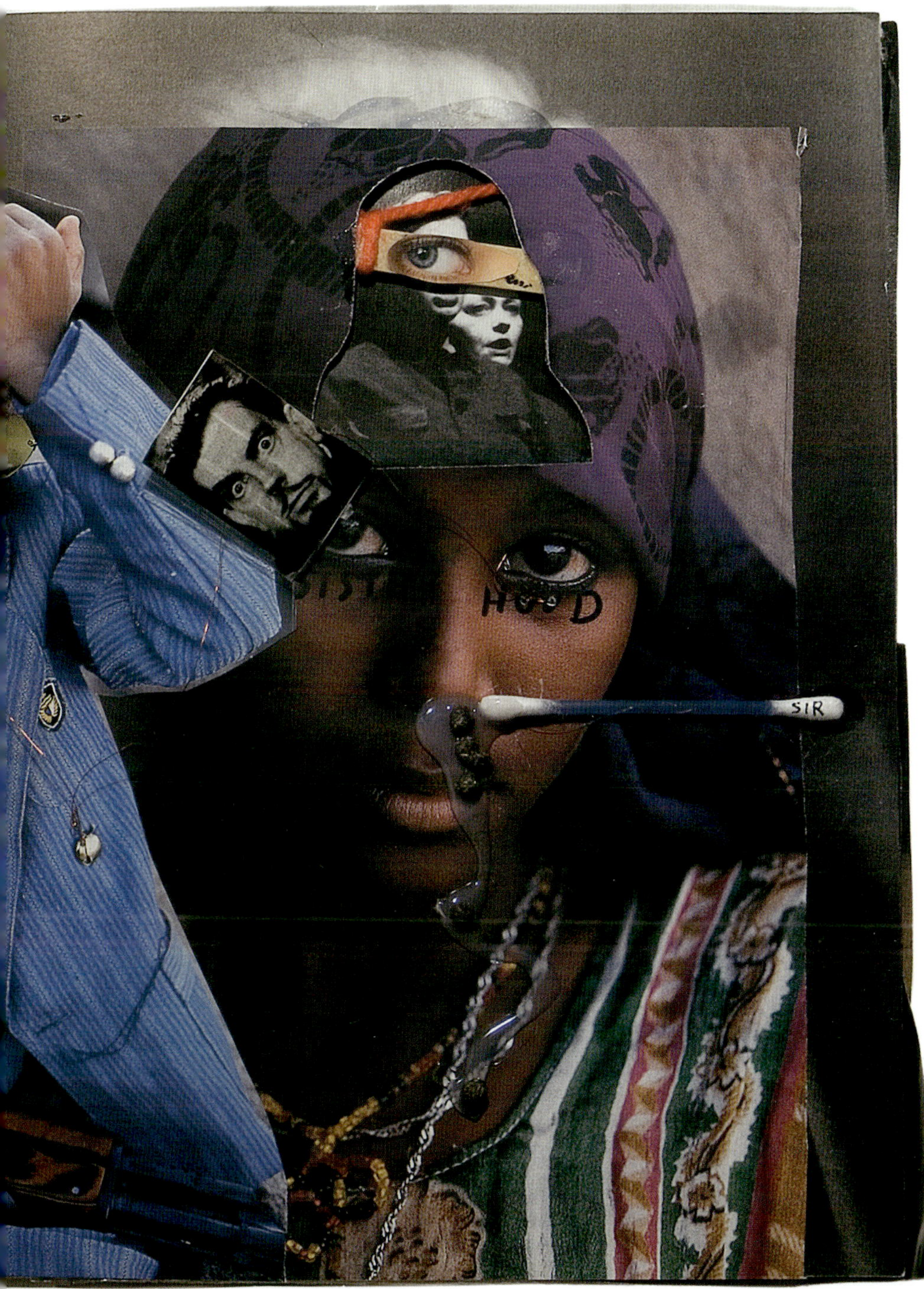
HOOD
SIR

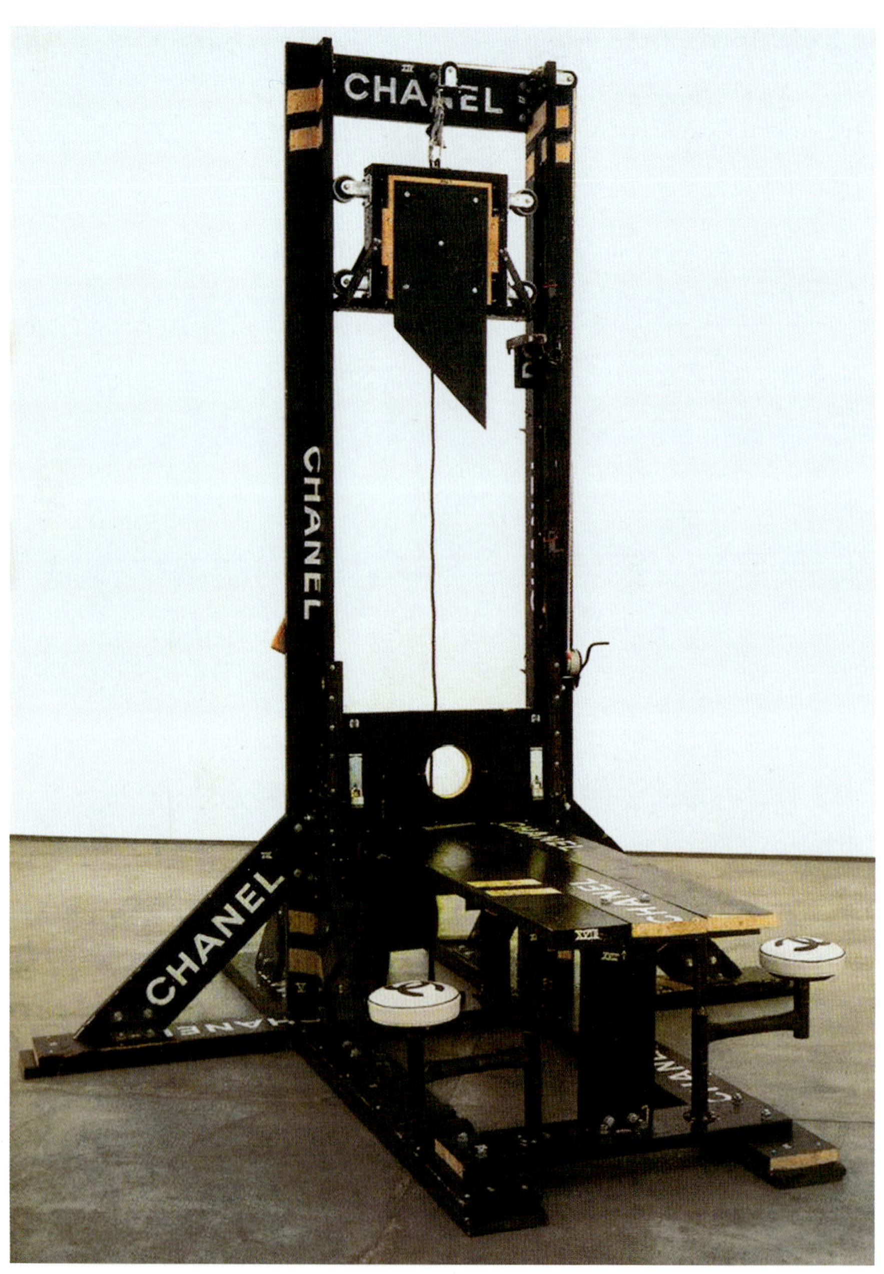

Tom Sachs *Chanel Guillotine*, 1998. Wood, metal, synthetic polymers, leather, nylon and rubber, 373.3 x 310 x 317.5 cm

Unhappiness negotiates at the highest price, while evil cannot be traded. It is impossible to make it an object of commerce.

Transcribing evil into unhappiness, and then transcribing unhappiness into commercial or entertainment value, in the majority of cases with the complicity or assent of the victims themselves. The fact that the victim is complicit in his/her own unhappiness is owed to the ironic essence of evil. From this derives the fact that no one wants their own good, and that nothing happens for the best in the best of all possible worlds.

[1] Ceremony performed by a number of Native American tribes of the northwestern US and Canada, whereby the entire community gathers to exchange the most extravagant and valuable gifts possible, then consume them. The study of these customs inspired the ethnographer Marcel Mauss to develop the theory of the 'gift economy'.

Jean Baudrillard, *D'un fragment l'autre, Entretiens avec François L'Yonnet*, Paris: Albin Michel, 2001.

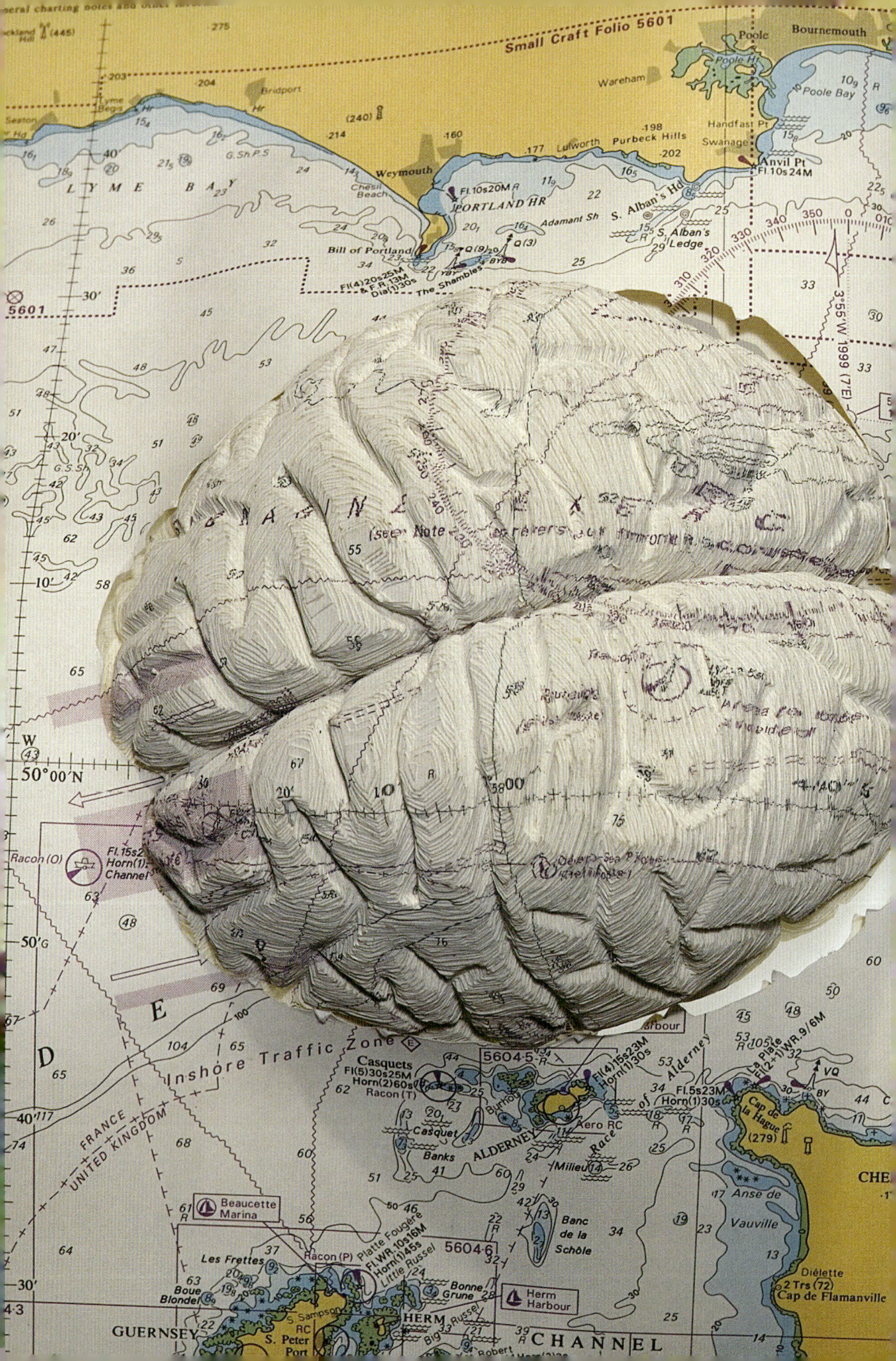

Small Craft Folio 5601
Poole
Bournemouth
Poole Hr
Poole Bay
Wareham
Bridport
Lyme Regis
Seaton
Handfast Pt
Swanage
Anvil Pt
Fl.10s24M
Lulworth
Purbeck Hills
Weymouth
Chesil Beach
LYME BAY
Fl.10s20M
PORTLAND HR
Adamant Sh
S. Alban's Hd
S. Alban's Ledge
Bill of Portland
Fl(4)20s25M
& F.R.13M
Dia(1)30s
The Shambles
5601
3°55'W 1999 (7'E)
50°00'N
Racon (O)
Fl.15s2
Horn(1)
Channel
Inshore Traffic Zone
FRANCE
UNITED KINGDOM
Casquets
Fl(5)30s25M
Horn(2)60s
Racon (T)
Casquet Banks
ALDERNEY
5604·5
Fl(4)15s23M
Horn(1)30s
Race of Alderney
Aero RC
Milieu
Fl.5s23M
Horn(1)30s
Cap de la Hague
(279)
Anse de Vauville
Banc de la Schôle
Beaucette Marina
Platte Fougère
Fl.WR.10s16M
Horn(1)45s
Racon (P)
Little Russel
5604·6
Les Frettes
Boue Blondel
Bonne Grune
Herm Harbour
GUERNSEY
HERM
S. Peter Port
Big Russel
CHANNEL
Diélette
2 Trs (72)
Cap de Flamanville

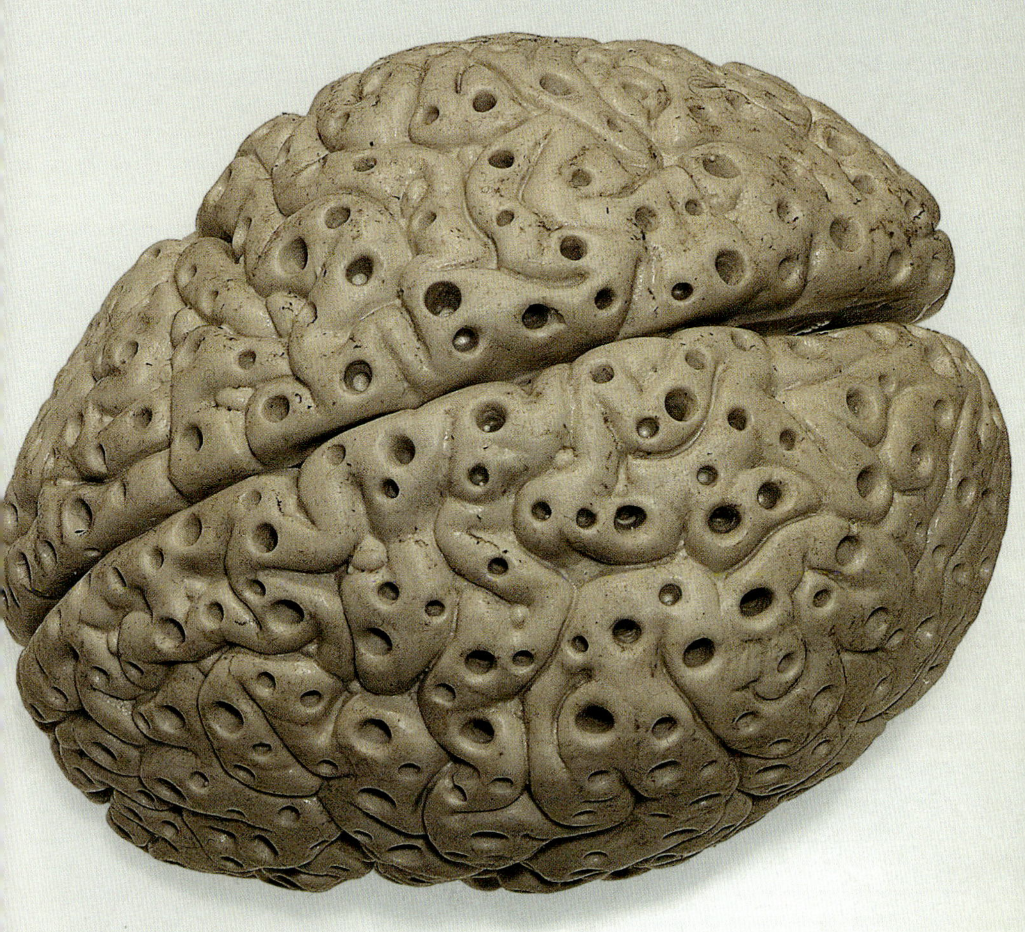

Mona Hatoum *Untitled (Brain)*, 1999. Silicon rubber, 10 x 15 x 12 cm

Left
James Hopkins *Horizontal Scan*, 2002. Sculpture in geographic paper, 59 x 42 cm; brain 12 x 15 x 16 cm

Overleaf
Tony Oursler *Influence Machine*, 2003. Video projected on a tree at Magasin 3, Stockholm

Angels and Demons

... But that's precisely the point! There isn't all that great a difference between angels and demons. In popular lore, an angel is not always a benevolent being. Who knows how many children, especially in Tuscany, have been scolded by their mothers, saying 'You'd better stop making those faces in the mirror or the angel will come and say "Amen!" and you'll stay like that forever!' In Neo-Platonic thought, as we've seen, angels and demons are considered to be one and the same thing, and can be either good or evil. Philo explains: 'If you consider that souls, demons and angels differ only in name and are in truth the same thing, you will be free from the burden of a base superstition'. Angels and demons, therefore, are 'relatives', or as Augustine puts it, 'the term "angel" is the name of the function [that of the messenger], independent of their nature'. In other words, since the earliest angelogical speculation, the name 'angel' refers to supernatural spirits, without necessarily intending the kind of moral judgement that has become implicit in the word today. They can operate at the service of good or evil.

Indeed, it was often necessary to use a qualifying adjective ('good' or 'bad') to specify the nature of an angel. And let us not forget the fact that, in the Christian tradition, demons are nothing but fallen angels.

Marco Bussagli

Marco Bussagli, *Storia degli angeli. Racconto di immagini e di idee*, Milan: Bompiani, 2003.

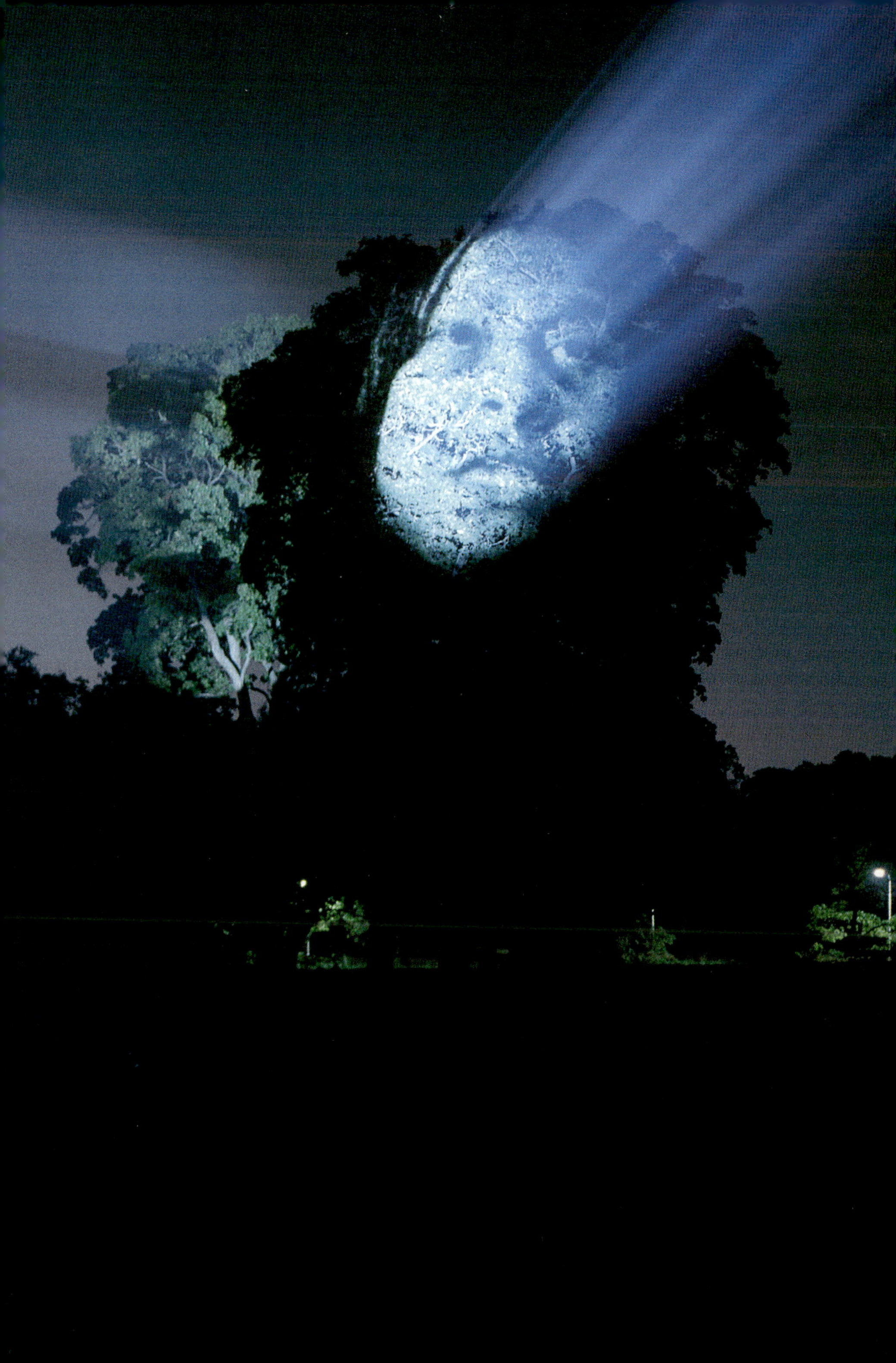

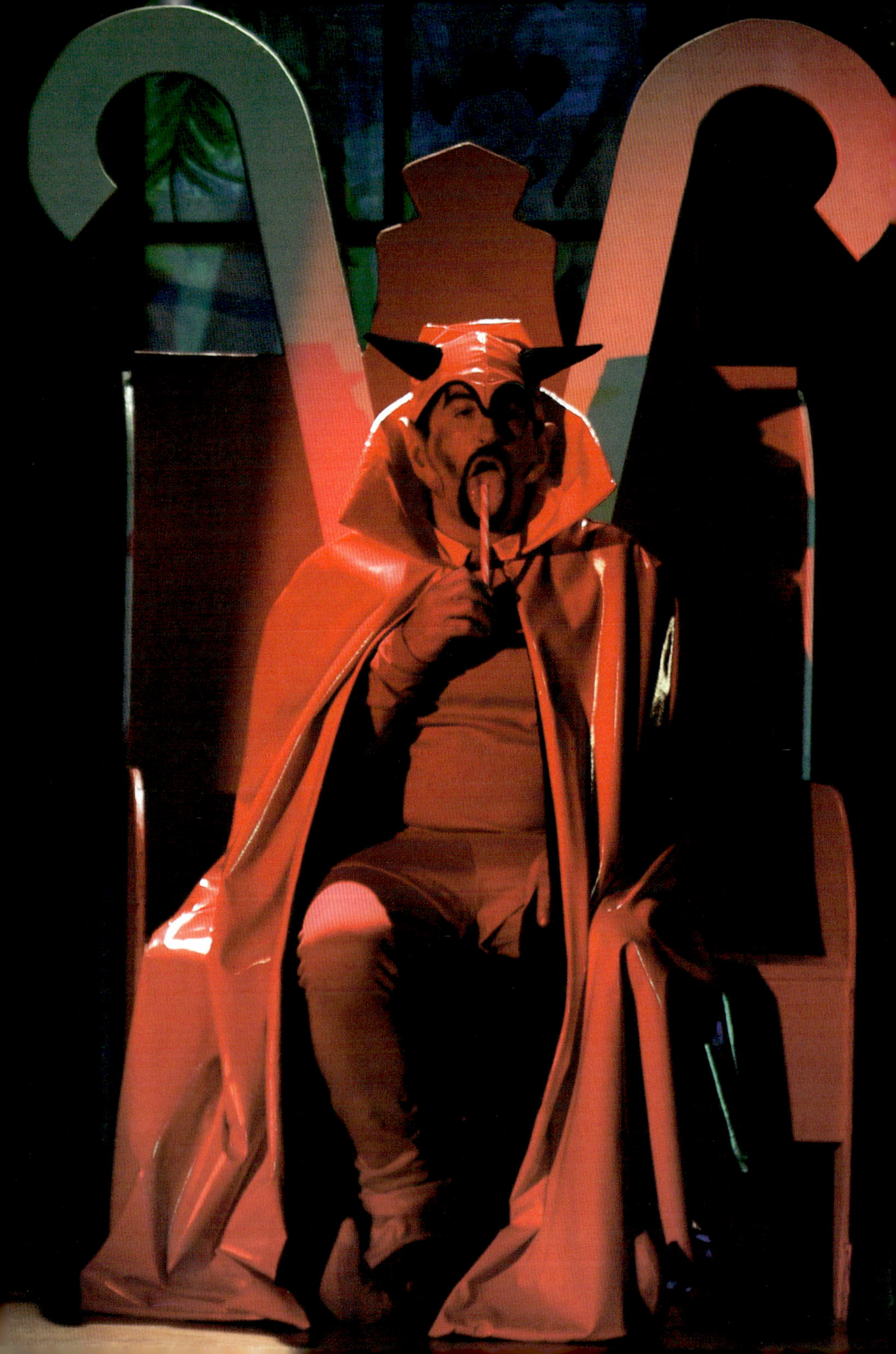

The Devil's Side

Michel Maffesoli

There's nothing worse than someone who wishes to do good, particularly if they want to do good for others. The same applies to those who champion 'right thinking'. These people all have the irresistible tendency to think for others, in their stead. Behind the protective cloak of their certainty, doubt cannot touch them. Consequently life, in all its complexity, escapes them. This would be of little importance in itself, were it not for the fact that these dispensers of lessons decree themselves as legitimate custodians of the word, with the right to dictate what society and the individual *should* be.

This moral mission — or more accurately, this moralism — is dangerous. Leave aside that which common sense has long told us (i.e., 'The road to hell is paved with good intentions'), forget the corroborative wisdom of Heraclitus, who equates the opinions of mankind with 'children's playthings': moralists of every stripe posit as absolutes the cultural values of a world whose permanence is anything but clear.

The 'good' is the ultimate justification of Judeo-Christian messianism. The theories of emancipation and modern universalism, their latest transmutations, also stand upon this fundamental principle. It is in the name of this principle that the various inquisitions have been able to freely operate. It is in its name that all the cultural ethnocides have been perpetrated and all the economic and polit-

Mike Kelley *Movement Portfolio #8 (Devil: Master of Ceremonies)*, 2005.
Chromogenic print, 76.2 x 61.6 cm

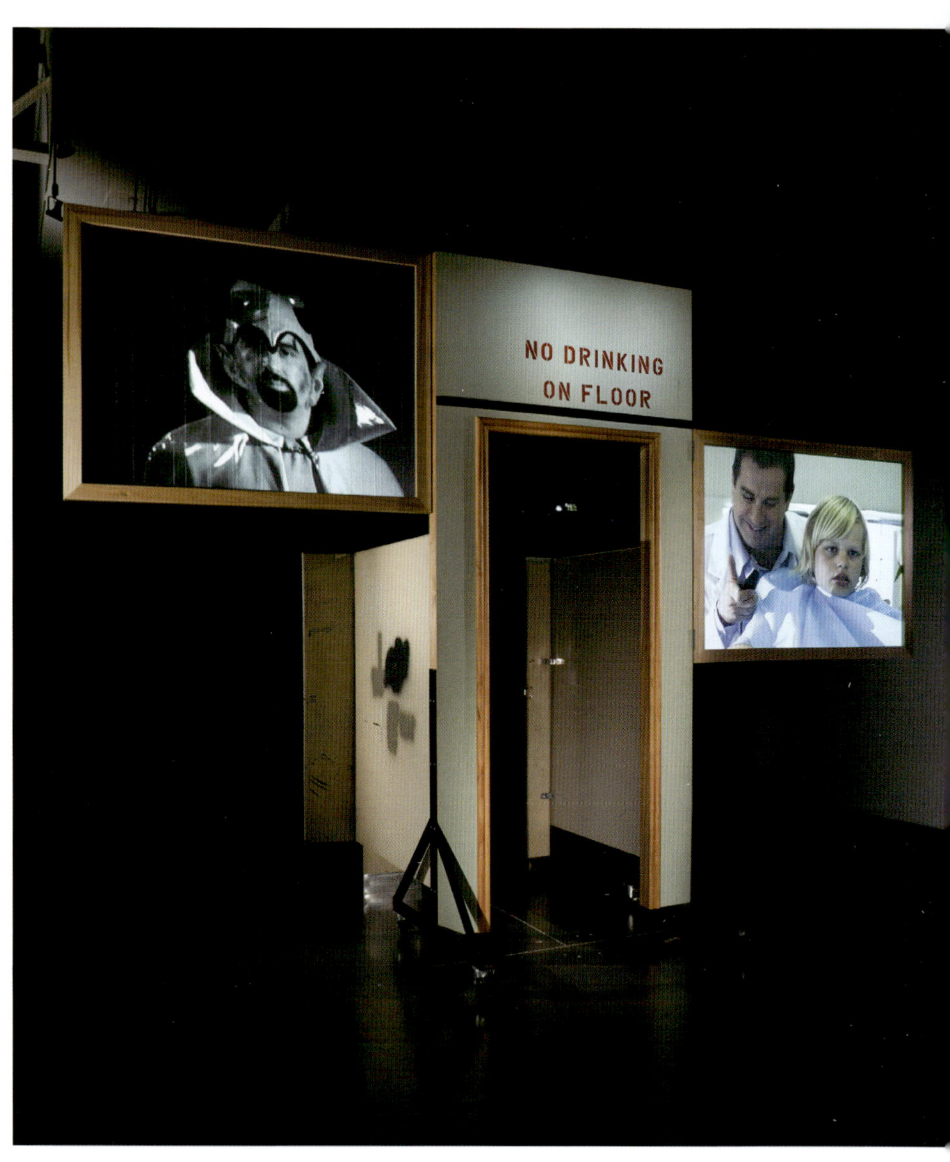

Mike Kelley *Devil's Door*, 2005. Mixed media with video and photographs, 287 x 396.2 x 203.2 cm

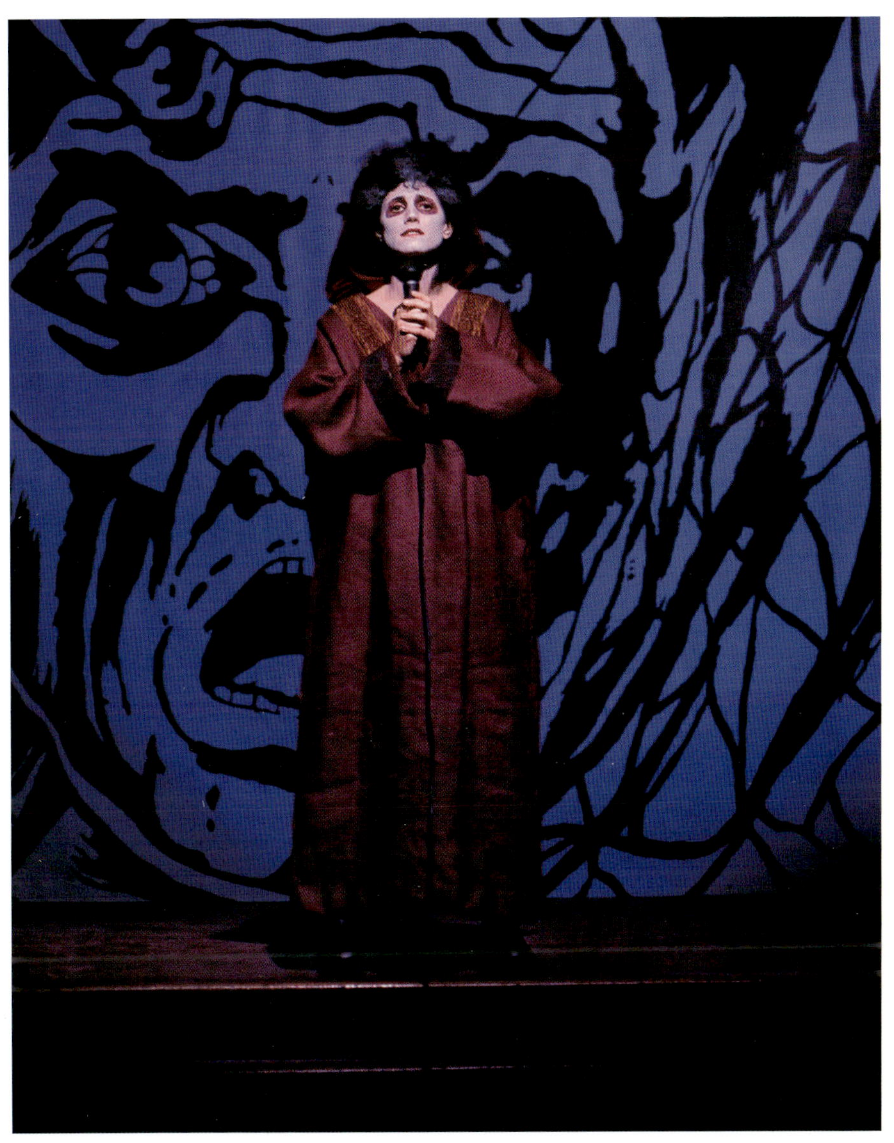

Mike Kelley *Movement Portfolio #5 (Shy Satanist)*, 2005. Chromogenic print, 76.2 x 61.6 cm

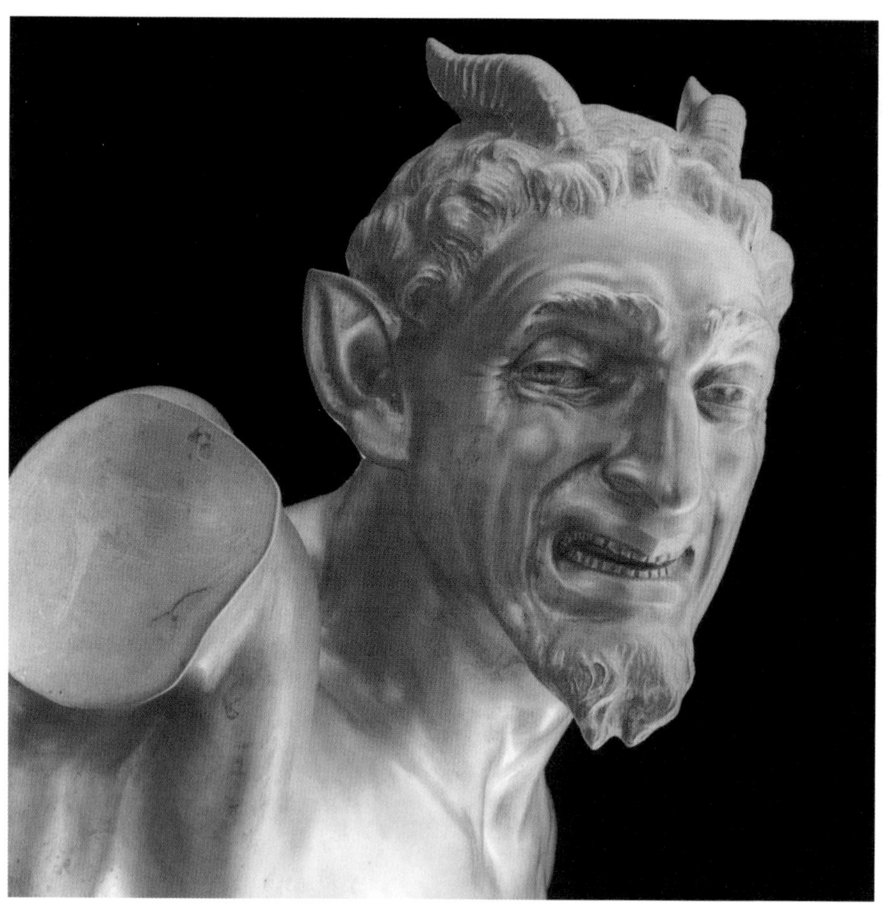

Robert Mapplethorpe *Italian Devil*, 1985. Silver gelatine print, 60 x 50 cm

ical imperialisms justified. It is invariably in its name that the parameters of how we should live and think are established, of how certain ways of life or objects of thought are taboo.

This is the same universalism that has justified all colonialism, all cultural ethnocide; it is indeed the very trademark of the Westernization of the world from the late nineteenth century forward. Insufferable conformism, because it's no longer fashionable. Dangerous conformism, because that which negates its existence — increasing complexity, cul-

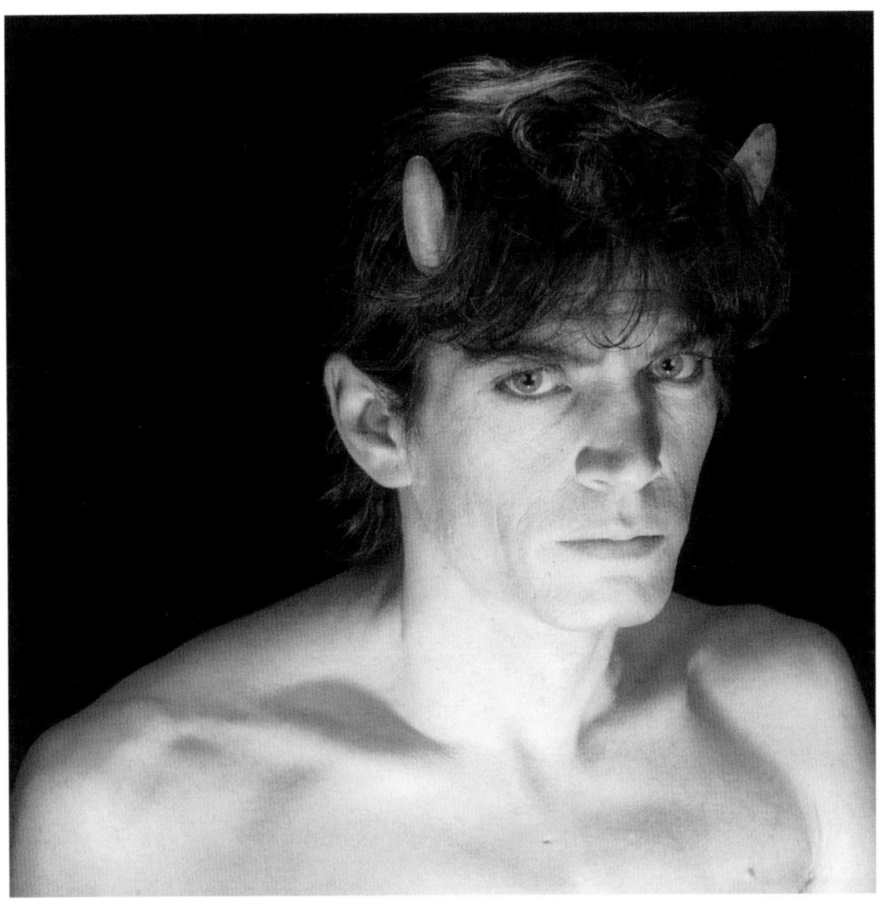

Robert Mapplethorpe *Self-portrait*, 1985. Silver gelatine print, 50.5 x 40 cm

tural relativism, emotional tribalism and other feelings of belonging — no longer compatible with right-thinking theories, risks becoming perverse. Meaning that it risks deviating, therefore, onto paths that are no longer controllable. Futile academic disputes, intellectual and political, are simply the expression of the cloistering off of intelligence in a world destined to end, unaware of when. Which leads it to seek vengeance through excesses of every sort. The most evident signs of this are the return of fanaticism in all its forms, of terrorism, even the more or less

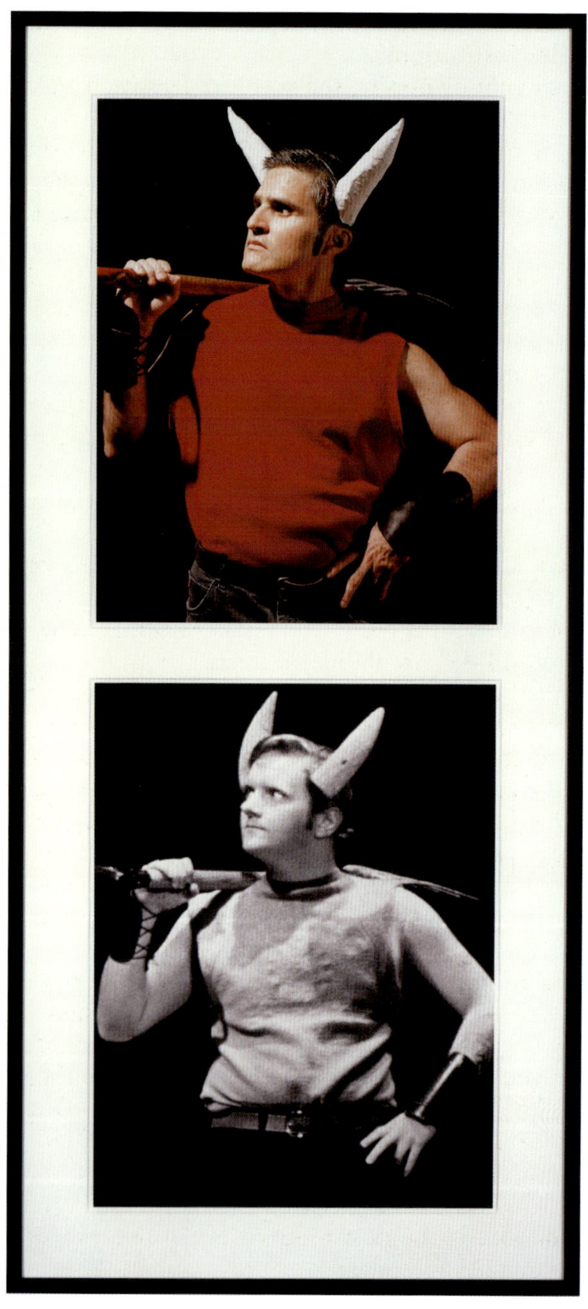

Mike Kelley *Extracurricular Activity Projective Reconstruction #30 (Pitchfork Maneuvers)*, 2005.
Piezo print on rag paper (black & white) and chromogenic print (colour), 76.2 x 51.6 cm

violent rebellion of suburban youth, without forgetting the abandonment of sundry institutions.

Whether silently or noisily, the revolt makes itself heard. When silent, it takes the form of the passivity, isolation and inactivity of young people. When noisy, it manifests itself as car rodeos, assaults on the police, the jeering when the *Marseillaise* is played at the Stade de France. There is no shortage of examples. Like a new *secessio plebis*, like the Roman populace gathered on the Aventine, there is no longer any adhesion to superficial values that no longer have any bearing on the reality of existence. This rebellion, at once underground and effective, means that there is no longer any doubt that the cycle of the consecration of the absolute value of the 'good' is about to end.

Well before this consecration, in other times and other places in the world, what counted was a form of polytheism of values, a polyculturalism, or that which could be called a compositional effect: culture and crudity, good and evil, death and life. At regular cycles, there is a '(re)birth' of this compound world. A plural reality is reborn, again. A moulting period based on the relativization of values. Moreover, this is how the mutation inaugurated by the Enlightenment at the dawn of modernity can be understood: faced with a fixed and rigid world, it placed the accent on dynamic force and the circulation of ideas.

Today, faced with apparently immutable social statutes (classes, socio-professional categories), the need for mobility is asserting itself. And the same is true of the multiplication of transactions, thanks the circulation, both real and virtual, of news sources and books: the trading of goods, of love. Elsewhere I have shown how this generalized exchange was the sure sign of society's various 'revolutions'. Urban tribes stand as the profile of this profound transformation, the importance of which is by now undeniable, along with the widespread hedonism of our societies, though it is more customary to call it 'the crisis'.

It is a revolution in the etymological sense of the return of that which was thought to have been surpassed. As Lévi-Strauss notes, 'man has always thought equally well'. One might say that he has always lived equally badly. And yet, at the centre of the tragic beauty of the world, he lives.

Against this Judeo-Christian progressism, which desperately tries to explain (from *explicare*, meaning to eliminate folds) absolutely everything, a truly *progressive* way of thought is emerging, a form of knowledge that incorporates all ways of being and thinking, that encompasses difference and deviation. This is the post-modern mutation, that which accepts the 'folds' of pre-modern archaisms.

For decades now I have been trying to draw attention to a reality that today is irrefutable: work is no longer the essential value. Clearly unemployment is still perceived and experienced as a disgrace. However, there are a large number of young people who have no desire to find steady work. They are happy to go back and forth between work and unemployment, from temporary jobs to being on the dole. In short, anything but a career as a minimum-wage grunt or postal clerk. Let us not forget that work has long been the privileged instrument of action on oneself and on the world, the vehicle for reaching the 'good', for achieving the perfect future. Work was the cause and effect, the means and the end of *homo œconomicus*, of the individual reduced to a production rate, and whose entire ideology was about productivism.

Insinuating himself into this modern prometheism is the more complex figure of Dionysius. Environmental hedonism, latent wildness. Serene animality. Even here, calmly or furiously but always obstinately, the plural person is asserting him/herself. The composite person ('I am another'), antagonist, contradictory. And this Dionysian wholeness implies, of course, 'evil'.

As often happens, the arts — music, cinema, painting, dance — emphatically underscore the implications of their time. In the ideology of *homo œconomicus*, the fact of having cast the individual as the self-sufficient cornerstone of society led to the banishment of imperfection, or at least to the postulation of its having been overcome. With the reaffirmation of the plural person in a polycultural world, evil ends up being incorporated as an element like any other. This can be experienced tribally. Thus 'homeopathised', it becomes more or less inoffensive. It's possible to imagine that part of the problem of teachers in so-called 'difficult' secondary schools comes from their propensity to perceive a class as a sum of individuals to be shaped and perfected, rather than as a group with its difficulties but also with its collective potential.

This is what is at stake in the post-modern transformation. Acknowledging the 'side of the devil', knowing how to use it so it doesn't overtake the social body. Among the interpreters of this same extraordinary wisdom was Marcus Aurelius, who wrote, 'Troubling oneself over that which is, is like abandoning universal nature, a part of which contains the natures of all other beings'.

It must therefore be recognized that the anomic is part of the spirit of the time, without canonizing it, but also without stigmatizing it *a priori*. Let us recall the programme of Rimbaud: 'The poet becomes a seer through a long, immense and reasoned derangement of the senses. All forms of love, suffering and madness; he searches himself, exhausts all poi-

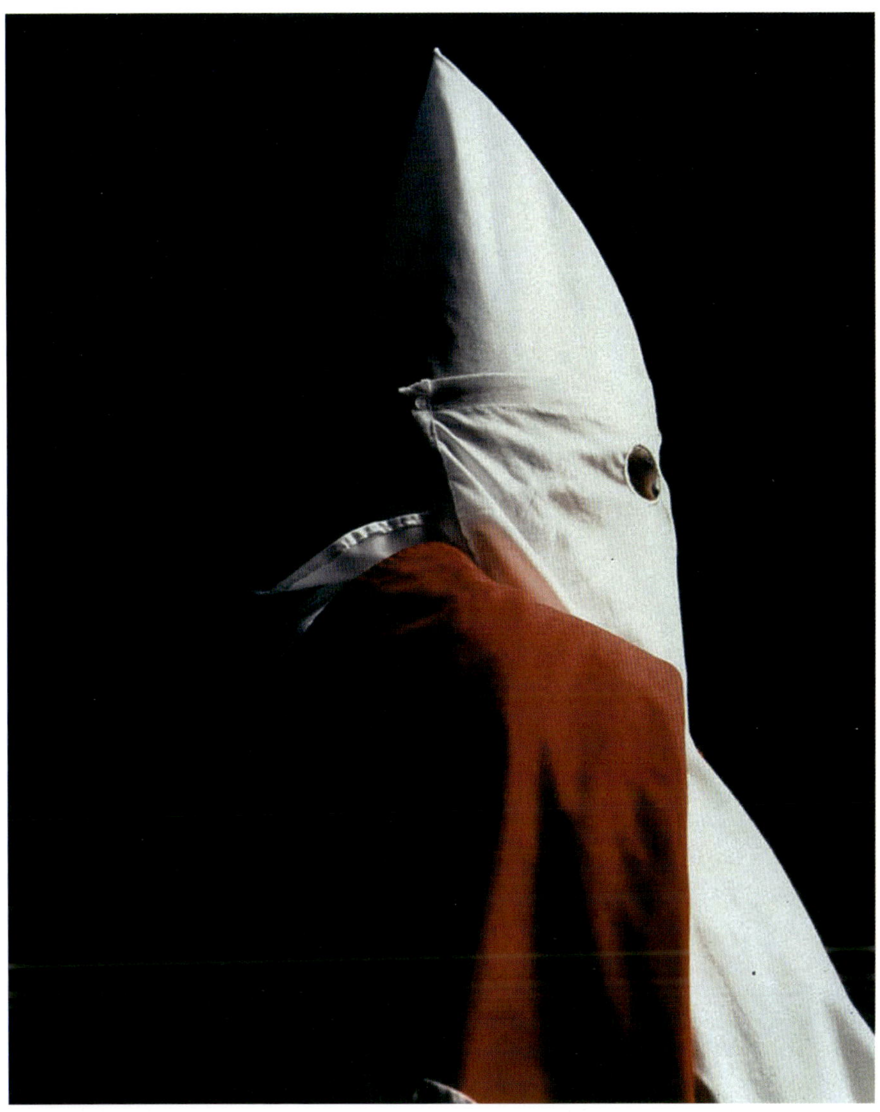

Andres Serrano *Klansman (Great Titan of the Invisible Empire)*, 1985.
Cibachrome, plexiglass, silicone and wooden frame, 101.6 x 68.5 cm

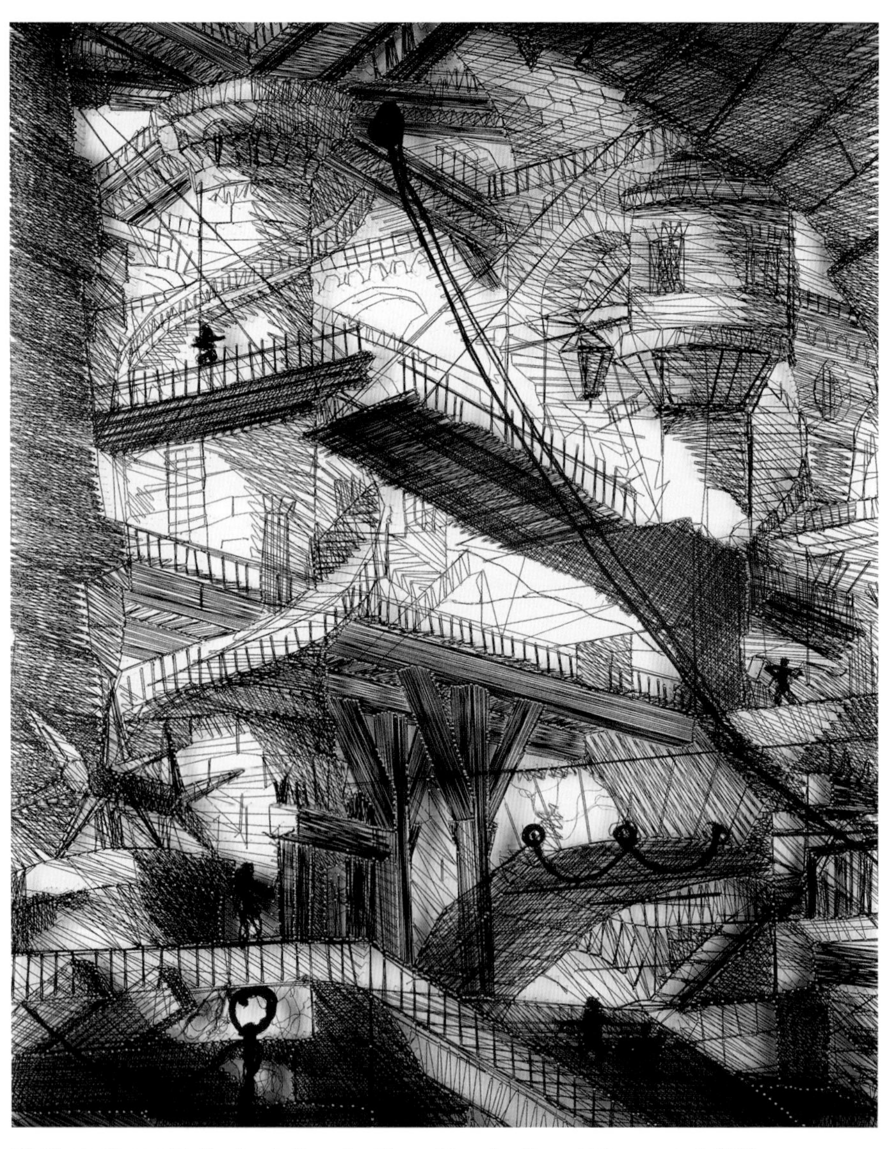

Vik Muniz *Carcere VII, The Drawbridge, after Piranesi* (from the *Piranesi Prisons* series), 2002.
Chromogenic print, 254 x 183 cm

sons in himself, to keep only the quintessences. Ineffable torture...' Rimbaud the seer became an academic reference, but his poetic 'gluttonization' has contaminated a significant number of youthful practices, an echo of which are the lipstick traces left by the Sex Pistols and other rebels of rock, of house and later of techno.

Excess, demonism: the multiple overflows of various sorts confirm that Dionysius is the 'clandestine king' of our epoch. The secret history of the twentieth century becomes, at the dawn of the twenty-first, a marked destiny. We will call it 'the eternal child', noisy, cruel, generous, non-conformist, reinvigorated not for reasons of age but of attitude, a state of being, a 'situationism' that is progressively generalized into the arc of generations.

A mystique of violence, the lines of which George Sorel traced, though in another context? Perhaps. Particularly insofar as it unites those that share its mysteries, those that have the same myths in common. What is certain is the revival of an erotic social realm, of a widespread organism — or, to say it more academically, the return of the *libido sentiendi*, that which feels and which cannot understand by way of the categories like the *libido sciendi*, which is concerned merely with abstract knowledge, or the *libido dominandi*, for which only politics and power are important, all structures erected by the 'living dead' who have the presumption to think on behalf of the world, to rule it. It is precisely for this reason that integration by way of 'civic education' — that is, imparting knowledge about the institutions and powers that be, is an empty deception and can only generate further frustration.

A theoretical change is insinuating itself. An epoch can only be understood by sniffing its scent. Social moods and instincts tell us much more than any amount of scholarly treatises. For there is where an epoch's feelings, passions and beliefs are expressed. Through them are spoken the wildest dreams with which it plays, or of which it is the game. It is the means for understanding the 'destructive side', the excess or the effervescence, the same that invariably precedes a new harmony. But one cannot comprehend the effective impact of this revival without some degree of desire for its arrival. Not adhesion necessarily, but comprehension in the sociological sense. Analysis does not have to be critical by definition. It is also possible to 'be in syntony', to accept and experience in the right way the positive charge that drives an epoch; but, I repeat, it is necessary to cultivate a sort of 'thinking from the gut'. After all, towards all, sometimes against all — life is there. One simply must be able to recognize it.

Dissidence is spreading, and it can no longer be judged solely on political grounds, for that is not where it identifies itself. Economic ideology cannot account for an ever more widespread desire to consume, to waste and burn objects and sentiments and relationships. It is here that the arrogance of the 'right-thinkers' hits the limit. They have the official press on their side, that which was described during the first uprisings of the 1960s as the 'organ of all power'. Today it would be more apt to call it the organ of total impotence, for the protagonists of that era have since become the rulers of a world without light or imagination. The official press is read less and less by young people, who prefer the transversality of the web, with its discussion forums and possibilities of contact, be they sexual, philosophical, religious or otherwise.

Official knowledge/power, that which contents itself with distributing certificates of conformity, that which strives to knowingly render society and knowledge aseptic, has become too abstract. Non-compliance is the only response sent to all those responsible. It is important to repeat: youthful energy no longer holds vindication, or a hand in planning history, as its goals. It manifests itself and consumes itself in the moment — parties, the solidarity of urgency — and has nothing whatsoever to do with an abstract political translation. Thus the mass non-compliance we see, like not registering to vote and other forms of indifference. What I have called the transfiguration of the political.

To think the material, in all its incarnations, has thus become a pressing intellectual requirement. Leaving the 'guard dogs' to their kind, one must walk the dangerous roads of the underlying sociality. It is true that one can simply take the 'correct path' marked out by modern rationalism, but one must instead proceed with richer motives, open to paradox and therefore able to grasp the kind of polysemy we have discussed here. To understand the social phenomena of today, it is necessary to change perspective: no more criticising and explaining, but instead comprehending, allowing. Without repeating, apart from philosophical and political representations, the saturation of which is apparent, we must set about, phenomenologically speaking, to present things as they are. Suggest the raw material of the enigma represented by evil. Not in the interest of a low-grade aestheticism, but in order to grasp the urgency of the phenomena that dominate present social reality. Even if its name is variable — State, Individual, God, Contract, etc. — there will always be enough advocates of God. *Oportet haereses esse*, there must also be heretics, advocates of the devil.

This is a delicate matter. Perhaps for this reason the philosophy of evil has long been either eradicated or confined to art, poetry and a handful of damned thinkers. Damned in their time. In fact, we remember the

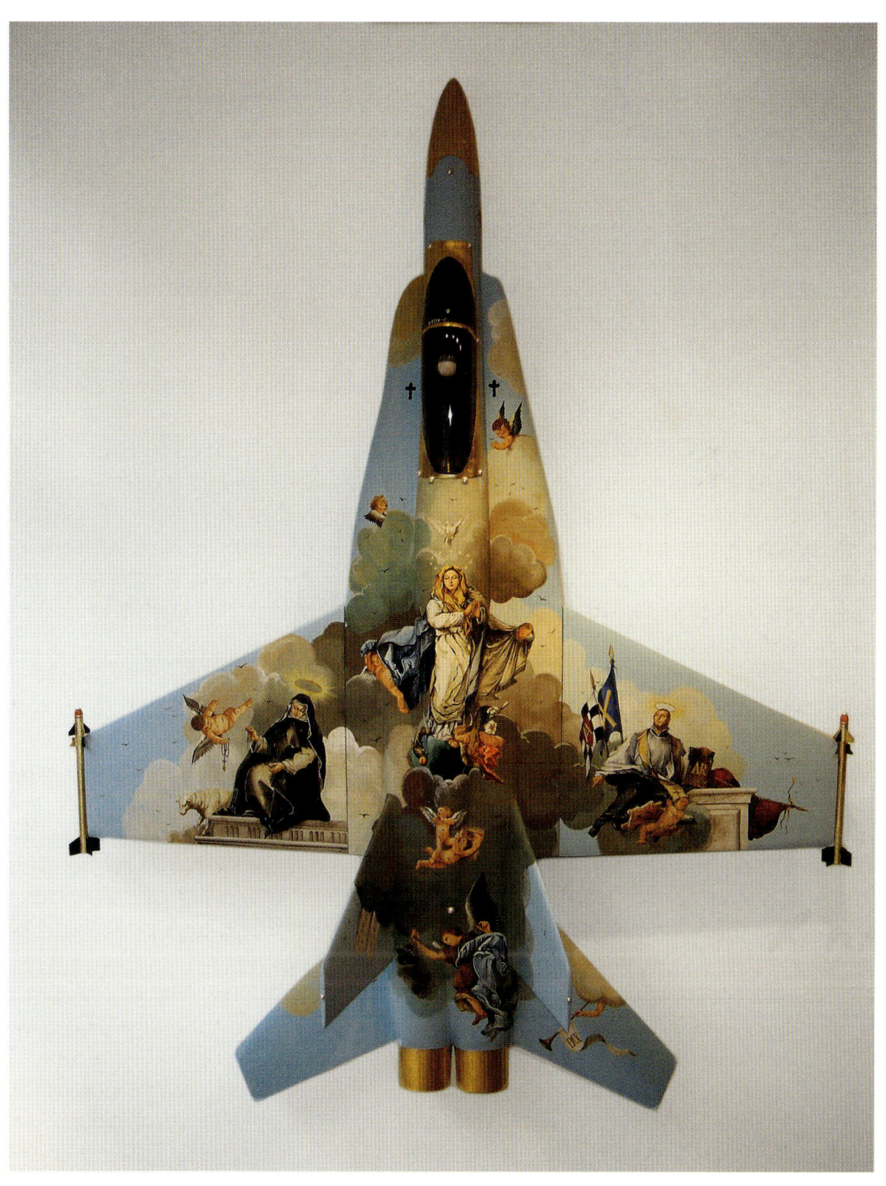

Antonio Riello *Kt35*, 2006. Fibreglass and metal, hand-painted with acrylic, 250 x 140 x 40 cm

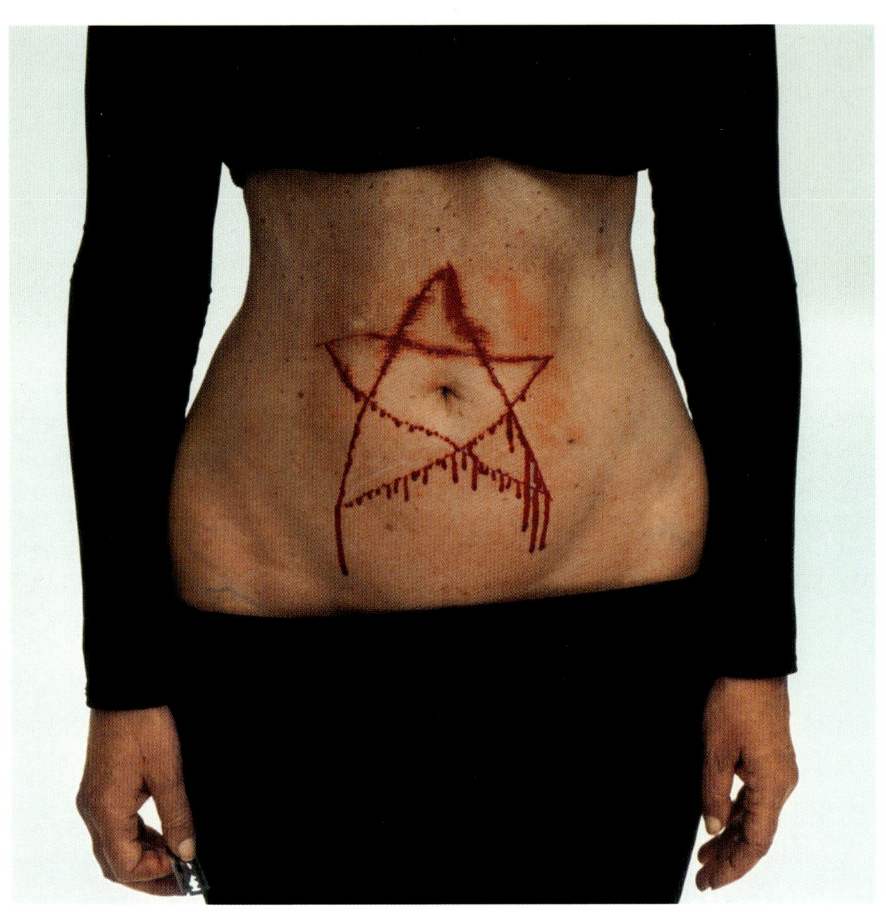

Marina Abramović *Lips of Thomas*, 2002 (photo still from the performance, 1975–97). Cibachrome, 129 x 129 cm

names and thought of Schopenhauer, Nietzsche, Baudelaire, Rimbaud, Rimmel and Max Weber, condemned in their own time. But who recalls the names of their detractors? It is safe to assume that the arrogance of today's right-thinking academics and policy makers and other hacks will enjoy the same fate. They will be consigned to oblivion.

The aim is that of identifying a basic tendency in post-modern life: the natural connection between good and evil, the tragic and the joyous. The astonishing paradox is that, by accepting evil in its various modulations, one can find a certain joy in living. Nietzschian *amor fati* that becomes a love of the world for what it is. Love of empirically experienced need that therefore must apply itself to thought.

Empirical life, which must be our final referent, 'knows' this perfectly well. There is nothing original, these ideas are already in everyone's minds. But one must have the courage to formulate them. There can be nothing original in that which is originary.

Perhaps it was exactly this that Heidegger wished to emphasize by noting the proximity that exists in Greek between 'pain' and 'language' (*algos* and *logos*). For our purposes, I would say that the pain of the 'lost word' incites us to give the word to rediscovered pain, and in this way to (re)turn to a total humanism. The kind that is capable of recognizing the devil's side.

Michel Maffesoli, *La part du diable. Précis de subversion postmoderne*, Paris: Editions Flammarion, 2002.

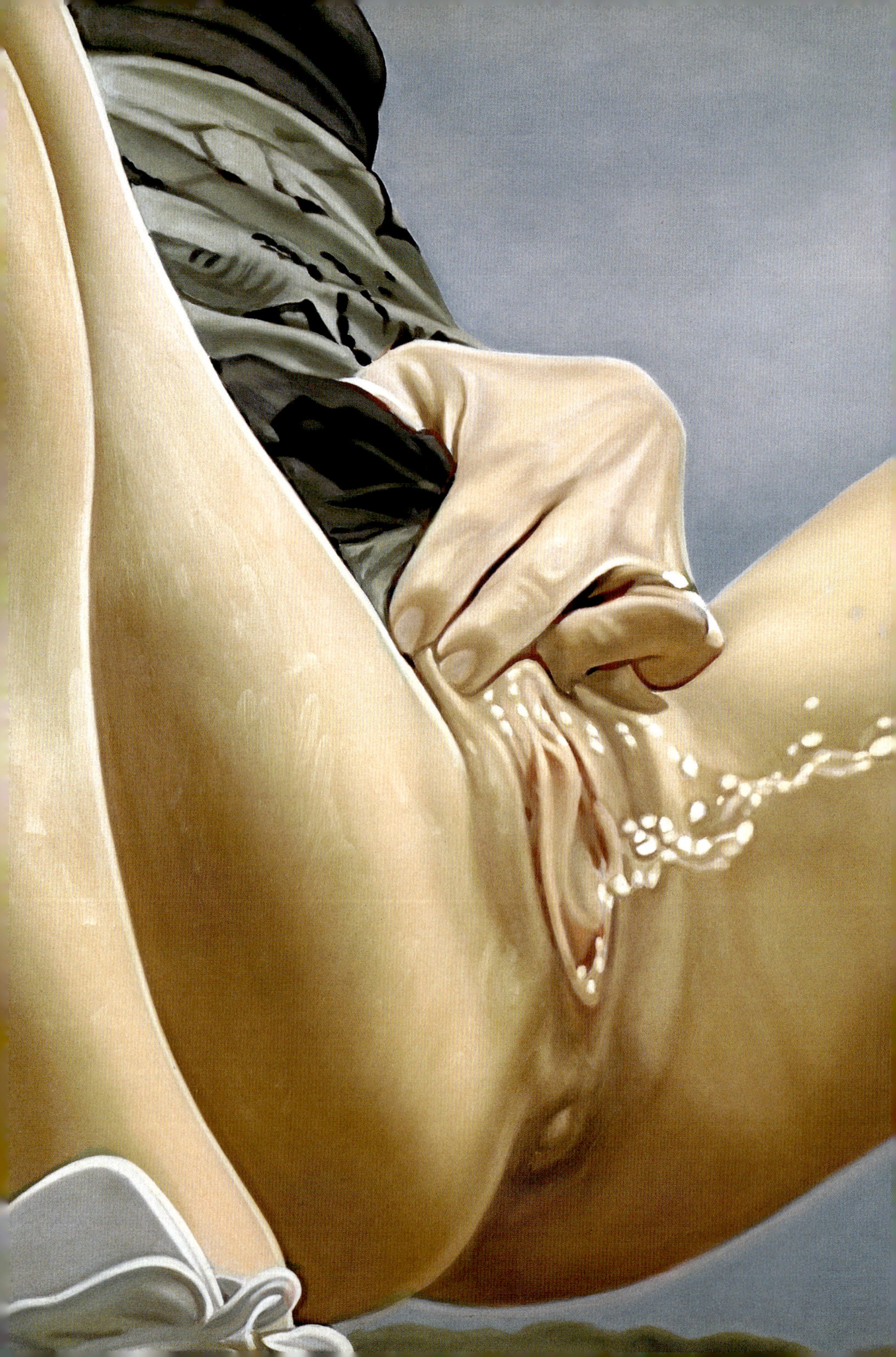

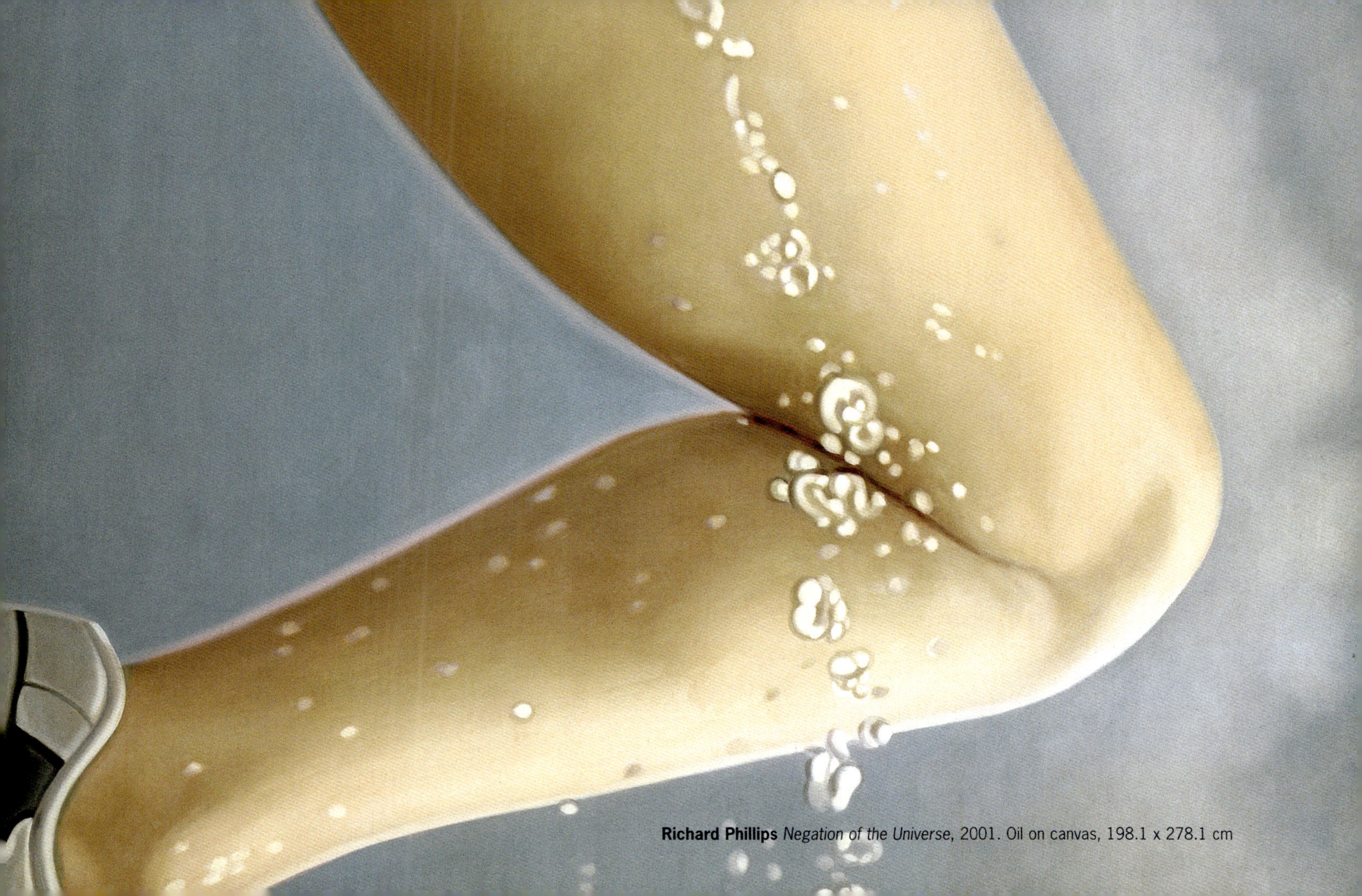

Richard Phillips *Negation of the Universe*, 2001. Oil on canvas, 198.1 x 278.1 cm

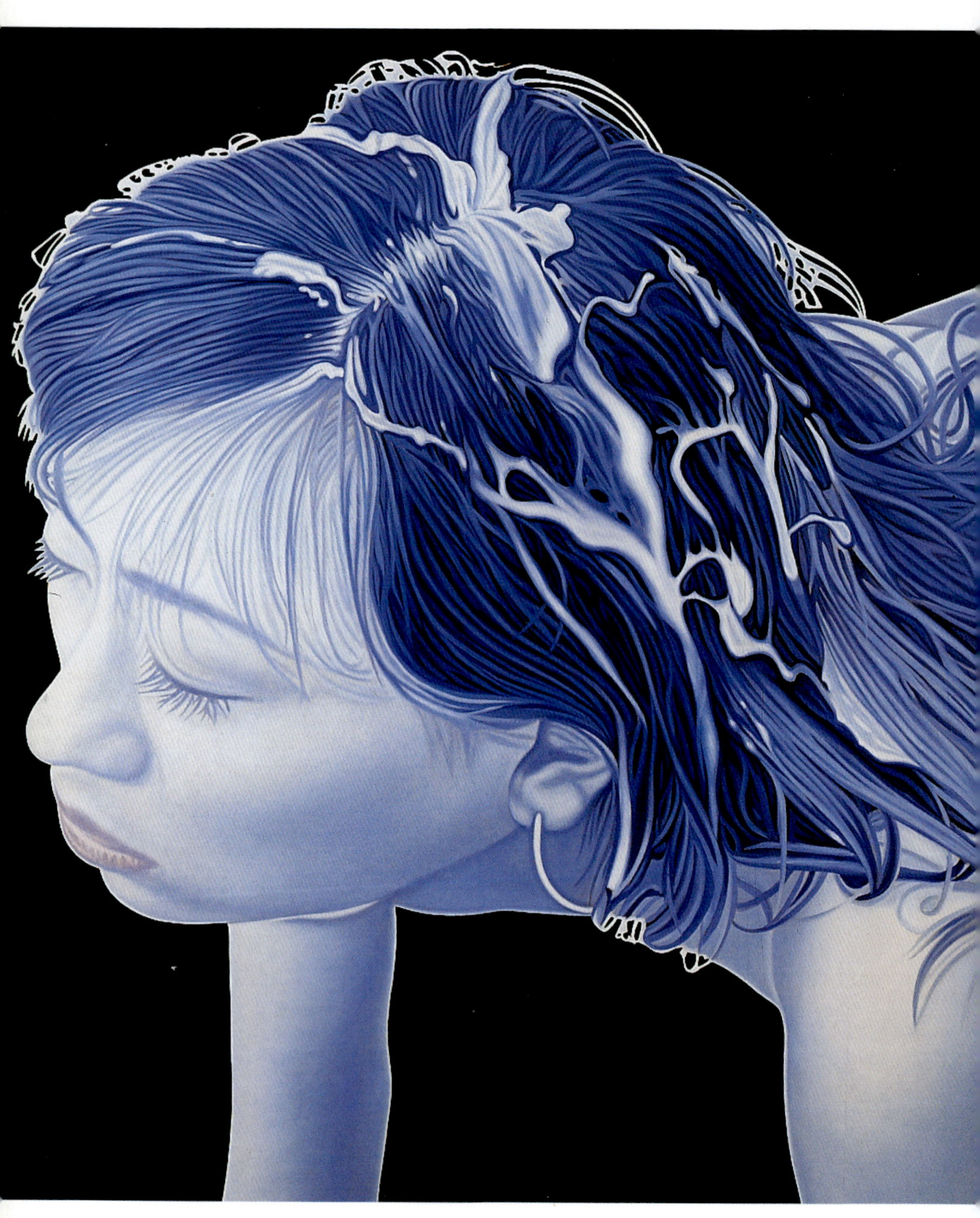

Richard Phillips, *Bukkake*, 2004. Oil on canvas, 217.8 x 198.1 cm

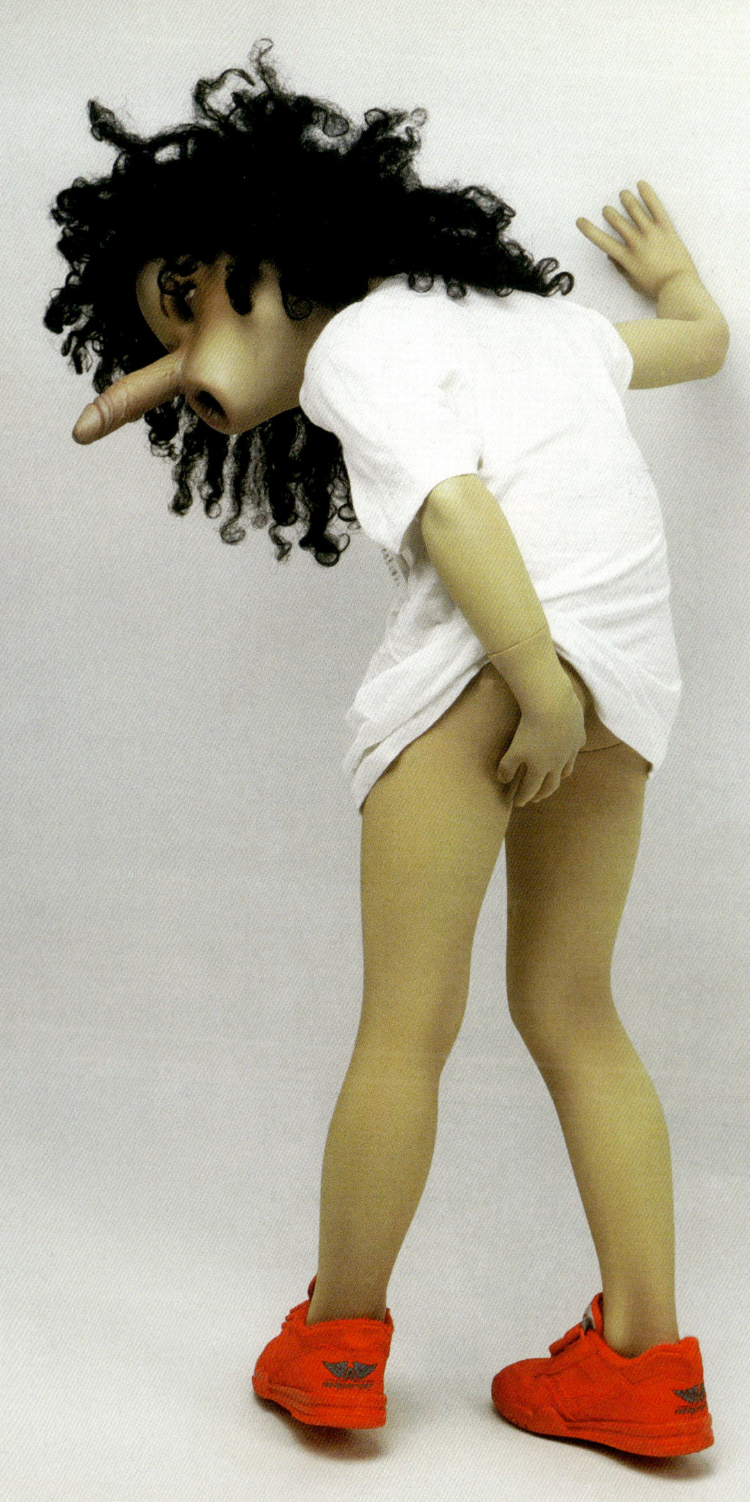

Jake and Dinos Chapman *Fuck Face*, 1994. Mixed media, life size

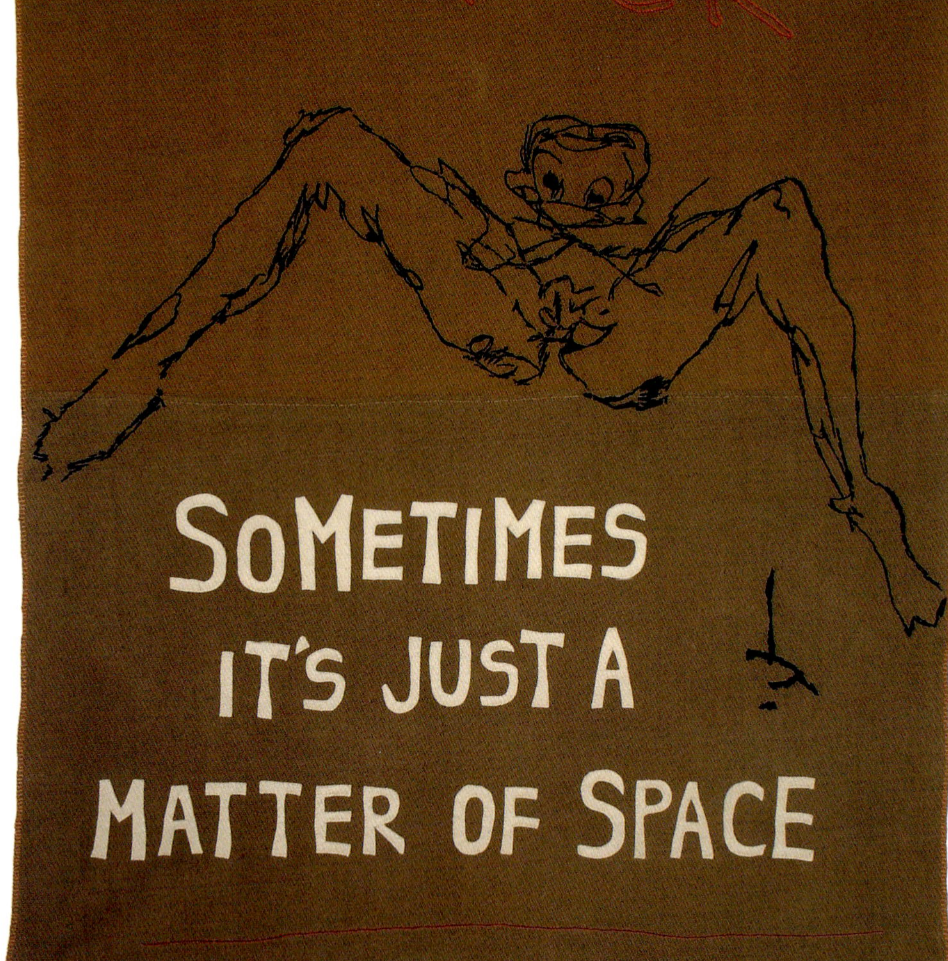
OH FUCK
SOMETIMES
IT'S JUST A
MATTER OF SPACE

Pornography

Gore Vidal

The origins of erotic jokes are so deeply-embedded in time and place that no sexual archaeologist will ever have the time to disembed them. But on the subject of pornography, a key joke did surface at the dawn of the age of the Kinsey Report now, 50 years later, under faith-based attack.

Joke: handsome young couple are making abandoned love until the achieve of an (unlikely) mutual orgasm! The earth moves, as Hemingway used to gasp. Then she whispers, 'I'll tell you who I was thinking of if you tell me who you were thinking of'. This exchange was the ultimate intimacy in those long-ago feather embedded times. Today, of course, if pop culture has it right, each would say 'Brad Pitt', giving that young man's astral image yet another, no doubt unpleasant, workout, flitting like Puck all 'round the world from couple to couple like a start-up battery.

Sexual stories and drawings probably go back to our hunter-gatherer ancestors when we lived in co-ed tribes where the stronger alpha males got the best females, thus developing the skills of all the females in the art of detaching at least one hirsute dummy off one of her rivals in order to acquire his gene pool to add to one of her eggs. And... Sorry that, alas, is the origin of French farce, not today's sermon on pornography.

Of course, males are equally driven to promiscuity for the same biological reasons. One learns of a tribe of ancestral apes which used to travel in processions, led by alpha males, their ladies close to hand while back of *them* beta — and worse — males slithered alongside, slipping

Tracey Emin *Oh Fuck*, 2002. Appliqué and embroideries on blanket, 180 x 150.3 cm

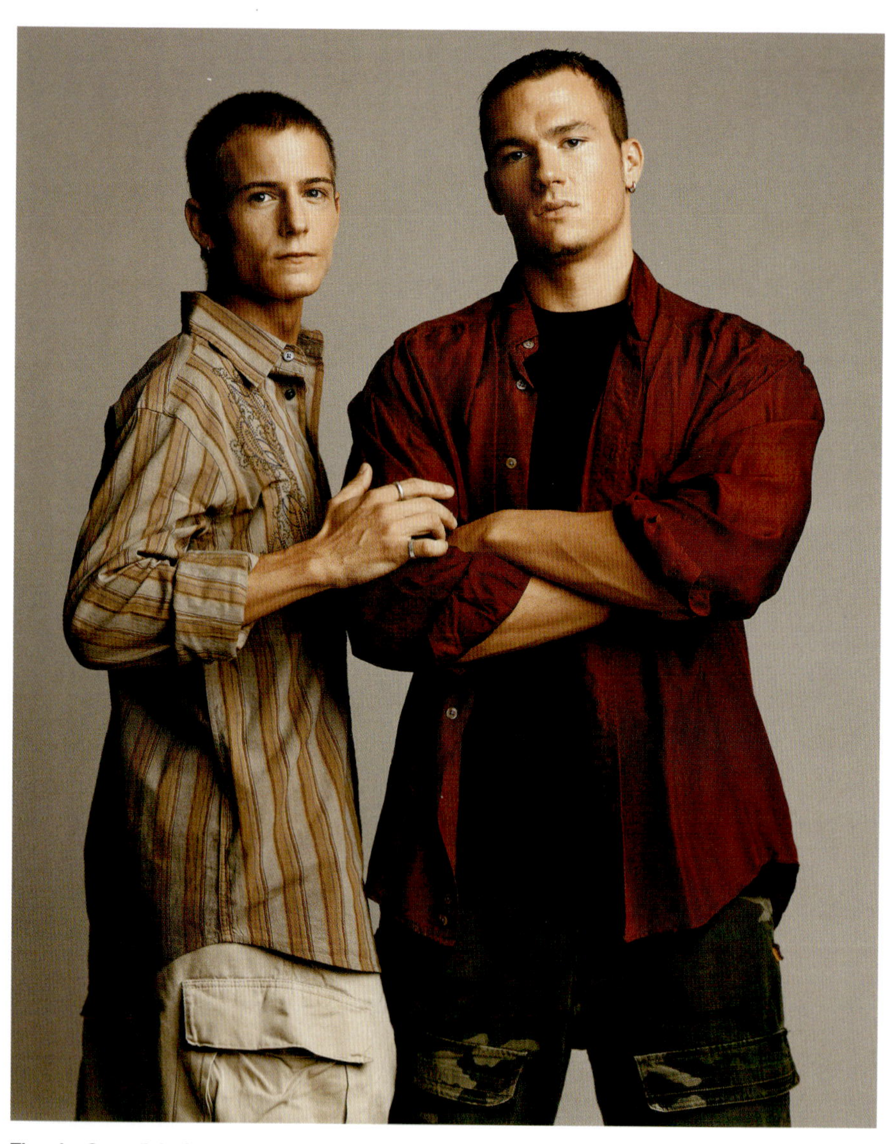

Timothy Greenfield-Sanders *Jeremy Jordan & Jason Hawke* (diptych), 2004
Photographic prints, 153 x 122 cm each

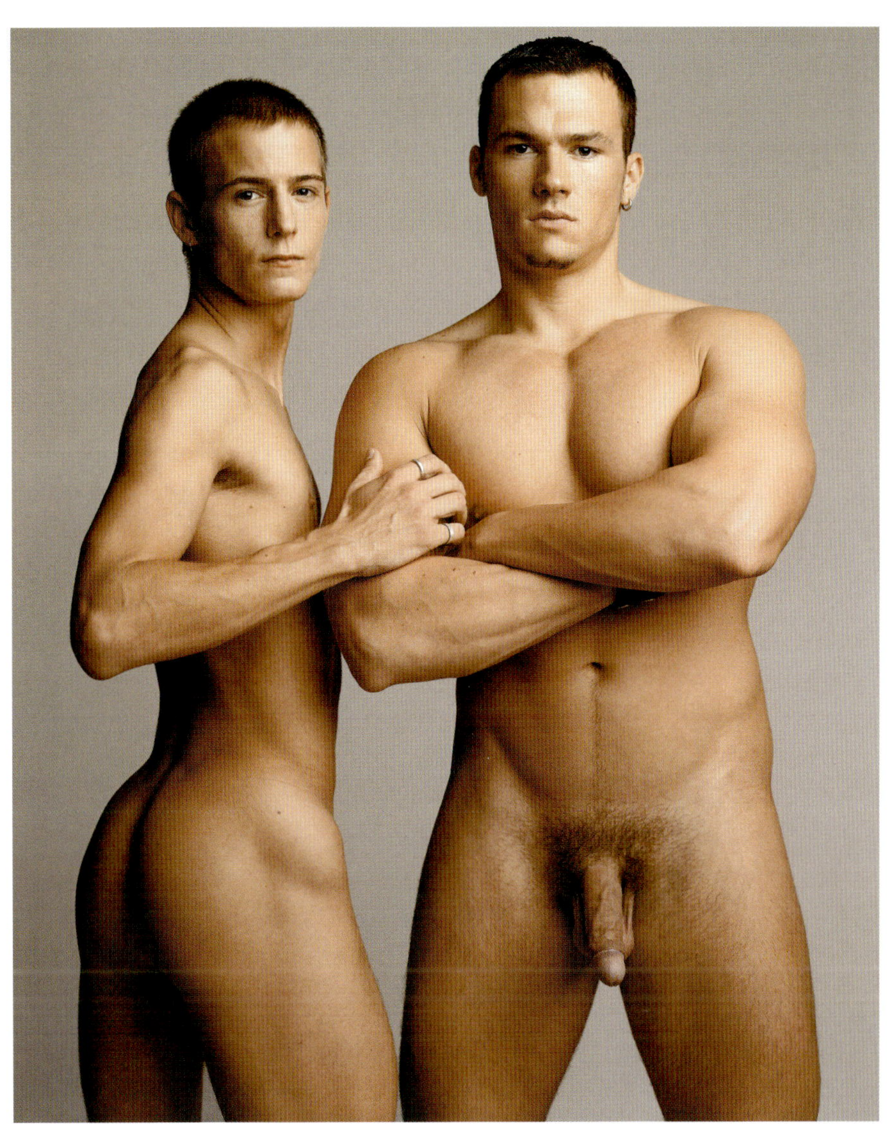

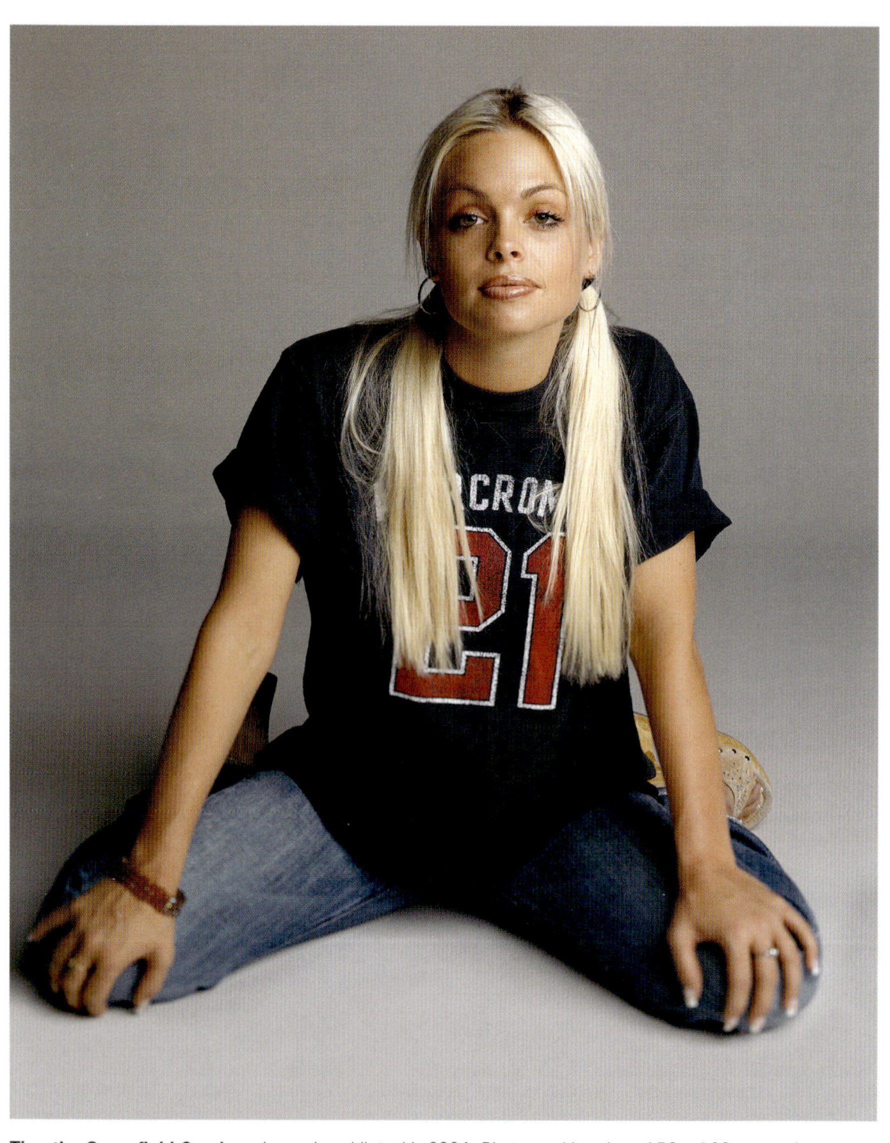

Timothy Greenfield-Sanders *Jesse Jane* (diptych), 2004. Photographic prints, 153 x 122 cm each

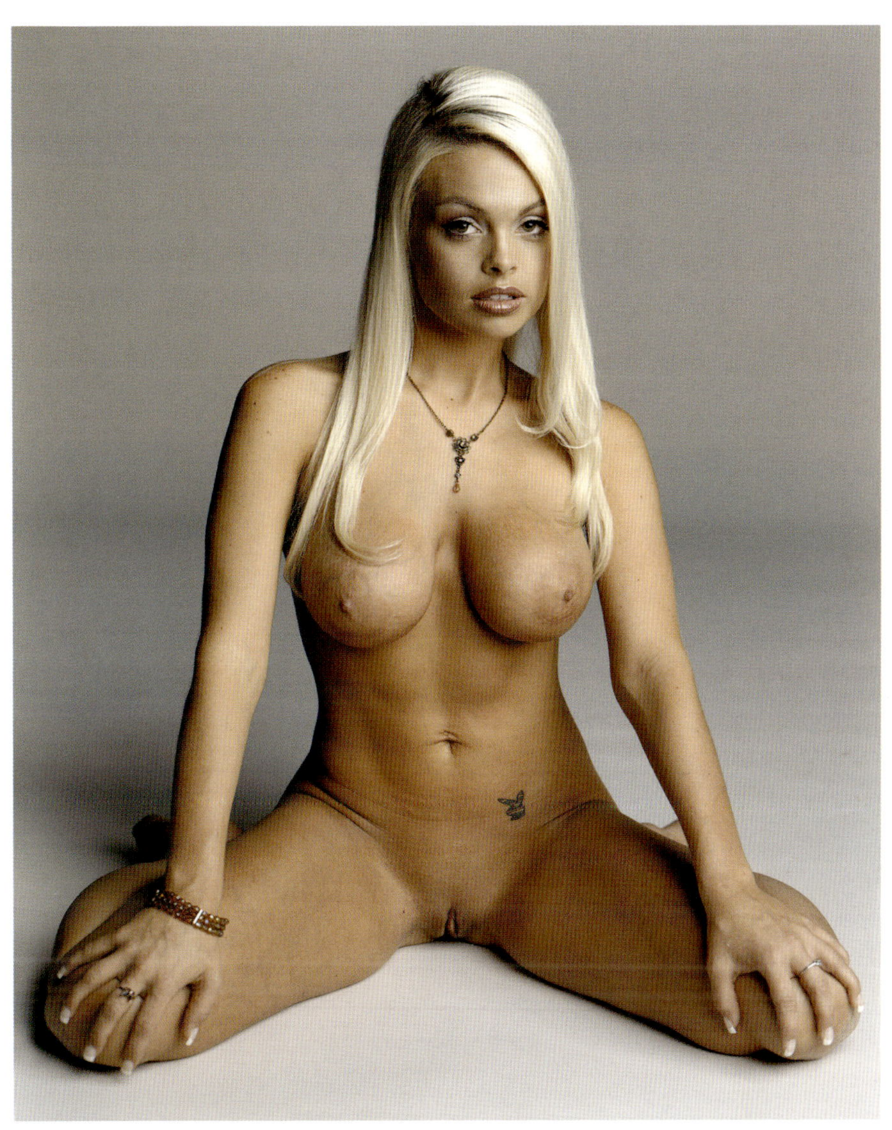

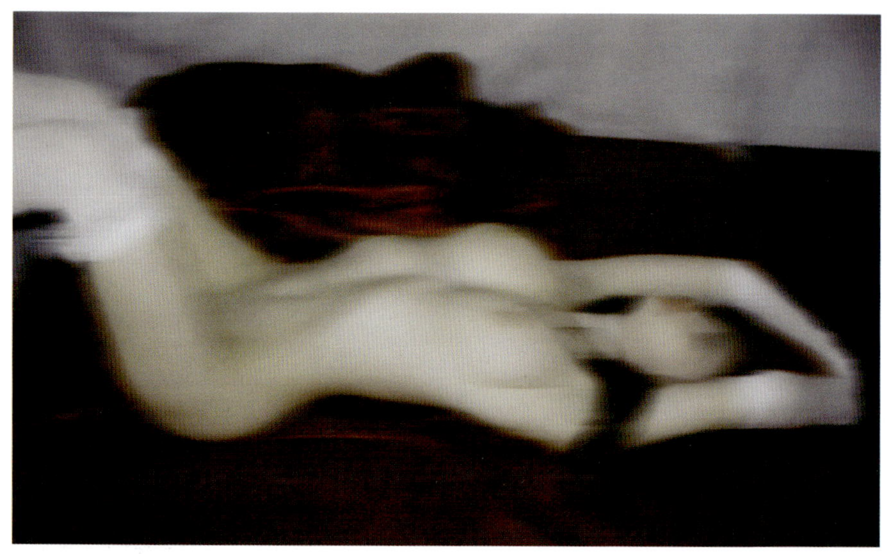

Thomas Ruff *Nude gr 20*, 2003. Chromogenic print, 109 x 165 cm

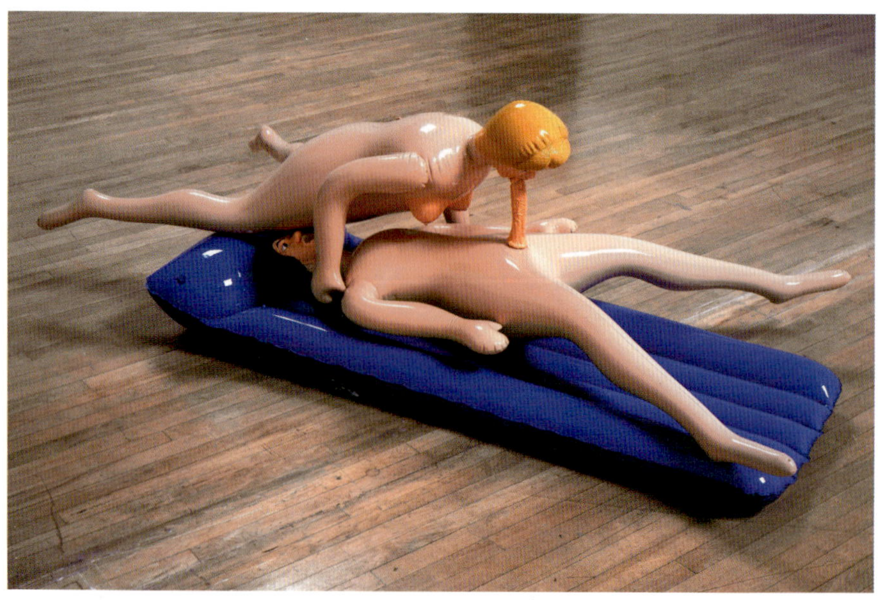

Jake and Dinos Chapman *Death I*, 2003. Painted bronze, 73 x 218 x 95 cm

unnoticed into the progress, speedily impregnating an alpha lady of choice, who never ceases to sport a Mona Lisa smile as she loyally follows her alpha man. All this, I fear, is news to that gambling dude William Bennett, keeper of all Morals, particularly Monogamy and Family Values that were so close to our Lord's heart ('Woman, what art thou to me?' he said somewhat pointedly to his lady mother).

So we start with *the* fact of Life, literally: that we are designed only to continue our species, preferably by bettering our DNAs with new additions through sexual contacts with as many members of the opposite sex as possible, not to mention sporting rehearsals with the same sex. For some reason, all this is horrifying to a lot of Bush guys and gals, who couple in marriage as often as they can afford a good lawyer to let them part from each other, not to mention from their money. The essential fact of our being is ignored which is — dare I say it — nothing more than our common humanity and likeness to each other.

I am carefully moving, I hope, to why pornography exists. Doubtless, sex tales were told about the Neanderthal campfire and perhaps instructive positions drawn on cave walls. Meanwhile, the human race was busy establishing such exciting institutions as slavery and its first cousin, marriage. In the tribes, the alpha males began to curb polymorphic activities as a patriarchal society was born in which the legitimacy of the children became all-important.

Then, telescoping the glorious story of how we got into our current mess, an ambitious politician and world conqueror called Constantine, decided to make Christianity — a mish-mash of Jewish tribal law, Mithraic cults and Egyptian monotheism — into a compulsory world religion. Why did this politician do this? First, he needed an organization that could govern the vast wreck of the Roman Empire over which he presided. Only the Christian Church had the organization, systems of communication and finance not to mention terrifying dogmas to keep the people at large, if slaves, obedient in their chains, if 'free', to keep them in order by stern laws regarding sexual behavior outside marriage, which would, they preached, involve millennia of suffering.

I shall leave to your friendly nearby theologians to walk you through this exciting story. Meanwhile, once the industrial revolution got going in the early eighteenth century and actual slavery more or less ended in the civilized world (the United States was not yet a player on the civilization team) economic slavery was promptly invented: avid consumers and docile workers were developed in order to operate new machinery instead of tending sheep.

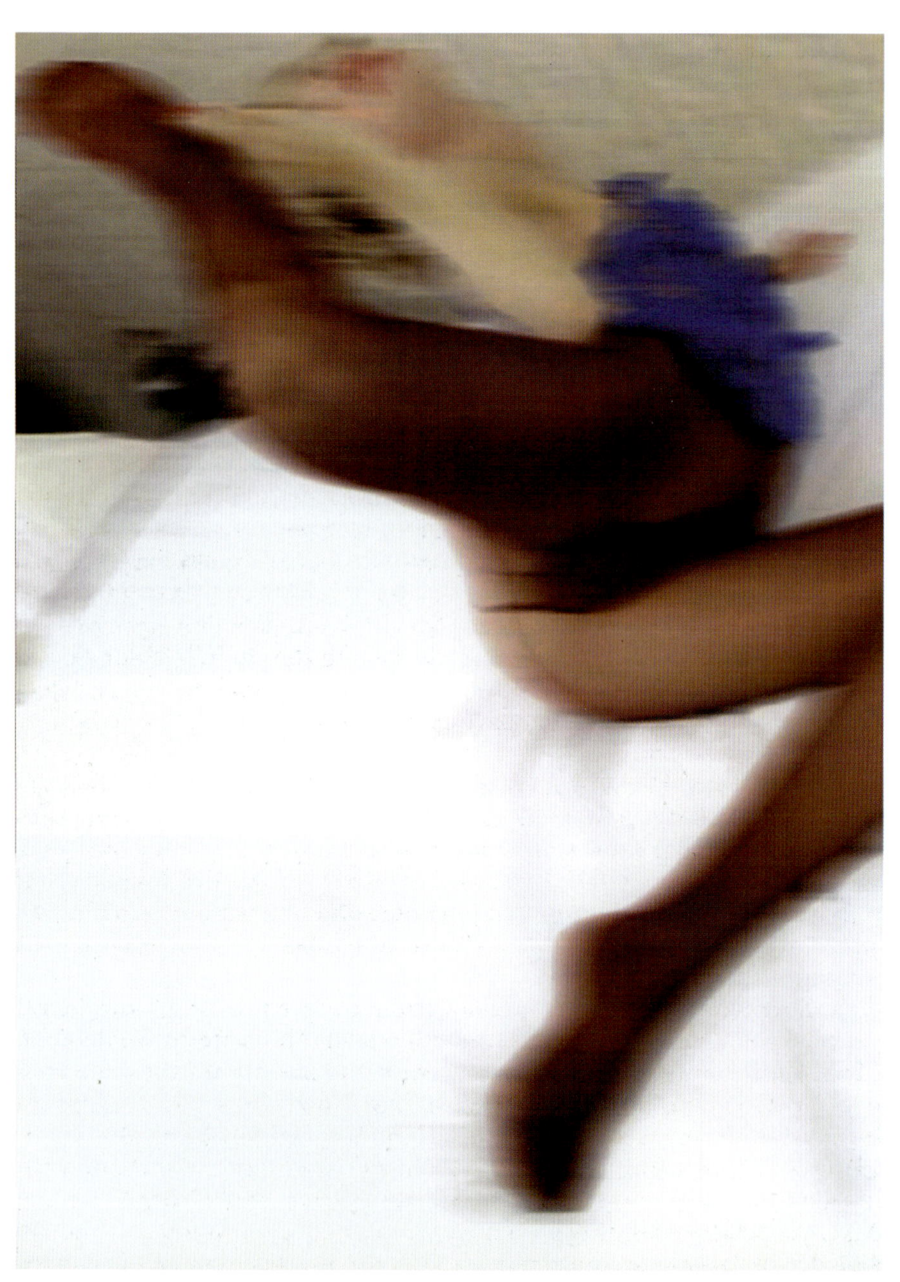

Thomas Ruff *Nudes ft 26*, 2003. Laserchrome, 140 x 110 cm

Then the great debate began. One hears the arguing voices in the novels of Thomas Love Peacock: country house stories peopled with the likes, thinly disguised, of the Reverend Malthus, Lord Byron, Shelley and other radical intelligences for and against educating the masses to read and write. Utilitarians said if we are to have great manufactures we must teach the lower orders to read and write, otherwise, they'll botch up the machines. Conservatives said no. Reading will make them think and thought, dangerously, gives them ideas and they'll overthrow us. The utilitarians won. The first novels were simple morality tales, or sermons, on the perils of drink, and adultery. But in the long run conservatives got it right.

Although young men were encouraged to marry early and have many children, so that all would suffer if they were fired for disobedience yet, even so, learning saved them. They formed unions, labor parties and the great fear of the upper classes was symbolized in the first quarter of the twentieth century by the novel *Lady Chatterley's Lover:* in which a lower class lad, like one of those Speedy Gonzalez's monkeys on safari, bedded a Lady of high degree, to her delight and that of D. H. Lawrence's readers. Conservatives fought back. But the new readers were betraying boredom with tracts describing the perils of alcohol, and so stories of shipwreck and adventure became popular. Masterpieces were written in our language, particularly.

Conservatives next staged religious revivals. Sex for the unmarried was demonized. Paradoxically, books on the subject (not to mention expensive paintings and crude cartoons) flourished; well, not so paradoxically: pornography was coming into fashion in a way not seen since the first century AD when sailors hit a hot town like Pompeii, full of brothels with a wide range of pornographic murals and graffiti (the street-corner man-size phalluses were a symbol of good fortune not invitations to lust).

Triumphant Christianity was not about to take this lying down! Ever fiercer laws were proposed by the church for the state to implement. Monogamy became the rock upon which the family and the state rested. One God, one Pope, one emperor, one factory boss and one mate at hearthside. Needless to say, prostitution, heavily punished, also flourished as did pornography, not only as an aid to solitary masturbation but a spur to the weary imagination. Today inner images of Brad Pitt and Marilyn Monroe still shore up many a too dutiful encounter — though Marilyn is largely a transference preferred by the more sophisticated lovers — the ladies.

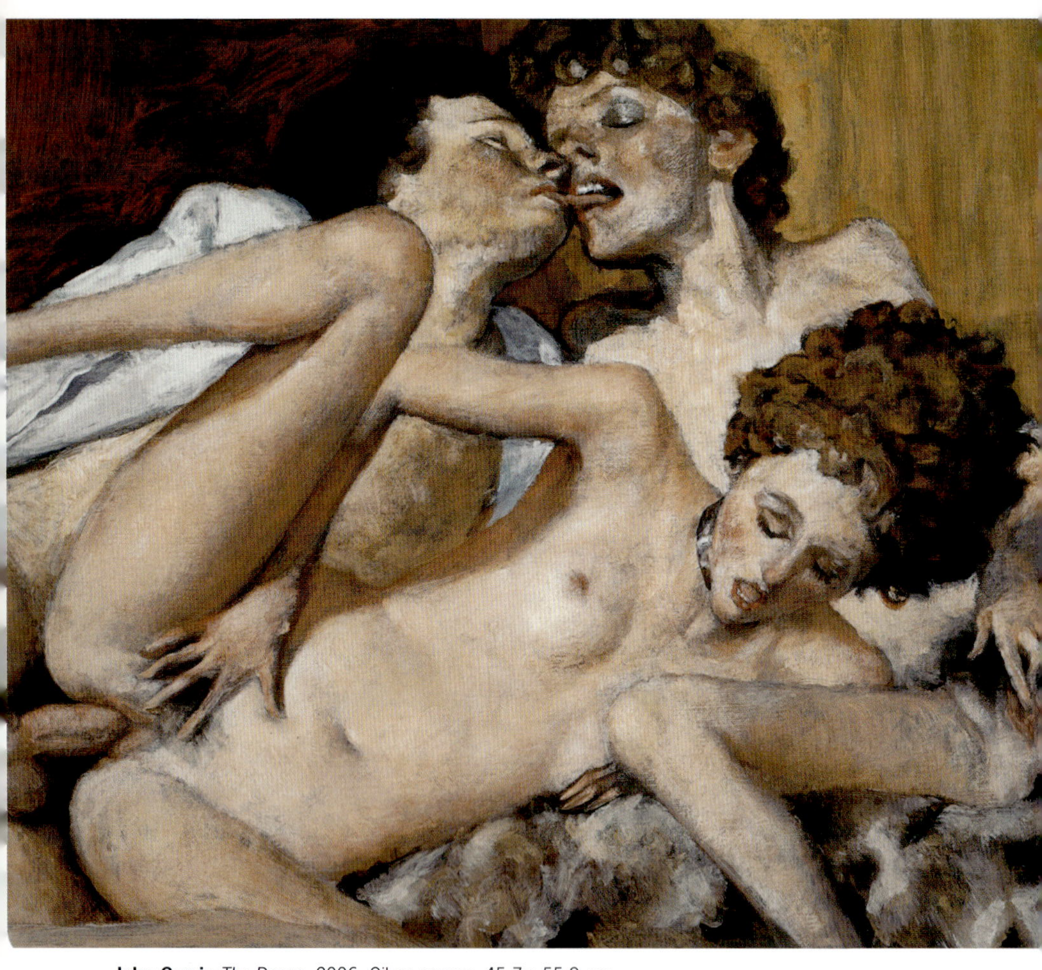

John Currin *The Danes*, 2006. Oil on canvas, 45.7 x 55.9 cm

Karl Kraus, a great Viennese wit of the last century, said, 'Sex with a woman can be as exciting as masturbation but it requires more imagination'. So there we are. And here you are, with some splendid new images to ponder in the dark before dawn. Timothy Greenfield-Sanders is a splendid photographer who has had the truly original idea of photographing porno stars backstage.

Timothy Greenfield-Sanders, *XXX: 30 Porn-Star Portraits*, New York: Bulfinch, 2004, by kind permission of the Author.

Courtesy and Photograph Credits

Marina Abramović
© of the artist
Courtesy Lia Rumma, Milan–Naples

Nobuyoshi Araki
© of the artist
p. 86: Courtesy Gianfranco Zonca Collection, Milan

Atelier Van Lieshout
© of the artist
p. 14: Courtesy photo Krinzinger Gallery, Vienna

Matthew Barney
© of the artist / Barbara Gladstone Gallery, New York
p. 60: Courtesy Rosella and Carlo Nesi Collection;
p. 145: Courtesy Paolo Consolandi Collection, Milan

Vanessa Beecroft
© of the artist
Courtesy Lia Rumma, Milan–Naples

John Bock
© of the artist
p. 160: Courtesy Klosterfelde, Berlin; Anton Kern, New York; camera editing Knut Klaflen; editing Marc Aschenbrenner
pp. 202–08: Courtesy Paolo Consolandi Collection, Milan; photo Jan Windszus
pp. 222–23: Courtesy Paolo Consolandi Collection, Milan; photo Mario Tedeschi

Monica Bonvicini
© of the artist
Courtesy Emi Fontana Gallery, Milan and West of Rome Inc., Los Angeles
photo Roberto Marossi

Maurizio Cattelan
© of the artist
p. 132: Courtesy Galleria Massimo De Carlo, Milan; photo Attilio Maranzano
p. 139: Courtesy Galerie Emmanuel Perrotin, Paris; photo Attilio Maranzano
p. 210: Courtesy Paolo Consolandi Collection, Milan; photo Mario Tedeschi

Jake and Dinos Chapman
© of the artist
Courtesy Jay Jopling / White Cube, London
pp. 157, 158–59, 249 and 256: Courtesy Jay Jopling / White Cube, London; photo Stephen White

Chuck Close
© of the artist
p. 109: Courtesy David Adamson, Washington, D.C.

John Currin
© of the artist
Private collection, Courtesy Gagosian Gallery, New York

Tracey Emin
© of the artist
p. 144: Courtesy Nicolò Cardi Collection, Milan;
p. 250: Courtesy Galleria Lorcan O'Neill, Rome

Gérard Garouste
© of the artist
Courtesy Galerie Daniel Templon, Paris

Robert Gober
© of the artist
Courtesy Matthew Marks Gallery, New York
p. 42: photo Russell Kaye

David Godbold
© of the artist
p. 68: Courtesy Almuth Spiegler & Thomas Tenkler Collection, Vienna
p. 99: Courtesy Galerie Bernd Kluser, Münich

Timothy Greenfield-Sanders
© of the artist
pp. 252–53 and 254–55: Courtesy Paolo Curti and Annamaria Gambuzzi, Milan

Andreas Gursky
© of the artist
Courtesy Lia Rumma, Milan–Naples
pp. 168–69

Mona Hatoum
© of the artist
pp. 118–19: Courtesy Galleria Continua, San Gimignano–Beijing; photo Ela Bialkowska
p. 227: Courtesy Paolo Consolandi Collection, Milan; photo Mario Tedeschi

Thomas Hirschhorn
© of the artist
pp. 184 and 195: photo Pasquale Di Stasio; Courtesy Galleria Alfonso Artiaco, Naples;
p. 195: Courtesy Vittorio Gaddi Collection, Lucca
pp. 216–17: Courtesy Paolo Consolandi Collection, Milan; photo Mario Tedeschi

Damien Hirst
© of the artist
Courtesy Jay Jopling / White Cube, London
p. 32: photo Mike Parsons; pp. 46, 47: photo Mike Parsons;
p. 49: Private collection, Milan; photo Stephen White

James Hopkins
© of the artist
Courtesy Cosmic Galerie, Paris
p. 226: Courtesy Paolo Consolandi, Milan; photo Mario Tedeschi

Jörg Immendorf
© of the artist
Courtesy Michael Werner Gallery, Cologne –New York

Mike Kelley
© of the artist
Courtesy Gagosian Gallery, New York; photo Fredrik Nilsen

Michael Joo
© of the artist
pp. 110–11: Courtesy of the artist and Anton Kern Gallery, New York; photo Tom Powel Imaging
pp. 112–14: Courtesy The Denver Art Museum; photo Artsonje Center

Regina José Galindo
© of the artist
Courtesy Galleria Prometeo, Milan

Robert Mapplethorpe
© Robert Mapplethorpe Foundation

Paul McCarthy
© of the artist
Courtesy Hauser & Wirth, Zurich
p. 166: Courtesy Gemma De Angelis Testa Collection, Milan
p. 211: Courtesy Paolo

Consolandi Collection, Milan

Jonathan Meese
© of the artist
Courtesy Paolo Curti and Annamaria Gambuzzi, Milan
p. 124: photo Roberto Mascaroni, Milan
p. 134 and 140: photo Efrem Raimondi

Ottonella Mocellin and Nicola Pellegrini
© of the artist
Courtesy Lia Rumma, Milan–Naples

Ron Mueck
© of the artist
Courtesy James Cohan Gallery, New York

Vik Muniz
© and Courtesy of the artist
p. 240: Courtesy Nicolò Cardi Collection, Milan

Shirin Neshat
© of the artist
p. 125: Courtesy Paolo Consolandi Collection, Milan
p. 221: Courtesy Lia Rumma, Milan–Naples

Tim Noble & Sue Webster
© of the artists
Courtesy Bortolami Dayan, New York and Modern Art, London
p. 126: photo Andy Keate
Courtesy Nicolò Cardi Collection, Milan

Luigi Ontani
© of the artist
Courtesy Galleria Lorcan O'Neill, Rome
p. 71: photo Stefano Elena

Tony Oursler
© of the artist
Courtesy photo Galleria In Arco, Turin

Richard Phillips
pp. 246–48: Courtesy Thomas & Janine Koefer Film AG, Zurich

Pierre and Gilles
© of the artists
Courtesy Galerie Jerome de Noirmont, Paris

Marc Quinn
© of the artist
Courtesy Jay Jopling / White Cube, London
cover and p. 34: photo Stephen White
p. 76: photo Stephen White; p. 172: photo Stephen White

Antonio Riello
© and Courtesy of the artist

Bernardi Roig
pp. 17–18: Courtesy Claire Oliver Gallery, New York

Thomas Ruff
© of the artist
Courtesy Lia Rumma, Milan–Naples
p. 88: Courtesy Gemma De Angelis Testa, Milan;
p. 256: Courtesy Nicolò Cardi Collection, Milan;
p. 258: Courtesy Lia Rumma, Milan–Naples

Tom Sachs
© of the artist
Courtesy Sperone Westwater, New York
p. 48: Courtesy Nicolò Cardi Collection, Milan;
p. 224: Courtesy Centre Georges Pompidou, Paris

David Salle
© of the artist
Courtesy Mary Boone Gallery / Deitch Projects, New York
pp. 146–47: Courtesy Nicolò Cardi Collection, Milan
pp. 178–79: Private collection, Milan

Jenny Saville
© of the artist
Courtesy Gagosian Gallery, London

Andres Serrano
© of the artist
Courtesy of the artist and Paula Cooper Gallery, New York

Cindy Sherman
© of the artist
p. 62: Courtesy Per Skarstedt Fine Arts, New York
p. 197: Courtesy Galleria In Arco Collection, Turin

Doug and Mike Starn
© and Courtesy Doug and Mike Starn, Artists Rights Society, NYC

Thomas Struth
© of the artist
p. 116: Courtesy Gemma De Angelis Testa Collection, Milan

Hiroshi Sugimoto
© and Courtesy of the artist
p. 105: Courtesy Rosa and Gilberto Sandretto Collection, Milan

Sam Taylor-Wood
© of the artist
Courtesy Jay Jopling / White Cube, London

Mark Wallinger
© of the artist
Courtesy Anthony Reynolds Gallery, London
p. 6: photo Peter White;
p. 9: photo John Riddy;
p. 78: Courtesy Gemma De Angelis Testa Collection, Milan

Andy Warhol
© Andy Warhol Foundation for the Visual Arts

Joel-Peter Witkin
© of the artist
Courtesy Baudoin Lebon, Paris / Colombo and Dolcetti, Turin

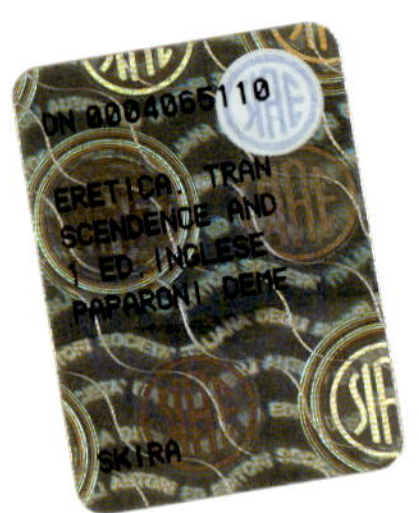
DN 0004065110
ERETICA. TRAN
SCENDENCE AND
1 ED. INGLESE
PAPARONI DEME
SKIRA